D0897580

From Wilderness to Empire

From Wilderness to Empire

A History of CALIFORNIA

BY ROBERT GLASS CLELAND

A Combined and Revised Edition of
From Wilderness to Empire (1542–1900) &
California in Our Time (1900–1940)
Edited and brought down to date

BY GLENN S. DUMKE

NEW YORK *Alfred A. Knopf* 1969

L. C. Catalog card number: 59–8037

© Alfred A. Knopf, Inc., 1959

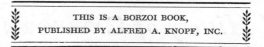

THIS IS A BORZOI BOOK,
PUBLISHED BY ALFRED A. KNOPF, INC.

Published April 27, 1959
Sixth Printing, July 1969

Originally published as two separate volumes: FROM WILDERNESS TO EMPIRE: A history of California, 1542–1900, in March, 1944 and reprinted three times, and CALIFORNIA IN OUR TIME (1900–1940) in August, 1947.

Preface

WALTER BAGEHOT began his classic study of the English Constitution with the words of John Stuart Mill: "On all great subjects much remains to be said." Mill's statement justifies the present volume. For, in spite of all the histories of California that have been written, the field has not yet been exhausted, nor its richness seriously impaired.

In undertaking this new venture I have had in mind two principal objectives—to avoid a local or provincial point of view, and, in so far as I was able, to give to scholarship a zest and flavor that would command the interest of the general reader without incurring the condemnation of the trained historian.

Out of consideration for the layman, the use of footnotes and references has been reduced to a minimum.

Nearly a quarter of a century ago Charles E. Chapman and I planned and carried through the publication of two independent, but closely related volumes that together covered the history of the state. Dr. Chapman's untimely death has denied me the benefit of his counsel and sound criticism in the preparation of the present work; but I am grateful to the Macmillan Company for permission to quote somewhat extensively from the two books just mentioned—Charles Edward Chapman: *A History of California: The Spanish Period;* and Robert Glass Cleland: *A History of California: The American Period.* In the preface to my earlier history I wrote:

"The writer has lived in California since 1889. He has known the state when it was still in a semi-pioneer stage, and has seen it rise to its present height of cultural development and material prosperity.

"At one time or another, too, especially within the last few years, he has visited nearly every section of the state, from Imperial Valley to Humboldt Bay. Sometimes travelling by railroad; sometimes by automobile equipped with camping outfit; and best of all, sometimes with saddle horse and pack train, he has sought to familiarize himself with that vast empire of desert and mountain, thriving cities and fruitful valleys, which stretches a thousand miles along the Pacific, from Oregon to the Mexican boundary. For that empire, which the world calls California, the writer confesses an absorbing love; and for those who laid its foundations, an abiding admiration. This book, in the last analysis, is chiefly the product of that love and of that admiration."

It is sufficient to say that my feelings, as thus expressed so long ago, have only been intensified by the passing of the years.

To all those who have aided, either directly or indirectly, in the preparation of the volume, I am deeply grateful. Without exception, the members of the staff of the Huntington Library merit my special appreciation. Mr. Leslie E. Bliss, Miss Haydée Noya, and Mr. Phil Townsend Hanna, editor of *Westways*, have given me good counsel. With outward cheerfulness, and at least no audible word of complaint, Dr. Louis B. Wright, and my unfailing and incomparably generous friend Dan S. Hammack gave much assistance. I gratefully add the name of Edward A. Dickson, who furnished invaluable suggestions and material on the political developments in California from 1906 to 1920; and of James C. Sheppard, who placed at my disposal a large collection of documents, manuscripts, and data relating to the chaotic period from 1935 to 1939. I am also under obligation to Claude Dudley, the Automobile Club of Southern California, Miss Bessie Best, and many librarians throughout the state. Mr. and Mrs. Alfred A. Knopf have shown unexampled consideration in overlooking the repeated delays incident to the completion of the manuscript.

And, finally, there is one whose patience, understanding, quiet words of encouragement, and eager anticipation of the finished volume were never far absent from my thought and work. For her, life's little candle has gone out; and for me, the sunsets have lost their glory, and the shining mountains are wrapped in the shadows of the night. I wish this book were more worthy of her.

ROBERT G. CLELAND

Occidental College, Los Angeles, California

Editor's Preface

WHEN I was asked by Dr. Robert Glass Cleland to reduce his two books, *From Wilderness to Empire* and *California in Our Time*, to a single volume and at the same time to bring the history of the state up to date, I accepted the task with the feeling that it was a genuine privilege so to merit his confidence. From my early days at Occidental College, when I, with other freshmen, took his great course in the history of England, I had been impressed not only with his scholarship but also with his ability to make history a living thing, and certainly he was partially responsible for my choice of history as a profession.

I have, therefore, approached this work with the profound respect that a student has for a great teacher, and, except for occasional passages, the first two chapters, the concluding chapter, and the bibliography, the writing remains chiefly his. My efforts have been restricted largely to reducing the length of the book. At the same time I have used recent scholarship to revise and amend in the few instances where such changes seemed indicated.

Dr. Cleland's work in the field of California and southwestern history, his early association with Professor Charles Edward Chapman, his supervision of the Huntington Library's research project in the history of the Southwest with Rockefeller Foundation assistance, his sincere love of his subject—especially the "mountain men" of the fur-trapping era, and his many writings combine to make him one of the great historians of the American West. I hope I have done justice to the responsibility which has been mine.

I want to give special thanks to Dr. Theodore Treutlein, Dr. Arthur Foff, and Dr. Frank Fenton, all of the faculty of San Francisco State College, who took time out from a busy period to review the manuscript. Their suggestions have been most helpful. In addition, Dr. Kenneth Brough, Mrs. Virginia Reuss, Mr. Thomas

Roddy, Mrs. Constance King, and Miss Sheila Knights of the Library of San Francisco State College, and Mr. Carey Bliss and Mr. Erwin Morkisch of the Huntington Library have assisted effectively.

GLENN S. DUMKE

San Francisco State College

CONTENTS

Contents

ILLUSTRATIONS AND MAPS

MAPS

From Wilderness to Empire

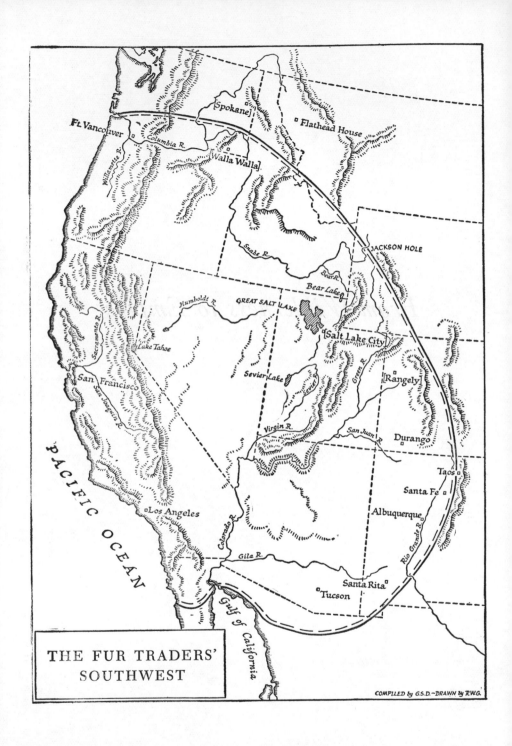

Spokane]

Ft. Vancouver

Columbia R.

Flathead House

Willamette R.

Walla Walla

JACKSON HOLE

Snake R.

Bear R.

Bear Lake

Humboldt R.

GREAT SALT LAKE

Salt Lake City

Lake Tahoe

San Francisco

Sacramento R.

San Joaquin R.

Sevier Lake

Sevier R.

Green R.

[Rangely]

Virgin R.

San Juan R.

Durango

Los Angeles

Taos

Santa Fe

Albuquerque

Colorado R.

Gila R.

Rio Grande R.

PACIFIC OCEAN

Santa Rita

Tucson

Gulf of California

THE FUR TRADERS'
SOUTHWEST

COMPILED by G.S.D.—DRAWN by R.W.G.

CHAPTER 1. Voyages and Discoveries

FOUR and a half centuries ago the Spaniards, in their search for Cathay and the wealth of the Indies, inadvertently discovered America. Attempting to make the best of what they considered to be a bad bargain, they stumbled upon California. The story of how this came about was a colorful one because it involved the love of man for gold, the adventurous spirit of the conquistadores of early Spain, and the building of a great empire whose outposts ran from the green islands of the Caribbean to the shores of the far-off Philippines and from the sun-drenched pueblos of New Mexico to the surging waters that beat against the Horn.

Within forty years of the time that Columbus discovered America, Spain had established two bases of operation in the western hemisphere which not only turned out to be treasure troves of tremendous richness, but also served as headquarters from which exploring parties quickly blazed trails over most of both continents. One of these was the Viceroyalty of Peru and the other was the Viceroyalty of New Spain or, as it was later to be known, Mexico. It is the latter that concerns us because it was from Mexico as a base that California was discovered.

The man who conquered Mexico was Hernán Cortés, one of the greatest of the conquistadores. He was described by one of his own soldiers in the following words: "He was of a good height and body and well proportioned and of strong limbs, and the colour of his face was somewhat ashy and not very merry and had his face been longer, he would have been handsomer and his eyes had a somewhat loving glance yet grave withal; his beard was dark and sparse and short and the hair which in those days was worn [long] the same as the beard, and his chest was high and his back of a good shape and he was lean and of little belly and somewhat bowlegged and his legs and thighs well set, and he was a good horseman and skillful with all weapons on foot or on horseback and knew very well how to handle them, and above all, a heart and a courage which is what matters." [1]

Cortés was a member of a group of lesser nobility who signed up under Velásquez, governor of Cuba, for an expedition which was to explore the unknown seas and lands to the West. Through an act which came near to being outright rebellion, he seized control of the expedition, coasted eastern Mexico, landed near Vera Cruz, and marched overland across the Sierra Madre Oriental into the lofty valley of Mexico, where, much to his satisfaction, he discovered the true goal of all conquistadores—a native people, the Aztecs, who had developed a great civilization. They had stone buildings and temples, a city, Tenochtitlán, much like Venice, whose traffic was carried on a complex network of canals, and, best of all, they had learned how to mine and refine gold and silver. The treasure of the Aztecs is said to have subsidized the Hapsburg wars in Europe for nearly three fourths of a century. Through battle, treachery, and a subtle playing upon the superstitions of the natives, Cortés succeeded in conquering the city of Mexico and establishing Spanish rule in that area.

It was ten years before Cortés was able to send out expeditions to the northern coastal waters. He was deeply interested in this area because folklore seemed to indicate that another treasure trove lay there which would multiply his fortune many fold. In 1532 he sent out two ships under the command of Diego Hurtado de Mendoza. Hurtado faced serious complications, including attack by the commandant of Nueva Galicia, who was himself a Spaniard but a great enemy of Cortés, and finally mutiny and shipwreck. The expedition was almost a total failure.

The next year two more vessels were sent out, and as the result of a mutiny a pilot named Fortún Jiménez found himself in command. Jiménez made his way northward to a bay on what he presumed to be an island. It was, in fact, the Bay of La Paz at the

---

[1] Salvador de Madariaga: *Hernán Cortés, Conqueror of Mexico* (1941), p. 103.

southern tip of the peninsula of Lower California. Here Indians set upon the members of the expedition and killed twenty-one men, including Jiménez himself, but reports came back of great wealth in pearls in those seas, which was stimulus enough for Cortés to send out still another band of adventurers.

This time, in 1535, Cortés himself went, leading an expedition of three vessels which attempted to set up a colony at La Paz. Here they encountered the same problem which was to be such a bugbear to later colonists of Alta California—the difficulty of getting supplies from Mexico. After much hardship, including the death of twenty-three of the colonists through starvation, Cortés, in 1536, abandoned the colony.

Cortés now faced further complications. In 1535 he was replaced as supreme commander of New Spain by its first official Viceroy, Antonio de Mendoza. The rivalry between Cortés and Mendoza on an unofficial plane was intense. Cortés determined to continue his explorations and, in 1536, he was greatly encouraged by the arrival in Mexico of one of history's greatest pedestrians, Alvar Núñez Cabeza de Vaca, who, being a member of an ill-starred Spanish expedition to the coast of Florida some years earlier, had made his way largely on foot from that peninsula all around the shores of the Gulf to Mexico itself. En route, Cabeza de Vaca had heard wondrous stories of legendary cities and wealthy tribes to the north, and in 1539 a Franciscan friar named Marcos de Niza traveled northward to confirm the tales of the wanderer. The friar saw what he thought were golden cities on the horizon and quickly returned to report the alleged truth of Cabeza de Vaca's legend. What Marcos had actually seen, of course, were Indian pueblos in New Mexico, but the excitement his report occasioned was sufficient to send out several official expeditions to the north, one the famous Coronado land party which explored the American Southwest. Another was a sea voyage commanded by Francisco de Ulloa, who took three vessels up the Gulf of California to the mouth of the Colorado, confirmed the fact that Lower California was in truth a peninsula rather than an island, and coasted it some distance up its westward shore before he and his vessel, with all on board, vanished into the empty seas.

Ulloa's expedition marked the end of Cortés's direct influence on northern exploration. By that time his own political position was threatened and he spent the remaining years of his life trying to regain the confidence of the Spanish monarch.

Francisco Vásquez de Coronado was given command of what was perhaps the most elaborate exploring party ever to be sent out by Spanish officialdom. There was basis for this, because Friar Marcos had apparently verified Cabeza de Vaca's tale of the Seven Golden Cities of Cíbola, and it was highly unusual for conquistadores to set out after anything but an unknown and highly amorphous goal. The expedition consisted of two hundred and fifty horsemen, seventy infantry, three hundred native allies, and more than a thousand Negro and Indian servants and followers.

Coronado started with great expectations, and his disappointment was the more bitter because of his overconfidence. For two years he searched the Southwest, marching north to Arizona, then east to New Mexico, struggling with normally peaceable Pueblo Indians who were disturbed by the invaders. He verified the fact that Friar Marcos's "golden cities" were in reality Indian pueblos built of mud and adobe, and, greatly disillusioned, he pursued another phantom of folklore, the "Gran Quivira," across the Texas panhandle and into the plains of eastern Kansas. Then, weary and sick with disappointment, he led his men back home to an obscurity which was in reality undeserved, for as a commander he was highly successful and suffered surprisingly few casualties on his long trek, and as an explorer he not only opened up the entire southwestern part of the future United States, but also laid the basis for Spain's claim to that vast and colorful area.

His connection with California was indirect, but important. The supporting expeditions of Ulloa, Alarcón, and Cabrillo would probably not have gone out if it had not been for Coronado's project, and the Indian gossip which Coronado picked up en route added further bits of information to the collection of disparate and often mistaken facts which men had about California.

The Coronado expedition stimulated the sending out of two more sea parties, one in 1540 commanded by Hernando de Alarcón, who was dispatched up the Gulf to make contact with the main force under Coronado. Alarcón reached the mouth of the Colorado and, sending some of his men ashore to drag the boats upstream against the current, he ascended the muddy river more than two hundred miles and thus became the "first European to see any part of the land which now comprises the state of California. It is possible that he even set foot on it for he went ashore several times, although on which side of the river he does not indicate." [2]

One of Coronado's men, Melchor Díaz, reached the Colorado by land and found there a tree on which was written: "Alarcón came thus far. There are letters at the foot of this tree." Díaz crossed the Colorado and explored a short distance into the deserts of Lower California.

The last, and greatest, expedition which the Coronado journeys stimulated started in 1542 under the command of Juan Rodríguez Cabrillo, a Portuguese adventurer who had served under several famous Spanish adventurers. Cabrillo set sail from Navidad in June in command of two ships, the *San Salvador* and the *Victoria*—two tiny, poorly built vessels, badly provisioned and inexpertly manned. Because of bad weather it took Cabrillo four days to cross the Gulf of California and he then proceeded up the western shore of Lower California, stopping frequently and making contact with the Indians. In several places on the coast he was informed by the Indians that there were white men farther east, thus indicating that reports of the Díaz or Coronado expeditions were drifting coastward by primitive grapevine.

Finally, on Thursday, September 28, 1542, after three months of journeying, Cabrillo entered a port which he named San Miguel. This, in fact, was San Diego harbor and Cabrillo, therefore, was

---

[2] Henry R. Wagner: *Juan Rodríguez Cabrillo* (1941), p. 6.

the first European to set foot on the shore of Alta California. After a brief stay at San Diego, Cabrillo sailed northward, landing at Catalina Island, San Pedro, Santa Monica, and Ventura. He proceeded up the Santa Barbara Channel and finally reached Point Concepción in mid-October. The weather then became troublesome and Cabrillo returned southward, landing at San Miguel Island, where he suffered a fall, breaking his arm near the shoulder. However, he made two subsequent attempts to sail northward beyond Point Concepción. Blustery winter weather prevented him from discovering the Bay of San Francisco or Monterey, but he did manage to reach Northwest Cape near Fort Ross. Forced back to San Miguel Island, Cabrillo died the following January as a result of the fracture he had suffered some months before. The command was then taken over by Bartolomé Ferrelo, who led the expedition to the Oregon coast as far as the mouth of the Rogue River. The chief goal of the expedition seems to have been the western mouth of the legendary Strait of Anián or Northwest Passage, which was popularly supposed to provide a water route through the North American continent. In April of 1543 Ferrelo returned to the expedition's home port of Navidad in Mexico after having named many of the prominent geographical configurations of the California coast—which names were not destined to endure, however, because they were largely renamed by the Vizcaíno expedition some years later.

Two, or perhaps three, years before Cabrillo made his memorable voyage along the California coast, the wife of Edmund Drake, a yeoman living on the edge of the wild wastes of Dartmoor, in Devonshire, England, had given birth to a son, named Francis, who was destined to become the leading navigator of his time and the foremost seaman of the English race.

Drake appeared on the high seas at a time when Elizabethan seamen were learning of the profits to be made from raiding Spain's galleon fleets carrying treasure from the New World to the Old. He gained experience with noted freebooters like Sir John Hawkins and in raids against Spanish settlements, and by

1577 he was ready for his great adventure—commanding a raiding expedition to the Pacific Ocean.

On November 15 five vessels sailed out of Plymouth harbor, ostensibly bound for Alexandria. The purpose of the voyage has been vigorously disputed by historians,[3] but it is generally agreed that Drake's major objective was to raid Spanish settlements on the Pacific coast of South America. The vessels were small but well armed, and prospects seemed good for a successful voyage. Drake encountered trouble, however, before he entered the Straits of Magellan, climaxed by a mutiny which he resolutely crushed by executing the ringleader. Stormy weather then separated Drake's flagship, the *Golden Hind,* from her sister vessels, and after fifty-two days of screaming gales and heavy seas Drake found himself alone in the Pacific.[4]

The Spaniards did not expect English freebooters in this area, and Drake found business very much to his liking. Sailing northward up the Chilean coast, he raided Valparaiso and Santiago. At Tarapacá one of his seamen wrote: ". . . we found by the sea side a Spaniard lying asleep, who had lying by him thirteen bars of silver, which weighed 4,000 ducats Spanish. We took the silver and left the man." Later Drake seized eight hundred pounds of silver from a llama pack train, found more treasure at Arica, and uncovered much loot in poorly defended vessels off Lima and Panama. The high point of Drake's success came when he encountered and captured one of the treasure galleons, the *Cacafuego,* out of whose hold he took "great riches, as jewels and precious stones, thirteen chests full of reals of plate, fourscore pound weight of gold, and six and twenty ton of silver." Drake

---

[3] In 1926, basing his conclusions upon a minute and objective examination of all available English and Spanish documents, Dr. Henry R. Wagner published an exhaustive study entitled: *Sir Francis Drake's Voyage Around the World, Its Aims and Achievements.* On most points the volume took uncompromising issue with the standardized treatment of the Drake expedition.

[4] For a convenient collection of the various accounts of Drake's voyage, see *The World Encompassed and Analogous Contemporary Documents* . . . , edited by N. M. Penzer (London, 1926).

then put into a deserted harbor to refit the *Golden Hind* for the long voyage home.

By this time the Spaniards were aware that strong measures were necessary, and Drake found it necessary to sail north along the Mexican coast to avoid capture. Because of the near approach of cold weather, Drake dared not plunge westward across the Pacific, but instead was forced to winter on the shore of California.

Here, after some searching for the Northwest Passage near arctic waters, Drake found an anchorage "in a fair and good bay, into which it had pleased God to send him." The actual identification of this bay has occupied the researches of many historians, and Drake has been variously placed in Trinidad, Bodega, San Francisco, and Drake's Bay, with some weight of evidence attaching to the last. Wherever he really landed, Drake made contact with the Indians, who showed him and his men every hospitality, and he formally took possession of the region by nailing upon a post a brass plate on which was inscribed Elizabeth's name, the date of arrival, the name which Drake bestowed upon the area, Nova Albion, and an English sixpence. The story of the discovery of this brass plate in the twentieth century, the arguments concerning its authenticity, and its final deposit in the Bancroft Library of the University of California constitute one of the most fascinating pieces of historical detective work which has ever been undertaken.[5]

On July 23, 1579, the *Golden Hind* sailed away from California and began her long voyage across the Pacific. Months later, after

---

[5] For Professor Herbert E. Bolton's spectacular story of the discovery of "Drake's Plate of Brass," the questions to which it gave rise, and the somewhat belated tests of the relic's authenticity, see *Drake's Plate of Brass* (California Historical Society, 1937), and "Drake's Plate of Brass Authenticated," in the *Quarterly* of the same society (December 1938). In a contribution, already cited, entitled "Sovereignty Rights through Symbolic Acts" (*Pacific Historical Review*, Vol. VII), Henry R. Wagner calls attention to a number of possible objections to the genuineness of the relic. For a popularly written and reasonably objective review of the story of the plate, see Joseph R. Ellison's article, "True or False" (*Saturday Evening Post*, April 3, 1943).

touching at the Moluccas, Java, and the Celebes, Drake rounded the Cape of Good Hope and set his course for England. On September 26, 1580, nearly three years after beginning the historic voyage "around the whole globe of the earth," the *Golden Hind* anchored again in the familiar waters of Plymouth harbor.

The expedition is said to have returned a profit of ten thousand per cent to the backers of the voyage; but the exact amount of the booty seized by Drake was never publicly revealed. Much of the treasure was secretly distributed; and when the remainder was transferred under cover of darkness from the Thames docks to the Tower of London, heavy wains, laden with the silver and gold of the Spanish king, creaked all night long through the narrow London streets.[6]

Drake's voyage affected the history of California chiefly by indirection. It showed the vulnerability of Spanish commerce in the Pacific and tempted other raiders, both English and Dutch, to follow his example; it stimulated new interest in the search for the Strait of Anián, and new efforts on the part of the Spaniards to block the advance of foreign interlopers; and in the European theater it hastened the inevitable conflict between Spain and England for the mastery of the sea.

---

[6] Despite Elizabeth's efforts to preserve Drake's famous flagship for posterity, the vessel was broken up during the reign of a later sovereign. But at least two relics, made from the good oak timbers of the *Golden Hind,* still remain—a table in Middle Temple Hall, in the heart of London; and a stoutly built, commodious armchair presented to the Bodleian Library of Oxford University in the year 1662.

CHAPTER 2. The Search for a Port of Call

CALIFORNIA suffered from the fact that it was an outpost of outposts, a far northern frontier in which the possibility of treasure was so remote that it became difficult to arouse enthusiasm for exploration. Still, despite this remoteness, it had, by the time of Cabrillo, already been named, and the circumstances surrounding the naming are of some interest and quite in line with the romantic tradition which has always been part of the region.

Spaniards of the 15th century enjoyed escape fiction as much as Americans of today and around 1500 a novelist named Garcí Ordóñez de Montalvo wrote a romantic novel called, *La Sergas de Esplandián.* One of the incidents in the book concerned a supposed siege of Constantinople in which the attackers received unexpected aid from a Queen Calafía of the Isla de California, which had the added interesting characteristic of supporting an amazon culture. This tale had a large reading public, and Chapman [1] said that the name "California" probably was first applied by Jiménez in 1533–34, although there is no direct evidence as to this. The term was later known by Cabrillo, for it appears in his journal. There are many other theories as to how the name came to be used, but whatever the reason, in its fictional form, it meant a land of wealth and treasure, and by the mid-16th century was generally accepted and applied to the general area.

Because California was so far distant from the centers of Spanish activity in the western hemisphere and also because the possibility of treasure there seemed so remote, the chief reason for its further exploration was utilitarian, and California appeared again in history as a possible port of call in the famous voyages of the Manila galleon.

----

[1] Charles Edward Chapman: *A History of California: The Spanish Period* (1936), p. 66.

The Manila galleon was a vessel which started from Acapulco on the Pacific coast of Mexico, sailed across the Pacific to the Philippine Islands loaded with silver and luxury products, exchanged the silver for the riches of the East including silks and spices, and then returned to New Spain. Several voyagers led by Magellan had sailed westward across the Pacific to the Philippines, but the eastward voyage was first attempted in an expedition led by Andrés de Urdaneta in 1565. Urdaneta's achievement led to a rich annual voyage, under rigid government control as was the Spanish custom, which often produced for its backers profits of one hundred to four hundred per cent.

The problems of the Manila galleon were many. The westward voyage was the easiest and could be accomplished in less than ninety days because of favorable winds and the direct route thus permitted, but the return voyage presented a problem. It was necessary for the galleon to sail far north along the Japanese islands until it could be aided by the Japan current; but this route brought it into the severe weather of the northern Pacific, through the typhoon belt along the east Asiatic Coast, and into the storms, fogs, and gales of the northwest coast of North America. Seven months was not unusual for a return voyage. An additional complication consisted of the fact that Spaniards were human beings and engaged in much graft and corruption in the loading of the galleon. Although certain parts of the hold were supposedly strictly reserved for food and water, bribery often filled these provision spaces with profit-making cargo. Because of the shortage of supplies and the lack of elementary scientific knowledge about diet, the return voyage was usually accompanied by many fatalities from scurvy and other nutritional diseases. Sanitation was poor on the galleon and vermin of all sorts afflicted the passengers, while tempers flared and human relations became difficult because of the long period in confined quarters.

There were two reasons why the Manila galleon helped to bring California to the attention of the world. One was that certain of the galleon commanders were urged to search for the western entrance to the Strait of Anián which Spaniards were still looking for under the delusion that it was possible to cross North America by a water passage. Another and more important reason was the fact that the galleon badly needed a port of call along the coast of California so that it could replenish its supplies and water and provide some fresh vegetables for those of its passenger list who were afflicted with scurvy.

Certain of the galleon commanders, Gali in 1584, Unamuno in 1587, Rodríguez Cermenho in 1595, and a passenger, Gemelli Careri, in 1597, left records of visits to California. Gali encountered currents which made him believe that the Strait of Anián did exist, and he described California as being "a very high and fair land with many trees, wholly without snow, and four leagues from the land you find thereabout many drifts of roots, leaves of trees, reeds, and other leaves like fig leaves, the like whereof we found in great abundance in the country of Japan, which they eat; . . . there likewise we found great store of seals; whereby it is to be presumed and certainly to be believed, that there are many rivers, bays, and havens along those coasts to the haven of Acapulco." [2]

Gali's successor in California exploration was an interesting adventurer named Pedro de Unamuno. During the summer of 1587 in command of a small, single-decked, three-masted frigate named the *Nuestra Señora de Buena Esperanza,* Unamuno began the voyage across the Pacific to Acapulco. Sighting the California coast late in October, he entered El Morro Bay near San Luis Obispo, and marched a considerable distance into the interior. Unamuno made formal claim to the land in the name of Philip of Spain, set up a cross on the site, and performed other ceremonies duly prescribed in the act of possession. He then continued his voyage to Acapulco.

Foreign pirates also stimulated the search for a port of call. In 1587 Thomas Cavendish, an English privateer, captured the Manila galleon near Cape San Lucas, and Spain consequently became more interested than ever in occupying California. In 1595,

---

[2] Ibid., p. 114. From Fernando de Navarrete, *Voyages.*

therefore, Sebastian Rodríguez Cermenho, a Portuguese, was appointed commander of the Manila galleon to search the California coast for a likely port. He located Drake's Bay and named it the Bay of San Francisco, not to be confused with the present port of that name. His vessel, the *San Agustín*, was wrecked, and he constructed a makeshift launch in which he continued his explorations, landing at many of the spots previously discovered by Cabrillo. Finally, in January 1596, he came to anchor in Navidad. But any glory which Rodríguez Cermenho deserved because of his persistence in carrying out his commission under difficulties was largely neutralized by the fact that he had lost the galleon and its cargo.

The most successful of the galleon commanders, at least insofar as exploring the California coast was concerned, was Sebastian Vizcaíno. Vizcaíno had previously engaged in the Manila trade, lost a considerable fortune when Cavendish took the *Santa Ana,* and participated unsuccessfully in exploration and pearl fishing in the Gulf. From all accounts he was a man with the knack of obtaining position and recognition out of all proportion to his talents.

The chief purpose of the voyage, which this time was to set out directly from Mexico, was to survey and map the coast and to examine likely harbors with the possibility of finding pearls. Though officially commander of the expedition Vizcaíno was subject to the authority of two councils: one to decide questions of navigation, the other to cope with military matters. He was under strict instructions not to explore the Gulf on the outward voyage, to make no attempt to establish permanent settlements, and to leave unchanged the names of landmarks already indicated on the maps. His expedition consisted of two fairly well equipped ships, the *San Diego* and the *Santo Tomás,* and a frigate, the *Tres Reyes*. He sailed from Acapulco in May 1602, with about two hundred persons in his crew.

Without difficulty the fleet reached Cape San Lucas, but thereafter the vessels encountered a succession of storms and adverse winds, and because the water barrels had been made of wornout materials, the expedition quickly found itself short of provisions. But despite such hardships the expedition came to anchor, on November 10, in Cabrillo's port of San Miguel, which Vizcaíno renamed San Diego. Vizcaíno described San Diego as an admirable haven for the Manila galleon and believed that vessels up to a thousand tons burden could be safely careened and overhauled in the bay. Sailing from San Diego, the Spaniards landed on an island which they named Santa Catalina, and the cove in which they came to anchor is today a popular resort known as Avalon. Here they were immediately surrounded by a multitude of Indians who "came out in canoes of cedar and pine, made of planks very well joined and calked, each one with eight oars and with fourteen or fifteen Indians, who looked like galley slaves." [3]

Leaving his Catalina Island anchorage, Vizcaíno sailed northward through the Santa Barbara channel, again encountering many Indians who handled their canoes with great dexterity. Threading their way with some difficulty through the islands above Santa Barbara and sometimes losing each other in the darkness, the vessels rounded Point Concepción and ran before a wind from the southeast until they found the anchorage called by Cabrillo the Bay of Pines. The day following the landing, the voyagers set up a tent and the friars said mass. Disregarding the fact that two of his predecessors had already named the port, Vizcaíno called it Monterey in honor of the Viceroy, the Conde de Monterey, under whose sanction the voyage had been undertaken, and pronounced it "the best port that could be desired." [4]

The great significance of the Vizcaíno expedition was, in fact, the new emphasis placed on the port of Monterey, which led, eventually, to that area's establishment as the provincial capital of Spanish and Mexican California. The diarist of the expedition, Father Ascensión, wrote that it was a very good port and well protected from all winds. There was, he said, wood and water in it and an immense number of great pine trees, smooth and

---

[3] Herbert E. Bolton, ed.: *Spanish Exploration in the Southwest, 1542–1706* (1952), p. 83.
[4] Ibid., p. 91.

straight, suitable for the masts and yards of ships. He pointed out that those coming from China in need of relief could very well resort to this port, and that it was the same region and parallel of latitude to Seville and was almost of the same climate. The Spaniards, he added, could settle here as an assistance to those sailing from China and to undertake the conversion of the numerous, docile Indians.[5]

The descriptions which the voyagers brought back of the superlative qualities of the port were so exaggerated that subsequent travelers, such as Portolá, when they saw it failed to recognize Monterey as the magnificent harbor so touted by Vizcaíno and his men. A further irony was the fact that just a few miles to the north lay a really magnificent port which today is known as San Francisco Bay.

From Monterey Vizcaíno sent one of his vessels south with the sick for the purpose of reducing the demands on his diminishing food supply while he took the other two ships and explored the coast to the northward. Again the storms of the northern coast with rain and fog plus the ravages of scurvy made the voyage an epoch of hardship. At one time only two of the sailors could climb to the main topsail. A furious south wind accompanied by fog and blinding rain made it "as dark in the daytime as at night."[6] The men believed that the currents and seas were carrying them full speed to the Strait of Anián and the flagship, struck by too heavy seas, was thrown about so violently that Vizcaíno fell against some boxes and broke several of his ribs. Finally, off Cape Mendocino, at the "head and end of the realm and mainland of California and the entrance to the Strait of Anián,"[7] one of the vessels was forced to turn back. The other continued northward to a debatable point which some have insisted was as far north as the 43rd parallel. But whether or not it achieved this latitude, little more was discovered because of the inclemency of the weather and the number of sick on board, and Vizcaíno decided to abandon further exploration and to return to Mexico.

---

[5] Ibid., p. 119.   [6] Ibid., p. 95.   [7] Ibid., p. 121.

Landing at Mazatlán, Vizcaíno managed to obtain supplies which aided the scurvy-stricken seamen. The other vessel which had turned south earlier arrived at Navidad with only six men alive in the crew.

Despite the difficulties both Vizcaíno and Father Ascensión remained ardent enthusiasts for the occupation of Alta California and continued to carry on an active propaganda for the establishment of a colony at Monterey. In addition to the contention that the port would provide a desperately needed refuge for the Manila ships, Father Ascensión advanced a number of other reasons for converting the harbor into a permanent Spanish base. Some of his arguments were based on his conviction that certain of the legends which Spaniards had heard about this northern country were true, but his basic reason for urging the occupation at Monterey was the opportunity which would thus be opened for the preaching of the Holy Gospel and the conversion of many souls. As a final clinching argument, Ascensión added: "As this realm of the Californias becomes pacified and its natives become converted . . . the Spaniards can go on settling other districts . . . suitable for effecting the conversion of souls, and affording them profits and advantages; for if the Spaniard does not see any advantage, he will not be moved to do good, and these souls will perish without remedy if it is understood that no profit will be drawn from going there. But if they are lured by self-interest they will go on discovering new lands every day. . . ." [8]

Meantime there had been a revival of Spanish interest in the region explored by Coronado half a century before and in the overland quest for the northern strait. In 1598 Juan de Oñate marched northward from Chihuahua to lay the foundation of a Spanish colony in New Mexico. Subsequent explorations carried him as far east as Wichita, Kansas, and into the Southwest by way of Bill Williams's Fork along the main Colorado to the head of the Gulf of California. Oñate and his companions brought back

[8] Ibid., p. 131.

Inscription Rock, New Mexico, showing both Spanish and American explorers' records, spanning more than two centuries.

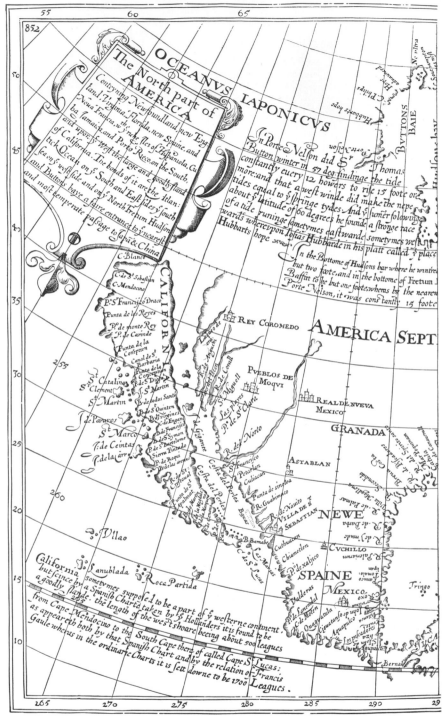

OCEANVS IAPONICVS

The North part of
AMERICA

Conteyning Newfoundland, new England, Virginia, Florida, new Spaine, and Noua Francia, wth ye rude Isles of Hispaniola, Cuba, Iamaica, and Porto Ricco on the South, and vpon ye West the large and goodly Iland of California. The bonds of it are the Atlantick Ocean on ye South, and East sides ye South sea on ye west side and only North Fretum Hudson and Buttons haue a faire entrance to ye nearest and most temperate passage to Iapan & China

In Porte Nelson did Sr Thomas Button winter in 57 deg: finding the tide constantly euery 12 howers to rise 15 foote or more: and that a west winde did make the nepe tides equal to ye springe tydes. And ye sumer folawinge about ye latitude of 60 degrees he founde a stronge race of a tide runinge sometymes eastwarde sometymes westwardes whereuppon Iosias Hubbarde in his platt called ye place Hubbarts hope

In the Bottome of Hudsons bar where he wintred but two foote, and in the bottome of Fretun Baffin to the but one foote, whems by the nearen Porte Nelson, it was constantly 15 foote

C:Blanco

C. de S Sebastian
C. Mendocino

P:S Franci ro Draco

Punta de las Reyes

P. de monte Rey
P. le Carinde

REY COROMEDO

AMERICA SEPT.

Punta de la
Conceptton

Canal de St
Barbaria
Punta de la
Conception
P. de S Dio

St Catalina
St Clement
St Martin

B. de todos Santos
B. de S Quinten
C. de Engaño

B. de Francisco
B. de S Virgines
P. de S Symon
P. de S Bartolome
Sierra Pintado
P. de Roqui
R de las arecas

**PVEBLOS DE
MOQVI**

**REAL DE NVEVA
MEXICO**

GRANADA

J. de Paraxos

St Marco
J. de Ceintas
P. de la Carr

R. de Norto

ASTABLAN

R. de S.
Cathoual
Ce Ra del Peñol
P de cual
La Mexter
La Meguela
C de las arca

Ce Ra del Peñol
Francisco
Petlarlan
Culiacan

Punta de singloa
R. Guahmelus

de Nanito y
**VILLA DE S
SEBASTIAN**

NEWE

R. de Diaba

CVCHILLO

Vlao

B. Barnaba
C de las Moxas
Cuthason

R de Palerman

Chiamelen
P de Alexaljeco

SPAINE

California
but since by a Spanish Charta taken by ye Hollinders itis found to be a goodly Islande. the length of the west shoare beeing about 500 leagues from Cape Mendocino to the South Cape there, ye called Cape S Lucas; as appeareth both by that Spanish Chart and by the relation of Francis Gaule who as in the ordinarie Charts it is sett downe to be 1700 Leagues.

Janublada
sometymes supposed to be a parte of ye westerne continent,

Roca Partida

Malleras

MEXICO

P de Sancdad
C de Moten
Ouagratula
Cieuatan so op uojt
Aquapulco
Aquipalco
Tema
Los piscadores

Tringo

Bernal

California and New Spain, c. 1625. In this map California
is depicted as a "large and goodly Iland."

Mission San Xavier del Bac, nine miles southwest of Tucson, was the headquarters of Father Garcés when he was making his great journeys of exploration.

Mission San Carlos Borromeo, founded at Monterey in 1770, moved a year later to Carmel.

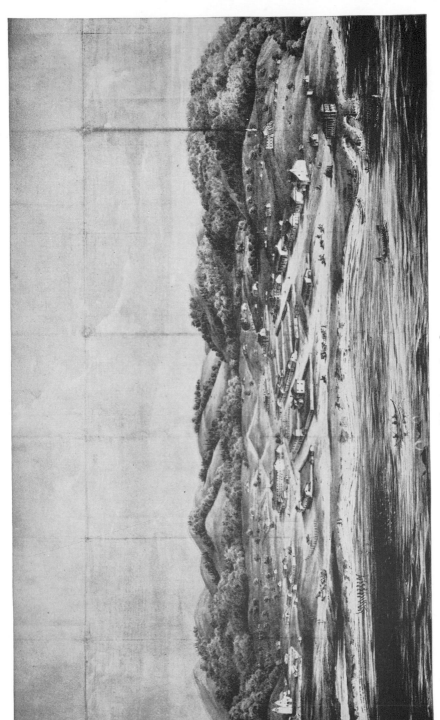

Monterey in 1842.

"Death on the Desert" (Rabbit-Hole Springs). A sketch by J. Goldsborough Bruff, one of the Argonauts of '49, showing some tragedies of the trail.

John C. Fremont, military explorer, opened many western trails
and was the officer to whom the Californians surrendered in 1847.

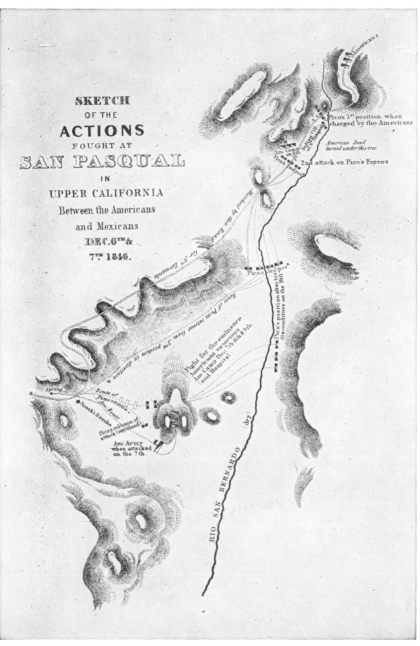

Diagram of the Battle of San Pascual, fought between Kearny
and the Californians under Pico during the Mexican War.

Sutter's Fort on the Sacramento, drawn by William Rich Hutton in 1849.
This was the headquarters of Sutter's barony.

curious and alluring tales of this Mediterranean Sea of California which some called the Mar de Cortés and others the Mar Vermejo. According to reports obtained from the Indians, the harbors yielded pearls as big as hazelnuts, and an amazon Indian queen who ruled over an island town had a priceless pearl breastplate and was accustomed to add finely ground pearls to the beverages which she drank. The Indians also reported rich deposits of silver and told of a lake whose shores yielded large quantities of gold. The legends, in other words, multiplied through Oñate's journeys and additional stimulus was given to the further exploration of California.

CHAPTER 3. Revival of the Plan of Settlement

DURING the long-extended interval between the voyage of Vizcaíno and the actual colonization of California, Spain's claim to a monopoly of North America was successfully disputed by one after another of her European rivals. France established and lost an empire in the valleys of the St. Lawrence and the Mississippi. England planted her colonies on the Atlantic seaboard and eventually extended her dominion from the Gulf of Mexico to Hudson Bay. Far to the northwest an advance guard of fur hunters, adventurers, and criminals crossed the narrow strait from Asia and erected a bastion of the Russian Empire in Alaska.

The viceroyalty of New Spain, in the meantime, had become a stabilized, well-ordered, well-developed kingdom. Mexico City, its capital, "was the metropolis of European life and culture in all North America"; its trade was the envy of every maritime nation in Christendom; and the fame of the extent and richness of its mines had spread throughout the world.

By 1750 New Spain's northern borderlands, which corresponded both in nature and in importance to the historic western frontier of the United States, extended in a great arc from the presidio of Los Adaes, in Louisiana, to a chain of recently established Jesuit missions in Lower California. At irregular intervals the long frontier was marked by presidios, missions, mining camps, cattle ranches, and rude adobe pueblos—the characteristic outposts of Spain's wilderness advance.

This advance had been achieved only through much travail, and while explorers and seamen blazoned their deeds on the pages of history, the more significant northward progress of the frontier had been brought about by hundreds of less picturesque miners, ranchers, churchmen, and soldiers. The frontier line had crept steadily toward California from Central Mexico, hastened at times by mineral discoveries such as the great silver hoards at Zacatecas and Durango, delayed occasionally by native hostility such as the Chichimeca War which for half a century, in the late 1500's, retarded the settlement of the Zacatecas region. But the advance was inexorable. Month by month, year by year, the Spaniards in Mexico pushed northward and westward and came ever closer to the borders of California.[1]

The chief figure in the expansion to the northwest, until the Spanish frontier touched the waste borderlands of Alta California itself, was the Jesuit friar Eusebio Francisco Kino. Herbert E. Bolton, Kino's authoritative biographer and devoted admirer, speaks of him as "the most picturesque missionary pioneer of all North America—explorer, astronomer, cartographer, mission builder, ranchman, cattle king, and defender of the frontier." [2]

Kino's contact with Lower California began in 1683, when he accompanied an unsuccessful colonizing expedition across the gulf. From that time on he was consumed by a passion to preach the gospel to the heathen of the peninsula, to bring light to those that sat in darkness, and to show the way of redemption to those that had no hope.

The friar began his labors in northern Sonora, in 1687, with the erection of the mission of Nuestra Señora de Los Dolores, in the valley of the San Miguel River, about a hundred miles south of Tucson. In the interval between that incident and his death, twenty-four years later, Kino founded twenty-nine missions, eight of which were in southern Arizona; he baptized four thousand neophytes, and made more than fifty overland expeditions, at least one of which carried him nearly a thousand miles.

Often alone, or with only one or two white companions, the missionary journeyed on horseback over unknown trails, traversed the most arid regions of the Southwest, braved the fierce midsummer desert heat; followed the forbidding Camino del

---

[1] For an excellent account of life on the Mexican frontier and, more particularly, of the Chichimeca War, see Philip W. Powell: *Soldiers, Indians, and Silver* (1952).

[2] Herbert Eugene Bolton: *The Rim of Christendom* (1936), p. vii.

Diablo between Sonoíta and the Gila; threaded his way through the grim, trackless mountains of the Sonora-Arizona wastes; and mapped the courses of the streams that feed the lower Colorado. The "steel-thewed friar" made nothing of riding fifty miles a day; once he covered a hundred and twenty-five miles in thirty-six hours; and on another expedition he averaged eighty miles a day for three successive days.

In his role of geographer Kino set himself to determine whether Baja California was an island, as most of his contemporaries believed, despite the reports of earlier navigators to the contrary, or a peninsula. As a missionary, he had a consuming desire to bring not only Sonora and Arizona into the fold of the church, but Baja and Alta California as well. With these dual objectives in mind, the great missionary explorer made several journeys down the Gila River to its junction with "the very voluminous, populous, and fertile Colorado River . . . the true Río del Norte of the ancients." Once Kino descended the Colorado from the Gila to the Gulf; on another occasion he crossed the lower Colorado into California; again, he stood with one of his fellow friars on "the very high hill of Santa Clara which is exactly north of the head of the Sea of California, and from which it is seen most plainly that this sea ascends no higher up, and that California has a continental connection with this mainland of New Spain."

Kino embodied the results of his observations in a treatise entitled: "Cosmographical Proof That California Is Not an Island but a Peninsula. . . ." Apparently the manuscript was never published; and the delusion of California's insularity remained so persistent and widespread that Juan de Ugarte and Fernando Consag, two of Kino's Jesuit successors, again found it necessary to refute the error. Kino's efforts to determine the true cartography of the Southwest were inspired primarily by his determination to open an overland supply route to the prospective mission fields in Baja and Alta California from the settlements and ranches of Sonora.

In his work both as missionary and as explorer Kino was supported by the inspector of Jesuit missions in Sonora and Sinaloa, "the square-jawed, hawk-nosed, clear-headed Juan María de la Salvatierra." It was Salvatierra, in fact, serving as "priest, officer, sentry, governor of the province and cook for the army, all rolled into one," who established, at Loreto, the first permanent European settlement in Baja California, and erected the first Jesuit missions on the peninsula.

By the time of Salvatierra's death in 1717, there were five such missions in Lower California. During the next half-century the chain was extended southward almost to the tip of the peninsula, and northward perhaps two thirds of the way to the present international boundary line. Despite the failure of later explorations to discover a practical overland route round the head of the gulf (which would link the Lower California foundations with those of Arizona and Sonora), and the sterility, malignance, and isolation of the country itself, the Jesuit outposts on the peninsula became an indispensable base of operations for the exploration and settlement of the immense wilderness to the north—the land of Alta California.

By 1750 the Spanish frontier had pushed across Sonora and Arizona as far as the Gila and the Colorado rivers; Lower California had been occupied; through the surveys and explorations of early navigators much was known of the ports of San Diego and Monterey; and for more than a century and a half the Manila galleon had been sailing within sight of the California coast. At that juncture, like a cloud no bigger than a man's hand, the threat of English and Russian advance appeared on Spain's colonial horizon. The Seven Years' War effected profound changes in the map of North America, and New Spain came under the direction of José de Gálvez, a vigorous, ambitious expansionist.

As a result of such a fortuitous combination of circumstances, Spain's intention to occupy California—a measure often proposed, but as often postponed or forgotten—finally became a reality. Ostensibly, at least, the momentous decision grew out of the government's perennial fear of foreign aggression. On the one hand, the Russian colony in Alaska furnished a potential threat to

Spanish sovereignty both in the Pacific and along the Northwest coast; at the same time it supplied timely and effective ammunition to the propagandists for the California venture. Reports also gained headway that the French and Dutch were seeking to gain a foothold on the Pacific, presumably at the port of Monterey, and the Seven Years' War further intensified Spain's chronic dread of England.

Besides the fear of foreign aggression, other factors also played an important part in bringing the California venture to a head. Charles III, one of the most capable of the enlightened despots of the eighteenth century, was rapidly restoring to the Spanish throne a measure of the vigor, initiative, and prestige it had enjoyed under the Emperor Charles V and his son Philip II, and introducing into colonial affairs long-needed fiscal changes, sweeping administrative reforms, and a new era of frontier expansion.[3]

In 1765 Charles appointed José de Gálvez Visitor-General of the Kingdom of New Spain. Gálvez was a man of complex, contradictory personality—cruel, vindictive, deeply religious, afflicted with megalomania (at times to the point of insanity), imaginative, energetic, capable of petty intrigues and reprisals, and equally capable of statesmanship of the highest order.

Although Gálvez came to Mexico primarily to reorganize the treasury and overhaul the royal taxes, his activities reached into almost every field of government concern. None of the enterprises in which he engaged, however, took such hold of his imagination as the possibility of expanding the northern frontier, and especially of developing the latent resources of Sonora and Alta California. As a step in that direction, the Visitador planned to reorganize the fiscal administration of New Spain by establishing a system of intendancies throughout the Kingdom. One of the proposed intendancies included the frontier provinces of Durango, Sonora, and the Californias.

Gálvez further recommended the separation of the provinces of Nueva Vizcaya, Sinaloa, Sonora, and the Californias from the

---

[3] Charles I, King of Spain (1516–56), is better known as the Emperor Charles V. Charles III, King of Spain, ruled from 1759 to 1788.

viceroyalty of Mexico, and their erection into a separate political body, to be known as a commandancy general, with its capital in northern Sonora, perhaps at the junction of the Gila and Colorado rivers. As part of the plan Gálvez also proposed to establish a port at San Blas, from which colonists and supplies could be sent by sea to the northwestern frontier; and planned to open an overland route to California from the Gila-Colorado settlements.

Partly because of opposition in Spain, Indian revolts in Sonora, and the Visitador's own temporary madness, the commandancy general was not established until 1776, and the system of intendancies was postponed a decade longer. In the meantime, however, Gálvez had gone rapidly ahead with his ambition to bring about the exploration and settlement of Alta California, a measure in which he had the full support and collaboration of the able Viceroy, Teodoro de Croix.

In the spring of 1768 Gálvez arrived at San Blas, preparatory to making an extended visit to the peninsula. Before crossing the gulf, he called a council, or junta, consisting of Miguel Costansó, an engineer and cosmographer; Vicente Vila, "a Pilot famed on all the seas of Europe"; and two other no less renowned navigators and mathematicians, to devise a feasible plan for carrying out the settlement of Alta California.

The council agreed that the *San Carlos* and the *San Antonio,* the largest and most seaworthy vessels on the coast, should be dispatched, either from San Blas, or Cape San Lucas on the peninsula, to Vizcaíno's "good port of Monterey"; and that a second expedition, using the northern missions of the peninsula as a base, should set out by land for the same destination.

Gálvez sailed from San Blas in May; but storms and contrary winds delayed his arrival in Lower California until July. The Visitador remained on the peninsula nearly ten months, seeking to increase the royal revenues, reorganizing the missions, and supervising the preparation and dispatch of the California expeditions.

By a drastic decree of the crown issued in 1767, the Jesuit order had suddenly been expelled from all the Spanish dominions, in-

cluding the Kingdom of New Spain, and their foundations divided
among the other monastic orders. In the distribution the Franciscans of the College of San Fernando in Mexico City had fallen
heir to the missions of Lower California.[4] In the spring of 1768,
accordingly, a band of fourteen friars, with the fifty-five-year-old
Junípero Serra in charge, landed at La Paz to take possession of
the new field.

The unexpected legacy the Franciscans had received, however,
was none too alluring. Due to the ravages of disease, the scarcity
of arable land, and the lack of water for irrigation, most of the
missions of Lower California were seriously impoverished and
showed faint prospect of returning to their former prosperity.
Despite its poverty, however, the peninsula was the logical base
from which to make the contemplated move into Alta California;
and with characteristic energy Gálvez set about assembling the
necessary equipment and getting the expeditions under way.

In accordance with the plan outlined at San Blas, the Visitador
first gave his attention to outfitting the two ships. Command of
the *San Carlos* was entrusted to the experienced navigator
Vicente Vila. The latter's sailing companions included Miguel
Costansó, the distinguished engineer already mentioned, whose
business was to "mark and map the ports and lands that might be
discovered," and to lay out the royal presidio at Monterey; Don
Pedro Prat, an Army surgeon, who "went for whatever might
come up"; a chaplain, Hernando Parrón, who had the somewhat
staggering task of providing for "the consolation of everybody";
and Don Pedro Fages, captain of a company of twenty-five
leather-jacket troops of Catalonian volunteers.

The *San Carlos* sailed from La Paz on January 9, 1769, and
six days later rounded Cape San Lucas. The voyage was un-
propitious from the start. Polluted water from a brackish stream

---

[4] At the time of the expulsion of the Jesuits, the crown took over a fund,
made up of gifts and donations, with which the Jesuits had supported the
peninsula missions. This "Pious Fund" was held in trust for the Franciscans
and Dominicans, and later became a matter of diplomatic negotiation between the United States and Mexico.

on Cedros Island apparently caused an epidemic among the crew; and scurvy, as usual, added its quota of misery and suffering. To make matters worse, storm, calm, and the lack of knowledge of the coast so delayed the voyage that the *San Carlos* was unable to reach San Diego until the afternoon of April 30. There she found the *San Antonio,* which had been lying at anchor in the harbor for nearly three weeks.

Except for scurvy, the voyage of the *San Antonio* had been uneventful. Overhauled "from keel to pennant," she had sailed from Cape San Lucas on February 15, under the special protection of St. Anthony of Padua, with a full complement of seamen, two Franciscan friars, and a number of carpenters and blacksmiths for the California settlements. Her commander, Don Juan Pérez, was an experienced navigator, and a former master of the Manila galleon.

Ironically enough, the safe arrival of the *San Carlos* at the port of San Diego marked the beginning of the most tragic chapter in the history of the expedition. Scurvy, in its most violent form, and perhaps other plagues as well, struck down the crews of both vessels, leaving only five seamen alive on the *San Carlos* and seven on the *San Antonio.*

Half the company of Catalonian volunteers likewise succumbed; and despite the transfer of the victims to a makeshift canvas hospital on shore, and the heroic efforts of the physician, Don Pedro Prat, the death list grew longer every day, until at last, as Costansó gloomily wrote, "this whole expedition, which had been composed of more than ninety Men saw itself reduced to only Eight Soldiers and as many Mariners in a state to attend to the safeguarding of the Barks, the working of the Launches, Custody of the Camp, and service of the Sick." [5]

In addition to these two vessels, Gálvez had dispatched a third, the *San José,* but it was lost with all hands.

Meanwhile the two land expeditions, upon which the success of the California enterprise chiefly depended, had left Velicatá,

[5] "Narrative of the Portolá Expeditions of 1769–1770," Academy of Pacific Coast History, *Publications,* Vol. I, p. 125.

a frontier post about a hundred and fifty miles south of the present international border, and were well on their way to San Diego. The personnel of the overland companies deserves special mention. The two principal figures were Don Gaspar de Portolá, civil and military commander of both the land and the maritime contingents, and the renowned Franciscan, Fray Junípero Serra.

Portolá was a soldier, born and bred on the frontier. According to contemporary opinion, except as that was colored by prejudice and petty dislike, he had all the qualities of a true leader—courage, resourcefulness, loyalty, tenacity of purpose, and the saving leaven of dry Spanish humor. Serra, the most popular name in California history, was a man of striking and heroic mold; but unfortunately, the real Junípero is difficult to find in the legendary figure created by fiction and too fervid religious zeal. We know, however, that the distinguished Franciscan was a scholar, a good administrator, a penitent, and a mystic. He was interested in soils, irrigation, and handicrafts. He gloried in suffering, often displayed extraordinary physical endurance, and had a consuming desire to preach the gospel to the heathen and to die a martyr's death. Chapman fittingly describes this St. Paul of California as "an enthusiastic, battling, almost quarrelsome, fearless, keen-witted, fervidly devout, unselfish, single-minded missionary." [6]

The first division of the overland expedition left Velicatá on March 24. With the commander, Fernando Rivera y Moncada, marched Fray Juan Crespi, gratefully remembered in California history because of the daily record he kept of the journey to San Diego, and the vivid descriptions.

Rivera's party also included a number of muleteers, forty-two Christian Indians, and twenty-five *soldados de cuero,* or leather-jacket troops, from the royal presidio of Loreto. These troops were hard-bitten veterans of the frontier, "men of great fortitude and patience in fatigue, obedient, resolute, and active and . . . the best horsemen in the world." They derived their name from the sleeveless leather jacket, or coat, "made of six

---

[6] Charles Edward Chapman: *A History of California: The Spanish Period* (1921), p. 353.

or seven plies of white deerskin," which they wore as protection against the missiles of the Indians. For further defense each trooper used a shield, covered with two thicknesses of raw bull's hide, and a sort of leathern apron, or *chaparejos*, which fell down on either side of the pommel of the saddle and thus protected thighs and legs. For offensive purposes the trooper carried a lance, broadsword, and short musket.

Except for the death of a number of the Christian Indians from some mysterious malady, and ample criticism from Father Crespi, directed against the commander, the food, and the length of time consumed on the journey, Rivera's party reached San Diego, on May 14, without serious misadventure.

The survivors on the *San Carlos* and *San Antonio*, who had been waiting long and anxious weeks for the relief anticipated from the arrival of the overland expedition, were overjoyed when the company came in sight; and Rivera's men, who had been on scant rations themselves for many days, were eagerly looking forward, in turn, to the prospect of food from the ships' stores. So the members of the two companies "saluted mutually with festive Salvos from their Weapons," and exchanged embraces and congratulations. But when it became known that neither side had much to share with the other, gloom and disappointment spread through both camps.

The second division of the overland expedition left Velicatá on May 15. Portolá himself was in command; Sergeant José Francisco de Ortega acted as his assistant; and Father Serra served as spiritual leader of the company. In the ranks were ten leather-jacket troops, forty-four Christian Indians (many of whom died or deserted on the way), four muleteers, and two servants. Several hundred head of cattle were driven along, both to augment the food supply and to furnish breeding stock for the proposed missions and settlements in Alta California. In the main, the company followed the trail already broken by Rivera.

At the outset Serra suffered so severely from an infected foot that Portolá advised him to turn back; but at the friar's request a muleteer named Coronel, some of whose descendants were later to acquire more than passing distinction in southern California, treated the sore with a preparation commonly used for the relief of saddle galls.

The Indians whom the expedition encountered presented a constant challenge to the missionary zeal of the friars. The savages wore little or no clothing, and otherwise showed scant evidences of decency or culture. "I saw that which I had hardly managed to believe," wrote Serra, "when I used to read it or they told me of it—which was their going totally nude, as Adam in Paradise before his sin." [7]

At times game was plentiful, and the company fed bountifully upon deer and antelope; again, the hunters returned empty-handed, for the "animals mocked at their shots, and remained walking about"; and of fresh meat the camp "had but the desire."

At times the company suffered from lack of water, and often the trail was made difficult by steep hills and deep barrancas. But there were other days when the road ran "level, straight, and happy"; and evenings when camp was pitched where there was "plenty of water and pasture, willows, tule, and a glad sky." So, if the dreariness, desolation, and stones of the desert took toll of both body and spirit, places of beauty and refreshment were also found along the way. "Flowers there are many, and beautiful as I have noted before," wrote Serra one evening in his diary; "and that there should be nothing lacking, today on arriving at the camping place we have met the Queen of them all, which is the Rose of Castile; when I write this I have before me a branch of rose bush, with three roses open, others in bud, and more than six impetaled. Blessed be He who created them!" [8]

Preceded by an advance party under Sergeant Ortega, Portolá brought his command to San Diego on July 1. With the arrival of this, the last of the four divisions, the first step in the occupation of California was accomplished, but only time could determine the ultimate outcome of the venture.

---

[7] "Diary of Junípero Serra; March 28–June 30, 1769," *Out West Magazine,* Vol. XVI, p. 405.

[8] Ibid., p. 636.

CHAPTER 4.   Portolá and Serra

A FEW days after his arrival at San Diego, Portolá formally recognized the port of San Diego as a royal presidio. But despite this brave beginning, the colony faced a gloomy and uncertain future. Of the three hundred men who had originally started on the expedition, less than half remained alive; and many of the survivors were "wholly prostrated, some half disabled, others on foot, without strength." Portolá's determination, despite such difficulties, to carry out the Viceroy's instructions and continue the march to Monterey answers effectually the charges of vacillation and weakness once unjustly made against him.

The force under Portolá which started for Monterey consisted of Costansó, the engineer; two friars, Juan Crespi and Francisco Gómez; twenty-seven leather-jacket troops, commanded by Lieutenant Pedro Fages; seven Catalonians; fifteen Christian Indians; and eight or nine muleteers and servants. As the company marched northward, traveling ten or twelve miles a day, the observant Spaniards noted the fertile valleys and watercourses where missions or settlements might be established, and gave to many landmarks the names they still bear. Flourishing cities, including one called Los Angeles, have also arisen on some of the pleasant sites where the expedition pitched its lonely evening camps.

Large numbers of Indians were encountered by the company, and the two missionary friars became increasingly enthusiastic over a field that seemed so ripe and ready for harvest. The men of most of the tribes went naked, but the women were modestly clothed with aprons of grass or skin from the waist down, and some covered their breasts with little caps of rabbit fur.

The diarists of the expedition noted many other salient characteristics of the California Indians—their complete dependence for food, in the absence of all agriculture, upon seeds, acorns, larvæ, small game, shell fish, grasshoppers, insects, or, indeed, anything else that ran, walked, crept, crawled, or wriggled; the bewildering diversity of languages and dialects in use among them; their love of music and dancing; the skill of certain tribes, notably along the Santa Barbara Channel, in making wooden boats and stone artifacts; and a tendency to steal everything in sight, or, more charitably, to "be very nimble with their fingers."

Four days out of San Diego the company passed through a valley, later the site of the Mission of San Luis Rey, "so green that it seemed to us it had been planted." Ten days later the explorers camped by a broad, shallow, tree-lined stream, called by Crespi "the River of the Sweet Name of Jesus of the Earthquakes," because, he says, "we experienced here a horrifying earthquake, which was repeated four times during the day." To the soldiers, the river was known as the Santa Ana.

From that camping-place the trail wound through La Brea Canyon, crossed the fertile valley of San Gabriel, and came to the east bank of the Los Angeles River, slightly below the Arroyo Seco. The entry in Crespi's diary for August 2 reads as follows: "After traveling about a league and a half . . . we entered a spacious valley, well grown with cottonwoods and alders, among which ran a beautiful river from the north-northwest. . . . Toward the north-northeast there is another river bed which forms a spacious water course, but we found it dry. . . . We halted not very far from the river, which we name Porciúncula. . . . The plain where the river runs is very extensive. It has good land for planting all kinds of grain and seeds, and is the most suitable site of all that we have seen for a mission, for it has all the requisites for a large mission." [1] Such was the first sight of the Los Angeles plain by civilized man.

Passing the next morning through "a large vineyard of wild grapes, and an infinity of rose bushes in full bloom," and noting with satisfaction the fertility of the soil and its adaptability to the production of every kind of grain and fruit, the party "saw some

---

[1] Herbert Eugene Bolton: *Fray Juan Crespi* (1927), pp. 146–7.

large marshes of a certain substance like pitch; they were boiling and bubbling, and the pitch came out mixed with an abundance of water. They noticed that the water runs to one side and the pitch to the other and that there is such an abundance of it that it would serve to calk many ships." The marshes were the asphalt exudes on the Rancho La Brea, now converted into Hancock Park.

Passing through the Santa Monica Mountains, by way of Sepulveda Canyon, Portolá crossed "a spacious pleasant Valley," which later came to be known as San Fernando, and entered the tangled range of the Santa Susana Mountains. Once across that difficult barrier, the explorers found themselves in a delightful valley, containing many oaks and cottonwoods, and watered by a tree-lined stream, whose waters frequently disappeared beneath the sandy bed. The valley was named the Santa Clara. Camp was made near an Indian village, which the soldiers called Ranchería del Corral. The site, now known as Castaic, was well suited for a mission, "with much good land, many palisades, two very large arroyos of water, and five large villages close together." [2]

Finding the valley an easy highway, the company followed the river to the coast and camped near an Indian village, now the site of Ventura, which the diarist called the Pueblo de la Asunción. The Spaniards estimated that the village had nearly four hundred inhabitants, and marveled at the Indians' skill in woodworking and other handicrafts.

From Ventura to the coast above San Luis Obispo the journey was measurably free from hardships and offered no particular problems. The route included what is now Carpinteria, Santa Barbara, Dos Pueblos, Gaviota, Point Conception, the Santa Inéz Valley, San Luis Obispo, the Cañada de los Osos (where the Spaniards had their first experience with the tenacity of a grizzly bear), and El Morro Bay.

Beyond that point the formidable barrier of the Santa Lucia

---

[2] Plans were actually made, some years later, for the erection of a mission on this site. The plan was abandoned because of a lack of missionaries and equipment.

Mountains marked the beginning of prolonged difficulty, hardship, and discouragement. "We set out in the morning," wrote Crespi of the crossing of the backbone of the range, "and the first thing was to begin to go over the crest, with a prayer in our mouths, for this day's journey called for nothing less." [3]

Several days later the exhausted explorers stood on a high ridge commanding a view of the entire range. Before them, mile after mile, lay an inhospitable and discouraging prospect, with apparently no breach in the mountain wall or outlet to the surrounding plains—"a sad spectacle for poor travelers, tired and worn out by the fatigue of a long journey." Cold, fatigue, and scurvy added to the general misery; but instead of losing heart, the men took courage and "rejoiced exceedingly, blessing our God and Lord and supplicating Him to grant health to everybody and success to the expedition."

Striking the Salinas River, near the present site of King City, the company followed the winding course of that wide, shallow stream until, on October 1, the scouts caught sight of "a very large bay and a beautiful point of pines," reaching far out into the sea. But the rejoicing and high hopes of the exiles soon turned to ashes. A scouting party sent out to investigate the harbor came back with the gloomy word that, except for a tiny bay, they found no trace "of any port large or small," from one end of the beach to the other. They paced the sands of Monterey, not recognizing the place whose advantages had been so glowingly described and exaggerated by Vizcaíno.

As a consequence of this report Portolá found himself on the horns of what might prove a life-or-death dilemma. Should he continue the march, with winter already at hand, supplies running low, and many of his men seriously ill? Or should he abandon the search for Monterey and turn back at once to San Diego, thereby defeating the purpose of the expedition and perhaps jeopardizing the whole plan of settling California? A council was called together to consider the critical situation. The opinion was

---

[3] Bolton: *Crespi*, p. 191.

unanimous: the expedition must go forward, at least until "the sick should get worse or their number should increase."

From the unrecognized port of Monterey, Portolá's trail ran to the Pájaro River (so called because there the Spaniards found a large bird which had been stuffed with straw by the Indians), through Pleasant Valley, across Soquel Creek and the San Lorenzo River, to the future site of Santa Cruz, and on to Half Moon Bay. On October 31 the expedition sighted Point Reyes and the Farallones, objects easily recognized and positively identified from the descriptions of early navigators.

It was now painfully evident that the expedition had long since passed Monterey; but Portolá determined to make a final reconnaissance of the surrounding country before ordering the company to turn back. A scouting party, under command of Sergeant José Francisco de Ortega, was accordingly sent on ahead. During the absence of this detachment, a band of hunters from Portolá's main command went into the adjacent hills to look for deer. From the crest of the range they gazed out over a succession of tree-covered plains and saw "the smoke of many fires, and an immense arm of the sea or estuary, which extended inland as far as they could see to the southeast."

The next day, November 1, Ortega and his scouts reached the shores of the same inland sea, and from the southern portal of the Golden Gate looked out across the lonely waters of the great bay—a port in which, as Crespi truly said, "not only all the navy of our most Catholic Majesty but those of all Europe could take shelter." But Portolá had been ordered to find Monterey, not to discover San Francisco Bay, and he was disappointed. The expedition's supply of food had long since been reduced to a bare minimum. Each man was limited to a tortilla for breakfast, two for dinner, two for supper, and a meager share of such game— deer, geese, sea gulls, and the like—as the weak, half-starved hunters were able to provide.

The alarming scarcity of provisions was accentuated by the threat of coming winter. Portolá consequently began at once to retrace the weary trail to San Diego. On the beach, near the

Point of Pines at Monterey, the Spaniards erected a large cross to attract the attention of any ship sailing into the bay, and inscribed on it the message: "Dig at the Foot and You Will Find a Letter." In the letter Portolá gave an account of the experiences the company had passed through, and closed with the words: "At last, disappointed and despairing of finding it [the Bay of Monterey] after such efforts and labors, with no provisions except fourteen sacks of flour, the expedition set out today from this bay for San Diego. It prays the All-Powerful God to guide it, and that His Divine Providence may lead thee, sailor, to the port of salvation. At the Bay of Pines, December 9, 1769." [4]

The return to San Diego was made under the most trying conditions; and the wanderers were reduced to such desperate straits by lack of food that they ate the tough, emaciated pack mules to keep alive. The flesh was roasted or "half fried in a fire made in a hole in the ground" and was eaten without salt or other condiment. But "we shut our eyes," wrote Portolá, "and fell to on that scaly mule . . . like hungry lions. We ate twelve in as many days, obtaining from them perforce all our sustenance, all our appetite, all our delectation." [5]

On January 24, "smelling frightfully of mules," the members of the futile Monterey expedition returned to San Diego. During their six months' absence scurvy had taken heavy toll of the occupants of the presidio; the Indians had become dangerously insolent; and, with most of the colonists, discouragement had turned to bleak despair. The situation was desperate enough, in truth, to warrant Portolá's abandonment of the California enterprise, and the expedition's immediate return to Mexico. But Portolá was made of sterner stuff. With the exception of a colorful incident in Palóu's biography of Junípero Serra, there is no evidence to show that, even in this extremity, the Governor proposed to withdraw from his half-finished task and order a retreat.

Captain Rivera was dispatched with a relief party to Velicatá

---

[4] Ibid., pp. 250–1.   [5] Quoted in Chapman: *History of California*, p. 226.

for food and cattle, and Portolá set about organizing a second expedition for Monterey.

The task was carried on both by land and sea. The overland party, again led by Portolá in person, reached the Bay of Pines on March 24, 1770, without particular hardship or serious difficulty, and made camp on the banks of the Carmel River. Many of the company were already half-convinced that the adjacent harbor was in reality the lost port of Monterey; and one evening as Crespi, Fages, and a soldier walked along the beach toward the river, they "perceived that the bay was locked by points Año Nuevo and Pinos, in such a manner that the great bay resembled a round lake like an O." Whereupon the three "broke out with one voice: 'This is the port of Monterey that we were seeking, for this is the letter described by Sebastián Vizcaíno and Cabrera Bueno.' "

With the identity of the port finally established, Portolá moved his camp to the beach at Monterey, and eight days later the *San Antonio* dropped anchor in the harbor. On June 3, 1770, under an arbor erected near the great oak underneath whose ancient boughs the Carmelite friars of Vizcaíno's expedition had worshipped a hundred and sixty-seven years before, Father Serra sang the Mass.

Thus the occupation of Monterey, talked of for two centuries, was at last accomplished. In Mexico the achievement was looked upon as so significant that the Viceroy "wanted the whole population forthwith to share in the happiness which the information gave him, and therefore he ordered a general ringing of the bells. . . ."[6]

---

[6] Francisco Palóu: *Historical Memoirs of New California* (1926); *Life and Apostolic Labors of the Venerable Fr. Junípero Serra* (1913), p. 103.

CHAPTER 5. Conquest of the Desert

HAVING discharged his mission by the occupation of San Diego and Monterey, Portolá, never an enthusiastic admirer of California, returned at once to Mexico, leaving Don Pedro Fages, captain of the Catalonian volunteers, as his successor. Although a blunt and irascible soldier, and frequently a thorn in the side to Father Serra and the other religious, Fages, on the whole, was well fitted both by temperament and experience to meet the peculiar problems and harsh conditions of his isolated post.

For the next five years, however, the fate of the Spanish foundations in California hung constantly in the balance. To bring supplies by sea from San Blas, or any other port on the mainland, involved a long and hazardous voyage and placed a heavy burden on the royal treasury. Lower California was too sterile and impoverished to serve as a food depot for the struggling communities to the north. There remained, accordingly, only one possible solution to the pressing economic problems of the California colony—the opening of an overland supply route from Sonora.

The chief initiative in the actual opening of the Sonora-California route was taken by three extraordinary men: the Viceroy, Antonio Bucareli, characterized by Chapman as "the greatest hero who has ever appeared in the field of California history"; Juan Bautista de Anza, a frontier captain "of heroic qualities, tough as oak, and silent as the desert from which he sprang"; [1] and the intrepid son of the desert and eventual martyr, Father Francisco Garcés.

In 1771, "with no other escort than his guardian angel," Garcés followed the course of the Gila to the Colorado; continued down that stream almost to the head of the gulf; then pursued a northwesterly course across the Lower California deserts to a place

[1] Herbert Eugene Bolton: *Anza's California Expeditions* (1930), Vol. I, p. vi.

called San Jacome. Beyond his camp at San Jacome rose a dark, rugged peak, still the most conspicuous landmark in the region, to which the explorer gave the name of Cerro Prieto, or Black Mountain. Near by, like a livid scar across the gray face of the valley, ran "a dirty salty arroyo with a deep bed"—the historic New River of present-day Imperial Valley. Frequently going incredible distances without water, Garcés continued through the valley until he sighted the high wall of the San Jacinto Mountains and noted two possible openings through the range.

By this extraordinary *entrada* Garcés made two invaluable contributions to the opening of the Sonora-California trail: he discovered a practical (though difficult) route from the lower Colorado River to the back side of the San Jacinto Mountains; and he won the goodwill of Salvador Palma, chief of the Yuma tribe, at the strategic junction of the Gila and the Colorado. In the hands of this extraordinary Indian lay the key to all overland travel between Sonora and the coast.

To Juan Bautista de Anza, who most of his life had dreamed of opening a route to Alta California, the explorations of Father Garcés brought both fresh inspiration and invaluable practical information. In May 1772 the Sonora captain accordingly petitioned the Viceroy to permit him to organize and lead an expedition to California, and offered to meet the major part of the expense out of his own pocket.

When consulted by the Viceroy, Serra, fortunately in Mexico at that time, argued convincingly and forcibly that the Alta California establishments could not rely either upon the problematical supply ships from San Blas or upon the meager and steadily decreasing resources of Lower California, but must look to the development of an overland line of communication and supply from Mexico. Instead of the Gila-Colorado route proposed by Anza, however, Serra advocated the exploration of an overland trail from New Mexico direct to Monterey—a route that the celebrated Domínguez-Escalante expedition attempted unsuccessfully to open in 1776.

In September 1773 Bucareli approved the overland expedition

from Sonora and commissioned Anza to organize and lead the company. The choice was wisely made.

As Bolton writes: "Anza was of good stock. For thirty years his grandfather had served on the Sonora border. For another thirty years his father had fought Indians on the same frontier and had been killed in battle with Apaches. Juan Bautista the grandson ran true to family tradition. Born on the Arizona border, he became one of its best representatives. He was a frontiersman by inheritance. Tales of Indian raids mingled with his childish prattle. When still a youth he took up his father's calling of arms. In early manhood he learned the smell of powder and the creeping chill of the war whoop. When his father was killed by Apaches he carried on the ancestral task of guarding the Sonora frontier. While Portolá was leading his expedition to Monterey, Anza was engaged with Gálvez and Elizondo in suppressing an uprising of Pimas and Seris in Sonora, an enterprise in which Anza won fame for his personal prowess. In a hand-to-hand fight he killed a famous chief. He was now in his prime—thirty-seven years old." [2]

After a discouraging beginning, including the loss of many of his horses and mules in an Apache raid, Anza found himself at the head of a company composed of two friars, Fathers Garcés and Juan Díaz, twenty volunteers from the presidio garrisons, numerous muleteers and servants, and a few others of various callings.

In addition to the usual pack train of provisions and supplies, the expedition also took with it sixty-five head of cattle and a hundred and fifty horses. One of the most interesting members of the party was an Indian, Sebastián Tarabal, who had recently run away from the Mission of San Gabriel and fled across the desert to the Yuma villages. Because of that remarkable exploit and the long journeys he later made with Padre Garcés, a kindred adventurer with restless feet, Tarabal was fittingly known as "El Peregrino," or "The Wanderer."

[2] Ibid., pp. 43–4.

From Caborca, the last settlement on the frontier, Anza followed the well-defined but perilous route, not inappropriately known as El Camino del Diablo, to the Colorado-Gila junction. There he was fortunate enough to cement the friendship with Palma that Garcés had begun three years before.

The Yuma Indians, who today appear so unprepossessing to the casual tourist, were then distinguished both for their physical superiority and for certain features of their cultural development. "The people who live on this Colorado River," wrote Anza, "are the tallest and the most robust that I have seen in all the provinces, and their nakedness the most complete." The sexual practices of the Yumas were, from a civilized viewpoint, scandalous and their habits abominably filthy; but the knowledge they showed of agriculture excited even the admiration of the Spaniards.

Beyond the Colorado, Anza encountered the dreaded belt of sand whose waterless expanse constituted the worst feature of any of the overland routes to California, even during the great migration of the Gold Rush. For six fruitless days, much of the time suffering acutely from thirst, the company struggled to cross the shifting dunes, only to be forced in the end to retreat to a small lake, or lagoon, called Santa Olaya, near the Colorado.

After a rest of two weeks Anza left part of the baggage and some of his men at Santa Olaya and followed down the river, seeking to turn the southern flank of the great barrier of sand. Finally crossing the Cócopa Mountains, the company followed a long diagonal course through the Colorado Desert, from about the present site of Mexicali to the foot of the San Jacinto Mountains.

The ascent of the great range began near the junction of Carrizo Creek and San Felipe River. Travel was difficult, for the trail ran through a rough, wild canyon. To a gap near the crest Anza gave the name of the Royal Pass of San Carlos. "From it," he wrote, "are seen some most beautiful valleys, very green and flower strewn; snowy mountains with live oaks and other trees native to cold lands. The waters, too, are divided, some running on this side to the Gulf, and others to the Philippine Islands." [3]

Descending to the valley, the expedition camped a few miles above the present city of San Jacinto, on the little river of the same name, and the next day crossed a fertile plain, covered with wild flowers and "useful for the raising of cattle . . . as many as one might wish." San Jacinto Lake, now entirely dry, was then several leagues in circumference and "as full of white geese as of water." The trail ran on by way of Riverside, the Santa Ana River, the Arroyo of the Bears or San Antonio Creek, Ontario, and the San Gabriel River. Finally, on March 22, two months after leaving Caborca, "as the southern California sunset blazed upon the peaks, Anza knocked at the gates of San Gabriel Mission."

The soldiers and friars, scarcely believing "that people could have come from Sonora," received the members of the company with the ringing of bells, the discharge of muskets, and such unfeigned demonstrations of joy that "tears sprang to their eyes." Owing to an alarming scarcity of provisions at the mission, however, Anza was soon compelled to send most of his men back to the Colorado; but the captain himself, with a small escort, rode on to Monterey.

A day at that presidio, a few hours longer with the hospitable friars at the Mission Carmelo, and the indefatigable leader was again in the saddle, setting out on his return to San Gabriel and the Colorado. When he reached Tubac, on May 26, Anza had been absent four months and a half and had ridden nearly twenty-two hundred miles. His discovery of a passable trail from Sonora to the coast was "hailed as a great service to God and the king, and a universal benefit" to the California missions.

As a reward for his exploits, Anza was raised to the rank of lieutenant colonel and warmly praised by Bucareli. Because of an increasing enthusiasm for California, and a determination to hold the territory against the ever-growing threat of Russian and English aggression, the far-sighted Viceroy at once proposed, "with generous heart and fervent zeal," not only to send reinforcements

---

[3] Ibid., pp. 151–2.

and supplies to the existing settlements in the province, but also to found a presidio and two additional missions in proximity to San Francisco Bay. Bucareli further endeavored to strengthen the Spanish hold on California by sending a complementary maritime expedition to investigate and check the Russian advance, to explore the coast as far as Alaska, and to examine San Francisco Bay.[4]

Preparations for Anza's colonizing expedition were pushed steadily forward, and recruiting stations were opened in Sinaloa and Sonora. Thanks to Bucareli's generous support, Anza was able to offer far greater inducements to volunteers than the usual colonizing venture could afford. All recruits and their families, children as well as adults, were promised complete outfits of clothing, daily rations of food for five years, and mules for transportation. The pay of the soldiers and settlers began, moreover, on "the very day when they took their places."

The colonists enticed by the promise of such rewards to embark on the California venture were far removed from the traditional hidalgo type. Many of them came from the sweepings of the cities and villages; almost none knew how to read or write; and the majority were "so submerged in poverty and misery that they could not be trusted with money with which to outfit themselves because they would immediately gamble it away." On the trail, however, those same humble, unpretentious, scapegrace recruits exhibited extraordinary fortitude, patience, kindness, courage, and good humor.

Horcasitas, a small frontier post in Sonora, served as the starting-point of the march. The expedition, assembled there in September 1775, consisted of approximately two hundred and forty members, more than half of whom were children! Fray Pedro Font, a trained mathematician endowed with a natural gift for ob-

---

[4] In 1773–4 Juan Pérez sailed as far north as 55°. The following year Bruno Hezeta discovered the Columbia River; Juan Francisco de la Bodega y Cuadra sailed to 58°; and Juan Manuel de Ayala sailed through the Golden Gate and spent several weeks exploring the many branches of San Francisco Bay.

servation and a felicity of phrase, went with the party as diarist and chaplain.

The military detachment of the expedition consisted of ten veterans from Anza's own garrison at Tubac, who acted as the commander's personal escort; eight other seasoned troops from Sonora presidios; and twenty volunteer recruits. Juan Pablo Grijalva served in the capacity of sergeant; and José Joaquín Moraga, who for eighteen years "had gallantly fulfilled his obligations" as a soldier on the frontier, accompanied Anza in the capacity of lieutenant commander.

On the eve of the company's departure from Horcasitas, the Apaches repeated the surprise attack they had made against Anza's first expedition, and drove off fifteen hundred animals from the *cavallada,* or horse herd. Thanks to this crippling loss, most of the colonists were forced to make the eleven-hundred-mile journey to Monterey "without change of mounts, in some cases with two or three children on a single horse."

On October 30, after an uneventful journey, the colonists reached the Gila River and the journey down the Gila to its junction with the Colorado consumed another full month. The crossing of the swollen Colorado, probably an impossible task if undertaken by the Spaniards alone, was rendered comparatively easy through the help of the Indians under Palma's direction. Before leaving the river, Anza presented the friendly giant with a gift from the Viceroy—an elaborate costume consisting of "a shirt, trousers, a jacket with a yellow front, and some decorations, a cape or cabriole of blue cloth decorated with gold braid, and a cap of black velvet adorned with imitation jewels and a crest like a palm."

Following the plan previously agreed upon, Fathers Garcés and Eixarch remained at the Yuma villages when Anza resumed his journey to California. But the main expedition was scarcely out of sight before Garcés set out on his own responsibility to explore a route from the Colorado to Monterey. He was able to obtain guides to lead him over the so-called Mojave Trail to San Gabriel. This ancient route between desert and coast "led up the Mojave

River into the San Bernardino Mountains, up Sawpit Canyon to the summit, and descended the southern slope of the range by the ridge lying west of Devil Canyon." [5]

Garcés reached San Gabriel on March 24, and thus broke a new path from the Colorado basin to the Spanish settlements in California. As Bolton has well said, "Few journeys by a lone white man ever equalled this remarkable feat of pioneering." It was, in truth, "one of the epic journeys of all North American history."

While Garcés was pursuing his solitary way across the Colorado and Mojave deserts, Anza, like Moses of old, was leading his motley company toward the Promised Land. Fatigue, thirst, an occasional threat of Indian attack, cold, rain, sickness, and petty bickerings between Father Font and the commander marked the slow progress of the expedition. No major difficulties were encountered, however, until the company reached the base of the San Jacinto Mountains. There storm, cold, and a dearth of pasturage and water made the passage of the range an experience long to be remembered.

On January 4, 1776, the expedition reached the friendly shelter of the Mission San Gabriel, to be jubilantly welcomed by the ringing of bells, the firing of guns, and the great rejoicing of everybody. According to Father Font, the location of the mission (then at the turn of the hills above Montebello) offered "such fine advantages for crops and such good pastures for cattle and horses that nothing better could be desired." An irrigation canal supplied the fields with ample water; a fair start had already been made in the development of a cattle herd; the cows were fat and gave an abundance of rich milk; and the hogs, sheep, and hens were rapidly increasing.

The mission buildings, made of adobe, logs, and tule, consisted of a very long shed, serving both as a habitation for the fathers and as a granary and storehouse; a guardhouse for the eight soldiers stationed at the mission; a rectangular shed used as a church; and

---

[5] George William Beattie and Helen Pruitt Beattie: *Heritage of the Valley* (1939), p. 3.

some small tule huts for the use of the Indians. Great live-oak trees grew near the mission, furnishing an ample supply of firewood and assuring sufficient timber for building needs in the future.

But despite the effective mission settlements, the country had certain grim and sinister aspects. The Indians at San Diego rose in revolt, attacked the mission, killed a number of its inmates, stripped Father Jaime of his robes, filled his body with arrows, and pounded his head and face with stones and hunting sticks until the martyred friar could be recognized "only because of the whiteness of his body and somewhat from his tonsure or crown."

When Anza arrived at San Gabriel, Governor Diego de Rivera was already there, en route to San Diego to suppress the revolt. Anza joined the Governor's party, and the presence of his veteran border soldiers almost certainly prevented a general Indian uprising, and perhaps the destruction of all the Spanish settlements in California. At the end of a month Anza returned to San Gabriel and resumed his march northward. Three weeks, over trails flooded with heavy rains, were required to complete the journey to Monterey. There the colonists found a disheartening situation. The presidio buildings were rudely made of mud and logs; living conditions were wretched; Governor Rivera showed himself neither very cordial nor encouraging; and Anza fell seriously ill.

As soon as he was able to ride, Anza set out for the Bay of San Francisco to select appropriate sites for the two missions and the presidio authorized by Bucareli. Fort Point was chosen for the presidio; and a beautiful, manzanita-fringed glen, called the Arroyo de los Dolores, furnished the location for the first of the missions. The second, named Santa Clara, was later established farther down the peninsula. Anza and his companions found the great bay "a marvel of nature, and worthy to be called the harbor of harbors." To Father Font the region was the most pleasing he had ever seen. "I think," he wrote, "that if it could be well settled like Europe there would not be anything more beautiful in all the world, for it has the best advantages for founding in it a most beautiful city . . . with that harbor so remarkable and so spacious, in which may be established shipyards, docks, and anything that might be wished." [6]

On June 1, after an absence of eight months, Anza returned to the presidio of Horcasitas. The frontier captain had, in truth, accomplished a heroic, history-making task and attained first rank among the explorers of the Southwest. Without his services, indeed, there is little likelihood that Spanish settlements in California could have escaped destruction at the hands of the savages or maintained themselves against the other dangers of the wilderness.

Unfortunately the trail between Sonora and California, which Anza labored so heroically to open, was all but abandoned after 1781 because of a savage uprising by the Yuma Indians. The outbreak resulted in the destruction of two recently established missions, San Pedro y San Pablo and Purísima Concepción, near the Gila-Colorado junction, and the massacre of a considerable number of Spaniards, including Rivera y Moncada, a former governor of California, and the heroic Padre Francisco Garcés. Because it led to the permanent disruption of the one overland line of communication with Mexico, the Yuma massacre also played a large part in determining the pattern of California's future colonial development.

---

[6] Bolton, Vol. IV, p. 341.

CHAPTER 6.   Impact of the Foreigner

WITH the completion of the work of the pioneer explorers
and colonizers, life in California assumed a pastoral simplicity whose tranquil routine was rarely broken by anything
more exciting than the building and dedication of a mission, the
occasional threat of Indian uprising, the coming of a new governor, or the rare appearance of an exploring expedition sponsored by some foreign government.

Le Comte Jean François de Galaup de La Pérouse was the
first of the distinguished European navigators to reach California. Engaged in a voyage around the world on behalf of the
French government, La Pérouse was instructed to visit the California coast "to make a strict search in these parts not yet known,
to see whether there be not some river, or some narrow gulph,
forming a communication by means of the interior lakes with some
part of Hudson's Bay"; and, finally, to investigate the extent and
condition of the California settlements and the colony's military
strength.

La Pérouse reached Monterey in September 1785. There he was
cordially welcomed by Don Pedro Fages, who had returned to
the province to serve a second term as governor, and by the Franciscan friars under Father Lasuén. Though sharply critical of certain features of mission life, in reference especially to the treatment of the Indians, the French explorer expressed his sincere
admiration for the missionaries themselves, and fell completely
under the spell of Lasuén's Christlike personality.

During his ten-day stay at Monterey La Pérouse forwarded an
extended account of his voyage, containing an enthusiastic description of California, to the Minister of Marine in Paris. He
added that he had discovered and taken possession of a harbor,
unknown to other navigators, that "a hundred men might easily
defend against a considerable force." The port offered extraordinary advantages for the establishment of a trading post, and was

so rich in sea otter that in two weeks' barter with the natives the expedition obtained a thousand skins. The harbor at which the French Empire for a brief fortnight thus found foothold on the Pacific coast has tentatively been identified as Lituya Bay, in latitude 58° 38′.

By confirming the fears of the Spanish officials that the Russians were advancing down the Northwest coast and had established a port as far south as latitude 56° 30′, La Pérouse's friendly call at Monterey helped to bring about a serious international crisis. In 1788 Viceroy Manuel Antonio Flores sent José Martínez, in the *Princesa*, and López de Haro, in the *San Carlos*, to investigate La Pérouse's report. The two commanders brought back word that both Russian and English ships, engaged in the sea-otter trade, were poaching in waters claimed by the Spanish crown, and that the foreign interlopers even asserted the right of permanent occupation along the coast.

The situation was so critical that Martínez advised the establishment of a garrison on Nootka Sound—a measure which he believed would assure Spain control of all the coast between that port and San Francisco. "I say this," added Martínez, "at the same time offering myself to carry out the project; and to prove the feasibility of it, I will sacrifice my last breath in the service of God and the King, if you approve."

In accordance with his urgent recommendation, Martínez was sent north again in 1789 to establish a garrison at Nootka. Upon his arrival he found one American and three English vessels in the Sound, and an armed trading post established on the shore. Without much ado, the Spanish commander seized the English vessels, confiscated their cargoes, and made prisoners of some of their officers and crew.

The incident brought about a diplomatic crisis between the Spanish and British governments. Pitt, the English Prime Minister, prepared a large fleet called the Spanish Armament, and threatened a declaration of war. Falling back on the terms of the Family Compact, Spain appealed to France for assistance; but the Revolution was then in progress, and after a brief outburst of enthusiasm for the Spanish alliance, the National Assembly, occupied with weighty matters of its own and having no real interest in the overseas problems of the Bourbon monarch of Madrid, declined to come to the rescue of the hard-pressed Spanish crown.

Deprived of any hope of support from her former ally, Spain thereupon reversed her centuries-old policy and abandoned all attempt to exclude foreign trade and settlement north of the present California line. Great Britain, in turn, contracted "not to navigate or fish within ten leagues of any part of this coast which Spain already occupied." The agreement, known as the Nootka Convention, was ratified October 28, 1790. During the next three years Spanish interest in the perennial mystery of the north, the legendary waterway called Anian, flared up for the last time. The stubborn hope that had outlived two and a half centuries was finally abandoned, but only after four expeditions had been dispatched, between 1789 and 1793, to look for the fabled strait.

The day of Spanish expansion on the Pacific coast, in truth, was over; and after a half-hearted attempt to occupy Bodega Bay, the government was content to take a defensive position and merely maintain the *status quo* in California. The policy was at once a confession of weakness and a sign of the impending collapse of the Spanish Empire.

In the spring of 1792 a fleet commanded by Captain George Vancouver was sent to the Northwest coast to protect British interests under the Nootka agreement. The following November Vancouver sailed down the coast and spent some time both at San Francisco and Monterey, receiving a cordial welcome at the presidios, and such entertainment as their limited resources would permit. Before he finally returned to England, Vancouver made two subsequent visits to California, on one of which he sailed as far south as San Diego. At every turn the observant and practical-minded navigator was impressed by the defenseless state of "New Albion" (as he habitually called California), by the primitive conditions under which the people lived, and by the flagrant neglect of the rich economic resources of the province. There was, in consequence, no doubt as to the ultimate fate of California. "Should the ambition of any civilized nation tempt it to seize on these unsupported posts," he wrote, "they could not make the least resistance, and must inevitably fall to a force barely sufficient for garrisoning and securing the country; especially that part which I have comprehended under the denomination of New Albion, whose southmost limits lie under the thirtieth degree of north latitude."[1]

Within California itself during this period, there were few noteworthy developments. Political and economic matters were regulated by a series of decrees and instructions, chief of which were the *Reglamento Provisional*, of Juan José Echeveste, adopted in 1773; a number of regulations issued by the great Viceroy, Antonio María Bucareli; and a famous *Reglamento*, drafted in 1779 by "California's first lawgiver," Governor Felipe de Neve.

Although the subject of much criticism by the missionaries, the Neve *Reglamento* remained the fundamental basis of California government until the close of Spanish rule. It may be added that in all frontier provinces, and especially one so remote and restricted in communications as California, the governor, except as he was bound by the orders of his superiors in New Spain and by the provisions of the Laws of the Indies, was "the state."

In 1782 Pedro Fages, "the fiery but lovable Catalan," returned to California from Sonora to serve a second time as governor. Though characterized by frequent disputes with the missionaries over questions of policy and jurisdiction, Fages's second administration, like his first, justifies Priestley in speaking of him as "one of the ablest, if not the outstanding, governor of the Spanish period."

One measure alone, indeed, was sufficient to give Fages a lasting place in California annals. In 1784 three of the soldiers who had served as leather-jacket troops in the Portolá expedition sought the concession of certain tracts of land near the Los Angeles River for grazing purposes. Fages approved the petitions of the three soldiers, writing to the Commandante General in Chihua-

---

[1] George Vancouver: *A Voyage of Discovery to the North Pacific Ocean, and Round the World;* etc. (1798), Vol. II, pp. 499–503.

hua: "The cattle are increasing in such manner that it is necessary in the case of several owners to give them additional lands; they have asked me for some *sitios* which I have granted provisionally, namely to Juan José Domínguez who was a soldier in the presidio of San Diego and who at this moment has four herds of mares and about 200 head of cattle on the river below San Gabriel, to Manuel Nieto for a similar reason that of la Zanja on the highway from said Mission along by the oak tree, and to the sons of the widow Ignacio Carrillo that on the deep creek contiguous to the foregoing. . . ." [2]

Many months later Fages was notified that his action had been confirmed in Mexico, with the proviso that the tracts tentatively conceded must not encroach upon the four square leagues of "water and pasture, wood and timber" allotted to a pueblo, upon the holdings of a mission, or upon the land occupied by any Indian village or ranchería. The recipient of each grant was also required to build a stone house, stock the ranch with cattle, and provide a sufficient number of vaqueros and sheepherders to care for his stock and keep the animals from running wild. The concessions granted by Fages thus inaugurated the system of private land grants, commonly known as ranchos, that later became the most distinctive and lasting of Spanish-Mexican economic institutions in California.

During the closing years of his administration Fages became involved in a long and epic quarrel with his wife, Doña Eulalia, who proved herself a sort of California counterpart to Katharina the Shrew. The serio-comic farce began when Fages resorted to a stratagem to induce the lady to come to California. Quickly tiring of the discomforts and restricted life of the frontier, Doña Eulalia demanded to be sent back to Mexico. Fages and Doña Eulalia finally settled their feud by a compromise. Don Pedro agreed to resign the governorship (on the grounds of ill health) and accompany his victorious lady home.

In 1794, after brief administrations by José Antonio Roméu and

---

[2] See Robert G. Cleland: *The Cattle on a Thousand Hills* (1941), text and footnotes, pp. 8–10.

José Joaquín de Arrillaga, Diego de Borica became governor. A man of education and culture, Borica introduced a new note of gaiety and sophistication into the restricted social life of Monterey, and wrote such enthusiastic reports of the attractions of the new land that he deserves to be adopted as a sort of patron saint by all chambers of commerce throughout the state! "To live much and without care, come to Monterey," he advised in one of his letters; and again: "This is a great country; climate healthful, between cold and temperate; good bread, excellent meat, tolerable fish, and *bon humeur* which is worth all the rest. . . . The climate is so good that all are getting to look like Englishmen. This is the most peaceful and quiet country in the world; one lives better here than in the most cultured court of Europe." [3]

Borica's successor was José Joaquín Arrillaga, who had served as governor *ad interim* from 1792 to 1794. Arrillaga's administration, longer by far than that of any other governor of either the Spanish or the Mexican regime, was characterized by at least three notable developments: a further exploration of the immense hinterland east of the Coast Range Mountains; the opening of the historic fur trade between New England, California, and Canton; and the consummation of the long-feared Russian advance to California.

Expeditions primarily designed to chastise marauding Indians, or to discover locations for a proposed chain of inland missions to parallel the foundations along the coast, were responsible for the principal exploring expeditions sent into the interior of California after 1800. Such expeditions visited the Sacramento and San Joaquin valleys; discovered most of the important rivers rising in the Sierra Nevada Mountains; retraced the trails across the Mojave Desert opened by Fages and Garcés more than a quarter of a century earlier; and found again the natural gateways, provided by the Tehachapi and Tejón passes, through the southern wall of the Sierra.

Foremost on the list of second-generation explorers was Gabriél

---

[3] Chapman: *History of California*, p. 408.

Moraga, son of José Joaquín Moraga, who had come to California in 1776 as lieutenant commander of the Anza colonists. His trail as explorer and Indian fighter ran from the Cajón Pass and the Mojave villages to the upper Sacramento; it made him familiar with a score of inland rivers, such as the Feather, the American, the Merced, the Tuolumne, and the Kern; and it led him farther into the depths of the majestic Sierra Nevada Mountains than any white man had ever gone before. Moraga's record of forty-six expeditions against the Indians probably stands unequaled in the annals of American border warfare.

But despite extensive inland explorations and repeated punitive expeditions against the Indians, Spanish control and civilization never succeeded in getting a foothold beyond the Coast Range. Until the coming of the Americans the narrow band of Spanish settlements along the coast was blocked on the east by a tangled wilderness of mountain and desert, unrelieved by mission, pueblo, or presidio. Furthermore, except for the route opened by Anza in the extreme south, and virtually abandoned after the Yuma massacre of 1781, there were no trails, or regular lines of communication of any kind, across this eastern barrier.

The failure of the Domínguez-Escalante expedition of 1776 to find a passageway from New Mexico to Monterey ended all attempts to breach the wall between the Great Basin and the coast until the historic expedition of the American fur trader Jedediah S. Smith in 1826. But if the isolation provided by nature on the east was so complete, on the west for a thousand miles the province bordered the universal highway of the sea; and over that highway, near the close of the century, Russian and American adventurers began to find their way to California.

In the course of time New England vessels came to the quiet harbors and the long, sunlit reaches of the California coast. There, for many years, the interest of Yankee merchant adventurers centered in the sea-otter trade with Macao, or Canton—a trade that helped lay the foundations for the traditional friendship between the United States and China and unwittingly represented the first important step in the American acquisition of California.

It is a truism to say that the course of world history has often been changed by some obscure economic factor. Certainly this was true in the case of the sea otter. In pursuit of the precious skins the Russians crossed from the Siberian mainland to the Aleutian Islands and, using those steppingstones between the two continents, came finally to Alaska. The extraordinary profits derived from the sale of a few vermin-infested skins in the Canton market awakened British interest in the commercial possibilities of the Northwest coast; and, as previously explained, the presence of English poachers in waters claimed by the Spanish crown, brought about the historic Convention of Nootka Sound. American interest in California likewise owed its beginning to the same trade. As Adele Ogden tersely remarks, "The commercial opening of the Pacific Ocean was begun because of man's desire for the fur of an animal."

The sea otter was found along the American coast from the Aleutian Islands to Sebastián Vizcaíno Bay, in Lower California. On the upper California coast the animal flourished in great numbers in the kelp beds of the Santa Barbara channel islands; off the bold, rocky coast between San Luis Obispo and Monterey, where fortunately a small herd still survives; and in many of the harbors of the mainland, including the Bay of San Francisco. The skin of a full-grown sea otter was described by William Sturgis, a Boston trader, as "about five feet long and twenty-four to thirty inches wide, covered with a fine fur about three-fourths of an inch in length, having a rich, jet black, glossy surface and exhibiting a silver color when blown open. Those are esteemed the finest skins which have some white hairs interspersed and scattered over the whole surface, and a perfectly white head.

Substantial progress had been made by the Spaniards in the development of the sea-otter trade before the close of the eighteenth century. Between 1786 and 1790 nearly ten thousand skins, valued at over three million dollars, were shipped to China in the Manila galleon. On the return voyage the galleon brought back quicksilver for use in the all-important mining industry of New Spain.

Prior to 1800 a few American sea captains engaged in contra-

band fur operations along the California coast. But the trade did
not assume significant proportions until after the turn of the century. In 1803–4 four New England ships, the *Alexander, Hazard,
Lelia Byrd*, and *O'Cain*, made their appearance in California harbors, pleading sickness or the need of wood, water, and fresh supplies as an excuse for coming to anchor, and carrying on an extensive clandestine trade in sea-otter skins under cover of such
feigned necessity. As high as twenty-five hundred pelts were collected by some of the vessels on a single voyage. The Americans
carried their cargoes to Canton (then the only port through which
Western trade could enter China), where the skins found a ready
and profitable market.

One of the best-known sagas of the California-Canton trade is
the narrative of the voyages of the *Lelia Byrd*, a brig of a hundred
and seventy-five tons, jointly owned by William Shaler and Richard Cleveland. On her maiden voyage to the coast, in 1803, when
"the circumvention of alien customs regulations was, if not an
American virtue, at least a patriotic failing," the *Lelia Byrd* became involved in difficulties with the Spanish officials, engaged
in the bloodless "Battle of San Diego," obtained sixteen hundred
sea-otter skins in one clandestine transaction, sailed to Canton, by
way of the Hawaiian Islands, and there exchanged her cargo of
furs for teas, silks, and other Eastern commodities, to the great
profit of her New England owners.

After two voyages to the California coast, and some further
service in the trade with the Sandwich Islands and Canton, the
Lelia Byrd was converted into a receiving ship for opium and
came to a shabby end in the crowded harbor of Whampoa, gateway to the ancient city of Canton. In 1830, after a distinguished
career as United States consular agent and diplomat in Algiers,
Shaler died of cholera at the home of his friend and former partner, Richard Cleveland, in Havana. Shaler's "Journal of a Voyage
between China and the Northwest Coast, Made in 1804," reached
the public through the medium of the *American Register*, in 1808.
The narrative was the first extensive account of California to be
published in the United States. Shaler wrote with a vivid pen;

and his descriptions of the richly endowed, poorly defended Spanish province on the Pacific made a special appeal to seafaring New England readers—an appeal no less effective because it closely paralleled, as befitted the writings of an avowed contrabandista, a passage from the English navigator George Vancouver.

As the possibilities of the sea-otter trade became better known, and the problem of obtaining skins by contraband barter grew more difficult, the New Englanders entered into co-operative agreements with the officials of the Russian American Fur Company of Alaska. In 1803 Captain Joseph O'Cain, representing the Winships of Boston, and probably the outstanding American merchant navigator engaged in the trade, made a contract with Alexander Baranov, variously called the "Little Czar," and the "Lord of the North Pacific," for a joint undertaking along the California coast. Under the terms of the engagement, the Russian company agreed to supply the American vessel with a force of Aleutian Indian hunters and all necessary equipment, including skin canoes, or bidarkas, in return for half the proceeds of the hunt.

The contract system thus developed between O'Cain and the Russians proved mutually so satisfactory that it was generally adopted by other New England traders and remained in effect for almost ten years. Baranov on his part favored the arrangement, not so much because it paid highly satisfactory dividends as because it enabled him to extend the hunting grounds of his company far to the south; laid the groundwork by which he hoped to obtain a monopoly of all the California-Northwest trade; and brought nearer to reality his dream of creating "a great Russian commercial empire in the North Pacific."

In 1805 Baranov purchased a New England vessel, the *Juno,* and dispatched her down the coast as far as San Francisco Bay to obtain grain, meat, and other supplies for the half-starved, scurvy-stricken settlers in Alaska. Baranov was also eager to find suitable locations for Russian colonies farther south, and was especially determined to gain a foothold within striking distance of San Francisco Bay. On board the *Juno* were Georg Heinrich von

Langsdorff, an eminent Russian surgeon, and Nikolai Rezánov, the Chamberlain of the Czar. The Californians gave the Russian visitors a cordial welcome and supplied the provisions the Alaskan colonists required.

The voyage of the *Juno* gave rise to California's most famous and best-loved romance. While the ship lay anchored at San Francisco, Rezánov met and successfully wooed Concepción Argüello, a famous beauty, and daughter of the commander of the port. Soon after the two became engaged, Rezánov sailed away in the *Juno*, giving Concepción his promise to return. The days went by, the weeks, the months, the years; but no word came to the waiting girl from her absent lover. At last Concepción took the robes of a nun, giving her life to the relief of suffering and the lightening of grief, while old age brought to her, in return, its gracious benediction of serenity and peace. Then a chance meeting with Sir George Simpson, of the Hudson's Bay Company, who told of Rezánov's death in Siberia, soon after leaving California, dispelled the tragic mystery of Concepción's unfulfilled romance.

The *Juno's* visit to San Francisco was the initial move in Baranov's program of establishing Russian control over California. A few years later the Russian American Fur Company broke away from its partnership with the New England traders, organized full-scale hunting operations of its own, and planted its long-planned settlement on California soil. The site, reputedly purchased from the Indians for "three blankets, two axes, three hoes, and a miscellaneous assortment of beads," overlooked the ocean, north of Bodega Bay.

The first colonists consisted of a hundred Russians and eighty Aleut hunters. A large establishment called Fort Ross, well defended by a stockade of timbers eighteen feet high and eight inches thick, assured immunity from attack by the Spaniards. Four twelve-pound carronades protected each corner of the enclosure; four six-pound brass howitzers guarded the main entrance; and two octagonal blockhouses furnished protection for the musketeers. Altogether there were over sixty buildings at the fort.

For generations the Spaniards had been fearing the Russian advance into California; now, when it came, they were in no position to resist. Governor Arrillaga, it is true, sent out a number of reconnoitering expeditions to report on the intentions and activities of the colonists; but no serious attempt was made to dislodge the intruders or to prevent them from engaging in sea-otter hunting along the coast.

By 1823, when the Mission of San Francisco Solano, the last of the Franciscan foundations in California, was finally erected at Sonoma as a barrier against further Russian expansion to the south, the Czar's dream of a trans-Pacific empire had vanished, and the establishment at Fort Ross no longer possessed any political significance.

For nearly two decades longer, however, the Russian colonists continued to engage in farming, sea-otter hunting, and a certain amount of mutually profitable trade with the Californians; and it was not until 1841, when John A. Sutter, the self-appointed lord of the Sacramento marches, purchased the livestock and other movable property at the fort, that the last vestige of the Czar's frontier in California, the extreme outpost of Baranov's bold dream of empire, finally disappeared.

The establishment of Fort Ross, and the evident purpose of Russia to use the colony as a base for further expansion along the coast, aroused some fear on the part of the United States. The obvious Russian threat to California, and the ukase of 1822 by which the Czar sought to exclude foreign vessels from the North Pacific and gain exclusive possession of the Northwest coast, played an important part in President Monroe's historic message of December 2, 1823, and furnished specific grounds for asserting that "the American continents . . . are henceforth not to be considered as subjects for future colonization by any European powers." [4]

[4] For a more extended discussion of the Russian "menace," see Robert G. Cleland: "The Early Sentiment for the Annexation of California," *Southwestern Historical Quarterly*, Vol. XVIII, pp. 6–9.

CHAPTER 7.   Politics, Missions, and Ranchos

WITH the opening of the nineteenth century, Spain's vast New World empire, after having withstood the storm and stress of three hundred years, began to fall apart. In Mexico the revolutionary movement started with the uprising of Hidalgo, in September 1810, and continued until the Convention of Córdova, eleven years later. The several revolutions, or so-called Wars of Independence, that followed Hidalgo's call to arms were bloody, complex in motives and objectives, immensely destructive, and all too clearly illustrative of Machiavelli's pronouncement: "Every revolution contains the seeds of another, and scatters them behind it."

No sooner had Mexico won her independence than she entered upon a prolonged period of political instability, dissension, and civil war that frequently threatened her very existence as a nation. Eventually such near-chaos in the mother country profoundly reacted upon the destiny of California. But while Mexico's prolonged struggle against Spain was actually in progress, the isolated province on the Pacific suffered almost no change in the rhythm or tempo of its tranquil life. During all that time, in fact, only one disturbing incident directly related to the wars of liberation affected California.

In 1818 a French-born Argentinian sea rover, Hippolyte de Bouchard, arrived at Monterey in two ships, the *Argentina* and *Santa Rosa,* with the announced purpose of aiding the Californians in their struggle for freedom, and also with the possible intention of making the remote province a place of refuge for the revolutionary cause in case it became too hard pressed in the other Spanish colonies. But the people of Monterey were not interested in raising the standard of revolt, or in forming an alliance with one of Bouchard's dubious reputation; and Governor Solá not only refused to furnish the supplies Bouchard requested, but even ordered his troops to fire on a landing party from the *Argentina.* Incensed by Solá's action, the self-styled liberator sacked the town and burned most of the buildings.

Having thus destroyed all hope of winning the co-operation of the Californians, Bouchard sailed down the coast, throwing most of the inhabitants into a dither by his presence, and occasionally doing actual damage. He burned the Ortega ranch at Refugio, threatened to seize Santa Barbara, caused a near-panic at Ventura, pillaged San Juan Capistrano, destroying "much wine and spirits and all the private property," and kept San Diego in a fever of suspense. With his motley company of "heretics, excommunicated persons, heathen, and a few Moors," to use the description of those who looked upon him only as a pirate, Bouchard then disappeared, never to return; and the peaceful inhabitants of California thanked the blessed saints for their escape and gratefully relaxed.

During the half-century of Spanish rule, and indeed for seven years thereafter, revolution was almost unknown in California. In 1825, however, Colonel José María Echeandía, "a tall, thin, juiceless man, possessing but little enterprise or force of character," came from Mexico to take over the reigns of government. Four years later, after a quarrel between Echeandía and José María Herrera, the central government's fiscal agent in California, a revolt broke out among some half-starved soldiers at Monterey, who found a leader in the person of Joaquín Solís, ex-convict and ranchero.

The revolt reached its climax in the bloodless but wordy Battle of Santa Barbara. According to James Ohio Pattie, an American fur trader who assisted in putting down the revolt, both armies kept up a continuous fire for three days, "at the expiration of which Gen. Solis, having expended his ammunition, and consumed his provisions, was compelled to withdraw, having sustained no loss, except that of one horse!" [1] Solís and the other leaders of the movement were subsequently captured at Monterey, put in irons, and deported to Mexico.

---

[1] *Narrative of James Ohio Pattie*, p. 293.

From the time of the Solís revolt to the coming of the Americans, seventeen years later, a succession of conspiracies, pronunciamentos, and small-scale civil wars, most of which were barren of historical significance, became the order of the day. Such disorders were due in large part to the character of the governors sent from Mexico, most of whom were arrogant, tactless, self-seeking, and incompetent. The Californians naturally resented such appointments; and, having little to fear in the way of reprisals from the distant federal capital, usually revolted against each new arrival and sent him post-haste back to Mexico. After Governor Echeandía's administration this practice became so habitual that California had nine governors in fifteen years!

But political unrest was not limited to outbreaks against Mexican-appointed governors. The California *hijo del país*, like his fellows elsewhere in the disintegrating Spanish Empire, was catholic and broad-minded in the matter of revolutions. His creed recognized many justifiable causes for issuing pronunciamentos and flying to arms to save the imperiled state. So the Californians not only revolted against the interloper; they revolted almost as readily against one another—faction against faction; the North against the South; defenders of Monterey, as the provincial capital, against the upstart champions of Los Angeles.

The Mexican governors ruled a politically troubled land. Figueroa, Chico, Gutiérrez, Alvarado, Carrillo, Micheltorena, Castro, and the Pico brothers engaged in plots, counter-plots, intrigue, and some military action. But by the 1840's the long reign of "anarchy and confusion" in California politics had reached its climax. Before the next act could be presented, the Anglo-American conquest abruptly rang down the curtain, scattered the players, and brought the serio-comic drama forever to an end.

However, the dissension and revolution that kept the California provincial government in such constant turmoil before the Mexican War apparently had little effect upon the routine life of the people themselves. On the contrary the stormy years of domestic politics following the death of Governor José Figueroa in 1835 closely coincided with what many are accustomed to call the Golden Age of California history. It was "the day of the Dons," the era of the private ranchos, the idyllic interlude during which a people of simple wants, untroubled either by poverty or by the ambition for great wealth, gave themselves over whole-heartedly and successfully to "the grand and primary business of the enjoyment of life."

The landholding system, of which the rancho grants were a part, originated in an ancient principle of Spanish law whereby title to all colonial lands and other natural resources was vested in the crown. Out of the inexhaustible patrimony thus placed at his disposal, the King built and financed the Spanish Empire. In border provinces, such as California, the presidios or fortresses, pueblos or civilian settlements, and missions, upon which Spain relied for the conquest of the frontier, were all supported by these royal concessions. Presidio and pueblo lands were granted in fee simple, in accordance with general laws or decrees; but the missions received only usufructuary rights, which might be canceled at any time. Consequently, as the United States Land Commission afterwards declared, the lands included in such concessions "did not become the property of the missions or of the church or of the priests having charge of them, or of the Neophytes who, while they lived in the Mission community, enjoyed the benefit of their use." Temporary though they were in character, all California mission grants were of enormous size.

During the first decade of Mexican rule the California missions reached the height of their spiritual influence, and at the same time almost completely dominated the economic life of the province. Paraphrasing the account of the distinguished French traveler Duflot de Mofras, Dwinelle writes:

At the end of sixty years, (in 1834) the missionaries of Upper California found themselves in possession of twenty-one prosperous Missions, planted upon a line of about seven hundred miles, running from San Diego north to the latitude of Sonoma. More than thirty thousand Indian converts were lodged in the Mission buildings, receiving religious culture, assisting at divine worship, and cheerfully performing their easy tasks. Over four hundred thousand horned cattle pastured upon the plains, as well as sixty thousand horses, and more than three hundred thousand sheep, goats and swine. Seventy thousand bushels of wheat were raised annually, which, with maize, beans and the like, made up an annual crop of one hundred and twenty thousand bushels; while, according to the climate, the different Missions rivalled each other in the production of wine, brandy, soap, leather, hides, wool, oil, cotton, hemp, linen, tobacco, salt and soda.[2]

The variety of industries and occupations at San Gabriel was summed up in even greater detail by Hugo Reid, the eccentric "Scotch Paisano," whose story has been told in fascinating form by Susanna B. Dakin.

"Thus people were divided into various classes and stations," wrote Reid. "There were vaqueros, soap makers, tanners, shoemakers, carpenters, blacksmiths, bakers, cooks, general servants, pages, fishermen, agriculturists, horticulturists, brick and tile makers, musicians, singers, tallow melters, vignerons, carters, cart makers, shepherds, poultry keepers, pigeon tenders, weavers, spinners, saddle makers, store and key keepers, deer hunters, deer and sheepskin dressmakers, people of all work, and in fact everything but coopers, who were foreign; all the balance, masons, plasterers, etc., were natives."[3]

But the very wealth and prosperity thus described, were destined, in time, to bring about the downfall of the missions. As early as 1826 Governor Echeandía presented a plan to organize the Indian neophyte communities into pueblos, replace the friars with members of the secular clergy, and strip the missions of their temporal holdings. The movement reached its climax in the historic Secularization Act, passed by the Mexican Congress in August 1833. Actual enforcement of the measure was begun by Governor José Figueroa in 1834, and completed by Governor Manuel Micheltorena a decade later. The following passage summarizes the far-reaching effects of the decree: "Ostensibly, the Secularization Act was designed to benefit the Indians and make them a self-sustaining people. Actually, it led to the rapid disintegration of

---

[2] John W. Dwinelle: *The Colonial History of San Francisco* (1863), p. 44.
[3] Hugo Reid: *The Indians of Los Angeles County* (1926), pp. 54–5.

the mission-controlled communities, scattered the partly civilized neophytes like sheep without a shepherd, ushered in a half century's tragic aftermath of wretchedness and poverty, brought about the virtual extinction of the mission system in the province, and, by throwing open millions of acres to private denouncement, revolutionized the departmental land system and made the rancho the dominant economic and social institution of California."[4]

As indicated earlier, the private land-grant system was introduced into California in 1784, during the second administration of Governor Pedro Fages. Because of a lack of responsible petitioners, or the pre-emption of most of the available lands by the missions, the Spanish governors who succeeded Fages added less than twenty grants to the three initial concessions.

Following the attainment of independence and the collapse of the Empire under Iturbide, Mexico sought to encourage the settlement of her sparsely populated frontier provinces by the unusually liberal Colonization Act of 1824. This law, together with an important supplementary measure known as the *Reglamento* of 1828, furnished the legal pattern for all subsequent land grants in the border provinces, and established a principle in Mexican law which, "with slight modifications, remained in force down to the enactment of the constitution of 1917."

Even under the stimulus of such favorable legislation, however, few private grants were made in California during the first decade of Mexican rule. But with the addition to the public domain of the millions of acres formerly held by the missions, the conservative land-grant policy, followed by both the Spanish and the early Mexican governors, gave way to one of prodigal liberality. Mexican law fixed the minimum size of a grant at one square league, or about four thousand five hundred acres; and although eleven square leagues constituted the maximum limit, the statute did not affect the size of family holdings, or even restrict the amount of land a rancher might acquire by gift, purchase, or bequest.

---

[4] Cleland: *The Cattle on a Thousand Hills,* p. 32.

It has been estimated that between 1834 and 1846 Mexican governors confirmed at least seven hundred private rancho grants. When the United States acquired California, most of the desirable land lying west of the Coast Range Mountains, and even in the lower Sacramento and San Joaquin valleys, was thus in the hands of private owners. In its effect upon nearly every phase of California's subsequent development—agriculture, immigration, land titles, social progress, the location and growth of cities—the rancho system accordingly proved to be the most important legacy the state inherited from Mexico and Spain.

In applying for a land grant under Mexican law, the petitioner stated that he was a native-born or naturalized Mexican citizen; set forth the location, boundaries, approximate size, and identifying landmarks of the desired tract; testified that none of the land in question had been included in a previous concession; declared that he was prepared to stock the holdings with the number of horses and cattle required by law; listed the names of the neighboring ranches; and supplied a *diseño,* or rough topographical map, of the property. The *diseño* showed not only the boundaries of the grant, but also the hills, watercourses, marshes, wastelands, and other landmarks mentioned in the petition. "A blotter copy, or *borrador,* was retained in the governor's office and a minute of the transaction was entered in a record book, called the *toma de razón.* The petition, *diseño,* and *borrador* were then assembled in a file called an *expediente* and placed in the provincial archives." [5] As a final step in the procedure the land was officially surveyed and juridical possession bestowed upon the owner.

Surveys made under the conditions just outlined were at best only rough and ready makeshifts, and in later years their inaccuracies proved the source of much controversy and led to an immense amount of litigation. Corner posts on a grant were sometimes branded with the owner's iron, or cattle mark; but often the most convenient objects at hand—a steer's skull fixed in a bush, a clump of cactus, a few notches on a tree-trunk, the place where

[5] Ibid., p. 34.

two roads crossed, a mound at the entrance to a coyote's den, the edge of a dry barranca or gully, a ramada or pile of brush, on the banks of a stream, a spring of running water—were made to serve as boundary marks.

With the passage of the years, such landmarks usually disappeared or became almost impossible to locate and identify, thus adding another prolific source of confusion to the muddled state of California land titles. Even now, after the lapse of nearly a hundred years, the boundary lines of a few old Spanish-Mexican grants are occasionally before the courts for adjudication.

Down to the time of the Gold Rush, the economic life of California centered almost exclusively in the cattle industry. The few hundred head of stock brought from Mexico by early colonists multiplied into the thousands before the end of the eighteenth century. Within another twenty-five years hundreds of square miles of grazing lands were required to support the herds of even a single mission. After secularization, as already stated, the province became a succession of great ranchos whose "black cattle and beasts of burden" numbered into the tens of thousands.

Life on one of the great ranchos followed, in the main, the ancient customs, laws, and practices brought to Mexico by the early Spanish conquerors, there adapted to the conditions of the country, and thence transferred to California. Stock was grass-fed the year round, and ran almost wild on the open ranges. California cattle had slim legs, short noses, and sharp, widespreading horns. "The general carriage of a Spanish cow," said Hittell, "is like that of a wild animal: she is quick, uneasy, restless, frequently on the lookout for danger, snuffing the air, moving with a high and elastic trot, and excited at the sight of a man, particularly if afoot, when she will often attack him." [6] The meat of California cattle was nutritious; but it was neither as tender nor as juicy as that of American-bred beef.

Cattlemen were required to have three registered brands—the *fierro*, or iron; the *señal*, or ear mark; and the *venta*, or sale brand.

---

[6] John S. Hittell: *The Resources of California* (1874), p. 277.

At least once a year every ranchero held a general roundup, or rodeo, presided over by one or more *Jueces del Campo*, or Judges of the Plain, for the purpose of segregating the cattle belonging to different owners and of branding the calves. The occasion was one of traditional hospitality. Neighboring landowners and their retainers came as a matter of course; and friends and relatives of the ranchero traveled great distances to share in the days and nights of dancing, gambling, horse-racing, cock-fighting, and occasional bear- and bull-baiting. The following passage catches something of the color and excitement of a California rodeo in the days of the great ranchos:

A roundup . . . was one of the most picturesque events of early California life. The vast herd of cattle, sometimes half a mile from center to circumference, the thick clouds of dust that rose from thousands of moving feet, the sudden dash after some escaping steer, the surprising feats of horsemanship, which were performed continually by the *vaqueros,* the bellowing of frightened and maddened bulls, the clash of horns striking horns, the wild shouts and laughter of the cowboys, all lent an air of excitement and interest that the printed page cannot begin to reproduce.[7]

As already indicated, stock-raising was the center and circumference of California life during the pre-American period. Cattle furnished the chief source of wealth, trade, food, and occupation. Beef, much of which was cut into strips and dried in the sun to become the universally used *carne seca,* constituted the most essential article in the provincial diet. Tallow supplied fat for cooking and grease for the manufacture of soap and candles. Rawhide, the general "repair-all," was put to innumerable uses. It was made into *reatas,* bridle reins, chair bottoms, bedsprings, lashings, and even floor mats.

The extensive export of hides, horns, and tallow gave California almost her only commercial contact with the outside world during the whole of her existence as a Mexican province. A hundred

---

[7] Cleland: *History of California,* pp. 39–40.

years ago Richard Henry Dana first made the American public aware of the extent and nature of that trade. In time, no doubt, some economic historian will produce an exhaustive, carefully documented study of the subject; but the graphic descriptions preserved for posterity by Dana in his *Two Years before the Mast* will never be surpassed.[8]

The trade began in 1822, when two English partners, William P. Hartnell and Hugh McCulloch, succeeded in negotiating a three-year contract with the California missions for hides and tallow. A month later William A. Gale, at one time a sealer on the Farallones, arrived at Monterey to obtain shipments of hides for Bryant and Sturgis, a Boston firm which had formerly engaged in the fur business on the Northwest coast.

California hides were cured by the simple process of pegging them out in the hot sun. Later they were scraped free of bits of fat and meat, and then beaten with sticks or flails to rid them of dust and insects. "Stowage of a vessel," writes Miss Ogden, "was an art of great importance. To ballast the ship, salted hides were laid in the bottom of the hold as far up as the keelson. Over the top of the salted hides was put a layer of salt and loose hides for dunnage. As dried hides were piled in the hold, lime was strewed over them. When the ship's hold was filled to within a few feet of the beams, steeving began. Beginning in the aft of the ship a 'book' of from twenty-five to fifty hides was inserted by a mechanism of ropes, pulleys and beam dogs, until a hundred or a hundred and fifty additional hides were forced in. When the last hide was stowed, bulkheads were put in the hold and the hatches well caulked down." [9]

The fat of slaughtered animals was rendered, or tried out, in large iron kettles (usually obtained from some whaling ship) and poured into rawhide bags, or *botas*, the largest of which were capable of holding upwards of a thousand pounds. Cattle were killed for food as they were needed; but the *matanza*, or whole-

---

[8] The book was first published in 1840.

[9] Adele Ogden: "Hides and Tallow . . . ," *California Historical Society Quarterly*, Vol. VI, pp. 262-3.

sale slaughtering, was carried out only at certain specified times of the year.

Money was little known and seldom used in California, and almost all business transactions were carried on by barter. Hides, or "California bank notes," as they were called along the coast, had a fluctuating value of from one to three dollars. With the exception of a few simple household crafts, the Californians had no manufacturers of any kind, and consequently depended upon foreign ships to supply nearly everything they required. A trading vessel's cargo contained an amazingly heterogeneous assortment of dry goods, liquors, cigars, raisins, sugar, spices, silks, hardware, cutlery, guns, powder, caps, shoes, pins, calicoes, stockings, combs, shawls, furniture, an occasional billiard table or piano—almost everything imaginable, indeed, from "Chinese fireworks to English cart wheels." According to Dana, profit on a voyage frequently ran as high as 300 per cent. Long-term credit was extended by the foreign merchant or his agent to the rancheros; and losses on bad debts, except perhaps in those cases where merchants or traders were dealing with one another, were very rare.

In addition to furnishing an all-important commercial outlet for the Californians, and providing much of the raw material for New England's extensive leather industry, the hide and tallow trade came to be a powerful factor in arousing American interest in California and in laying the foundation for the ultimate annexation of the province by the United States. As Dana wrote in his classic narrative: "In the hands of an enterprising people what a country this might be!"

During the pre-American period the so-called white inhabitants of California were roughly divided into three groups. Most numerous were the lower-class cholos of the pueblos, always a desperately poor and sometimes a dangerously vicious and unruly lot. A considerable body of Americans and other foreigners constituted a second division in the population. Many of these immigrants of the better class intermarried with the *gente de razón*, closely identified themselves with the Californians, and became large landowners or outstanding merchants. Among such influential foreigners were men of the type of Abel Stearns, Thomas O. Larkin, William Heath Davis, Benjamin D. Wilson, John Marsh, William Workman, John Rowland, William Wolfskill, John Temple, and John A. Sutter.[1]

After the secularization of the missions, the rancheros constituted the third and most important element in provincial society. The picture of California life during the so-called Golden Age, long ago created by romantic writers and deeply embedded in popular tradition, will probably never be greatly changed by historians of a more realistic school. The truth is, however, that the California ranchero lived in an environment of curiously contrasting elements. On the one hand, even the wealthiest of the landholding families were shut off from almost all cultural resources and amenities. With rare, inconsequential exceptions, there were no schools in California (barring those attached to the missions for purposes of indoctrination) during the Spanish or Mexican periods. By the same token, there was no post office, newspaper, magazine, library, museum, theater, art gallery, or any such thing; and many of the largest landowners were so unlettered that they were forced to make the sign of the cross even on wills and similar important documents.

Most of the rambling adobe houses, especially in the early days, were neither very comfortable nor inviting, from the modern standpoint. They had earthen floors, little furniture, and that often of the crudest type, and almost no conveniences. Later dwellings were both more comfortable and attractive.

"Adobe was the material generally employed for the walls, which were sometimes two or three feet thick, making a deep embrasure for the rather small window openings," writes Mrs. Sánchez. "The poorer houses were thatched with straw or tules smeared with mud or asphalt, while the better ones had roofs of overlapping tiles. As a rule the rooms were few but quite large, and the houses were comfortable, roomy, warm in winter and cool in summer, as is coming to be recognized in our day.

---

[1] About half of these married "native daughters."

"At first there was no glass in the windows, and sometimes the doors were made of rawhide stretched over sticks, while the more ambitious had painted wooden doors. None of these doors had locks, for there was little fear of thieves where there was nothing to be stolen. The rafters were made of straight young trees with the bark stripped off. Often no nails were used, but these rafters were tied to the cross-beams with thongs made of oxhide. . . .

"After 1834, when a large number of colonists came in, some of them from the better class in the city of Mexico, material changes took place in California. A more luxurious mode of living was adopted, and some of the wealthier residents constructed commodious and even handsome houses after the Spanish fashion, built around an inner court filled with luxuriant plants watered by a fountain in the center. All around the court ran a corridor, upon which opened the large, dimly lighted rooms, with low ceilings, furnished sparsely, after the manner of the abstemious Spaniard." [2]

The clothing of the common people was mean and shabby, as it is in Mexico today. But most foreigners who visited California found the dress of the *gente de razón* both colorful and attractive. According to Don Francisco Coronel:

The dress worn by ladies of some means in 1834 and 1835 consisted of a narrow skirt made of muslin or silk, a high, tight waist, trimmed with ribbon or flowers or in any way that the caprice of the lady dictated, and an underskirt of red or any other color according to the taste of the person. . . . The manner of dressing the hair was to draw it smoothly back into a braid and tie it together with a silk ribbon or cord, with a small knot or flower of ribbon at the lower end of the braid, gracefully arranged. A small silk shawl was worn around the neck, the points crossed on the breast. Some of the women wore a *comorra*, which consisted of a black silk handkerchief tied gracefully around the head. . . .

The dress of the men consisted of short breeches reaching a little above the knee, open for about six inches on the outside seams of the legs, where they were trimmed with ribbon or braid and some four or

---

[2] Nellie Van de Grift Sánchez: *Spanish Arcadia* (1929), pp. 90–1.

six buttons of silver or other metal, according to the means of the individual . . . a vest of cloth, velvet, silk, or cotton (according to the resources of the man) coming down over the abdomen, and fancifully trimmed.

The jacket was of the same materials but a little longer than the vest. . . . The leggings were made of a single piece of deerskin, tanned, black or red, embroidered in parts with silk, according to the means of the wearers. . . . The shoes were made of cowhide or deerskin, of four or six pieces, each piece in two colors, red and black, embroidered on the toe piece with agave thread or silk. . . . The hat had a broad brim and round crown; it was made of wool, and was very strong; it was held on by a chin strap of ribbon about two inches wide, tied in the shape of a large flower under the chin. Nearly all the men wore a kerchief tied around the head.[3]

Thanks to a vigorous, outdoor life, simple diet, appreciation of leisure, and freedom from the tensions of our modern life, the Spanish Californians of a hundred years ago knew almost nothing of the ills of the civilization of the present day. If their culture lacked some of the amenities of a more advanced, sophisticated society, it possessed the greater virtues of simplicity, sincerity, and unaffected happiness. Families, closely organized on the patriarchal tradition, were usually very large, often including fifteen or twenty children. Hospitality was spontaneous and unaffected; the whole tenor of life, leisurely and gracious. California was in truth, "the land of the large and charitable air."

---

[3] Antonio Francisco Coronel: "Things Past." Translated by Nellie Van de Grift Sánchez, *Touring Topics*, Vol. XXI, No. 9, p. 20.

CHAPTER 8.   The Era of the Mountain Men

A FEW years after the beginning of the hide and tallow trade, companies of American fur hunters broke through the wall of mountains and desert behind which California had remained so long isolated, and opened the first overland lines of communication between the western American frontier and the California coast.

The Rocky Mountain fur trappers, of which the vanguard that came to California were a part, filled a unique place in American history. They were the pioneers of all Far Western frontiersmen, the trail blazers for subsequent explorers, the pathfinders of the course of empire to the western sea. As Hill well said: "The trapper's domain knew no artificial boundaries. . . . Trapping parties setting out from Taos for the Gila River might, as likely as not, trap on the Yellowstone and the Snake rivers before returning to Taos or Santa Fé with their furs; or they might cross to California and trap on the San Joaquín and Sacramento rivers. Ewing Young's party did both. Dick Wootton was with a party that set out from Bent's Fort and trapped the waters of the Grand, the Green, the Snake, the Columbia, the Sacramento, the San Joaquín, and the Gila rivers before its return to the fort." [1]

One of the most distinctive and romantic chapters in American history closed forever when the use of the silk hat and the advance of civilization to the Rocky Mountains and the wilderness beyond reduced the beaver trade to a casual occupation. But when the historic day of the Mountain Men thus came to its early setting, the rivers they had trapped, the passes they had crossed, the routes they had discovered, and the valleys in which they had held their rendezvous lay open to an endless procession that marched behind them to the West. The first overland emigrants to California, the hordes of the Gold Rush, the thousands of

---

[1] Joseph J. Hill: "Mountain Men," *Touring Topics*, Vol. XX, No. 9, p. 24.

covered wagons of later settlers, and every great railroad that now spans the continent made use of the trails the trappers pioneered. Even today's huge airliners, as they shuttle back and forth between the coasts, look down on the sweeping deserts, the hidden valleys, and the high shining peaks first seen by the Mountain Men.

The life of the fur trader was hard, lonely, and beset on every hand with violence and danger. Men of all races, types, and cultural backgrounds entered the calling; and most of those who came under the spell of the wild, free life never shook off its subtle fascination. Though primarily concerned with trapping, the fur traders readily turned their hands to any other enterprise that offered profit or excitement. Some developed the historic trade between St. Louis, Santa Fe, and Chihuahua; others undertook the operation of Mexican mining properties; many engaged in cattle ranching; a few opened a traffic in horses and mules between California and the markets of New Mexico, Louisiana, and Missouri. In later years, when the fur trade was nothing but a name, the remnant of the trappers became emigrant guides, Army scouts, employees of the overland stage companies, or professional hunters.

On August 22, 1826—a year of great import for California and the western advance of the United States—a fur-trading brigade left the Bear River Valley, in northern Utah, to penetrate the country between the Great Salt Lake and the Pacific—a daring enterprise undertaken and abandoned by the Domínguez-Escalante party a half-century before. The expedition was the initial venture of a newly organized partnership, composed of David E. Jackson, William L. Sublette, and Jedediah S. Smith, to which Colonel William Henry Ashley had just completed the transfer of his fur-trading interests, at a rendezvous in Bear Valley a short time before.

Jedediah Smith, a man whose heroic qualities, desperate adventures, and extensive explorations have only recently begun to emerge after a century of almost complete oblivion and neglect, was placed in command of the party. Smith was then only twenty-eight years of age; but he had served an eventful apprenticeship under Ashley, most distinguished of the fur traders operating out of St. Louis, and had already won an honorable place as a seasoned Indian campaigner in the fraternity of the Mountain Men. His reputation as an explorer was also assured by the discovery of the historic South Pass and an early expedition to the shores of the Great Salt Lake. His personal courage and hardihood were exceptional, even when measured by the rigorous standards of the Mountain Men themselves.

To his arduous training and Spartan-like qualities, Smith added strong Christian virtues and a singular nobility of character. It is said that he carried a Bible among his personal effects on all his explorations, even through the most difficult and perilous regions; and those who knew him testified that his religion was a living principle of daily life from which nothing could ever swerve him.

The party with which Smith started on his historic expedition into the Southwestern wilderness included eighteen men and fifty horses. The venture was not merely another routine trapping expedition: it represented a well-organized, carefully planned attempt on the part of the three ambitious young partners to exploit the virgin beaver country lying between the central Rocky Mountains and the Pacific; to trap the rivers and lakes of California, and perhaps those of Oregon as well; and to explore the possibilities of establishing "a place of deposit," such as Astor sought to set up on the Columbia, for the shipment of furs by sea, either to China or to American ports on the Atlantic.

From the Bear Valley rendezvous the company traveled southward, passing east of Great Salt Lake and Utah Lake, to the Sevier River. Following that stream to its source, Smith crossed the divide between the Sevier and Virgin rivers, struck the east fork of the latter stream (which the trappers called the Adams, "in compliment to our President"), and continued down the river until it entered the mountains southwest of St. George. From that point on, the trail is difficult to trace. It is probable that the company swung west, then south, finally reached the banks of the Virgin, and followed the desolate course of that stream to the Colorado.[2]

Crossing the muddy waters of the Colorado, which he recognized as the lower reaches of the Green or Siskadee, Smith continued along the east bank until he came to the villages of the Ammuchaba, or Mojave Indians.

After remaining there fifteen days to recuperate, the trappers found two runaway Indians from the San Gabriel Mission to guide them across the grim wastelands that lay between the Colorado and the California settlements. Travel on the desert is often intolerable, and the company suffered acutely from thirst and fatigue before reaching the banks of the Mojave River.

Because the water of the Mojave so frequently disappeared beneath the surface, Smith appropriately called the river the "Inconstant." Following the stream to its upper reaches, the company crossed the lofty San Bernardino Mountains, by way of the old Mojave Trail, first used more than half a century earlier by Fages and the wandering Garcés, and so came to the fertile plain between the Sierra Madre Mountains and the sea.

The company reached San Gabriel on November 27. The arrival of the rough, ragged band caused prodigious excitement in the isolated and uneventful life of the mission; but the historic implications of the incident were far too big for trapper, priest, or Indian neophyte to grasp. For the coming of Smith and his half-starved, sorry-looking band of Mountain Men wrote, in truth, a new chapter in the American advance to the Pacific and opened a new epoch in the history of the entire West.

For nearly two months—a grateful interlude between the hardships already experienced and the greater hardships and tragedy ahead—the trappers lived as the guests of the hospitable friars. Food was abundant, the weather continued mild, and the colorful and varied activities of mission life each day afforded new interest and entertainment.

But the American trappers, having entered California without

---

[2] En route the party crossed Beaver, or "Lost River"; the Santa Clara, or "Corn Creek"; and Beaver Dam Wash, or "Pauch Creek."

adequate passports, or official permission of any kind, were subject by Mexican law to summary arrest and expulsion. Smith consequently went to San Diego to present his plea to Governor Echeandía; but the latter declined to permit the foreign interlopers either to remain in the province, or to travel up the coast on their way to Oregon.[3]

Returning to San Gabriel from his fruitless visit to San Diego, Smith ostensibly planned to obey the Governor's orders and leave California by the trail over which he had come. Recrossing the Sierra Madre range to the desert by way of the Cajón Pass, Smith turned northward along the eastern side of the mountains, traversed Antelope Valley, and entered the San Joaquin Valley, probably through Oak Creek Pass. The party trapped as far north as the Kings River, or perhaps the Stanislaus, and established a base camp from which scouting expeditions continued up the valley, possibly beyond the American River.

Early in the spring the trappers attempted to cross the high wall of the Sierra Nevada and return to Salt Lake; but deep snow and bitter cold forced them to abandon the undertaking. About a month later, however, Smith and two of his men, after an eight-day struggle and the loss of three of his nine animals, forced a passage of the snow-covered range and followed the course of the West Walker River to the Nevada plains. In the simple language of a trapper's journal Smith tells the story of the crossing of the bitter land that lay between "Mt. Joseph" (as he called the Sierra Nevada, possibly because of the proximity of the Mission San José), and the valley of Salt Lake. It was a barren, waterless country, broken only by dreary, volcanic hills, white wastes of alkali and sand, and endless miles of fantastic, curiously twisted vegetation—a region continually fretted by the wind, and lonely as when Time itself began.

On July 3 the exhausted trappers reached the rendezvous at Bear Lake, previously agreed upon with Jackson and Sublette. The account Smith gives of his reception is noteworthy for its

[3] See *The Ashley-Smith Explorations . . . 1822–1829,* edited by Harrison Clifford Dale (1941).

modesty and restraint. "My arrival caused a considerable bustle in camp," he wrote, "for myself and party had been given up as lost. A small Cannon brought up from St. Louis was loaded and fired for a salute."

After remaining only ten days at the rendezvous, Smith, with eighteen men, set out again on the long trail to California. In addition to relieving the portion of his company left to trap in the San Joaquin Valley, Smith proposed to make a further "examination of the country beyond Mt. Joseph and along the sea coast." Because of the inhospitable nature of the Nevada desert, which he had crossed on his return from California to Salt Lake, he made no attempt to use that more direct route to the Sierra Nevada Mountains, but followed his old trail to the Colorado.

Reaching the river without incident, Smith spent several days at the Mojave villages, whose inhabitants, to all appearances, were as friendly as he had found them on his visit the previous year. Deceived by the Indians' hospitality and well-concealed treachery, the trappers relaxed their vigilance and, after a few days' rest, started to swim the horses and ferry the baggage across the Colorado. While the unsuspicious and carelessly armed whites were thus engaged the Indians fell upon them in overpowering numbers, killed ten of the company at the first onslaught, and seriously wounded Thomas Virgin (for whom the Virgin River was subsequently named) by a blow with a war club. Less than half the company succeeded in crossing the river to temporary safety; and the lot even of these survivors seemed utterly hopeless. Behind them, blocking any possible return to Salt Lake, lay the impassable Colorado; the great wastes of the Mojave Desert stretched between them and California; their horses had fallen into the hands of the Indians; and out of all their baggage and equipment, they had succeeded in saving only five guns, a little ammunition, and fifteen pounds of dried meat.

Following a skirmish with the Indians, Smith and his men marched across the desert to the California settlements. Nine and a half days after leaving the Colorado the exhausted trappers descended the western slope of the San Bernardino Mountains and dragged themselves into the confines of the friendly *asistencia* of San Gabriel. Here again the generous Father Sánchez supplied the needy men with horses and supplies. Leaving Virgin and another trapper at the *asistencia*, Smith recrossed the Sierra Madre Mountains, followed his old trail into the San Joaquin Valley, and rejoined the company from which he had parted the preceding spring.

During their leader's absence, the company had passed "what hunters called a pleasant summer." The weather had been delightful, the Indians friendly, and game, chiefly deer, elk, and antelope, unusually abundant. To obtain supplies necessary for a continuation of the expedition, Smith and three of his men set out from the camp in the San Joaquin for the Mission San José. Here, in striking contrast to the hospitality exhibited by Father Sánchez, the trappers received a frigid welcome from the father president, Fray Narciso Durán. Fearful of estranging Governor Echeandía if he proved too friendly to the interlopers, Durán placed the trappers under guard until the civil authorities took them into custody and transferred them to Monterey.

There Smith spent several weeks in verbal fencing with the Governor, finally winning his release under a bond of thirty thousand dollars, supplied by Captain John R. Cooper and other Americans in Monterey, and making his way to San Francisco, where he was joined by the remainder of the company. Disposing of the year's catch of furs, Smith used the proceeds to purchase food, ammunition, and several hundred head of horses; then in December 1827 the party set out for Oregon, by way of the San Buenaventura, or Sacramento Valley. Excessive rains presently turned the whole region into one vast lake or morass, making travel difficult and slow and adding greatly to the hardships of the march. But the abundance of beaver and other game more than offset the added inconvenience and delay.

In a bear-infested region in the upper part of the valley, Harrison G. Rogers, clerk of the expedition, was badly mauled by a grizzly; and Smith himself had two narrow escapes. Rogers's wounds, which Smith treated "with cold water and salve of Sugar and Soap," proved so serious that the expedition was compelled to lie over several days until the injured man was able to travel. Finding the route along the Sacramento becoming more and more difficult, Smith turned toward the coast. The country was indescribably rough and broken, and travel became "amazing bad."

On July 5, more than seven months after leaving San Francisco, Smith reached the Umpqua River. Here, only a few days' travel from the shelter of Fort Vancouver, the entire company was almost wiped out in an Indian massacre. Several versions of the affray still survive. Smith's own account, as reported by Peter Skene Ogden, ran as follows: "Having prolonged my stay for two days, to recruit the worn-down animals I had purchased at St. Gabriel, on the third morning I directed Mr. Rogers, my assistant, to have everything in readiness, desiring the men also to clean their rifles, preparatory to start on the morrow. I then, accompanied by two men, embarked in a canoe, and proceeded in search of a suitable crossing-place, the banks opposite our encampment being too steep for the horses to surmount. On my return, after an absence of three hours, when within half a mile of the tents, I observed a number of Indians running towards us along the bank, yelling most fearfully. Immediately suspecting what had happened, we crossed over, and secreted ourselves in the bushes, the Indians discharging their guns at us without effect. Anxious to ascertain the fate of my party, I then ascended an eminence, from whence I could plainly perceive that the camp was destroyed, and not a vestige of man, horse, or mule, to be seen." [4]

Traveling by night and lying hid by day, Smith and his companions made their escape to Fort Vancouver. There the next day they were joined by John Black, the only other survivor of the massacre. Dr. John McLoughlin, chief factor of the Hudson's Bay Company and benevolent despot of the Northwest, treated

---

[4] *Traits of American Indian Life and Character,* by a Fur Trader (original ed., London, 1853) (1933), p. 8.

the refugees with extraordinary kindness and sent an expedition into the Umpqua territory to rescue the furs, traps, and other equipment stolen by the Indians.

Upon the return of the rescue party to Fort Vancouver, Smith, accompanied only by John Black, followed up the Columbia almost to the present Canadian border line; turned southeast along Clark's Fork until he fell in with a company of Jackson's men in the Kootenais; and finally, after a two-year separation, rejoined Sublette on the Snake River.

Smith's remarkable expeditions place him among the foremost of American explorers. After the expedition of 1827–28 his trail never again ran to California. But he and his rough followers had done their work. By breaking through the barriers that guarded the province on the east, they had prepared the way for the opening of the emigrant trails to California. The American advance to the Pacific followed the footsteps of this unassuming, seldom honored, almost forgotten man.

It was fitting that death should come to the great pathfinder in the West, to which he rightfully belonged. Having attained financial independence through his fur-trading ventures, Smith resolved to leave the mountains and establish a permanent residence in St. Louis. But the spirit of the wilderness was not so easily exorcized, and the spring of 1831 found Jedediah again turning his back on civilization to take command of the largest trading caravan that had ever left St. Louis for Santa Fe.

While crossing the arid region between the Arkansas and Cimarron rivers the expedition ran short of water; and when the men and animals began to suffer dangerously from thirst, Smith set out to find relief. Reaching the banks of the Cimarron, he was rewarded by signs of water in the sandy bed. But his rejoicing was suddenly cut short by the appearance of a band of hostile Comanche Indians. Resorting to the common ruse of waving blankets and flashing mirrors, the Indians frightened Smith's horse and distracted the rider's attention. Then, in the words of Maurice Sullivan, "the horse turned and Smith was exposed to a Comanche lance. Wounded, he fired and killed two of his attackers.

The rest closed in upon him, and, on the twenty-seventh of May, in the year 1831, Jedediah Smith came to the end of his last trail."

Smith's expeditions marked the beginning of an influx of fur traders into California that continued, with varying degrees of intensity, for approximately ten years. The names of some of the Mountain Men, such as Benjamin D. Wilson, Peter Lassen, Joe Walker, and Kit Carson, were attached to rivers, passes, lakes, peaks, and other landmarks in California, and thus preserved in perpetuity. Many of the fur traders eventually made their homes in the province, married into landholding families, and took an active part in California affairs. Some of their colleagues, however, notably Peg-Leg Smith and "Old Bill" Williams, were charged with instigating horse-stealing raids and committing other reprehensible and lawless acts against the Californians.

The first band of fur traders to enter California, after the pioneer expeditions of Jedediah Smith, was led by the two nomadic Kentuckians Sylvester Pattie and his son James Ohio. Of all the vivid accounts of Western adventure, hardship, and hairbreadth escape, none is quite comparable to the narrative of the younger Pattie. The critical historian may point out discrepancies in dates, confusion in routes, and misstatement of fact; but the tale still remains a classic adventure story of the West—an epic saga of the Mountain Men.

Between 1824 and 1827 James Ohio's trapping, trading, and mining ventures carried him from Missouri to Santa Fe, thence southward to Chihuahua and Sonora, westward to the Colorado, and northward to the Yellowstone and the upper reaches of the Arkansas and Platte rivers. A later trapping expedition down the Gila River and on to the gulf finally led the Patties across the terrible sand wastes of the lower Colorado basin to the Mission of Santa Catalina, in Baja California. From Santa Catalina the refugees were sent to San Diego; and there Governor Echeandía, still upset over his experience with Jedediah Smith, threw the hapless Americans into jail.

The harsh treatment meted out to Sylvester Pattie, added to the privations through which he had passed in crossing the desert, soon brought about his death. Somewhat later the younger Pattie was given his liberty on condition that he vaccinate the hundreds of Indians living at the various missions, as well as the other inhabitants of the province, to protect them against a virulent epidemic of smallpox then sweeping through the country. In carrying out this novel commission Pattie visited all the missions and settlements from San Diego to Sonoma, bearing the impressive title of "Surgeon Extraordinary to His Excellency, the Governor of California," and inoculating a multitude of wondering patients at every stopping-place.[5]

A quarrel with the Governor and the mission authorities over the matter of compensation for his services intensified Pattie's violent dislike of the Californians and led him to seek asylum on an American ship at Monterey. Later he volunteered to join the revolution which General Solís set on foot against Governor Echeandía; but after some initial success Solís showed such strong anti-American feeling that Pattie swallowed his hatred of Echeandía and took an active part in suppressing the revolt.

Subsequently he engaged in a short but successful sea-otter hunt along the coast, and then sailed for Mexico to lay his grievances and claims for damages before the Mexican government. His visit is mentioned in letters from the United States Legation to the Department of State in Washington; but there is no record that the Mexican government made any response, favorable or otherwise, to the American trapper's claims. From Mexico Pattie returned to Kentucky, broken in fortune, failing in health, and a stranger among his few surviving kin. There is some evidence to show that he returned to California during the days of the Gold Rush; but the glimpse is fleeting, and the figure too vague for positive identification.

Ewing Young was another trader of that period to whom California history is indebted. In 1829, after extensive trapping experience in the Southwest, Young set out for California at the head of a large expedition. By way of the Colorado and the Mo-

---

[5] Vaccination against smallpox first had been successfully developed by Dr. Edward Jenner in 1798. It was still a rather crude technique.

jave villages, he arrived at San Gabriel and thereafter spent an eventful year in California. His wanderings carried him through the San Joaquin Valley and back to Los Angeles, whence he returned to Taos in 1831 with two thousand pounds of beaver pelts. Subsequently he participated in the wagon traffic between Independence, Missouri, and Santa Fe.

Another adventurous mountain man was Joseph Reddeford Walker. Like Young a native of Tennessee, Walker early entered the fur business and joined the Bonneville expedition to the Great Salt Lake country. Bonneville commissioned him to strike westward with a detachment and to return the following summer. Walker followed the Humboldt River, then turned south to the Walker River and the Sierra Nevada. He and his men negotiated a crossing of the great range and on their descent of the western slope discovered the Yosemite Valley, whose wonders were largely lost on the exhausted men. The company broke out of the mountains just in time to be greeted by the spectacular meteor shower of November 12–13, 1833.

Walker wintered at Salinas, reorganized his party, and headed back to Salt Lake, crossing the Sierra via Walker Pass into Owens Valley. After additional adventures and hardships, characteristic of almost all of these expeditions, Walker intersected his old trail from the Humboldt and rejoined Bonneville's group on the Snake River in 1834. For nearly forty years thereafter Walker continued to blaze wilderness trails, serving in addition as guide to Fremont. Washington Irving called him "one of the bravest and most skillful of the mountain men."

Smith, Pattie, Young, Walker, and many others whose adventures cannot here be detailed constituted a vanguard of pioneers whose search for the elusive beaver opened up the empty places of the Southwest and brought California into the ken of Americans. The trappers blazed the trails; the pioneer settlers followed in their footsteps.

CHAPTER 9.   Propaganda and Emigration

HARD on the heels of the Mountain Men, a vanguard of pioneer settlers, whose interest in California had been awakened by an extraordinary advertising campaign that began early in 1840 and continued with growing effectiveness until the Mexican War, crossed the continent to find homes and fortunes in the new land.

Except for the intensity with which it was carried on, the publicity the province received during that period was not new in California history. Almost from the time civilized man first visited the region, California's resources and attractions have been advertised more widely and more enthusiastically than those of any other country. The narratives of some of the early explorers, even before the time of Vizcaíno, began the tradition maintained today by radio programs, newspapers, magazines, motion pictures, official government agencies, commercial bodies, and tens of thousands of captivated visitors and super-loyal citizens.

It must be confessed, however, that California's modern press agents often fall far short of the vivid color and imagination employed by their long-dead predecessors. One, William Frederick Martyn, happily stated: "In California a vast quantity of dew falls every morning which, settling on the rose-leaves, candies, becomes hard like manna, and possesses all the sweetness peculiar to refined sugar, without its whiteness." [1]

Many of the descriptions of California in the early forties, though less inspired than that of Martyn, were no more restrained. The publicists of that day spoke in extravagant phrases of the endless extent, boundless fertility, matchless climate, and inexhaustible natural wealth of the province. They described the harbor of San Francisco as the best in the world, the Califor-

---

[1] William Frederick Martyn: *Geographical Magazine* (1785).

nia forests as the largest on earth, and the valleys of the Sacramento and the San Joaquin, as capable of supporting a population of twenty millions of people. Southern California, one might note, was seldom even mentioned by such panegyrists!

From the standpoint of the Western settler, almost fanatical in his belief in manifest destiny and the expansion of the United States to the Pacific, contemporary accounts of the political situation in California also offered a strong appeal. According to such reports, the land was thinly populated, its government about ready to disintegrate, and Mexico's hold on the province "miserably weak and ineffective." Military defenses were described as inadequate and widely scattered, and the Californians themselves were portrayed as unambitious, pleasure-loving, and well-disposed toward Americans.

Such, in brief, was the picture presented to the American people just before the outbreak of the Mexican War. Its effect upon the restless, land-hungry, adventure-seeking settlers of the Western frontier can scarcely be overemphasized.

During the winter of 1840 Antoine Robideaux, a member of the famous fur-trading family of St. Louis, and a well-known trapper in his own right, set the Missouri frontier agog by vivid, first-hand accounts of California. "Robideaux described California," wrote John Bidwell, a schoolteacher who had recently come to Missouri from Ohio, "as a land of perennial spring and boundless fertility, and laid stress on the countless thousands of wild horses and cattle. He told about oranges, and hence must have been at Los Angeles or the mission of San Gabriel, a few miles from it. Every conceivable question that we could ask him was answered favorably. Generally the first question which a Missourian asked about a country was whether there was any fever or ague. I remember his answer distinctly. He said that there was but one man in California that ever had a chill there, and that it was a matter of so much wonderment to the people of Monterey that they went eighteen miles into the country to see him shake. Nothing could have been more satisfactory on the score of health. He said that the Spanish authorities were most friendly, and that the people were the most hospitable on the globe; that you could travel all over California and it would cost you nothing for horses or feed. Even the Indians were friendly. His description of the country made it seem like a paradise." [2]

As a result of such enthusiastic descriptions many of the settlers of Platte County, Missouri, formed a company to migrate without delay to California. "We called ourselves the Western Emigration Society," said Bidwell, the leading spirit in the enterprise, "and as soon as the pledge was drawn up every one who agreed to come signed his name to it, and it took like wild-fire. In a short time, I think within a month, we had about 500 names; we also had correspondence on the subject with people all over Missouri, and even as far east as Illinois and Kentucky, and as far south as Arkansas."

As soon as the first excitement died down, however, most of the prospective California emigrants, in some instances encouraged by merchants fearful of losing so large a number of customers, withdrew their names from the agreement and abandoned the undertaking. Conservative settlers likewise sought to discourage would-be emigrants by pointing out the dangers and difficulties of the journey, and branded the expedition as "the most unheard of, foolish wild goose chase that ever entered into the brain of man."

From the standpoint of logic and common sense, the condemnation was thoroughly sound. Not one of the sixty-nine members of the expedition that finally started for California could qualify as an experienced frontiersman or possessed more than the vaguest knowledge of the plains, deserts, and mountains the company proposed to cross.

From the financial standpoint, members of that first California settlers' train had little to distinguish them from the so-called "Dust Bowl" immigrants of a later day. The entire company could muster only about a hundred dollars in cash; and even Bidwell, who later became one of the most influential landowners in the

---

[2] John Bidwell: *Echoes of the Past about California,* edited by Milo M. Quaife (1928), p. 14.

Sacramento Valley, had scarcely enough money to outfit himself with a gun, a wagon, and provisions. "Cheyenne" Dawson, a member of the party, started the trip with only seventy-five cents in his pocket.

The organization of the company was effected, according to the usual custom, by drafting a set of rules and regulations for the conduct of the expedition and selecting a leader. The ill-advised choice of John Bartleson to serve as captain was responsible for much subsequent friction, lack of co-operation, and inefficient leadership. By good fortune, however, the inexperienced emigrants were able to travel as far as Fort Hall with a band of fur traders, commanded by the renowned Thomas Fitzpatrick, and accompanied by Father De Smet, a heroic Jesuit missionary, whom Bidwell, though a devout Protestant, characterized as one of the saintliest men he had ever known.

The mixed expedition, consisting, as Charles L. Camp remarks, "of gentlemen and roughnecks, missionaries, schoolteachers, and frontiersmen, an embezzler, and a future candidate for the presidency," left Sapling Grove, a few miles from West Port, the modern Kansas City, on May 19, 1841.[3] "This morning," wrote Bidwell, "the wagons started off again in single file; first the four carts and the small wagon of the missionaries, next eight wagons drawn by mules and horses, and lastly five wagons drawn by seventeen yoke of oxen. . . . Our direction was west."

From Sapling Grove the party proceeded, by way of the Platte River and the old trading post of the American Fur Company at Fort Laramie, to Independence Rock. Leaving that historic landmark the route kept along the Sweetwater to its source, followed the Big Sandy and Green rivers, and crossed the divide into Bear Valley. Before reaching the Platte the emigrants encountered the enormous buffalo herds which then roamed the Western prairies.

At Soda Springs, on Bear River, the company divided. The

---

[3] *Narrative of Nicholas "Cheyenne" Dawson* . . . with an Introduction by Charles L. Camp (1933). The quotation is taken from the unpaged Introduction.

trappers, the missionaries, and about half the emigrant company took the trail for Fort Hall, en route to Oregon. The remainder of the settlers, including Bidwell and John Bartleson, continued the westward march to California. By way of Salt Lake, the Humboldt, and the Walker, the emigrants reached the frowning wall of the Sierra Nevada.

But a peril vastly greater than any the wanderers had yet encountered still lay ahead. Autumn was far advanced, and heavy snows, such as Walker's hard-bitten band of fur traders had barely survived in the same region eight years before, were already overdue. The company's one chance of escape lay in crossing the Sierras and reaching California before a storm blocked the way.

With the odds thus heavily against them Bidwell and his companions began the ascent, and after the greatest exertion reached the crest of the range, crossed the divide (probably through Sonora Pass), and struck a branch of the Stanislaus River, flowing toward the west. As the company followed along that stream, the mountains became ever more majestic and terrifying, and the route grew increasingly difficult. "Several horses and mules fell from the mountain side," wrote Bidwell on October 28, "and rolling like huge stones, landed at the foot of the precipice."

A cold, bleak rain, accompanied by the ever present threat of snow, intensified the misery of the emigrants. Most of them were now on foot, many so weak from hunger and fatigue they could scarcely travel. "Once, I remember," "Cheyenne" Dawson wrote in his reminiscences, "when I was struggling along . . . I looked back and saw Mrs. Kelsey a little way behind me, with her child in her arms, barefooted, I think, and leading her horse." [4]

The emigrants had already killed the last of the oxen and were eating the mules to keep alive. Some of the members of the company were so hungry that when a mule was killed, they gulped down the tough, raw meat without waiting to make a fire; others ate the flesh "half roasted, dripping with blood."

---

[4] *Ibid.*, pp. 23–4.

At last, after weeks of painful effort, the company came within sight of the San Joaquin Valley and saw the line of the Coast Range Mountains on the other side—"a faint blue mass pencilled against the glowing sky." The more pessimistic thought that the settlements along the coast were still five hundred miles away!

A few days later, fortunately, all such gloomy delusions were dispelled. On October 31 the company left the mountains and camped on the floor of the San Joaquin Valley, feasting, for the first time in weeks, on deer, antelope, and wild geese. The following day a vaquero came upon the caravan and guided the emigrants to the ranch of his employer, Dr. John Marsh, at the foot of Mount Diablo. The vanguard of American settlement had at last reached California.

Only a few weeks after the Bidwell-Bartleson company made its appearance at Marsh's ranch, a mixed expedition of Americans and New Mexicans from Santa Fe arrived in Los Angeles. The party, about twenty-five in number, was led by William Workman and John Rowland, merchants and traders of long standing in New Mexico. The company started for California early in September 1841, and followed the old Wolfskill Trail. The expedition drove a flock of sheep along for food, and met with no adventures worthy of the name. Many of the colonists, including Workman, Rowland, and Benjamin D. Wilson (universally known to the Californians as "Don Benito"), acquired large landholdings and played an important part in the affairs of southern California.

In 1843 a party of forty settlers, led by Lansford W. Hastings, the potential Sam Houston of California, came into the Sacramento Valley by way of the Oregon territory. During the same year Joseph B. Chiles, a member of the Bidwell-Bartleson company of 1841, started from Missouri with a large California-bound party. At Fort Hall, however, the company divided. Some of the members continued with Chiles over the Oregon Trail, reaching California in November.

"Fourteen wagons have arrived at Sutters from the U States with families in all about 100 souls all under the direction of one

Capt Childs who was with us about two years ago and appeared a smart intelligent man," wrote William S. Hinckley to Abel Stearns. "You see how immigration progresses and the Yankees will not be stopped unless by the Pacific Ocean." [5]

Meantime the settlers who separated from Chiles at Fort Hall were following "Old Joe" Walker over the route he had pioneered through the Owens Valley a decade before. South of Owens Lake the party was compelled to leave its wagons, pack its goods on horses, and abandon some heavy mill machinery it had succeeded, in some incredible fashion, in transporting half-way across the continent.

Keeping along the edge of the desert, the company turned "the point of the mountain" and entered the San Joaquin Valley by way of Walker Pass. A long, dreary march, more exhausting than anything they had experienced up to that time, brought the emigrants to the secluded valley in the Coast Range Mountains where Walker and his trappers had found winter quarters in 1833. Remaining there until January, the settlers then scattered to various parts of California.

A party consisting of thirty-six members, led by Andrew Kelsey, and a larger train, known as the Stevens-Murphy party, entered California during 1844. The latter company, for the first time in Western immigration, succeeded in bringing wagons all the way from Missouri to the California settlements; and one of its divisions opened the important trail along the Truckee River to the crest of the Sierra Nevada divide.

By the spring of 1845 the anticipated migration to California was giving rise to all sorts of rumors along the excitable American frontier. Seven thousand settlers, according to one report, were preparing to leave Independence for the coast; a New York editor assured his readers that a hundred thousand persons would reach California by the spring of 1846; and even the most conservative estimate of the coast-bound emigration reached several thousand. In point of fact, however, the actual migration to Cali-

[5] Hinckley to Stearns, November 18, 1843. Gaffey MSS., Huntington Library.

fornia for the year did not exceed a total of two hundred and fifty persons, nearly half of whom came in what was known as the Grigsby-Ide party, over the Humboldt-Truckee route.

By the mid-forties the publicity campaign, especially designed to influence American migration to California, was in full swing. The movement was supported by numerous influential newspapers and magazines, such as the New York *Sun,* the New York *Herald,* the *Journal of Commerce,* the Boston *Advertiser,* the *Whig Review,* Hunt's *Merchants Magazine,* and others of similar standing. American residents in California furnished much of the ammunition for such publicity. Two of the most effective propagandists were Dr. John Marsh, the American physician, already mentioned, living near Mount Diablo; and a newly appointed United States Consul, Thomas O. Larkin, of Monterey.

In letters to the various American journals, for which he served as a regular correspondent, Larkin combined practical advice to prospective settlers with a long list of the extraordinary attractions they could expect to find in California. "Immigrants leaving Independence for the Pacific," he said in one of his well-known communications, "should furnish themselves (if a family of five or six persons) with one good wagon, four or five yoke of oxen, three or four cows, three horses, and to each person two hundred and fifty pounds of flour, one hundred and fifty pounds of bacon, thirty pounds of coffee, fifty pounds of sugar, twenty pounds of rice, two good blankets, and a few cooking utensils. Every male person over fourteen years of age should have one good rifle, ten pounds of powder, thirty pounds of lead, two thousand percussion caps and a good horse. On arriving on the banks of the Sacramento and finding a convenient piece of land that the immigrant can occupy, he should begin sowing wheat from December to February; beans, peas and corn in April or May; and should also procure himself cows two years old, worth from four to five dollars; young bulls at two or three dollars; thirty or forty mares at five or six dollars; a stallion at fifteen or twenty dollars, and a few sheep at two dollars each. One hundred cows will produce from seventy to ninety calves between the 2d and 12th months.

From $1,000 to $1,500 in cash will start an enterprising man in breeding animals for a California farm." [6]

News of the outbreak of hostilities between the United States and Mexico, which occurred in April 1846, did not reach the western frontier in time to prevent the departure of the California-bound emigrant companies during the early spring. The annals of one of those expeditions contain the grimmest tragedy in the history of Western travel. [7]

In May 1846 a large number of emigrants, including several units of a family named Donner, started from Independence, Missouri, with ample provisions and adequate equipment to take them into California. Owing, however, to a series of costly delays, arising about equally from poor judgment, misinformation, and unavoidable mishaps, the company did not reach the foot of the Sierra Nevada Mountains until late in the fall.

By that time the emigrants were in a thoroughly demoralized and wretched state; their food supply was almost gone; and the arrival of a small relief train from Sutter's Fort provided barely sufficient supplies, even under the most favorable conditions, to enable them to cross the mountains. But despite the desperate need for haste, further time was required to permit the party's worn-out animals to recuperate. This brief delay spelled tragedy and disaster.

When the train finally began the passage of the mountains most of the emigrants were physically at the end of their resources, correspondingly discouraged, and destitute of spirit. The company was also disrupted by individual and factional disputes, and its members proved incapable of making any concerted effort to solve their common problems.

But such difficulties were merely incidental. As the emigrants

---

[6] Larkin to the Secretary of State, December 31, 1845. *Official Correspondence*, Part II, No. 32, pp. 94–100, Bancroft Collection.

[7] The standard authority is Charles F. McGlashan: *The History of the Donner Party* (Truckee, 1879 and numerous subsequent editions). Recent versions are George R. Stewart, Jr.: *Ordeal by Hunger: The Story of the Donner Party* (1936); and Bernard De Voto: *The Year of Decision* (1943).

neared the crest of the mountains, the stark Sierra winter broke over them with sudden and appalling fury. In a few hours one division of the caravan was snowbound, near what is now known as Donner Lake; and the remainder of the company found itself stalled at Prosser Creek, some six miles distant.

Roaring winds swept through the treetops above the crude cabins and makeshift canvas shelters the emigrants erected. Deeper and deeper grew the snow, more bitter the cold, more pitiless the grip of famine. Death took ghastly and impartial toll, both of the victims who remained in the camps and of those who sought to escape to the settlements on the Sacramento. In an extremity of hunger the starving emigrants ate everything available—boiled strips of oxhide, a glutinous, nauseating mess; baked, marrowless bones; tiny field mice; the bark and twigs of trees; and finally even the flesh of their dead companions.

Seventy-nine persons, all but twenty of whom were women, children, or nursing babies, entered the mountains in October; only forty-five survived. But because of the fortitude, self-sacrifice, and steadfast courage of common people, the epic of the Donner party holds an immortal place, both in the history of California and in the heroic tradition of the frontier West.

CHAPTER 10. Washington, Mexico, and California

AS THE influx of American settlers into California steadily increased, the United States government conducted an active diplomatic campaign to obtain possession of the province. The movement began as far back as 1835, when Andrew Jackson endeavored in a mild way to sound out the Mexican government on the cession of San Francisco Bay. The idea was apparently suggested to Jackson almost simultaneously by Anthony Butler, United States Chargé d'Affaires in Mexico, and William A. Slacum, a purser in the United States Navy and an associate of Ewing Young in the Oregon cattle trade.

Butler, a man whom Jackson later denounced as a rogue and a liar, in whom there was "neither truth, justice, or gratitude," assured the Secretary of State that half a million dollars, "judiciously applied," would put the United States in possession both of Texas and "of the whole of that tract of territory known as New Mexico and Higher and Lower California, an empire in itself, a paradise in climate." [1] Butler made no headway in his negotiations with Mexico; and Jackson, after "wriggling along and snapping at the bait like a mackerel after a red rag"—to use the spleenish figure employed by John Quincy Adams—violently denounced the unprincipled diplomat and ousted him from his position.

After Butler's dismissal, however, Jackson made two further efforts to obtain San Francisco Bay, then the only part of California considered of any value to the United States. In discussing the question of mediation between Mexico and Texas with General Santa Anna after the Battle of San Jacinto, Jackson proposed to offer Mexico three and a half million dollars for that part of California lying north of 38°. About the same time he urged the

---

[1] Robert G. Cleland: "The Early Sentiment for the Annexation of California," *The Southwestern Historical Quarterly*, Vol. XVIII, p. 14.

new Republic of Texas to extend its boundaries to include California. Such a move, he believed, by assuring control of the chief harbor on the Pacific, would reconcile New England and other commercial sections in the North to the annexation of Texas. "He is very earnest and anxious on this point of claiming the Californias, and says we must not consent to less," wrote W. H. Wharton, the Texan Minister to Washington. "This is in strict confidence. Glory to God in the highest!"

After the retirement of Jackson from the presidency all negotiations for the acquisition of California were suspended until Tyler brought them to the fore again in 1842. In the interval, however, the first of several government exploring parties, some of which frankly combined political objectives with scientific pursuits, reached the California coast. The expedition was under the able command of Lieutenant Charles Wilkes of the United States Navy, and spent five years in the Pacific. On the basis of its contributions to various branches of science, the Wilkes expedition is looked upon as one of the most successful undertakings of its kind in the history of American exploration.

In the fall of 1841 Wilkes visited the port of San Francisco, traveled extensively through the surrounding country, and gathered valuable material on the economic, social, and political life of the province. The American commander was equally impressed by the possibilities and incomparable natural advantages of San Francisco Bay, and by the complete vulnerability of the province to invasion. Among the Californians the expedition was believed to be a definite part of an American program of annexation.

A year after Wilkes's visit to San Francisco, Commodore Thomas Ap Catesby Jones, commander of the United States Pacific Squadron, who had begun his naval career by seeking "to chase the pirate Jean Lafitte from his bayou stronghold," received a false report, while at Callao, Peru, that the United States was at war with Mexico and that the latter country intended to cede California to Great Britain to prevent it from falling into American hands. Jones accordingly sailed post-haste for Monterey. When he reached the port, on October 18, 1842, "most of the garrison were off at work in the fields; fort and guns were in their usual state of decay . . . and everything . . . was quiet, peaceful, and normally dilapidated." But despite the fact that he found no sign of war, of warlike preparations, or of the British fleet, Jones formally demanded the surrender of the port, set a landing force ashore to occupy the city, issued a proclamation to the bewildered inhabitants, and raised the American flag.

Two days later, convinced that he had been misinformed on the outbreak of hostilities and had acted too hastily in seizing the California port, Jones restored Monterey to the Californians, replaced the Mexican flag, formally apologized for his precipitate action, and sailed down the coast to pay his official respects to Governor Micheltorena in Los Angeles. Not to be outdone in courtesy, the California Governor, who had previously pictured himself in the role of "a thunderbolt to fly and annihilate the invaders," gave Jones a formal ball, "well and brilliantly attended," and extended him other hospitalities.

As Micheltorena's attitude made clear, the Monterey incident created surprisingly little ill will in California; but in Mexico it caused a violent and inopportune reaction against the United States, and compelled the Tyler administration, at least for the time being, to suspend negotiations, which had recently been revived, for the purchase of California.

The movement for the annexation of California found its chief advocate, at that time, in Waddy Thompson, American Minister to Mexico. Thompson was a California enthusiast of the most ardent type. In his official communications to the Department of State he described the province as "the richest, the most beautiful, the healthiest country in the world." [2] Daniel Webster, who once said that he considered the Bay of San Francisco twenty times more valuable than the whole of Texas, was Secretary

---

[2] See Cleland: "Early Sentiment for Annexation"; and *A History of California, passim.* In a later dispatch Thompson added that the acquisition of California would be "by far the most important event that has occurred to our country."

of State during the first years of the Tyler administration, and took an active part in furthering Thompson's plan of annexing California. Webster's most distinctive contribution to the program was the so-called tripartite agreement—a plan to unite in one measure the acquisition of California, the satisfaction of the claims of American citizens against Mexico, and the settlement of the Oregon boundary dispute between Great Britain and the United States. Webster's proposal involved the sale of California to the United States; the liquidation of American claims against Mexico; and a substantial payment to British creditors and holders of defaulted Mexican bonds from the funds made available by the United States. Britain, in return, would then be asked to accept the line of the Columbia as the boundary between Canada and the United States. Although Webster's suggestion lay within the realm of practical politics, and promised substantial benefits to each of the three governments involved, the measure aroused little interest and died before it reached the negotiation stage.

With the appointment of John C. Calhoun as Secretary of State in 1844, California became more than ever an object of interest to the United States. Three major factors accounted for this increasing government concern: a well-grounded fear of English designs upon the territory; the rapidly expanding volume of American overland emigration; and apparently authentic reports that California was about to separate from Mexico and become an independent republic.

With such far-reaching events in the making, the United States obviously needed an official representative in California to safeguard American interests, political as well as economic. Tyler accordingly appointed Thomas O. Larkin, the well-to-do and long-established merchant at Monterey, to serve as American Consul for California. In addition to fulfilling the usual functions of his office, Larkin became an active promoter of American immigration, the chief California correspondent of Eastern newspapers and magazines, a repository of fact and rumor on everything that took place in the province, and an accurate and efficient information bureau for the Department of State in Washington.

When Tyler left the White House in March 1845, he was succeeded by James K. Polk, an expansionist as resolute and zealous as Andrew Jackson himself. The new President began his administration with a fourfold program that included the settlement of the Oregon boundary; a reduction in the tariff; the establishment of the subtreasury system; and the annexation of California. Before his term was over, he had carried through all the items on the agenda.

Unfortunately, most early American historians suffered from a severe anti-slavery complex that led them to resolve the movement for the acquisition of California, from beginning to end, into a simple plot to obtain "bigger pens to cram with slaves." But Polk was an expansionist, not because he came from the South, but because he belonged to the West. He was an extreme Jacksonian nationalist. Manifest destiny, with its cardinal doctrine that the United States must eventually expand across the continent and control the shores of the Pacific, was as deep-rooted in his convictions as the rigid Calvinistic theology to which he subscribed. As a political realist Polk also recognized the obvious fact that Mexico's weak and tenuous grasp on California was rapidly slipping; and that, when her last hold gave way, the province would inevitably either fall within the orbit of the British Empire, or unite, voluntarily or by compulsion, with the United States.

At the time of Polk's accession to the presidency, the Mexican government seemed hopelessly demoralized. Mexico was manifestly able to exercise only nominal control over California. Overland communication between the two countries had practically ceased; official advices from Mexico City reached Los Angeles and Monterey only once or twice a year; and one experienced traveler even asserted that Mexico had "more intercourse with China than with California."

Within California itself political organization was becoming less and less effective. On his visit to San Francisco Bay, previously mentioned, Lieutenant Wilkes reported that he found "a total absence of all government in California and even its forms

and ceremonies thrown aside." The arrival of General Micheltorena, with tatterdemalion troops, and the report that the Mexican government proposed to turn California into a sort of Botany
Bay, naturally added to the turmoil and confusion in the province.

From a military standpoint conditions were equally deplorable.
The four presidios along the coast were manned by only a handful of troops; most of the guns were dismantled or rusty from dis-
use; there was little or no ammunition; and Mexico had neither
troops, supplies, nor transport facilities with which to reinforce
the province. For naval defense California was forced to rely
on "a mere apology for a coasting cruiser"—"an old, cranky
craft, not mounting a single gun, and so badly manned that she
was unable to make any progress when beating against the wind."

In the light of such conditions, California's imminent separation from Mexico was accepted in informed quarters, both
within and without the province, as a foregone conclusion.
Some of the Spanish Californians cherished the vague hope of
erecting California into a sovereign state and setting up an independent government; but the idea of creating a new republic appealed far more to the bold imagination of American adventurers
than to the less vaulting ambitions of the *paisanos*.

In 1842 the explorer and potential filibuster, Lansford W. Hastings, came to the coast for the express purpose of uniting California and Oregon and making himself president of the new republic. With that end in view he sought to promote the American occupation of California, organized immigrant families to
settle in the province, carried on extensive correspondence, and
succeeded in enlisting widespread support for his ambitious
schemes.

The idea of an independent republic such as Hastings en-
visaged was advocated by many of his contemporaries, and, indeed, frequently came to the fore long after California was admitted as a state. Dr. John Marsh, the American ranchero-
physician, prophesied that the union of Oregon and California
would create a new empire on the Pacific, whose capital, located

on San Francisco Bay, "possibly on the site occupied by the miserable village of Yerba Buena," would eventually become "one of the great emporii of the world." About the same time Sam Houston declared that the union of Texas, Chihuahua, Sonora, California, and Oregon would create a nation equal to any in existence. "It is impossible," he wrote, "to look upon the map of North America and not perceive the *rationale* of the project."

Instead of an independent republic, many well-informed persons looked to see California ultimately become either a British colony or some sort of British protectorate. The possibility of such a step, despite the failure of the British government to give the movement any official backing, was not a figment of American expansionists seeking to concoct effective propaganda to hasten the annexation of California, but constituted a very real danger, down to the actual outbreak of the Mexican War, to the rapidly maturing plans of the United States to obtain the territory, or at least to sponsor a movement for California's independence.

A half-century earlier George Vancouver had given a hint of the revival of Britain's interest in Drake's old claim to "Nova Albion." In 1839 Alexander Forbes, British Vice-Consul at Tepic, published his popular history of California, the first extended treatise in English on the province. The book was authoritative, interesting, well written; but its primary purpose, as the author frankly stated, was to encourage British colonization of California. And Forbes even went so far as to outline a definite plan by which British sovereignty could be extended over the territory. The volume, with its startling implications, aroused widespread interest in the United States. The reaction to the author's proposals was thus voiced by the Baltimore *American:* ". . . to make the Rocky Mountains the boundary of the United States on the west; to hold the spacious valley between the range and the ocean . . . thus possessing the seaboard, by means of which the commerce with China and the East Indies would be secured to British interests—this would be an attainment worthy of no small effort on the part of Great Britain."

In keeping with the traditions of American expansion, the more deeply the United States interested herself in California, the more suspicious of Britain's purpose did our people and government become. Commodore Ap Catesby Jones explained his seizure of Monterey as a move to forestall the "occupation of California by Great Britain under a secret treaty with Mexico." Waddy Thompson, Duff Green, and other representatives of the State Department, whether in Mexico, England, or California, voiced the same fear. "I know that England has designs on California," wrote Thompson to Webster, "and has actually made a treaty with Mexico securing to British creditors the lands there in payment of their debts and that England will interpose this treaty in the way of a cession of California and that in ten years she will own the country." [3]

Reports were later sent to Washington that British creditors held a mortgage on California for $26,000,000; that the British fleet in the Pacific had been reinforced for the express purpose of taking and holding the province, in case of war between the United States and Mexico; and that several of the leading powers of Europe proposed "to compose the Mexican trouble" by setting up a monarchy in the country, thereby effectually blocking the annexation of California by the United States.

As further evidence of British designs on California, it was pointed out that the Hudson's Bay Company, characterized by an American diplomat as "that embryo East India Monopoly," had established a post in San Francisco; and that James Alexander Forbes, a British agent at Monterey, was using every opportunity to undermine the influence of the United States among the Californians. Admiral Seymour of the British Pacific fleet was also charged with supporting a movement to lead California to declare its independence and seek the protection of Great Britain.

Finally, it was common knowledge that a priest named Eugene Macnamara (who seemed to Larkin much more familiar with politics than with theology) had received permission from the

---

[3] See Cleland: "Early Sentiment for Annexation," pp. 82–97, for a full discussion of the rumors of European interest in California.

Mexican government to establish a large Irish-Catholic colony in California. On July 2, 1845, Macnamara's petition for a grant of land was presented to the California Assembly. The tract lay between the San Joaquin River and the Sierra Nevada Mountains, and extended from the Cosumnes River on the north to Tulare Lake in the south. Macnamara promised to bring two thousand sober, industrious, Catholic families into California. The colonists would defend the province against invasion, keep peace in the interior, and devote themselves to developing the resources and increasing the prosperity of the country.

Confronted by the prospective separation of California from Mexico and the threat of British domination of the province, President Polk sought to negotiate with Mexico for the sale of the territory to the United States, and appointed John Slidell of Louisiana to carry out the mission. Slidell was authorized to offer as high as forty million dollars for the cession; but violent anti-American feeling in Mexico, coupled with the explosive state of Mexican politics, forced Slidell to return to the United States empty-handed and thoroughly disgruntled.

While Slidell's appointment was under consideration, Polk quietly initiated a program within California itself that promised to bring about ultimate annexation. The spearhead of the movement was the American Consul, Thomas O. Larkin, of Monterey. On October 17, 1845, James Buchanan appointed Larkin confidential agent of the State Department and instructed him to keep himself informed on all matters relating to the province, to counteract the influence of foreign governments, and to encourage the Californians to look to the United States for counsel and assistance. "Whilst the President will make no effort and use no influence to induce California to become one of the free and independent States of this Union," wrote Buchanan, "yet if the people should desire to unite their destiny with ours, they would be received as brethren, whenever this can be done without affording Mexico just cause of complaint." [4]

---

[4] Cleland: "Early Sentiment for Annexation," pp. 73–4. The letter is printed in full in James A. B. Scherer's *Thirty-first Star* (1942), pp. 326–9.

Larkin fulfilled the responsibilities of his new appointment with energy and discretion. His reports to Buchanan were clear, detailed, and reliable; he made himself thoroughly conversant with the political and military problems of the province, and worked adroitly to encourage the Californians to seek independence and ask protection from the United States.

In support of the movement, Larkin enlisted the services of some of the most influential native and foreign-born citizens of California. Among the number were Mariano Guadalupe Vallejo, the most powerful political figure in California, and General José Castro, author of a confidentially circulated plan for "declaring California independent in 1847–1848, as soon as a sufficient number of foreigners should arrive." To Jacob P. Leese, of Sonoma, J. J. Warner, near San Diego, and the wealthy merchant and landowner Don Abel Stearns, of Los Angeles, Larkin sent secret circular letters, inviting their assistance and co-operation.

Supported by Stearns, Vallejo, Castro, and other leading Californians, Larkin's plan of an independent California was well on its way to realization by the spring of 1846, and gave every promise of reaching a successful climax within the ensuing year. At that juncture three events, occurring in rapid succession, completely disrupted Larkin's smoothly working plans and ushered in a new and all-important chapter in California history. First came a threatened clash between the Californians and the noted explorer John C. Frémont; second, an uprising of the American settlers in the Sacramento Valley, usually called the Bear Flag Revolt; and third, the outbreak of the Mexican War.[5]

---

[5] Copies of the Larkin letters cited in the chapter and documents relating to the Macnamara project are in the manuscript collections of the Huntington Library.

CHAPTER 11. From Bear Flag to Statehood

DURING the mid-forties, when American interest in California was rapidly approaching its climax, John Charles Frémont—hero, villain, or adventurer, according to one's individual point of view, but in any case a man who experienced "one of the stormiest, the most erratic, and the most adventurous of American careers" [1]—made his first dramatic entrance into California.

Following a preliminary reconnaissance to the Rocky Mountains in 1842, Frémont led five separate expeditions across the Great Basin to the Pacific coast. Three of these immediately antedated the outbreak of the Mexican War. A fourth, undertaken during the winter of 1849, ended in starvation, cannibalism, and the death of a third of the party in the San Juan Mountains of New Mexico. Four years later, in attempting to discover a central railroad route to the Pacific, Frémont almost lost his own life in the snow-covered fastnesses of southern Utah.

In some respects, thanks in part to Frémont's flair for the dramatic and his extraordinary sense of timing, the exploits of the so-called Pathfinder were greatly exaggerated. Many of the less spectacular but equally important aspects of his Western expeditions, on the other hand, failed to receive appropriate recognition.

Frémont's chief contributions did not consist in the opening of new trails or the exploration of unknown lands, but arose from the observations and impressions of a well-trained mind, the correlation of the discoveries of his predecessors, and accurate, systematized descriptions of the West beyond the Rocky Mountains and its Indian inhabitants. A mastery of narrative and descriptive writing also enhanced Frémont's popularity. Thousands of stay-at-homes who read his reports saw the poppies and lupin of early spring miraculously transform the valley of the San Joaquin into an unbelievable carpet of orange, gold, and blue. They chilled to

---

[1] Allan Nevins: *Frémont: Pathmarker of the West* (1939), p. 1.

the very marrow of their bones in the smothering snows and roaring winds of a Sierra storm, or shuddered with dread at the bloody give-and-take of a sudden Indian attack upon a sleeping camp, while the smoke of a smoldering fire hung suspended in the dark branches of the pine trees or drifted down across the faces of dying men.

To supplement his own very considerable scientific knowledge, Frémont included a few specialists such as Charles Preuss, botanist and skilled topographer, and Edward M. Kern, artist, in the personnel of most of his expeditions. His reports consequently proved of extraordinary value from a scientific as well as from a historical and literary point of view.

Frémont first came to California in 1843–4 as commander of an expedition, authorized by the War Department, to link the explorations of the preceding year in the Rocky Mountains with "the surveys of Commander Wilkes on the coast of the Pacific Ocean, so as to give a corrected survey of the interior of our continent."

At the time Frémont entered California, the dominant figure in the Sacramento Valley was the romantic rover, adventurer, dreamer of empire, and jack-of-all-trades, John August Sutter. During the interval between the summer of 1834, when he reached New York a penniless emigrant from Germany, and his arrival at San Francisco five years later, Sutter's wanderings carried him into the mountains of New Mexico and Colorado, across the continent to Oregon, from there to Hawaii, and to the Russian settlement of Sitka in Alaska.

When Sutter landed at San Francisco, he brought with him a highly original, well-matured plan by which he hoped to make himself the feudal lord of the Sacramento Valley. He proposed to acquire an immense tract of land, develop it with the aid of Kanaka and Indian labor, erect upon it the strongest military post in the province, and eventually settle it with American and other foreign immigrants. With surprising readiness, impelled by the desire to set up a buffer colony against Yankee invasion from the East, Governor Alvarado responded to Sutter's request for land by promising to give him nearly fifty thousand acres, the maximum grant permitted under Mexican law, in the very heart of the Sacramento Valley. To this principality Sutter gave the name of New Helvetia. Gathering together a motley force of "sailors, Kanakas, Mexican cowboys, and friendly Indians," the future "lord of the marches of the Sacramento" began to build his fortress and develop his domain.

Frémont spent something over two weeks at Sutter's Fort, recuperating his men, purchasing fresh animals and supplies, and gleaning extensive information on the rising tide of American emigration to California, the country's inadequate military defenses, the widespread agitation for independence, and the rumored designs of British annexation. To one of Frémont's large ambition and fertile imagination, the fast approaching crisis in California affairs promised dazzling opportunities. But the record is silent as to the actual dreams that ran through his eager mind, or the commanding part he reserved for himself in the forthcoming drama, soon to be enacted on the fertile plains of the Sacramento.

Upon his return to Washington, Frémont occupied himself with the preparation of his reports, met many members of Congress and the Cabinet, and undertook to organize a second expedition to California. By that time the province had come to hold a prominent place in diplomatic and political circles, as well as in public interest; and with the support of his influential father-in-law, Senator Benton, and other pronounced expansionists in Washington, including George Bancroft, Secretary of the Navy, Frémont had little difficulty in securing the necessary authorization for the undertaking.

Leaving Bent's Fort in June 1845, Frémont traveled up the Arkansas to the heart of the Colorado Rockies, visited the Great Salt Lake, and crossed the desolate Nevada plains to the Ogden River. This dreary but historic stream Frémont gratuitously renamed the Humboldt, in honor of a European geographer who never saw the river, the Rocky Mountains, or any part of the Far West, at the expense of one of the foremost explorers of the Great Basin and the Pacific coast.

After making an extensive exploration of the region between Humboldt River and Walker Lake, Frémont divided the expedition and with fifteen men struck almost directly west to the Sierra Nevada Mountains. Ascending the Salmon Trout or Truckee River to the summit, he followed down the course of the American River into the Sacramento Valley, and reached Sutter's Fort on December 10. Meantime Walker was leading the other division of the expedition over his old trail into the San Joaquin Valley. Skirting the eastern base of the Sierra, traversing the long extent of Owens Valley, rounding the "point of the mountains," and crossing through Walker Pass, the party moved leisurely down the San Joaquin to meet their companions at a previously designated rendezvous.

A misunderstanding, however, as to the place agreed upon for the rendezvous prevented the reunion of the two detachments. Walker stopped at the Kern River, while Frémont waited a hundred miles farther north, on the banks of the King's River. It was then late in December; but despite the ominous threat of winter, Frémont made his way up the swift-running stream, penetrating deeper and deeper into the snow-covered mountains until he reached the majestic solitudes in which the headwaters of the river find their source.

Disappointed in his efforts to effect a junction with Walker's party in the San Joaquin, Frémont returned to Sutter's Fort to await the arrival of the absent men. The interval gave him the opportunity of visiting William A. Leidesdorff, the recently appointed American Vice-Consul at San Francisco, and of traveling as far south as Monterey. General Castro gave the Americans tacit permission to winter in California, provided they would agree to keep away from the settlements along the coast.

About the middle of February Frémont was rejoined by the party under Walker from which he had separated east of the mountains and which had vainly waited for him at the delusive rendezvous on the Kern River. The united company then went into winter quarters on the Rancho La Laguna, some thirteen miles south of San José. In this comparatively isolated spot there was little chance of the Americans coming into conflict with the Californians. But at the end of two weeks the company broke camp and marched across the mountains into the Salinas Valley. The action, directly at variance with Frémont's implied pledge to keep his men away from the coast, placed the small but heavily armed band of foreigners within easy striking distance of Monterey and reawakened all the fears and suspicions of the Californians.

José and Manuel Castro, commandant and prefect respectively of the district, both sent curtly worded messages to Frémont, ordering him and his men to leave the province. Without condescending to make a written reply to the Castro communications, Frémont moved his camp to a strong position on a commanding landmark, known as Gavilán, or Hawk's Peak, that overlooked the surrounding plain, and openly defied the Californians.

While these events were taking place, General Castro had gathered a considerable body of cavalry at the Mission San Juan Bautista, and summoned all loyal citizens of the countryside to enlist at his headquarters. Though the Americans and Californians threatened for three days to come to blows, no blood was actually shed by either side; and on March 9, under cover of darkness, Frémont left his fortified position and retired slowly up the Sacramento Valley toward Oregon.

The Hawk's Peak affair completely disrupted Larkin's plan of peaceful annexation. It affronted the Californians, caused grave concern among responsible, long-established American residents, and encouraged newly arrived overland immigrants in their truculent attitude toward the provincial government. Two months after the incident Lieutenant Archibald H. Gillespie, of the United States Marine Corps, arrived in California with confidential messages from Washington, and succeeded in overtaking Frémont in the depths of the forests near the southern end of Klamath Lake. The precise nature of the communications Gillespie delivered to Frémont has been the subject of endless speculation and disagreement, among both historians and near-historians, from that day to this.

The whole affair, indeed, including Frémont's assertion that even a secret family cipher was involved, constitutes one of the most persistent mysteries of California history and "the most baffling problem of Frémont's career." Whatever the exact tenor of the messages, however, it is clear either that Frémont considered himself bound, explicitly or by implication, to return to California and take such part in forthcoming events as circumstances required, or else that he saw in the situation an opportunity to make John Charles Frémont the Sam Houston of California.

Owing in part to preoccupation with the critical decisions he was called upon to make as the result of this new turn of events, Frémont neglected to post sentries about the camp the night of Gillespie's arrival, and his carelessness gave the Klamath Indians an opportunity to attack the sleeping men. Three of Frémont's men and the Klamath Indian chief were killed in the affray. When morning came the Americans exacted savage retribution for the loss of their companions.

Following this bloody incident, Frémont retraced his steps to the Sacramento. Here events were moving swiftly to a crisis, and rumors of all kinds were circulating among the settlers. Though some of these reports were obviously exaggerated, American residents on the Sacramento had genuine reason to be alarmed; and when Frémont returned to the valley, the settlers naturally turned to him and his formidable band of frontiersmen, many of whom were known on every Western trail for their prowess in border warfare, for assistance and protection. How far Frémont was responsible for instigating the ensuing uprising among the settlers is still a subject of debate. Larkin, and many other long-established American residents in California, outspokenly blamed him "for moving in the affair of the Bear party"; and certainly his presence and promise of co-operation supplied the confidence necessary for any such revolt.

The first clash with the Californians occurred on June 10 when a company of settlers, under the leadership of Ezekiel Merritt, a tall, raw-boned, tobacco-chewing, fearless, illiterate frontiersman, seized a band of horses that had been collected by Lieutenant

Arcé for the use of General Castro. The incident set the Sacramento Valley ablaze. Four days later a much larger body of settlers occupied the village of Sonoma and seized its principal citizens. Among the prisoners was Don Mariano G. Vallejo, the wealthiest, most influential citizen in California, a strong supporter of American interests, and one of the native leaders upon whom Larkin had counted most heavily for success in his plan of peaceful annexation! Vallejo was sent to Sutter's Fort and held there, despite Sutter's protest, for nearly two months.

Edward M. Kern, previously mentioned as a member of Frémont's company, was given charge of the fort and custody of the prisoners. Meanwhile, under the direction of such men as Ezekiel Merritt, Robert Semple, William B. Ide, John Grigsby, and William Knight, the settlers' uprising took on the character of an organized revolt. The insurrectionists proclaimed the Republic of California; raised a crudely designed flag, on which appeared what purported to be the figure of a grizzly bear; and issued a formal proclamation justifying the revolt and setting forth the democratic principles of the new government.

The proclamation, signed by Ide and dated: "Headquarters Sonoma, June 15, 1846," invited "all peaceable & good citizens of California" to assist in establishing and perpetuating "a Republican government which shall secure to us all Civil & religious liberty, which shall encourage virtue and literature, which shall leave unshackled by fetters Agriculture, Commerce & Mechanism." [2]

Less than a month after the events just mentioned, the Bear Flag Revolt and the California Republic had run their meteoric course. In the intervening weeks a "motley array of voyageurs, trappers, scouts, former sailors, frontier farmers, and ranchmen . . . a body unlike any other that has ever fought on American soil," had been organized into the California Battalion under Frémont's personal command. In a skirmish near San Rafael the Bear Flag settlers had routed a considerable force under Joaquín de la

---

[2] Huntington Library, MS. No. 4116.

Torre, three American settlers had been massacred, and the same number of harmless Californians had been waylaid and shot.

Who can say what historic exploits the rough frontiersmen who rallied to the standard of the Bear Flag might not have accomplished, or what fate, glorious or ignominious, the California Republic might not have experienced had the movement for independence been left to run its full course? The answer must be left to speculation. On July 9 a courier brought word to Frémont that war had broken out between the United States and Mexico, and that Commodore John D. Sloat, with a strong American naval force, was already in undisputed possession of Monterey. At that moment the historic significance of the Bear Flag movement came to an end, but the passage of nearly a century has built about the revolt a highly romantic tradition, and made it, in the popular mind at least, the means by which California won her independence, and the United States obtained possession of an incomparable empire on the Pacific coast.[3]

The occupation of Monterey, which brought the Bear Flag movement to such an abrupt end, was carried out by Commodore Sloat, commander of the United States Pacific fleet. In the spring of 1846 Sloat was on the west coast of Mexico with a force of five vessels. Upon receipt of unofficial but apparently authentic information that hostilities had broken out with Mexico, Sloat sailed for California waters, reaching Monterey on July 2. There the American commander found himself in a difficult quandary. Formal notice of a declaration of war between the United States and Mexico had not arrived; but if he waited to take possession of Monterey until official dispatches came from Washington, the long delay would almost certainly jeopardize the government's plan of swift and bloodless occupation of the California ports, and might even afford Admiral Seymour, of the British Navy, an opportunity for prior intervention.

A more resolute commander would have found in the circumstances ample justification for immediate action, but Sloat, wary

---

[3] The Bear Flag is now California's official emblem and must be flown on all state buildings.

because of his predecessor Jones's experience, pursued a hesitant policy. On July 7, however, he sent a formal demand for the surrender of the presidio (a demand no one in Monterey had authority to answer), disembarked a force of bluejackets and marines, seized the customhouse, raised the American flag, and declared California a possession of the United States.

Once in control of the port, Sloat issued a proclamation to the Californians emphasizing the attitude of goodwill and conciliation which all along had been the keynote of Polk's California policy. Two days after the seizure of Monterey, Captain John Montgomery took peaceable possession of the port of San Francisco. On July 15 Commodore Robert F. Stockton arrived at Monterey to relieve Sloat and to assume command of the Pacific fleet. A much more aggressive officer than his predecessor, Stockton proceeded at once to occupy the remaining California ports and to complete the conquest of the province.

As part of the program, the members of the Bear Flag battalion were sworn in as volunteers in the United States Army, Frémont was made a major, and Gillespie was raised to the rank of captain. Both San Diego and Los Angeles were occupied without opposition, and the situation appeared so hopeless to the California leaders, Pío Pico and José Castro, that they disbanded their forces and sought to escape to Mexico. With all organized resistance to the American forces thus brought to an end, Stockton dispatched Kit Carson across the continent to inform President Polk that American sovereignty had been extended over the whole of California and that the province was entirely free from Mexican domination. The report was gratifying, but unhappily not in accordance with the facts.

Deceived by the ease with which the country had been occupied, and misled by the submissive attitude of the bewildered and divided Californians, Stockton made the dual mistake of placing Captain Archibald Gillespie in command of Los Angeles, and of leaving only fifty men to maintain order in that notoriously unruly city. Gillespie was unsuited, both by temperament and by personality, for the responsible task to which he had been assigned. Benjamin D. Wilson described him as arbitrary and dictatorial, and concurred in the common charge that he "established very obnoxious regulations to annoy the people, and upon frivolous pretexts had most respectable men in the community arrested and brought before him, for no other purpose than to humiliate them."

The turbulent citizens of Los Angeles, ready, even under their own rulers, to revolt at the slightest provocation, were quick to resent Gillespie's arbitrary conduct and equally prompt to take advantage of the weakness of his position. In the early morning of September 23 a band of Californians, "filled with patriotism and perhaps with wine," made a blustering attack upon the sleeping Americans. No blood was shed at the time, but upon Gillespie's attempt to arrest the leaders of the mob, the Angelenos rose in open revolt. The movement thus begun swept across the countryside with the speed of a mountain fire; and the small American detachment in Los Angeles soon found itself closely surrounded by five or six hundred Californians under command of José María Flores. The plight of the besieged Americans finally became so desperate that John Brown, a former trapper, whom the Californians called Juan Flaco, or Lean John, offered to slip through the enemy lines and carry an appeal for aid to Stockton, who was then in Monterey.

With a brief message from Gillespie written on cigarette papers and concealed in his long hair, Lean John made his way by night out of the beleaguered camp. Brown rode day and night, without rest or sleep, until he reached Monterey, only to find that Stockton had gone on to San Francisco. After a few hours' respite Lean John resumed his epic ride. When he reached San Francisco, he had covered nearly five hundred miles on horseback and traveled an additional twenty-seven miles on foot—all in less than five days!

In the meantime a force of Californians had surrounded a considerable body of Americans, many of whom were related by marriage to influential native families, on Isaac Williams's Rancho del Chino, south of the site of the present city of Pomona. After some preliminary skirmishing the besieging force set fire to the highly inflammable roof of the large adobe house in which the Americans had taken refuge, and forced them to surrender. For a time it appeared that the Californians, incensed over the death of one of their number, would massacre the captives; but the courage and chivalry of Serbulo Varela, the California leader, prevented the threatened execution.

As the Californians approached Los Angeles with their prisoners, Gillespie was persuaded to capitulate and he and his men marched out of the pueblo for San Pedro, "with drums beating, colors flying, and . . . matches lighted." Stockton had already dispatched Captain Mervine in the *Savannah* to the relief of the besieged Americans; but the vessel did not reach San Pedro until September 7, and by that time Gillespie had withdrawn from Los Angeles, as already indicated, and established an encampment at the port.

Following the arrival of the *Savannah*, a force of some three hundred Americans, including Gillespie's command, set out over the dry, dusty plain to reoccupy the pueblo. Much of the route lay through immense fields of wild mustard which stood higher than the heads of the marching troops. The heat was insufferable; the air, unrelieved by even the faintest breeze, grew more and more oppressive as the day wore on; and the men suffered so acutely from thirst and exhaustion that camp was made early in the afternoon on a portion of the famous Rancho de Domínguez.

By the following morning, when the march was resumed, the enemy had mustered in sufficient force to threaten the advance of the invaders. For weapons the *paisanos* relied chiefly upon vicious eight-foot willow lances, the blades of which were made of files and rasps, and a bronze four-pounder, known as the "Old Woman's Gun," mounted on the front axle of an immigrant wagon. The gun was fired by applying a lighted cigarette to the touch-hole, and whisked out of danger by the lariats of the mounted Californians. Tradition says that the powder used in the gun was made at the Mission San Gabriel.

Exhausted by their futile efforts to capture the four-pounder or bring the Californians to a decisive engagement, Mervine gave up the proposed attack upon Los Angeles and began the return march to San Pedro. Harassed by the "Old Woman's Gun," under constant threat of the superbly mounted Californians, nearly prostrated by dust and heat, the American forces reached the landing a very dispirited and sorry lot. Four of their number were either dead or dying; six had been seriously wounded; and many others were in a state of near-collapse.[4]

While events were thus taking shape in California, a force of about a hundred men, under the command of Colonel Stephen W. Kearny, and called somewhat grandiloquently "The Army of the West," was marching overland from New Mexico, by way of the Gila River and the Colorado, to the coast. The long journey, especially the heat, dust, and thirst of the Colorado Desert, played havoc with the morale and physical condition of the men, and reduced the riding and baggage animals to walking skeletons.

In the rugged mountains between San Diego and Warner's Ranch (where the worn-out Americans stopped for a few days to rest), Andrés Pico waited with about a hundred Californians to dispute the further advance of the invaders. The two forces met near the little Indian village of San Pasqual. A clever feint by the Californians, who were armed with long lances and mounted upon fast, well-trained horses, drew the Americans into a rash, disorganized attack. When the pursuit was strung out over a mile or more, and the weakened American horses were beginning to show the effects of the charge, Pico's men suddenly wheeled and swept back over the surprised Americans.

The engagement—saber and gun butt against lance—was the bloodiest fought on California soil. Eighteen of Kearny's troops were killed in the affray, and a somewhat larger number, including the commander, more or less seriously wounded. Fortunately the Californians were accustomed only to a hit-and-run form of

---

[4] The so-called Battle of Navidad, a sharp encounter between a band of Americans, seeking to join Frémont at Monterey, and a hastily organized force of nearly a hundred and fifty *paisanos,* constituted the only important engagement of the revolt in northern California.

warfare and did not take advantage of their initial success to effect a complete rout of Kearny's badly crippled force. The position of the Americans, however, was still extremely critical. "Day dawned," wrote Major William H. Emory, "on the most tattered and ill-fed detachment of men that ever the United States mustered under her colors. . . . Our provisions were exhausted, our horses dead, our mules on their last legs, and our men, now reduced to one-third of their number, were ragged, worn-down by fatigue, and emaciated." [5]

In the emergency Alex Godey, Frémont's noted scout, and two others volunteered to carry word of the company's plight to Stockton's headquarters in San Diego. Many men could not have survived the courier's ordeal; but a few hours after delivering Kearny's message, Godey was on his way back to the American camp near San Pasqual. Fearing that the reply entrusted to him by Stockton might fall into the hands of the Californians, the scout committed its contents to memory and hid the note itself beneath the branches of an oak tree. [6] Years later a vaquero found the paper and brought it to his employer, Don Juan Bandini. The letter, now preserved in the Huntington Library, reads as follows:

Head Quarters San Diego Dec 7/46
8 A.M.

Sir

Your letter by Lt. Godoy communicating to me the sad Intelligence of the fight which took place yesterday at early dawn, reached me last night, and I would have instantly sent a detachment to aid you but unfortunately every horse that could travel had been sent with the riflemen, and left us without any means to transport our Artillery—We have not an Animal in the Garrison that can go two leagues, besides we have no conveyances [?] or means of any kind to transport the wounded—Under these circumstances and especially because Mr. Godoy says you have effective force enough to defend yourselves in camp or to march to San Diego, I have thought it most wise to postpone the

---

[5] W. H. Emory: *Notes of a Military Reconnaissance* (1848), p. 109.
[6] Ibid., p. 110.

march of my men till I can hear from you again as they will only consume provisions without being of any use.

Mr. Godoy returns to you Immediately with this.

Faithfully

Your obt. St.

[Signed] R. F. Stockton

To H. S. Turner

Captain U.S.A.

Cmdg at Camp near San Pasqual [7]

In the meantime the depleted American detachment renewed the march toward San Diego, harassed and threatened by the Californians as it moved through the mountains. Without waiting for Godey's return, Kearny dispatched Lieutenant Edward F. Beale, Kit Carson, and an Indian volunteer with a second urgent plea to Stockton for reinforcements. The messengers wormed their way through three lines of sentries, walked or ran barefoot over miles of rock and cactus, and reached San Diego more dead than alive, from hunger and fatigue. Responding to the appeal, Stockton sent a detachment of a hundred and eighty men to Kearny's relief; and on December 12 the combined force reached San Diego. After an undignified wrangle over the question of rank, from which neither Kearny nor Stockton emerged with credit, the American army of occupation—a band of six hundred ragged, poorly equipped troops, a small artillery force, and a baggage train drawn by weak, emaciated animals—marched up the coast to attack Los Angeles.

Near the present town of Montebello, on the heights overlooking the San Gabriel River from the west, José María Flores had mustered his horsemen for a last decisive stand. The Californians, about equal numerically to their opponents, held a distinct advantage in position; but they had only a small supply of ammunition, a serious division had developed among their leaders, and their morale was at a low ebb. With little difficulty the Americans forded the river, beat off a furious charge of the California horse, and drove the enemy from his natural defenses on the bluffs.

---

[7] Gaffey MSS., Huntington Library.

The next day a brief skirmish, dignified by the name of the Battle of the Mesa, marked the end of organized resistance by the Californians and cleared the way for the peaceful entry of the American forces into Los Angeles. On January 10 Stockton and Kearny occupied the city and marched their troops to the Plaza, where Gillespie raised the same flag which four months earlier he had been compelled to haul down.

While the forces under Kearny and Stockton were approaching Los Angeles from the south, Frémont started down from Monterey to invest the pueblo from the north. Under him was a motley, barbaric-looking band, some four hundred strong, of regulars, trappers, settlers, half-breeds, and even a few Delaware Indians.

Forewarned of an ambuscade near Gaviota, Frémont followed a seldom-used trail through San Marcos Pass to Santa Barbara. As the battalion marched through the Santa Clara Valley toward San Fernando, the Californians, under José Antonio Carrillo, hovered along the flanks, waiting a favorable opening for a hit-and-run attack such as Andrés Pico had carried out so successfully at San Pasqual. Some of the California leaders also proposed to surprise Frémont's men as they lay encamped on the Rancho Sespe, a few miles from the present town of Santa Paula. The plan was defeated, however, when a Mexican sentry inadvertently fired a musket, warning the Americans.

By the time Frémont reached the San Fernando Valley, the Californians had given up all hope of further resistance; and when he let it be known that generous terms of surrender would be granted, the leaders of the disorganized *paisano* forces readily consented to negotiate. Terms of an agreement, known as the Cahuenga Capitulations, were drawn up in an adobe house, still preserved as a historic monument, near the San Fernando entrance to Cahuenga Pass. Terms of the Capitulations were dictated by liberality and common sense.

The cession of California to the United States was formally recognized by the Treaty of Guadalupe Hidalgo, February 2, 1848. For several years thereafter the political status of the new territory, a matter of no great moment under normal conditions, was rendered ambiguous and confused by the immense influx of population into California due to the discovery of gold. Civil and military governors followed one another with bewildering rapidity; the air was filled with disputes over jurisdiction and authority; and the government was well described as "part military and part civil and part no government at all."

Deadlocked by the controversy over slavery, Congress failed, session after session, to establish a territorial form of government for California; while immigrants from the four quarters of the earth, attracted by the amazing richness of the Sierra Nevada mines, poured into the region by the tens of thousands, building cities that rivaled the imaginary creations of the *Arabian Nights* and giving rise to a society unlike anything the world had ever seen before. Amid such momentous changes California remained without properly constituted officials, legally established political institutions, or adequate laws for her heterogeneous and rapidly multiplying population.

In localities little affected by the new inrush of population, Mexican laws and institutions continued to function; the mining communities, following the traditional democratic practice, made rules and regulations of their own; and the cities newly created by the Gold Rush set up workable forms of government, some of which had no exact counterpart in either Mexican or American public law, to meet their simplest needs.

Such an anomalous situation, however, obviously could not last indefinitely; and since Congress showed no signs of taking immediate action in the matter, groups of citizens, notably in San José, Sacramento, and San Francisco, proposed that the people of California themselves should establish a territorial form of government. By the spring of 1849 the movement had become so widespread and the need for action so imperative that Bennett Riley, military governor of the conquered province, not only anticipated the proposed action of the local groups in reference to a territorial government, but even went so far as to issue a proclamation for a general election to a state constitutional convention. The election took place on August 1. Early in September the delegates met at

Monterey. Northern California had thirty-eight representatives; southern California sent only ten.

The convention hall was a schoolhouse built by Walter Colton (a Navy chaplain converted into an alcalde, or mayor, by Commodore Stockton) through the use of "the labor of convicts, the taxes on rum, and the banks of the gamblers." Dr. Robert Semple, six feet eight inches tall, a member of the Hastings party of 1845 and a prominent participant in the Bear Flag Revolt, was elected president, and Captain William G. Marcy served as secretary. The convention on the whole was fairly representative of the various groups into which California was then divided. Native-born rancheros including Mariano G. Vallejo, José Antonio Carrillo, and Pablo de la Guerra, and Americans long resident in the province, such as Thomas O. Larkin of Monterey and Abel Stearns of Los Angeles, mingled with delegates from San Francisco, Stockton, Marysville, Sacramento, and the mining districts, many of whom had come to California only a few months before.

Using constitutions of other states, notably those of Iowa and New York, for working models, the delegates at Monterey did a workmanlike job, and framed a sound and practical instrument of government for California. The most controversial subject before the convention was the location of the eastern boundary of the state. The "small state" faction advocated the line of the Sierra Nevada and the Colorado; the "large state" proponents argued for the Rocky Mountains—a boundary that would have included all of Nevada, nearly half of Utah, and a large slice of Arizona, and created a state so preposterously large that Congress probably would have refused to admit it to the Union. The extended boundaries also cut deep into Mormon territory and the proposed state of Deseret and would have led to friction and perhaps outright conflict with the Utah Saints. Finally, the difficulty of providing even a semblance of government for such an enormous wilderness and of maintaining effective control over settlements so scattered and remote was insurmountable. But the bigness of the idea was at least in keeping with the California tradition!

On the slavery question, then the most controversial and divisive issue in the nation, no debate was necessary. The convention voted unanimously to prohibit slavery in California. "There was no sign of the amazing importance of that decision, so easily reached in that little, far-off town on that day," wrote the Reverend Samuel H. Willey, one of the two chaplains of the convention, and a founder of the University of California. "The convention went on about its ordinary business as if nothing unusual had happened. The outside world was quiet; the forenoon sun had melted away the usual morning fog, and the deep, unceasing roar of the surf came up from the circling shore of the bay, and everything seemed peaceful—but something had taken place there, that morning, that was soon to convulse the nation." [8]

On October 13, after having been in session a little more than six weeks, the convention completed its deliberations and adjourned. A month later, in an election drenched by such a torrential rain that less than ten per cent of the qualified electorate of California went to the polls, the constitution was ratified by approximately twelve thousand votes.

The tempestuous congressional struggle then in progress over the slavery issue delayed for almost a year the admission of California, a state created under a highly novel and irregular procedure to say the least. Month after month the historic Compromise of 1850, which included the admission of California as one of its provisions, ran the gantlet of debate. Clay, Webster, and Calhoun —the great triumvirate who had dominated the Senate for a score of years—appeared in the lists for the last time. The nation reacted to passions, convictions, and political antagonisms it had never known before, out of which in time came the Civil War.

Meantime, undeterred by congressional obstinacy, constitutional scruples, or sectional animosities in Washington, the self-created state of California calmly set up necessary governmental machinery and began to function.

Although Clay's famous compromise was scuttled as a whole,

---

[8] Samuel H. Willey: *The Transition Period of California* (1901), p. 97.

each of its component provisions, including the admission of California as a free state, was finally enacted into law. The measure affecting California was signed by President Fillmore on September 9, 1850. News of the event reached San Francisco nearly six weeks later and touched off a state-wide celebration that continued for a fortnight. Communities everywhere, from isolated mining camps to the largest cities, gave themselves over to an orgy of speeches, flag-waving, parades, and ear-splitting salutes. So much enthusiasm was engendered, indeed, that Admission Day has been recognized as a state holiday ever since.

Monterey, despite its historic associations, was destined to be abandoned as the capital. San José hosted the first legislative session, then Vallejo prevailed for a year. But inconveniences moved the legislators to decide upon Sacramento, which they left briefly for Benicia, then to which they returned permanently in 1854. The movement there stimulated the growth of the interior valleys, but the desertion of Monterey robbed the capital of California of a rich historic tradition and, unquestionably, a more comfortable climate.

CHAPTER 12.   Gold

THE DISCOVERY of gold in California, like many another event that has diverted the stream of history into unexpected channels, came about by accident. In the winter of 1847–8 James W. Marshall, a member of the Clyman emigrant party of 1845, entered into an agreement with John A. Sutter to build a sawmill on the South Fork of the American River, about forty miles from Sacramento. During the afternoon of January 24, when the work was nearly completed, Marshall noticed some shining yellow particles in the tailrace of the mill.

Collecting a small quantity of the material, which had every appearance of gold, Marshall submitted it to various simple tests, and a few days later took about three ounces of the flakes to New Helvetia to show to Captain Sutter. Working behind locked doors, the two men tried the samples out with acid, weighed them in Sutter's apothecary scales, and experimented with them in other ways until they were sure the shining particles must be virgin gold.[1]

Though Sutter and Marshall sought to keep the secret to themselves, knowledge of the discovery gradually seeped out. Teamsters spread the news from one community to another; vaqueros carried the rumor from ranch to ranch; presently the word reached the coast, and newspapers in San Francisco and Monterey began to give the report casual publicity. Indifferent or frankly skeptical at first, people soon became curious over the reports, then mildly interested, and at last madly excited. As rumors of the extent and magnitude of the discoveries increased, the hysteria reached flood proportions, the dam burst, and virtually the entire population of northern California stampeded to the mines.

In a description of conditions at Monterey, now so familiar that

---

[1] For a somewhat different and more extended account, see *A Pioneer at Sutter's Fort, 1846–50* . . . translated, edited, and annotated by Marguerite Eyer Wilbur (1941), Ch. viii. Sutter's own brief version is given in *The Diary of Johann August Sutter* (1932), pp. 43–4.

it promises to become a classic, Walter Colton wrote: "My messenger sent to the mines, has returned with specimens of the gold; he dismounted in a sea of upturned faces. As he drew forth the yellow lumps from his pockets, and passed them around among the eager crowd, the doubts, which had lingered till now, fled. All admitted they were gold, except one old man, who still persisted they were some Yankee invention, got up to reconcile the people to the change of flag. The excitement produced was intense; and many were soon busy in their hasty preparations for a departure to the mines."

The effect of the stampede in other California communities was much the same as Colton found it in Monterey. "At Sonoma, or San Francisco Solano," wrote the French Consul, "where there were not more than five or six houses a year and a half ago, there are now more than sixty, and had it not been for recent events the plan of a large city subdivided into lots would have been carried out within a few years. But since the discovery of the gold region the progress of this town, like that of Yerba Buena and of Monterey and of the Pueblo of San José, has been suddenly brought to a standstill. Now, instead of its population increasing, it has lost two-thirds of its inhabitants. Most of its houses are empty, all work has stopped and here, as everywhere else, there is not a single carpenter left nor a joiner nor a blacksmith nor any laborer to do the least work. All have gone to the Placer or have come back from there too rich and too independent to resume their trades or to work for any man whomsoever." [2] Thomas Ap Catesby Jones, Commander of the Pacific Squadron, informed the Secretary of the Navy that the rush to the mines was demoralizing all normal business and taking the crews of his ships.

Those who reached the mountains in 1848 found gold in seemingly inexhaustible quantities. Stream channels, gravel beds, sand bars, pot-holes hollowed out by centuries of wear in solid rock, all alike yielded treasure. The year's operations marked the beginning of the greatest bonanza the world has ever known; and

---

[2] Jacques Antoine Moerenhout: *The Inside Story of the Gold Rush* (1935), p. 35.

as letters, newspapers, and official announcements carried word of the richness of the California deposits throughout the world, the hopeful, curious, and adventurous of all nations set out, first by hundreds, then by thousands, finally by tens of thousands, for the new El Dorado.

A combination of factors gave the California Gold Rush both an epic quality and a historic significance no other mining stampede in history has attained. From the standpoint of the westward movement of population and the settlement of the Pacific coast, Marshall's discovery was perfectly timed to exert its maximum effect. Even before 1848 the Pacific phase of westward emigration was rapidly gaining momentum, and the ardent believers in manifest destiny were impatiently waiting to go and occupy the land. The discovery of gold, like some prearranged signal, dropped the barriers and started the great stampede madly on its way.

Like the followers of Jason, from whom they took their name, the Argonauts consisted chiefly of young men, many of whom were under twenty years of age. They represented every profession, calling, and occupation. A surprisingly large number held college or university degrees. A small minority were criminals and ne'er-do-wells. Most of the immigrants were seeking fortune, adventure, or escape; and many combined the expectation of finding gold with the hope of acquiring land and building permanent homes in the new territory.

Numerous emigrant routes ran to California both by land and by sea. The voyage round the Horn, following the familiar track of the hide and tallow ships, was slow, monotonous, full of discomfort and boredom, but relatively safe. Emigrants preferring quicker arrival traveled by way of Panamá or Nicaragua and ran grave risk of contracting malaria, yellow fever, or some other tropical disease; while those who elected to cross Mexico, trusting to find a ship at one of the ports on the Pacific, found the country overrun with bandits, subject to virulent epidemics, and miserably supplied with means of transportation and accommodations for travelers.

Four principal overland routes, of which there were numerous variants, ran from the western American frontier to California. The southern trail crossed the state of Texas, intercepted the old fur-trading route from Santa Fe to the Gila-Colorado junction, and made its way across Imperial Valley to Warner's Rancho, or through San Gorgonio Pass to Los Angeles. From Santa Fe the Spanish Trail ran by way of the Green, Sevier, and Virgin rivers to San Bernardino.

The famous California-Oregon Trail followed the course of the Platte River, and crossed the South Pass to Fort Hall. There the California Trail branched off to Salt Lake and continued along the Humboldt and the Truckee rivers to Sacramento. The Oregon fork of the same trail ran from Fort Hall to the Columbia, whence the gold-seekers came south, by various routes, into the Sacramento Valley.

As a variant of the Humboldt Trail many emigrants followed Jedediah Smith's old route from Salt Lake along the course of the Sevier and Virgin rivers to strike the Wolfskill Trail to San Bernardino. This particular route gave the Mormons their greatest opportunity to participate in the Gold Rush, for guides like Jefferson Hunt led Argonauts southward from Salt Lake in some numbers. Many Mormons themselves, such as Sam Brannan, often against the strictures of the church, joined the travelers and sought the placer diggings. After reaching Humboldt Sink some companies also turned south over Walker's route, by way of the Owens Valley and Walker Pass, into the San Joaquin.

The immense volume of travel over the main emigrant routes turned the faintly defined trails of the fur traders into dusty, deeply rutted thoroughfares, visible for miles on the prairies or across the white alkaline face of the desert. Even the least experienced company could travel such a well-marked course; but a train that left the well-beaten road to take an unfamiliar cut-off all too often paid for its temerity in suffering and disaster.

Fortunately the Indian menace was not nearly so critical during the Gold Rush as in the later fifties, and the emigrant companies suffered comparatively little from the depredations of the savages.

Epidemic and disease, however, frequently took ghastly toll, especially among those who were ill-equipped physically to endure the months of hardship, privation, and exposure that the arduous trip entailed. Dysentery and mountain fever made heavy inroads on the companies; and when a cholera epidemic ravaged the wagon trains, the traveler had no need of signposts to mark the road ahead. Its course could be traced, mile after mile, by crude monuments and shallow graves.

Complete inexperience, aggravated in many cases by lack of common sense, led thousands of emigrants to start the long overland journey with a mass of bulky, ill-chosen equipment, much of which had to be abandoned along the way. One author supplies the following description of such folly: "The emigrants find they have made a great mistake in overloading the teams, for as a rule, when making up their outfits, they had but little idea what they needed. Hence, everything that a man's wife or a boy's mother could think of was piled in the wagons—sheet-iron stoves, feather beds, pillows, pillowslips, blankets, quilts and comforters, pots and kettles, dishes, cups, saucers, knives, and forks. . . . The road has been literally strewn with articles that have been thrown away. . . ." [3]

In 1849, and again in 1850, scores of miserable, badly outfitted companies reached the foot of the Sierra Nevada Mountains after winter had begun. Such companies were usually destitute of animals (since earlier trains left almost no grass behind), and the few surviving horses and oxen were little more than skeletons. Difficult enough even under the most favorable conditions, the passage of the mountains was thus rendered a desperate if not a hopeless undertaking. The most serious situation developed in September, 1850, when ten thousand emigrants were reported to be stranded east of the Sierra, with little hope of escaping starvation unless they received immediate assistance.

As word of the impending disaster to the unfortunate emigrants spread throughout the state, the people responded with unstinted,

[3] Archer Butler Hulbert: *Forty-Niners* (1931), pp. 122–3. The volume is aptly characterized as a synthetic narrative of the Gold Rush.

spontaneous generosity. Money and supplies poured in from every quarter, making it possible to send relief trains across the mountains, with sufficient food and other necessities to save the threatened companies.

Even the emigrant parties that escaped spectacular tragedy or unusual suffering experienced hardships which the average American, accustomed to the miracle of modern transportation, can scarcely comprehend. Sometimes two or three hundred destitute Argonauts, for example, reached the Rancho del Chino, gateway to the southern California settlements, in a single day. Often such emigrants, many of whom were women and children, had been forced to cross the desert on foot, killing their oxen and other animals, day by day, for food. Usually the refugees were penniless, and frequently "without a shoe to their feet."

Yet with all its discomforts, hardships, and occasional disaster the trip from the Missouri frontier to California was an experience many of the Forty-Niners cherished the remainder of their lives as a priceless memory.

"On the plains men learned to know their companions," wrote O. T. Howe. "All that was best and worst in human nature came out and the real man was revealed. Those who went by sea in after life remembered in a hazy way the uneventful voyage, but those who crossed the plains, though they lived beyond the age allotted to man, never forgot the ungratified thirst, the intense heat and bitter cold, the craving hunger and utter physical exhaustion of the trail, and the rude crosses which marked the last resting places of loved companions. But there was another side. Neither would they ever forget the level prairie, covered with lush grass and dotted with larkspur, verbena, lupin, and geranium; the glorious sunrise in the mountains; the camp fire of buffalo chips at night, the last pipe before bedtime and the pure, sweet air of the desert. True they had suffered, but the satisfaction of deeds accomplished and difficulties overcome more than compensated and made the overland passage a thing never to be forgotten and a life-long pleasure in remembrance." [4]

[4] Octavius T. Howe: *Argonauts of '49* (1923), p. 182.

The crowning tragedy of the Gold Rush migration was furnished by the sufferings of the so-called Death Valley party of 1849. The historic disaster involved a large emigrant train, at one time numbering over a hundred wagons and nearly five hundred cattle and horses, which left the Mormon settlement of Spanish Fork, some fifty miles south of Salt Lake, over the familiar Spanish Trail to Los Angeles. The party, organized in seven divisions, called itself the Sand Walking Company, and had engaged Captain Jefferson Hunt, a well-known Mormon mountaineer, to act as its guide.

At the resting-place called Las Vegas de Santa Clara, or Mountain Meadows, not far from the present town of Enterprise in southwestern Utah, the company divided. A few of the wagons, with Hunt in command, continued along the original route and reached Los Angeles without serious mishap. The remainder of the train elected to try a supposed cut-off leading through the desert more directly to Walker Pass and the southern mines. In the company were several loosely organized groups, variously referred to as the Manly-Bennett-Arcane party, the Jayhawkers, the Mississippi Boys, and the Brier family.

The cut-off proved to be a false trail and led the hapless emigrants into a veritable dwelling-place of evil and abomination— a region of arid ranges, waterless canyons, and incredibly barren wastes. Wandering for days, with no guiding landmarks, the travelers at last found themselves in a deep, Sahara-like valley— a place of fantastic formations, weird beauty, and the loneliness of chaos; or as Manly described it, a valley "of dreadful sands and shadows . . . exhausting phantoms . . . salt columns, bitter lakes, and wild, dreary, sunken desolation."

On every side rose such stark, high-walled mountains that escape from the valley seemed impossible. Here the emigrants remained week after week, gradually exhausting their provisions and killing the draft oxen, one by one, to supplement the dwindling supply of food. The situation finally became so critical that two members of the company, John Rogers and William Lewis Manly, chronicler of the expedition, set out in a forlorn effort to obtain relief. Crossing the Panamint Mountains and the vast expanse of the Mojave Desert, the exhausted men made their way through Soledad Canyon to the Rancho San Francisquito, near the present town of Saugus, and finally reached San Fernando. There they obtained three indifferent horses (all of which died on the return journey), a small mule, and a meager quantity of food.[5]

Looking more like skeletons than men and racked by uncertainty over the fate of their companions, Manly and Rogers recrossed the desert and entered the valley from which they had started twenty-six days before. Some distance from the emigrant camp they found the body of one of their companions, lying "upon his back with arms extended wide, and his little canteen, made of two powder flasks, lying by his side empty." Coming to the wagons, they saw no sign of people, of oxen, or of any other living thing. To relieve the unbearable suspense, Manly fired his revolver. "Then, as if by magic," he wrote, "a man came from under a wagon. . . . He threw up his arms high over his head and shouted, 'The boys have come! The boys have come!' . . . Bennett and Arcane caught us in their arms and embraced us with all their strength, and Mrs. Bennett when she came fell down on her knees and clung to me like a maniac in the great emotion that came to her, and not a word was spoken." [6]

Early in February the emigrants broke camp and began the ascent of the Panamints on the first stage of the long journey to the California settlements. As the refugees stood at the crest of the divide and looked down upon "the scene of so much trial, suffering, and death," they spoke the thought uppermost in their minds, saying: "Good-bye, Death Valley!"

Probably the most heroic role in the drama of the Death Valley party was played by Mrs. Juliette Brier, wife of the Reverend James W. Brier, and mother of three small boys, the oldest of

---

[5] The emigrants had little money, and consequently Manly and Rogers were unable to buy more than a small fraction of the supplies and animals actually needed.

[6] William Lewis Manly: *Death Valley in '49* (1929), pp. 201–3.

whom was only nine. Nearly half a century after the Death Valley experiences were only a memory, Mrs. Brier described the family's escape from the desert and told how she put two of the tired children, begging for water and whimpering for food, into raw-hide bags slung over the back of an ox, while she led the third little boy by the hand or carried him on her back over the rough, desolate trail.

An interesting reference to the escape of one faction of the Death Valley party appears in the diary of George W. B. Evans, a Forty-Niner then engaged in prospecting in the Mariposas mines. Under date of January 31, 1850, Evans wrote: "On Tuesday last a party of 12 men by accident came in here, in a starving condition. This party belonged to a train of 30 wagons, arrived at Salt Lake sometime in the month of August last, and at that place recruited their cattle for a few weeks. On leaving the Lake, they travelled almost due South for about 300 miles & then bore west, and soon found themselves in the great American Desert, near the west side of which the most of the party burnt their wagons & packed their cattle, with the intention of crossing the Sierra Nevada Mountains wherever they should reach it. A separation of the party had already taken place, & the fragment now in had reached Owen's Lake & here met with a party of Indians who directed them to go south along the mountain untill they reached Walker's Pass & through it pass to the west side. Following these directions, & subsisting upon Akorns, mule meat, and a few fish obtained from the indians they happily reached these mines without the loss of a man after having suffered intensely. These men think the other party about 20 days behind, and what renders this more painful is the fact that there are women & children suffering with those behind." [7]

The Gold Rush created two distinct, strikingly dissimilar Californias. A thinly populated cattle frontier, completely dominated by the great ranchos, extended south from Monterey to the Mexican border. Throughout that long coastal plain the great migra-

----

[7] MS., Huntington Library. See *Mexican Gold Trail*, Glenn S. Dumke, ed. (1945), p. 254.

tion that began in 1849 "destroyed little that was old, created little that was new. It brought about almost no increase in population, built neither city nor village, and left the established life and customs of the Spanish Californians almost undisturbed"—except for the boom conditions created by high beef prices in the mines.

North of Monterey, however, the effects of the Gold Rush were nothing short of revolutionary. "The huge immigration which poured into northern California from every quarter of the globe overwhelmed the native population, transformed drowsy adobe pueblos into sprawling, cosmopolitan cities, and supplanted the simple agrarian life of the Spanish-Californians with a frontier society of the most explosive type." [8] Any writer who attempts to present a picture of that society, especially in the brief compass of a single chapter, is driven to despair. Its elements were too varied, too incongruous, too violently in flux, to be described in summary fashion. In 1848, according to the best estimates available, there were about fifteen thousand persons of Spanish-Mexican, or Anglo-Saxon descent in California. The federal census of 1850, taken under extreme difficulties and making little pretense at accuracy, gave the state a population of nearly 93,000. Not content with those figures, two years later the state itself conducted a census which fixed the population at approximately 260,000! It may be added that Congress, for perhaps the only time on record, instructed an outraged Census Bureau to include the California state compilation as a supplement to the Bureau's own official returns.[9]

In both the state and national census the relative distribution of population throughout California was about the same. According to the federal figures the total population of the six southern counties was less than 8,000; while, by way of contrast, that of the remote mountain counties of Eldorado, Calaveras, Yuba, and Nevada ranged from 20,000 to 40,000! The contrast between northern and southern cities was even more surprising. San Francisco

---

[8] Cleland: *The Cattle on a Thousand Hills,* p. 3.

[9] The data were published in the *Seventh Census of the United States* (1850).

had nearly 40,000 inhabitants; Sacramento, about 7,000; Grass Valley, 3,000; Marysville, 4,500; Dry Diggings, later Hangtown, then Placerville, 5,600; and Los Angeles, the largest pueblo in southern California, only 1,600!

The huge migration which began to pour into northern California in 1849 came at a time when political organization and authority, as explained in a previous chapter, were confused, anomalous, and generally impotent. Social and economic conditions were even more chaotic. But despite the disorganization and lack of formal government, society did not disintegrate or capitulate to anarchy. Men lived together, worked together, and succeeded in giving to usage and custom something of the sanctity of law. They determined by popular vote what could and could not be done; substituted common sense for technicalities; set up people's courts that had the power of high, low, and middle justice; and eventually brought the disorganized, turbulent, highly individualistic society of the mining era under the control of recognized authority and legally constituted institutions.

Almost to a man the Forty-Niners were men of itching feet. A few days, a few weeks, at most a few months in one locality, and on they wandered to try their luck in another camp. The vaguest rumor of a new strike drew them to the spot like bees to a honey pot. As Francisco Gamboa, in his classic *Commentaries on the Mining Ordinances of New Spain,* had long before observed: "When a bonanza has been discovered the fame of the discovery spreads through the whole kingdom, and the odor of its richness brings crowds from the most remote parts to the newly discovered districts. What before was a waste becomes on a sudden an inhabited neighborhood." A thousand Sierra sand bars, gulches, and hidden canyons bore witness to the truth of Gamboa's statement.

Shorn of all romantic veneer, mining was a rough, monotonous job, from which the returns all too seldom justified the sacrifice and labor devoted to it. Gold was washed or panned from gravel beds and sand bars; picked out of crevices in the rocks with long-bladed knives; and gathered by means of such simple contrivances as the cradle, or rocker, the Tom, and the sluice. To the "wet diggings" of streams and rivers, the "dry diggings" of mesas, gulches, and hillsides were later added. American ingenuity was also supplemented by the methods and devices in use in other mining countries, especially in the century-old camps of Chihuahua, Sonora, Durango, and other Mexican states.

"To make work convenient," wrote one of the Forty-Niners, "the gold hunter must provide himself with a good, but light Pick, a round pointed shovel, a light Crow Bar, a Pan or a light cradle, a short strong knife & a horn spoon, and when thus equipped he is ready for the work. The cradle . . . is a machine from three to five feet in length, and from five to eight inches deep, the bottom of it crossed by kleets, called bars. On the head of this cradle or Rocker & sloping backwards, is a box generally four inches deep on the bottom of which is nailed a piece of Sheet Iron, Zinc or copper—punctured full of holes. This is the Sieve. Under this sieve is a board or slide also inclining backwards which receives the dirt gold & water from the sive & throws it into the bottom of the cradle and when the gold reaches the bars it lodges, & is saved to the laborer. To be worked with speed one man should rock & another dip on water yet one can do both. The Horn Spoon is part of the horn of an ox, opened, the peth taken out & considerably pointed at one end. This is then spread out according to fancy and looks something like a large oyster shell in shape. This instrument and the knife are found very convenient in searching the pockets & getting out the dirt & gold. Besides these things, the miner must have a good store of Pork & beans on hand, and then he can expect to lay up money; if he is industrious and saves his earnings." [1]

Accurate statistics of the production of the California mines during the Gold Rush are not available. Figures compiled by the California State Mining Bureau placed the yield at approximately $10,000,000 for 1849; $41,000,000 for 1850; $76,000,000 for 1851; and $81,000,000 for 1852. Economic changes of great magnitude followed the addition of such huge sums to the world's gold sup-

---

[1] *Mexican Gold Trail,* p. 233, Huntington Library.

ply. But only a small fraction of the gold produced by the Sierra Nevada mines remained within the state itself; and for many years California's economic progress, especially in all lines of agriculture, was seriously retarded by a chronic dearth of capital and the fantastic interest rates, running from two to ten per cent a month, compounded, that were customarily charged even on the most amply secured loans.

Life in the mines was a curious compound of robust virtues and elemental vices, of the traditions of decency, culture, and religion attempting to survive in an environment devoid of homes, churches, or feminine society. "How would you like to winter in such an abode?" asked "Dame Shirley" of her sister, "in a place where there are no newspapers, no churches, lectures, concerts, or theaters; no fresh books; no shopping, calling, nor gossiping little tea-drinkings; no parties, no balls, no picnics, no tableaus, no charades, no latest fashions, no daily mail (we have an express once a month), no promenades, no rides or drives; no vegetables but potatoes and onions, no milk, no eggs, no *nothing?*" [2]

People of every calling, background, and standard of conduct were transplanted to wild, unfamiliar surroundings, and there thrown together into rapidly formed and as rapidly dissolved communities, beyond the pale of formal laws, conventional customs, and polite taboos. Under such conditions men found their natural levels. Many of the miners drank and gambled to excess; many turned to crime, either for profit or for excitement; many spent their hard-earned gains in riotous orgies in city dives. As Clarence King trenchantly remarked, "Human character crumbled and vanished like dead leaves."

Describing the mines, from which he had just returned to Monterey, the ill, cynical, and despondent Hugo Reid wrote to his friend: "Don't go to the mines on any account. They are full of goods, and a rush of cattle streaming likewise to every digging. The mines are, moreover, loaded to the muzzle with vagabonds from every quarter of the globe, scoundrels from nowhere,

---

[2] *California in 1851. The Letters of Dame Shirley*, with Introduction and notes by Carl I. Wheat (1933), Vol. I, p. 79.

rascals from Oregon, pickpockets from New York, accomplished gentlemen from Europe, interlopers from Lima and Chile, Mexican thieves, gamblers of no particular spot, and assassins manufactured in Hell for the express purpose of converting highways and byways into theaters of blood; then last, but not least, Judge Lynch with his thousand arms, thousand sightless eyes, and five hundred lying tongues, ready under the banner of justice to hang, half, and quarter any individual who may meet his disapprobation, either because said individual wears his hair cropped instead of a wig, as the afore-mentioned judge does, or that his waistcoat a'n't doublebreasted, or some other serious grievance and eyesore to the respectable jurist." [3]

Reid's picture was drawn with a pen dipped in acid; for, despite the fact that society in the mines was rough, unrefined, and often lawless, and the lives of the miners "a rapid succession of strong sensations," the majority of the Forty-Niners retained their religion, their ethics, and a strong sense of decency.

Among the polyglot immigration that composed the Gold Rush, the members of certain races, notably Frenchmen, Chileans, Mexicans, and Chinese, were classed as "foreigners," and either excluded from the mining camps or forced to submit to various restrictions and indignities. Ironically enough, those most active in enforcing such harsh measures were often themselves only recent arrivals in the United States.

Prejudice against such groups led to the state's discriminatory foreign miner's tax; to the erection of racial barriers by many mining districts; to brutal attacks and bloody riots; and to the development of a deep-rooted anti-foreign tradition on the part of Californians generally—a legacy, it may be added, that long outlived many of the more spectacular and romantic features of the "days of '49."

---

[3] Reid to Abel Stearns, April 22, 1849. Gaffey MSS., Huntington Library.

CHAPTER 13. Society in Ferment

AS ALREADY suggested, the flood of immigration that poured into California after Marshall's discovery by-passed Los Angeles and Monterey, the chief political and social centers of Spanish California, and centered in the rough, busy, sprawling cities at the gateways to the mines. Sacramento, Stockton, Marysville, and, above all, San Francisco, were the products of such concentration.

Though unique from certain standpoints, the rise of San Francisco merely epitomized, on a large scale, the development of all other important Gold Rush cities in California. In 1848 the "miserable village of Yerba Buena," as John Marsh had characterized the small collection of adobe buildings three years before, boasted eight hundred inhabitants, two wharves, and two hotels. By 1850 the population had risen to perhaps thirty or forty thousand, and the city surged back from the beach to the hillsides and flowed down into the valleys and coves looking out across the bay.

"Of all the marvelous phases of the Present," wrote Bayard Taylor, "San Francisco will most tax the belief of the Future. Its parallel was never known, and shall never be beheld again. Like the magic seed of the Indian juggler, which grew, blossomed, and bore fruit before the eyes of his spectators, San Francisco seemed to have accomplished in a day the growth of half a century." [1]

It was indeed a lusty, polyglot, swashbuckling, devil-may-care sort of city—a city of extremes, contrasts, and superlatives. Its harbor was full of ships from every quarter of the globe; its buildings were flimsy things of frame and canvas; in winter drunken men sometimes drowned in its muddy streets; within its borders a constant stream of newly arrived immigrants bound for the gold fields, and of miners returning from the same diggings, formed a vast, fascinating, never ceasing human eddy.

[1] Bayard Taylor: *Eldorado* (1850), Vol. II, p. 55.

"We came in from the Mission by a trail over the sand hills and through thick chapparal," wrote one of the Argonauts in the late spring of 1849. "We found the first houses and tents at the corner of Kearney and Clay streets. Around Portsmouth Square were several adobe buildings. A frame hotel, the Parker House, was being built on the N. E. corner of Kearney and Clay. On Washington street to Montgomery and Montgomery from Clay to Jackson were occasional canvass houses and some scattering houses around the foot of Telegraph Hill. . . . Many ships were anchored a quarter of a mile or more from shore and of these a large number were deserted. Officers and crew gone to the mines. Apparently there were in San Francisco, people of every nation in the world, and a reckless confused state of things beyond any description." [2]

Early in the Gold Rush San Francisco became the cultural and literary center of the state, finding a certain complacent satisfaction in its schools, churches, theaters, magazines, newspapers, opera, and public library. Appeals for charity, such as those made by the emigrant relief committees of 1849 and 1850, met with instant and generous response from its citizens; and the tradition of the city's tolerant and cosmopolitan spirit took quick and sturdy root.

But there was another and less inviting side to the picture. No one knew how many saloons, brothels, and gambling dens the city supported. Notorious communities, such as that called Sydney Town, offered asylum to hoodlums and lawless elements of all kinds. An appalling record of violence and crime, growing in part out of the prostitution of the administration of justice, and indeed of all branches of government, twice forced the reputable citizens to resort to the dangerous remedy of setting up their own courts and organizing their own system of law-enforcement.

In 1849 a citizens' court summarily seized, tried, and banished the leaders of a lawless band, known as the Hounds, or Regulators; but the first of the true Vigilance Committees was not formed until 1851. Carefully organized, composed of civic and business

---

[2] From typescript by W. C. S. Smith, in the author's possession.

leaders of recognized integrity, and accepting full responsibility for its proceedings, the Committee set up a formal court, followed a prescribed judicial procedure, and made arrests with its own police. Of ninety-one persons taken into custody, the Committee hanged four and banished twenty-eight. Some hundreds of other criminals either fled the city or went into hiding to escape a similar fate.

Five years after the dissolution of the first Vigilance Committee a second reign of lawlessness and corruption reached its brutal climax in the murder of James King, editor of the recently established *Daily Evening Bulletin.* James King of William, as he preferred to be called, elected to play the part of a gadfly in San Francisco, as Socrates had done in Athens. California editors of the fifties had an extraordinary command of pungent and vituperative language, and James King was magnificently equipped in this respect. With impartial acrimony he attacked the powerful banking house of Palmer, Cook, and Company; David C. Broderick, the dictator of the Democratic Party; and James P. Casey, a notorious politician and racketeer.

Incensed by the *Bulletin's* onslaughts, Casey challenged the editor to a duel; King calmly ignored both the challenge and the open threats which Casey made against his life. But the latter was not merely bluffing; and one evening as King left the office of the *Bulletin,* Casey shot him down in cold blood. King's death, following a long series of murders and other major crimes, led, almost spontaneously, to the formation of the Second Committee of Vigilance. William T. Coleman, a well-known San Francisco merchant who had taken a prominent part in the Vigilance movement of 1851, became its natural leader. The Committee perfected its organization with remarkable rapidity. Three days after King was shot, a force of some two or three thousand men took Casey and another murderer named Cora from the city jail, tried them before a Vigilance tribunal, and sentenced them to be hanged. The execution was publicly carried out as the tolling bells announced the burial of James King of William.

Looking upon the execution of Cora and Casey as merely the

first step in its responsibility to purge the city, the Committee enlisted nine thousand members, established strongly fortified headquarters, known as Fort Gunnybags, and assembled an arsenal of thirty cannon, a large supply of ammunition, and several thousand muskets.

Perhaps because they sought to free the city from corrupt politicians as well as their henchmen, the cutthroats and gamblers, the Vigilantes were opposed by many state and city officials, and also by a large body of more conservative citizens who styled themselves the Law and Order men. The situation became dangerously tense; but the Vigilance Committee carried through its program, the criminal element ran to cover, and for many years the decent citizens continued to hold the upper hand. Describing San Francisco in 1863, William H. Brewer wrote:

It is the best-governed city in the United States—there is less rowdyism than in any other city I know of in America. This will surprise you. Previous to 1856 it was terrible—its fame for murder and robbery and violence spread over the world.[3]

As remarked earlier, the San Francisco of 1849 was a congested, hastily constructed city of wood and canvas. From time to time devastating fires, most of which were believed to be of incendiary origin, swept away whole blocks of the inflammable buildings, in both the residence and the business sections, and in the end destroyed some twenty-five million dollars' worth of property.

Other cities had similar conflagrations. In 1851 Stockton was completely gutted by a fire designed to effect a jail delivery. The next year a large part of Sacramento was burned by an incendiary blaze that left thousands of persons homeless and was said to have taken a toll of three hundred lives. There were reports that while the citizens fought the fire in one area, hoodlums were using burning shavings to start fresh conflagrations in other sections of the city. The loss and suffering caused by the fire were greatly augmented by flood waters from the swollen Sacramento River.

---

[3] William H. Brewer: *Up and Down California in 1860–1864*, edited by Francis Farquhar (1930), pp. 499–500.

Business in San Francisco, as indeed in all cities engaged in supplying the needs of immigrants and miners, was unconventional and highly speculative. Gold was plentiful, and men spent it recklessly and ostentatiously, or gambled it feverishly away in such popular resorts as the Bella Union and the El Dorado. The profligacy and extravagance of the miner, fresh from the diggings with his pile of dust and nuggets, were matched by the prodigal expenditures of the great landowner to whom the cattle boom of 1849 and the early fifties brought dazzling and unimagined fortune.

During the four years of the Gold Rush, rents and real-estate values in San Francisco and other cities skyrocketed to dizzy levels. Leases on hotels and gambling houses ran as high as a hundred thousand dollars a year. "Any room twenty by sixty feet," W. T. Sherman wrote of San Francisco, "would rent for a thousand dollars a month." Lots in Sacramento which originally sold for two hundred dollars brought thirty thousand a year later. Everywhere the tale was the same, and the inflated values of real estate were matched in every other field. Commodity prices fluctuated wildly, sometimes swinging in a few hours from one violent extreme to the other.

Insufficient storage facilities, a glut of the market when several ships came into port, or the interruption of shipments and travel to the mines by rain or snow were the chief causes of depression. But much merchandise sent to California was of no value there under any circumstances. "Many shipments were doomed to failure from the start," wrote O. T. Howe, "patent cradles, invented by men who were not practical miners, cooking stoves in a country where they were never used, spades and saddles of a pattern not liked, razors in a country where men rarely shaved, five thousand lady's hats and three thousand pieces of calico—one shipment to a city where there were few women; these, and a multitude of things of which there was already a surplus, were promptly dumped and left at the disposal of the passer-by." [4]

---

[4] Howe: *Argonauts of '49*, p. 120.

Saleratus, a prime necessity for making bread, was usually sold in small packages at from twelve to sixteen dollars a pound; but on one occasion some twenty barrels, containing at least eight hundred pounds, were auctioned off at a dollar for the entire lot! "In the winter," wrote one of the Forty-Niners, "I had seen tons of plug tobacco in cases, bundles of mowing scythes, crowbars, etc. thrown down in the streets of San Francisco for walks and crossings. . . . I bought a quantity of scythes, pitchforks, and whetstones for almost nothing. I took them to Marysville and sold the scythes for $25 each." [5]

Instances of even more extreme fluctuations than those just cited might be multiplied a hundred times. For the merchant, as well as the miner, lived in an atmosphere surcharged with speculation and excitement; and gambling was by no means confined to faro, monte, and roulette.

It was inevitable that the years of wild speculation and inflation, coincident with the mining boom, should be followed by a painful period of readjustment. The turning-point came in 1853. By that time the flush days in the mines were over, and thousands of disillusioned and impoverished gold-seekers were returning to the cities, eagerly looking for employment. The situation was aggravated by a severe drought that halted mining operations in many parts of the state and seriously reduced the purchasing power of cattle ranchers and farmers. European capital, attracted to California in the first instance by the fantastic interest rates of the time and loaned by reckless money brokers with no regard to security, had been frightened away by the heavy losses which it thus sustained. But the marked falling off in immigration, sure evidence that the golden era had run its course, was the worst blow of all.

The depression compelled Page, Bacon & Company and Adams and Company, whose banking and express offices were fast becoming a tradition in the West, to close their doors. Wells, Fargo and Company, together with several other large financial houses,

---

[5] W. C. S. Smith MS.

were almost equally distressed, and a great host of speculators and merchants became engulfed in the general ruin. Yet despite all the immediate suffering and disaster, the feverish era of speculation established California business on a more permanent and rational foundation.

As indicated in the preceding chapter, the Argonauts constituted a heterogeneous mixture of many races, types, and cultural backgrounds. Many of them were at heart soldiers of fortune. When the gold fever began to decline, such restless spirits instinctively turned to Mexico—politically unstable, poorly defended, traditionally rich in precious metals—as a natural outlet for conquest and excitement.

The imminent annexation of the northern half of Mexico by the United States, moreover, was then generally taken for granted; and that fact in itself was enough to encourage the more reckless and imaginative adventurers to dream of making themselves the Sam Houstons and John C. Frémonts of Sonora or Lower California.

Between 1851 and the early part of 1856 at least four companies of a military or semi-military character left California for Mexico. Two of the four were led by French noblemen—the first by the Marquis Charles de Pindray, who either committed suicide or was murdered in northern Sonora; and the second by the Count Raousset-Boulbon, "a quixotic and fantastic figure," who, after preparing a flag for an independent state and capturing Hermosillo, the capital of Sonora, suffered reverses and betrayal and died before a firing squad, "with his eyes unblindfolded and his knees unbent!"

Raousset's successor was the inveterate filibuster William Walker—small, red-haired, freckle-faced, gray-eyed, rash, taciturn, visionary, eccentric in manner and dress, yet possessed of an indomitable will and a singular appeal to the imagination and loyalty of reckless men. Like his predecessors, Walker began his first invasion of Mexico at Guaymas; but he soon transferred his interest to Lower California. With a force of only forty-five men, pretentiously called the First Independence Battalion, he occupied the harbor of La Paz, hauled down the Mexican flag, and proclaimed the Republic of Lower California.

After this grandiose beginning Walker sailed for Ensenada. There he issued a proclamation to the American people, appealed "to Him who controls the destiny of nations, and guides them in the way of progress and improvements," and formally organized a government. Receiving additional reinforcements from San Francisco, the audacious filibuster next proclaimed the Republic of Sonora, unfurled a flag containing two stars, and set out round the head of the gulf to effect the conquest of the mainland.

Scarcity of food and water, the impassable nature of the country, and the complete exhaustion of Walker's men stopped the expedition long before it reached its objective and almost led to its complete destruction. Walker and the other survivors of the foolhardy venture reached the international boundary, near Tijuana, and crossed over to the safety of the United States. A month later the "gray eyed man of destiny" was tried in San Francisco for a violation of the neutrality laws—and triumphantly acquitted!

Last, and most tragic, of the California-Mexican ventures was the Crabb expedition of 1857. As in the case of some of the other so-called filibustering companies, it is difficult to determine how far the Crabb undertaking was a legitimate colonizing and mining speculation and how far its leader intended to play the role of revolutionist.

Henry A. Crabb, a native of Tennessee and a boyhood friend of William Walker, had come to California in 1849. After a brief career as a miner and the attainment of some distinction in state politics, he married an "attractive Sonoran girl, Señorita Ainsa of a prolific but exiled clan." [6] Through this marriage Crabb became involved in the decayed and questionable fortunes of the Ainsa

---

[6] "On the fringes of Sonora's little conflict," writes Rufus K. Wyllys, "there skirmished hungrily and hopefully the half-exiled and ruined house of Ainsa. Once ranking high in wealth and social position, they had guessed wrongly in too many of Sonora's political turmoils." See "Henry A. Crabb—A Tragedy of the Sonora Frontier," *Pacific Historical Review*, Vol. IX, pp. 183–94.

family, and in the equally dubious political intrigues then in progress in Sonora—"the land of romance, the land of tragedy, the dream land of the filibuster."

In 1856 Crabb visited Sonora, met Ignacio Pesquiera, reputedly an ally of the Ainsa faction in its long-drawn-out feud with Governor Manuel María Gandara, and entered into a confidential agreement to enlist several hundred American colonists or adventurers for settlement in the state. On January 22, 1857 Crabb embarked at San Francisco, with less than sixty men, on the first stage of his tragic venture. Landing at San Pedro, the band marched inland to El Monte, there completed its organization, enlisted a few additional recruits, and took the name of the Gadsden Colonization Company. By the time the expedition reached the Colorado, the rapidly shifting currents of Sonora politics had effected a change in Pesquiera's fortunes and brought about an even more radical change in his attitude toward Crabb and the members of the Gadsden Colonization Company. Instead of looking upon them as friends and allies who had voluntarily come to his assistance, he now professed to regard them as enemies and invaders; and instead of making the Americans welcome, he prepared to attack them with the largest force he could gather together.

Apparently ignorant of Pesquiera's defection, Crabb and his men marched nearly fifty miles up the Gila River, where they established what later came to be known as Filibuster Camp, and then turned southeast across the desert into Sonora. In the early morning of April 1 the unsuspecting Americans rode into the outskirts of the little town of Caborca, only to discover that they had allowed themselves to fall into an ambush and that they were hopelessly entrapped by an overwhelming force of hostile Mexicans. Taking refuge in some adobe buildings facing the Plaza, the beleaguered company carried on a stubborn fight for six days. At the end of that time, after many of their number had been killed, their ammunition almost exhausted, and the thatched roofs of the houses set on fire by burning arrows, the battle-weary Americans agreed to surrender.

The sequel to Crabb's rash, ill-timed adventure added a chapter to the ruthless annals of Mexican warfare almost as terrible as that of the massacre of the Texans at Goliad. Violating their promise to spare the lives of the Americans and recognize them as prisoners of war, the Mexican leaders, probably at Pesquiera's command, executed all of their helpless captives, with the exception of one fourteen-year-old boy. Crabb himself was tied to a post with his back turned toward his executioners and his hands raised above his head, and in that position was riddled by a hundred balls. His head was then cut off and preserved in a jar of mescal as a trophy for Pesquiera. According to common report, the bodies of the victims were subjected to nameless indignities and sadistic mutilation.

A tablet on the old mission church at Caborca bears the following inscription:

A HUMBLE TRIBUTE OF GRATITUDE
TO PERPETUATE THE MEMORY
OF THE DEFEAT INFLICTED BY NATIONAL
FORCES AND INHABITANTS OF THIS TOWN
UPON THE NORTH AMERICAN FILIBUSTERS
ON THE 6TH OF APRIL, 1857, THIS CHURCH
HAVING SERVED THE DEFENDERS OF THE
FATHERLAND AS A BULWARK.
CABORCA, SON., APRIL, 1926 [7]

---

[7] Frank C. Lockwood: *Story of the Spanish Missions of the Middle Southwest* (1934), p. 68.

Chapter 14. California of the Ranges

THE VIGOROUS, exuberant society that characterized the
Gold Rush cities and mining regions of northern California
found no counterpart in the counties south of Monterey. In 1850
the "social and economic life of the people was still that of a typical Mexican cattle frontier. East of the Coast Range extended an
isolated hinterland of savage mountains, rich but uncultivated
plains, and almost illimitable deserts. Adjacent to the coast lay a
land of captivating beauty, diversified by ranges of low foothills,
infrequent watercourses, and pleasant valleys opening out upon
the sea. Here the traveler encountered a few despoiled, half-
abandoned missions, and an occasional unpretentious pueblo, or
presidial town, founded by Spanish colonists before the century
began. For the most part, however, the coastal area was occupied
by a succession of enormous private estates, called ranchos, which
were primarily devoted to cattle raising and served as California's
counterpart of the more familiar Mexican hacienda." [1]

Despite a gradual displacement of the original California owners by Americans, the ranchos remained the dominant feature of
southern California society for at least a decade after Marshall's
epochal discovery. On these great estates, created when land was
measured in square leagues instead of acres, and bestowed by the
government with prodigal liberality, life followed long-established
patterns. Thousands of "black cattle and beasts of burden" continued to graze on the unfenced ranges; and the rancher's simple
but often many-roomed adobe *casa* constituted the center of an
almost feudal life. There, as in the days before the conquest,
hospitality knew no bounds; and scores of servants and attendants,
like those of an ancient English manor, carried on the simple
handicrafts that made the estate virtually self-sustaining.

---

[1] Cleland: *The Cattle on a Thousand Hills*, pp. 4–5. Much of the ensuing
chapter is taken from the same volume.

In a statute entitled *Laws Concerning Rodeos and Defining the Duties of Judges of the Plains*, the first California legislature provided for the continuation of the usages and customs that had governed the cattle industry during the Mexican regime; and for nearly a generation after American annexation there were no material changes in the open-range practices or institutions under which the Californians had lived since the coming of the first Spanish settlers.

Early California law placed the cattlemen in a highly favored class. The statute most bitterly criticized by the settlers and small farmers was known colloquially as the no-fence or trespass law. Under the measure (which remained in effect until the early seventies), the farmer, or small landholder, had no recourse for damages if roving cattle entered his unfenced fields, destroyed his crops, or ruined his vineyards and orchards. Indispensable from the range-owners' standpoint, the law worked great hardship upon the settlers, became the source of bitter controversy, and proved a major deterrent to land settlement and agricultural development.

The year 1849 marked the beginning of the "Great Boom" in the California cattle industry. The rapid influx of population created an enormous and ever expanding demand for beef and led to a rise in cattle prices that far exceeded even the most extravagant imagination of the old Californians. Steers which had sold for four or five dollars a head in the days of the hide and tallow trade brought from seventy-five to a hundred dollars in the northern cities and the mines.

To the easy-going, pleasure-loving *paisanos*, the boom of the mining era brought sudden, extravagant, and, in the end, ruinous prosperity. For a few years the native rancheros lived to the limit of their hearts' desire—"princes in the keeping of their houses, and bountiful in all manner of things." According to Charles Nordhoff, the women covered the earthen floors of their adobes with expensive rugs, adorned their four-poster beds with costly lace coverings, and dragged "trains of massive silk and satin over the earthen floors."

Not to be outdone in extravagance, the men bought "saddles trimmed with solid silver, spurs of gold, bridles with silver chains," and clothing for themselves even more costly and elaborate than the equipment and trappings of their horses. During the boom era many a California Don spent two or three thousand dollars on a single costume, only to find, when the sheriff took possession a few years later, that he had unwittingly "worn a whole rancho on his back." Prodigal sums were also lavished on amusements, hospitality, and entertainment. The Californians were inveterate gamblers; and wagers (commonly made in land, cattle, and other livestock) often ran into the tens of thousands of dollars.

Living far beyond their means, even in the flush days of the Gold Rush, the Californians thus had neither the prudence nor the desire to make provision for the lean, hard years ahead. Consequently they were in no position to withstand the series of losses and misfortunes they were called upon to meet when the hectic prosperity of the Gold Rush began to ebb, and the seven fat years were succeeded by the lean.

First came the federal Land Act of 1851. The measure authorized the President to appoint a board of three "Commissioners to ascertain and settle the Private Land Claims in California." It also provided for submission to the board of all California land titles held under Spanish or Mexican grants; for outright forfeiture of claims not presented within two years; and for an appeal from the decisions of the commissioners to the federal courts, either by the claimant or by the government. The commission was originally established for three years, but its life was prolonged two additional years by subsequent legislation.

The board opened its session in San Francisco in February 1852. During the next five years it heard over eight hundred cases, involving title to approximately twelve million acres. More than five hundred claims were approved, about two hundred and seventy-five rejected, and the remainder withdrawn. In submitting the documents and testimony required to validate their claims, the Californians were put to great inconvenience and almost endless expense. According to Hittell, at least one landowner out of every ten was forced into bankruptcy by the cost of validating his title; and one legitimate grant after another was forfeited because its owner found himself unable to bear the cost of presenting his claim, as the law required, or of financing the subsequent hearings before the federal courts.

In a great majority of cases the commissioners' decisions were reasonable and fair; but at times the letter of the law took precedence over equity and common sense. In a letter to Frémont, Abel Stearns spoke of injustice and impoverishment: "The long lists of Sheriffs and mortgage sales in our newspapers, the depopulation of flourishing stock Ranches, and the pauperism of Rancheros, but a short time since wealthy, all attest the disastrous consequences of too much litigation and of this unsettled state of titles." [2]

From the standpoint of the Spanish-Mexican grantees, the federal Land Act thus worked gross and inexcusable injustice. Whatever the theory behind it, the measure violated repeated assurances given the Californians by the Polk administration, and contradicted a clear-cut provision in the Treaty of Guadalupe Hidalgo that the United States would recognize "legitimate titles to every description of property, personal and real, existing in the ceded territories."

Extravagance, gambling, and litigation also led most of the native California landowners deeper and deeper into debt. From that treacherous morass few ever found their way back to solid ground. Compound interest ranged as high as ten or twelve per cent a month, even in the case of notes secured by land or cattle worth many times the value of the loan; and it was simple economic suicide for a people conditioned for generations to a pastoral economy and a simple system of barter to borrow on such fantastic terms.

To make matters worse for the range-owners, large numbers of cattle and sheep from Texas, New Mexico, the Missouri Valley, and the border states of Mexico began to appear in the northern

---

[2] Ibid., pp. 58–59.

California markets; and as a result prices fell to less than half the levels to which they had risen during the Gold Rush. "Business is dull," wrote the editor of the Los Angeles *Star* in April 1856, "duller this week than it was last; duller today than it was yesterday. The flush times are passed—the days of large prices and full pockets are gone. . . . It is no use talking—business has stepped out and the people is asleep."

Indian forays, especially during the early fifties, also took heavy toll of livestock, both from the ranchos and from the trail-herds driven to the northern markets. The long eastern border of California was, in fact, an Indian frontier, for a time as grim and dangerous as any in the United States. Far to the south the Apache and Yuma Indians lay in wait for the wagon trains that sought to follow the Gila and cross the Colorado, and "inaugurated scenes of horror . . . for which the early history of the eastern states shows no parallel for cruelty and atrocity."

At the other extremity of the state the Klamath, Pit River, and Modoc Indians wantonly attacked and massacred small parties of whites—and in turn were wantonly attacked and massacred by other whites. The San Joaquin and Tulare valleys witnessed raids, sieges, ambushes, massacres, and reprisals as merciless as any of those recorded in Kentucky annals. Coming out of the illimitable deserts that stretched eastward from the Sierra Madre Mountains to southern Utah and Nevada, bands of Mojave and Paiute raiders harried the ranchos of the San Gabriel and Santa Ana basins, and at times approached the boundaries of Los Angeles itself.

During the fifties and early sixties Indians from the Owens River Valley carried off hundreds of horses and cattle from the ranchos of Los Angeles and Santa Barbara counties. The most serious Indian threat to the southern California settlements came from an abortive insurrection, in 1851, that attempted to unite all the southern tribes under a chief named Antonio Garrá, an able leader and an implacable foe of the whites. After plundering numerous ranchos, waylaying emigrant trains, gaining many recruits throughout the south, and boasting that "he would exterminate the white race in California," Garrá was captured by a chief of the Cahuilla tribe, friendly to the Americans, and surrendered to a company of rangers. A military court condemned the proud, stoical, unrepentant chief to death, and a firing squad quickly carried out the sentence.

Whatever savage glamour surrounds the long-drawn-out conflict between the whites and the hostile border Indians, the wild "Arabs of the West," the annals of the California domesticated Indians never rise above a drab level of wretchedness, degradation, and injustice. The depressing story began with the secularization of the missions, and grew progressively worse for upwards of forty years. After the mission communities were dispersed, nothing was done either by individuals or institutions to improve the lot of the California Indian. No attempt was made to raise his standard of living, provide him with even the rudiments of an education, or save his soul.

In many parts of the country the Indians supplied the only available unskilled labor for ranchos, farms, and vineyards. The landowners considered the natives lazy and inefficient, except in the capacity of sheepherders and vaqueros. In Los Angeles County, and perhaps elsewhere, local ordinances and custom established a virtual system of legalized peonage for the hapless native.

The Indian, whether wild or domesticated, had no monopoly on viciousness and crime. The cattle frontier was, in fact, even more lawless than the mines; and Los Angeles was responsible for more murders per capita than San Francisco boasted even in its wildest days. In September 1851, for example, the Los Angeles *Star* asserted that thirty-one homicides had been committed in or near the pueblo during the preceding year, and that in no instance was the murderer brought to justice.

Stock-rustling was almost a recognized profession. In 1851 Governor Burnett declared that the losses in cattle and horses sustained by the ranchers from such depredations constituted one of the state's major economic problems. Bands of rustlers, sometimes containing fifty or more members, preyed on the southern Cali-

fornia herds down to the very close of the cattle era. Many a
bloody and now long-forgotten battle was fought between such
raiders and the rancheros and their vaqueros. Justice was meted
out to captured rustlers without delay or ambiguity. A lariat over
the limb of a convenient tree, or fastened to the pommel of a
saddle, brought the outlaw's career to a swift and irrevocable end.

A number of bandit leaders, some of whom extended their activities from the northern mines to the Mexican border, attained
dubious fame during the fifties and early sixties. Most notorious
of such outlaws was Joaquín Murrieta, a cutthroat Mexican bandit
of the type produced by the score in the chaotic political and
social conditions south of the border, out of whom tradition, romance, and the history-be-damned brand of motion picture have
made a sort of bastard California Robin Hood.

At the head of a band of renegades of the worst type, Murrieta
and his lieutenant, the sadistic "Three-fingered Jack," terrorized
the state from 1851 to 1853. After committing innumerable rob-
beries and murders, some of which may have been done by
others and attributed to Murrieta because of his notoriety, the
outlaws were finally surprised by a company of rangers, under
command of Captain Harry Love of Los Angeles. Both Murrieta
and "Three-fingered Jack" were killed in the attack. Murrieta's
head, together with the mutilated hand of his lieutenant, was
preserved in aguardiente and exhibited to curious crowds throughout the state. According to one story, the head was treated by an
Army surgeon at Fort Miller and "reposed in Doctor Jordan's
Museum in San Francisco until 1906, when it was destroyed in
the fire which followed the earthquake."

In addition to Murrieta other notorious bandits, such as Tiburcio
Vásquez, Jack Powers, Salomon Pico, and a host of lesser fry,
equally villainous but less spectacular in their operations, infested
the state for at least a decade and a half after the Gold Rush.
In July 1856 a mob, composed "of the lowest and most abandoned
Sonoranians and Mexicans," killed the City Marshal of Los Angeles and threatened to seize and loot the pueblo. The next year
some fifty desperados, led by Juan Flores and Pancho Daniel,

ambushed and killed Sheriff Barton of Los Angeles and three of his posse on the San Joaquín Rancho, about fifteen miles north of San Juan Capistrano.

The act brought swift retribution. A detachment of United States troops, several companies of citizens, and a large number of Indians united to rid the country of the outlaws. Surrounding the bandits in the Santa Ana Mountains, the posses killed some of the company, made prisoners of others, and scattered the remainder to the four winds.

Flores was among the first of the outlaws to fall a prisoner; but taking advantage of the carelessness of his guards, he made his escape and, with two companions, took refuge in an almost inaccessible spot in the mountains. He was finally recaptured near Simi Pass, in the Santa Susana Mountains, taken to Los Angeles, and there hanged—a fate Pancho Daniel and eight or more of the other members of the band also suffered.

The pastoral era in southern California was brought to a close by two disastrous seasons, appropriately called the Great Drought, which afflicted the state from 1862 to 1864. During the preceding year there had been such unprecedented floods that the Sacramento and San Joaquin valleys were turned into an inland sea, "250 to 300 miles long and 20 to 60 wide," and so deep in places that the water covered the tops of the telegraph poles. Rivers everywhere overflowed their banks, spreading ruin and devastation for miles around; dry creeks and arroyos became raging torrents; and all the lowlands were converted into shoreless lakes. Until the floods subsided, business and transportation were at a standstill, thousands of cattle and other livestock perished, and possibly a fourth of the state's taxable wealth was destroyed.

On the southern ranges the damage done by the rains was inconsequential compared to the appalling losses caused by the two succeeding years of drought, when the grasslands reverted to desert, the earth became iron, and the sky turned to brass. Livestock died by the thousands on the sun-baked ranges; carcasses lay in heaps about the dry water holes and sand-choked springs;

and "the whole country from North to South was almost depopulated of cattle."

To add to the general distress, swarms of locusts swept across the land like a devastating fire; and, worst of all, a virulent plague of smallpox spread throughout the countryside, and brought its loathsome terror into every rancho, village, and city of the south. Deaths were so numerous in Los Angeles and panic became so widespread that the tolling of church bells was forbidden; the routine life of the city was paralyzed; and the district north of the Plaza, "from the Church to the mill, was almost depopulated."

The disastrous effects of the drought were naturally reflected in the collapse of property values in all the cattle counties. On assessment rolls pasture lands were reduced to ten cents an acre, and range cattle to only a dollar a head. By 1865 the total valuation of real and personal property in Los Angeles, the self-styled "Queen of the Cow Counties," had fallen to about eight hundred thousand dollars.

The Great Drought, as the long-forgotten, dust-covered, unromantic records of county archives testify, eliminated almost the last of the native California landowners and initiated the subdivision of many of the great Spanish-Mexican grants. But out of the widespread ruin and desolation a new economic order rapidly emerged. "Forbidding heaps of bones and skeletons, everywhere bleaching in the sun, symbolized the ruin of the universal industry of southern California. Thereafter, the 'cow counties' lost their distinctive appellation. The day of unfenced ranchos, of enormous herds of half-wild cattle, of manorial estates, and pleasure-loving *paisanos* came to its inevitable close. But in its passing, something of color and romance faded forever from the California scene."

CHAPTER 15. The End of Isolation

DESPITE the beginning of the new economic era in southern California, the northern part of the state continued, for many years, to enjoy an immense superiority in wealth, population, and political power. There was, in truth, at that time almost no community of interest between northern and southern California. As explained in the preceding chapter, the southern half of the state remained a thinly populated, semi-lawless cattle frontier until some years after the close of the Civil War. Its towns and so-called cities were limited to adobe settlements of eighteenth-century Spanish foundation, such as San Diego, Los Angeles, and Santa Barbara; to small, self-sustaining rancho-villages; and to a few towns established by American immigrants. El Monte, San Bernardino, and Anaheim were the largest of such communities.

El Monte, the first American settlement to be established in southern California, was founded in 1851 by immigrants from Texas. The following year the colony was enlarged by fifty additional families. The settlers, generally referred to as the "Monte Boys," were southern Democrats of the fire-eating type, excellent farmers and stockmen, quick on the trigger, hard drinkers, devout Protestants, and so true to the Texas tradition that the citizens of Los Angeles invariably turned to them for help when the lawless elements in the city's decidedly mixed population threatened to get beyond control.

San Bernardino was a Mormon colony, an outpost of Brigham Young's remarkable empire in the valley of the Salt Lake. It was designed to serve both as a shipping-point and as "the gateway settlement from the Pacific into the Mormon commonwealth." A chain of lesser settlements was designed to link the California city to the Mormon capital in Utah; but San Bernardino itself was expected to become "a second Salt Lake City," a metropolitan center of Mormon faith, trade, industry, agriculture, and influence on the Pacific coast.

Elders Amasa M. Lyman and Charles C. Rich commanded the train of a hundred and fifty wagons which brought the original colonists to San Bernardino. With characteristic foresight and energy the new Mormon settlers set about developing farms, building irrigation works, and laying out a city.

San Bernardino remained distinctly a Mormon community until 1858, when the Mountain Meadows Massacre and a threatened conflict with the federal government led Brigham Young to recall the colonists. At the time of the withdrawal there were approximately a hundred improved farms in the settlement, besides flour mills, sawmills, stores, shops, and extensive irrigation works. Most of this property the gentiles were able to purchase at a small fraction of its actual value.

The settlement of Anaheim, begun in 1857 on twelve hundred acres of the Rancho San Juan Cajón de Santa Ana, represented a successful venture in co-operative community development by a company of Germans from San Francisco. The land selected for the colony was cheap, extraordinarily fertile, and well supplied with water. With the exception of two hundred acres reserved for a town, the tract was divided into twenty-acre farms and planted to vineyards, gardens, and fruit trees. A deep ditch, or moat, and a quickset fence of forty thousand willow poles protected the land from roving cattle and other livestock. The venture prospered from the first, and within a year individual holdings had appreciated at least a hundred per cent in value.

In contrast to the pastoral character of southern California and its small scattered settlements, northern California had its well-populated cities, flourishing mining communities, and highly developed farms. San Francisco was potentially one of the world's greatest ports. Inevitably the city became the center and undisputed arbiter of the state's financial, commercial, industrial, and cultural life.

The contrast between the two sections, and the lack of any real community of interest with the north, led to various attempts on the part of the south to withdraw from the state and establish a territorial government of its own. One reason for such separatist movements was a well-grounded fear that the state legislature, so largely dominated by the mining and commercial population of the north, and interested in encouraging land settlement and diversified farming, would enact discriminatory taxes or resort to some other means of breaking up the great landholdings, a large part of which lay in the southern counties.

As early as 1850 a petition was sent to Congress from Los Angeles asking to have the southern counties organized into a separate territory to be called Central California. The next year, on the plea that the experiment of state government had proved only "a splendid failure" so far as southern California was concerned, a more vigorous attempt was made to separate the southern from the northern counties. In 1859, upon the initiative of southern representatives, the state legislature even went so far as to approve a bill to that end. The act provided for the withdrawal of the counties of San Luis Obispo, Santa Barbara, Los Angeles, San Diego, and San Bernardino from the remainder of the state and authorized their erection into a separate political entity to be known as the Territory of the Colorado. The measure was subsequently ratified by popular vote in the seceding counties; but because of the controversy over slavery, and the near approach of the Civil War, the bill was killed in the federal Congress.

For a decade or more after California's admission, the state's political control was divided between the mining counties, the large cities, and the farming sections of the north, with the sparsely populated "cow counties" playing but a minor part. During that time the state remained predominantly Democratic; and its political history, neither very interesting nor inspiring, centered chiefly in the acrimonious personal rivalry between Senator William M. Gwin, a native of Tennessee, who controlled the federal patronage, and David C. Broderick, an Irish Tammany Democrat, whose shrewdly organized political machine dominated the large northern cities and the state party conventions.

The struggle between the two reached its bitter climax in 1859. Charging that he had been betrayed by his rival in an unsavory bargain relating to the senatorial election of 1857, Broderick set out to destroy Gwin by every means, legitimate or illegitimate, at his command. Gwin retaliated in the same spirit. There ensued, in consequence, one of the most vicious political battles in the history of the state. Early one morning in September, in the seclusion of a little valley near the Golden Gate, the feud was brought to a sudden and dramatic close when Senator Broderick and Judge David S. Terry, a member of the state Supreme Court and a partisan of Gwin, met to settle their personal and political animosities in a duel. The incident was strikingly reminiscent of the meeting between Aaron Burr and Alexander Hamilton fifty-five years before. Broderick was reputedly a good marksman; but he was so nervous that when the word was given to fire, his shot went wide of the mark, while Terry's carefully aimed bullet inflicted a mortal wound.

Broderick's death had far-reaching repercussions. Terry was temporarily forced out of politics; the split in the Democratic Party was hopelessly widened; and in the election of 1860 Broderick's followers threw their support to the Republican candidates.

The opening of the Civil War placed California in an anomalous position. Thousands of Southerners had participated in the Gold Rush, and other thousands had joined the subsequent overland migration to the coast. Many of these settlers kept their Southern sympathies and openly supported a program of secession. Secret societies, such as the Committee of Thirty, the Knights of the Golden Circle, and the Knights of the Columbian Star, set on foot numerous schemes either to cripple the state's support of the Union or to bring California openly into the conflict on the side of the Confederacy. The San Joaquin Valley, southern California (notably Los Angeles, San Bernardino, and El Monte), and an influential faction in San Francisco furnished the chief support for the secession movement.

Union sympathizers, representing probably a safe majority of the population of the state, varied greatly in the degree of their devotion to the Lincoln government. A group of ardent crusaders, led by the notable Unitarian minister Thomas Starr King, constituted the militant wing of the Northern party. Most of the rank and file, however, were lukewarm in their attitude toward the war, and assumed a typical isolationist position.

A third group in the state, including Governor John B. Weller and other high public officials, contended that California should withdraw from the Union and constitute itself the nucleus of an independent Pacific republic. The idea, which appealed rather powerfully to the popular imagination, was in essence a revival of the movement sponsored by Lansford W. Hastings and other potential filibusters before the Mexican War.

Upon the outbreak of hostilities large numbers of Southern sympathizers, many of whom had seen service in the Mexican War, left California to join the Confederate forces. Among the number was Albert Sidney Johnston, one of the nation's foremost military geniuses, who had assumed command of the federal forces in California early in 1861. Speculation and conjecture in the field of history are never very profitable; but one wonders what the future of the West would have been if Johnston and his fellow Confederate sympathizers had elected to remain in California, organize an army, and make an active bid for the secession of the state. Such a movement might have led to the formation of the Pacific states into a new republic.

Some fifteen thousand volunteers, relatively few of whom ever saw active service, applied for enlistment in the Union Army from California. The National Conscription Act was never enforced in the state; and when the first call for volunteers was issued, the leading businessmen of San Francisco formally protested to the Secretary of War against the use of such troops outside the boundaries of California. In much the same spirit the federal government's Legal Tender Act of 1862 was nullified by the state legislature and disregarded by Union and Confederate sympathizers alike. With characteristic generosity, however, Californians contributed nearly a million dollars, over a third of which came from San Francisco, to the Sanitary Commission for the relief of the sick and wounded in the war.

In addition to creating a large demand for certain state products, such as gold, wheat, and wool, the Civil War bequeathed two important legacies to California: a great increase in population, which began even before Lee's surrender at Appomattox; and the construction of the long-awaited transcontinental railroad. The tide of immigration which characterized the late sixties and early seventies was a factor of major importance in the history and development of the United States. The return of millions of soldiers to civil life; the demoralization wrought throughout the Southern states by war and reconstruction; the appeal of cheap land and adventure to those uprooted by four years of military life, all alike contributed to the historic postwar westward movement. Thanks to widespread and systematic propaganda, European countries also added their quota to the stream of colonists and settlers coming to California.

The entire state felt the effects of the influx; and as a result California's population rose from slightly less than 380,000 in 1860 to approximately 560,000 in 1870. Until the completion of the transcontinental railroad in 1869, the relative increase was greater in southern California and the San Joaquin Valley, since most of the immigrants from the former Confederate States came by way of Texas or New Mexico and naturally settled in the southern counties.

By 1868 the population had increased sufficiently to bring about an embryonic real-estate boom in Los Angeles and other southern communities. Newspapers spoke of "the immense tide of immigration flowing into the southern counties"; and long caravans of covered wagons, a single train sometimes containing as many as a hundred wagons and five hundred settlers, were crawling across Texas, Utah, and Nevada toward the hoped-for paradise on the Pacific.

The postwar immigration assumed new proportions, and an altogether different character, with the completion of the railroad in 1869. The story of that great enterprise is both magnificent and sordid, heroic and corrupt. From the very beginning of Spanish occupation, California's economic, political, and cultural life had been limited by the primary factor of isolation. Distance and natural barriers alike, as explained in earlier chapters, cut off ready communication with the outside world, and imposed almost insuperable obstacles in the way of the development of any form of adequate transportation.

The Civil War awakened the federal government to the potential danger of the situation and drew attention to the obvious fact that the natural line of cleavage in the Union ran north and south at the Rocky or Sierra Nevada Mountains instead of east and west along the Mason and Dixon parallel.

The construction of a transcontinental railway was therefore looked upon primarily as a war measure. From an economic standpoint, however, the road would aid incalculably in the development and settlement of the West, in the opening of new markets for Eastern manufactures, and in the stimulation of trade with the Far East and the whole Pacific area.

In the meantime, while waiting for the construction of the railroad, the state was forced to devise various methods of meeting its transportation problems. Saddle horses, pack trains, and heavy wooden-wheeled ox-carts, called carretas, continued in use in many regions long after the American occupation. Modest provision was made for state highways by some of the early legislatures and a large number of toll roads were subsidized by local governments or operated, sometimes at enormous profit, under private management. Huge freight wagons, usually run in trains or caravans, plied between the mines and the cities or distributed goods, brought to the coast by steamer, to interior markets as distant as Salt Lake, Idaho, and Wyoming. So great was the traffic between southern California and Utah alone, for example, that it employed as high as six thousand men, five thousand wagons, and many thousand head of horses, mules, and oxen.

The opening of the Comstock Lode and of mines in the Owens Valley necessitated the transportation of tens of thousands of tons of ore and supplies—in the one case across the innumerable canyons and ridges of the Sierra Nevada Mountains; in the other over hundreds of miles of unbroken desert waste. Brewer has left us the following vivid picture of travel on the Placerville road, "the grand artery of travel to Washoe."

"It is stated," he wrote, "that five thousand teams are steadily employed in the Washoe trade and other commerce east of the Sierra—not little teams of two horses, but generally of six horses or mules, often as many as eight or ten, carrying loads of three to eight tons, on huge cumbrous wagons. . . .

"Clouds of dust arose, filling the air, as we met long trains of ponderous wagons, loaded with merchandise, hay, grain—in fact everything that man or beast uses. We stopped at the Slippery Ford House. Twenty wagons stopped there, driving over a hundred horses or mules—heavy wagons, enormous loads, scarcely any less than three tons. The harness is heavy, often with a steel bow over the hames, in the form of an arch over each horse, and supporting four or five bells, whose chime can be heard at all hours of the day. . . ."[1]

Mail, passengers, and express were transported by a network of stage lines running throughout the state. Many of these were purely local enterprises, plying within a radius of only fifty or a hundred miles, but some of the larger companies operated scores of vehicles and maintained regular schedules over routes hundreds of miles in length.

In 1854 the California Stage Company absorbed most of the independent lines in northern California, and thus began the era of transportation monopolies in the state. The organization was capitalized at a million dollars, and in time extended its business to cover 1,500 miles of stage lines. James Birch, the directing genius of the company, started his career in California with "an old farm wagon and four fractious mustangs." After becoming one of the principal figures in the development of transportation in the Old West, Birch, still a young man, lost his life in the foundering of the steamship *Central America* off the Atlantic coast.

---

[1] William H. Brewer: *Up and Down California in 1860–1864* (1930), pp. 439–40.

Prior to 1857 the federal government showed little interest in subsidizing the development of overland mail routes to California, but just before the close of the Pierce administration Congress passed the long-awaited Overland California Mail Bill, empowering the Postmaster General to select a route and contract for the transportation of mail between the Mississippi Valley and San Francisco. The Postmaster General, a Tennessean by birth, selected the southern route and awarded the contract to John Butterfield's Overland Mail Company, an organization largely financed by New York capital.

Butterfield was an administrative genius. In the twelve months allowed for inaugurating the service he equipped nearly three thousand miles of stage line, much of the way through uninhabited or hostile Indian territory, and had the line ready to function well within the allotted time. On September 15, 1858, the eastbound stage left San Francisco, and the next day the mail for the West started from St. Louis.

"The mail route adopted by the Postmaster-General had two eastern terminals on the Mississippi River, one at St. Louis and the other at Memphis, the two forks converging at Fort Smith, Arkansas. From Fort Smith, the line ran through Indian Territory to Colbert's Ferry on the Texas border, thence bore to the west, over the plains of Texas, to Franklin, opposite El Paso, Mexico, crossing the dreaded Llano Estacado en route. Leaving Franklin, the road traversed the arid lands of New Mexico Territory, and entered California near Fort Yuma, on the Colorado River. At this point it dipped southward into Mexico for a short distance and re-entered California in the neighborhood of the New River, crossed the mountains (by way of Warner's ranch) to Los Angeles, and proceeded north through the San Joaquin Valley and Pacheco Pass to San Francisco, the western terminal. The route was over 2,700 miles long, and the first run of the Butterfield stages, carrying the mail . . . was made in 23 days, 23 hours." [2]

In the magnitude of its operations, the resourcefulness dis-

---

[2] Waterman L. Ormsby: *The Butterfield Overland Mail*, edited by Lyle M. Wright and Josephine M. Bynum (1942), p. viii.

played in overcoming extraordinary difficulties, the hardihood and courage required of its drivers, the Overland Mail came to typify the tradition and spirit of the Old West. As a business enterprise it was ably organized and operated with extraordinary efficiency. Its equipment consisted of more than a hundred of the famous Concord coaches, fifteen hundred animals, and a line of stations, built at ten-mile intervals, reaching halfway across the continent. Nearly a thousand men were in the company's employ.

Stages were operated day and night, winter and summer, despite storm, flood, or Indian outbreak; and the run between St. Louis and San Francisco was usually made in twenty-three days, or even less. The fare normally ran from a hundred and fifty to two hundred dollars. Postage, which during the Gold Rush had ranged from a dollar and a half to four dollars a letter, was fixed by law at three cents per half-ounce.

The outbreak of the Civil War led to the abrupt abandonment of the Overland Mail's southern route and forced the company to transfer its movable equipment to the central or Salt Lake road.[3] John Butterfield gave place to Ben Holladay, the shrewd, domineering, ruthless "Napoleon of the West," who made himself the master of 3,300 miles of stage lines and brought Western transportation to the highest degree of efficiency it was to attain during the pre-railroad era.

No single factor during these early years testified more eloquently to California's isolation from the world at large than its slow and inadequate mail service. At least three weeks were required for even the most urgent communications to reach San Francisco from the Mississippi Valley by the Overland Mail, or from the Atlantic seaboard by the Pacific Mail and Panamá route.

To meet the demand for better service, and at the same time to open a northern offset to the Overland Mail's southern route, the firm of Russell, Majors, and Waddell, one of the principal stage and freighting companies of the West, inaugurated the spectacu-

---

[3] The last Overland Mail stage left St. Louis March 18, 1861.

lar, shortlived, and financially unprofitable enterprise known as the Pony Express. The venture typified the reckless daring and gambling spirit of the frontier.

The company, operating as a subsidiary of the Central Overland California and Pike's Peak Express, inaugurated its service in April 1860. By means of relays of fast horses stationed at twelve- or fifteen-mile intervals, and a corps of sixty to eighty riders, the "Pony" cut the time of mail delivery between California and Missouri from approximately twenty-three days to ten. On special occasions the time was even less. Thus the text of Lincoln's Inaugural Address, of March 4, 1861, was carried from St. Joseph, Missouri, to Sacramento, a distance of 1,966 miles, in seven days and seventeen hours.

The Pony Express riders, Mark Twain's "swift phantoms of the desert," who swept across the landscape "like the belated fragment of a storm," were reputedly the most carefully selected body of men in the history of the West. Physically they were lean, hard, and capable of incredible endurance; to those traits they added loyalty, resourcefulness, and a courage that became proverbial.

Upon entering the service of the company, all riders and other employees, according to Glenn D. Bradley, were required to take the following oath: "I do hereby swear, before the Great and Living God, that during my engagement, and while I am an employee of Russell, Majors & Waddell, I will, under no circumstances, use profane language; that I will drink no intoxicating liquors; that I will not quarrel or fight with any other employee of the firm, and that in every respect I will conduct myself honestly, be faithful to my duties, and so direct all my acts as to win the confidence of my employers. So help me God." [4]

On October 24, 1861, the Western Union Telegraph Company and its subsidiary, the Pacific Telegraph Company, opened a transcontinental line between Omaha, Salt Lake, and San Francisco; and the Pony Express, which from the beginning had been a losing venture financially, was soon driven out of business. But

---

[4] Glenn D. Bradley: *The Story of the Pony Express* (1920), p. 52.

if the enterprise thus ended disastrously from a business standpoint, it brought its backers some measure of fame and added an
unforgettable chapter to the story of Western adventure and romance.

After the failure of Russell, Majors, and Waddell, Ben Holladay dominated Western transportation until 1866, when, foresee-
ing the effects of the coming of the railroad upon the overland
freight and stage business, he sold his interests to Wells, Fargo
and Company.

Meantime, while the Overland Mail and the Pony Express were
doing their best to break down California's long-established wall
of isolation, the urgent necessity for constructing a railroad to
the Pacific coast had been the subject of an endless amount of
discussion, scores of well-meaning resolutions, and a very considerable amount of careful exploration and investigation. As far
back as 1845 the projected railroad had found an indefatigable
champion in the person of Asa Whitney, a crusading enthusiast
who spent eight years and much of his private fortune "seeking
to educate Congress and the American public to think in terms
of a continent."

The Gold Rush gave fresh impetus to the need of a transcontinental railroad; but unprecedented engineering problems, the
lack of detailed knowledge of available routes, and the tremendous cost of the undertaking precluded the beginning of the work
at that time. The problem was still further complicated by acrimonious disputes over the location of the route and the part to be
played respectively by the government and private enterprise
in the stupendous undertaking.

As a necessary preliminary step in the construction of the road,
Congress authorized Jefferson Davis, Secretary of War under
President Pierce, to make a survey of the possible routes from the
Mississippi basin to California. The survey was carried on from
1853 to 1855. It covered five major routes (four of which were
declared feasible for a railway), and resulted in the collection of
a vast amount of factual information and scientific data relating
to the West beyond the Rocky Mountains. Davis chose the south-

ern route as the most desirable of the four. Sectional bias may have influenced his decision to some degree, but financial and engineering considerations were apparently the deciding factors. One of the weightiest objections to the southern route was the fact that at one point topographical obstructions diverted it south of the international boundary line and compelled it to run some distance through Mexican territory. In 1853 this difficulty was remedied by the Gadsden Treaty, under which the United States acquired some 45,000 square miles, comprising what is now the southern portion of Arizona, from the Mexican Republic.

Owing in part to the growing antagonism between North and South over the question of slavery, sectional bickerings within California itself, and the powerful opposition of the Pacific Mail Steamship Company (which had no desire to expose its monopoly of west-coast transportation to competition), Congressional action on the railroad was delayed until Lincoln became President and the outbreak of the Civil War broke the deadlock over the location of the route. On July 1, 1862, the long-awaited Pacific Railroad bill accordingly became law. The measure provided for the construction of a railroad (the famous Union Pacific) which should start on the one hundredth meridian, between the Republican and Platte rivers, and run along "the most direct, central, and practical route to the western boundary of Nevada, there to meet and connect with the Central Pacific Railroad Company of California."

The organization of the "Central Pacific Railroad Company of California" was due primarily to the unquenchable enthusiasm of Theodore D. Judah, a young civil engineer who visualized the limitless possibilities of a railroad across the mountains and devoted his life to making that dream a reality. With heroic singleness of purpose and at great cost to himself, Judah personally examined a score or more of possible routes across the Sierra, assembled an enormous amount of engineering data and general information with which to support the feasibility and economic soundness of the proposed road, and sought financial support in

New York and Washington, as well as in California, for the undertaking.

Judah reached the culmination of his long, single-handed struggle when he persuaded a handful of businessmen in Sacramento to incorporate the Central Pacific Railroad and subscribe for a modest amount of stock. Collis P. Huntington and Mark Hopkins, dealers in hardware and mining supplies, and Leland Stanford and Charles Crocker, well-to-do dry-goods merchants of Sacramento, soon emerged as the dominant figures in the small group whom Judah lured, by the prospect of government subsidies and a lucrative freight and passenger service with the Washoe silver mines, into giving their cautious and limited support to his plans for a transcontinental railway.

A short time after the formation of the Central Pacific Judah found himself at loggerheads with his four principal backers and went to New York to obtain sufficient financial support to regain control of the company he had called into being through so much effort, sacrifice, and imagination. But fate had other plans. While crossing the Isthmus of Panamá Judah contracted yellow fever and lived only to reach the Atlantic coast.

Thanks to extraordinary teamwork, a remarkable combination of complementary abilities, and rare immunity to the influence of ethical precepts, the "Big Four," as Crocker, Hopkins, Huntington, and Stanford came to be known, soon created for themselves a dictatorial position in the state's political and business life. In the division of labor between the four, Crocker assumed responsibility for the actual construction of the railroads; Stanford concerned himself mainly with state politics and finance; Hopkins supplied counsel and management; and Huntington, the dominant member of the group, played the role of master lobbyist, political dictator, and financial wizard.

From the physical standpoint, the construction of the Central Pacific Railroad across the Sierra Nevada Range was a gigantic undertaking—a conspicuous example of American ability, ingenuity, boldness, and engineering skill. The burden of the task rested upon the broad shoulders of Charles Crocker—and upon the patient backs of 15,000 Chinese coolies whose amazing industry and endurance overcame even the rugged granite and choking snows of the great mountains.

The road was financed by private capital, by immense grants of land and loans from the federal government, and by subsidies of many kinds from state, county, and municipal sources. Without government aid it is probable that the road would not have been built for another generation. But the methods by which such aid was obtained, the extent to which the promoters of the road profited individually from the subsidies, and the scandalous abuse of the land grants in later years left an ugly blot upon the history of a stupendous and otherwise noble enterprise.

Following the familiar device that led to such notorious scandals in the case of the Union Pacific and the Crédit Mobilier, the "Big Four" formed a separate company, from which other stockholders were rigidly excluded, to undertake the actual construction of the railroads. The organization, first called the Charles Crocker Construction Company and later the Contract and Finance Company, made large profits for the four partners at the expense of both the government and the minority stockholders. As many important records were apparently deliberately destroyed, the amount of such profits is problematical, but was undoubtedly great.

The immediate objectives of the builders of the Central Pacific Railroad were the extensive federal grants of aid, provided for in the Pacific Railroad Bill, and the lucrative freights of the Washoe silver mines. The government grants or subsidies consisted of twenty sections, or twelve thousand eight hundred acres, of public land per mile; and a credit in United States bonds, ranging from sixteen thousand dollars for every mile of track laid across the plains to forty-eight thousand dollars for a like distance in the mountains.

Building westward from Omaha, the Union Pacific expected to reach the California boundary before the Central Pacific crossed the Sierra Nevada Mountains; but as construction progressed it became evident that the Union's time schedule would have to be drastically revised, and that the tracks of the competing lines would meet in Utah, rather than at the California border.

The rivalry of the two roads resulted in an epic race. In addition to control of future traffic, each road stood to gain over three million dollars in government credit, and 1,280,000 acres of public land for every hundred miles of track laid down at the expense of its competitor. At one time Huntington and his associates hoped to build as far east as Green River, thereby gaining control of the traffic of most of the Great Basin and blocking the Union Pacific's outlet to the Columbia and the Northwest. But the latter road, having made its escape from the toils of the Crédit Mobilier, successfully met the Central Pacific's challenge and carried its rails as far west as central Utah.[5]

The two roads met at the little desert junction of Promontory Point. The event was celebrated on May 10, 1869 by a formal ceremony typical of that mid-Victorian generation and strangely out of place in the wild, desolate heart of the Great Basin. With the accompaniment of top hats, long coats, numerous speeches, and endless toasts, a golden spike was used to unite the rails of the two roads, and a dramatic telegram was dispatched to resident Grant: "The last rail is laid, the last spike is driven. The Pacific Railroad is finished."

The construction of the Central Pacific served as a training school for the "Big Four." To realize their ambition to monopolize the commerce of the territory extending from the Columbia to the Gulf of California they proceeded by successive stages to build or acquire a network of short lines around San Francisco Bay; to extend the California and Oregon Railroad through the Sacramento Valley to Oregon; to build southward far enough to block the approach of any rival road along the coast; and to construct a transcontinental line up the San Joaquin Valley, across the Tehachapi Pass, through Los Angeles to Yuma, and thence along the so-called Sunset Route to New Orleans.

---

[5] The subsidy east of the Sierra Nevada was $32,000 per mile.

By 1885 the "Big Four" had built or purchased nineteen railroads, of which the Central Pacific of California was still the dominant company. But when Congress created the Pacific Railway Commission to investigate the affairs of the Union and Central Pacific railways, the Southern Pacific Company (a Kentucky corporation that still has its annual meetings in the little village of Spring Station) was hastily organized to serve as a holding company for the "Big Four's" intricate railroad interests.

For many years, under the ægis of the Southern Pacific Company, Huntington and his associates enjoyed a virtual monopoly of railroad transportation throughout the state. In the late eighties, however, the long dictatorship was successfully challenged by the Atchison, Topeka, & Santa Fe, which bought the charter of the Atlantic and Pacific Company. Running west from Kansas City through New Mexico, the Santa Fe found its way into California blocked at the Colorado by the Southern Pacific interests; but the new road finally reached San Bernardino by way of Barstow and the historic Cajón Pass, and after having absorbed a number of local lines, including the California Southern and the San Gabriel Valley companies, succeeded in entering Los Angeles on its own line early in 1887. For about a year and a half prior to that time it had used the Southern Pacific tracks from Colton.

The Santa Fe afterwards extended its lines from Mojave to San Francisco by way of the San Joaquin Valley and built southward along the coast to San Diego. The later history of railroad-building in the state included the construction of the Los Angeles, San Pedro, & Salt Lake Railroad and its subsequent absorption by the Union Pacific, and the completion of the Western Pacific across the Sierra Nevada Mountains, by way of Feather River Canyon.

It is difficult to make an accurate and objective estimate of the pioneer railroad-builders of California. They were, beyond question, one of the most constructive of the forces of a highly creative generation, and aided incalculably in the development and enrichment of the state. It is equally obvious, on the other hand, that they looked upon the railroads as their private, personal possessions and used them, both directly and indirectly, within the law or without the law as occasion demanded, to build up huge fortunes for themselves and to acquire tremendous economic and political power.

The "Big Four" clearly had no conception of a public utility as a public trust, and brushed aside the quixotic idea that the welfare of a community, or of a great commonwealth, was vastly more important than the ambitions and fortunes of four private citizens. Public opinion charged them with corrupting the fountainheads of government, setting up puppet legislatures and city councils, and making lackeys and henchmen out of public officials. To all such charges Huntington angrily replied: "We have served California better than any other set of men have ever served any other state in the Union."

In all fairness the practices of the California railroad-builders must be judged by the standards of the society to which they belonged and not by the ethics of a more socially-minded generation. But whether we condemn or excuse, the facts and their consequences remain the same. Long after the men who complacently accepted the title of the "Big Four" had been gathered to their fathers, the Southern Pacific machine still remained an arrogant and hateful reality to the people of California—the personification of all that was dictatorial and corrupt in state politics. And the builders of great enterprises, the initiators of a revolution in industry and transportation, were cast, by popular tradition, in the role of economic buccaneers.

CHAPTER 16. Speculation, Monopoly, and
Discontent

THE NEW era which began in California with the building
of the railroads was marked by economic and social changes
of the most fundamental character. The revolution in transportation effected a corresponding revolution in population, industry, markets, and agriculture. But though California's days of extreme isolation came to an end in 1869, and the development
of her resources went forward at an ever accelerated pace, the
first decade of the railroad era witnessed widespread economic
stagnation, and social unrest of a violent and explosive type.

The new era opened in the prosperous aftermath of the Civil
War. From a few simple handicrafts at the time of the Gold Rush,
California had developed a manufacturing business, largely in
flour, lumber, machinery, sugar, and printing, that ran to a total
of seventy million dollars a year. Gold was still being produced
at the rate of twenty millions a year; and quicksilver, chiefly from
the historic and legally entangled mines of New Almaden, near
San José, yielded about three millions.

Many sections of the state were witnessing an agricultural revolution. The sheep industry, for example, following the drought
of the mid-sixties and the demand for wool created by the Civil
War, entered upon a period of almost unparalleled prosperity.
Private ranchos, formerly the domain of the cattle herds, passed
into the hands of the sheep barons; and thousands of square miles
of public domain, much of it useless for other purposes, furnished
almost unlimited free grazing lands for the California flocks. Wool
production rose from five and a half million pounds in 1862 to
more than twenty-two million pounds in 1871. Profits in the industry were enormous, often running from fifty to a hundred per
cent a year; and, like almost everything else in California, sheep
farming was carried out on a scale undreamed of in Eastern or
Midwestern states.

Small farming in California during this early pioneer period, thanks especially to drought, pests, and lack of transportation, was too often a hand-to-mouth affair that broke the spirits of those who sought a livelihood from it and created a shiftless, discontented, antisocial class. To such impoverished settlers the seventies added some thousands of "wandering, gypsy-like poor whites," commonly called "Pikes," who lived almost wholly off the country and added little to the economic or cultural welfare of the state. "The true 'Pike,'" wrote Nordhoff in 1872, ". . . often lives with his family in a wagon; he rarely follows steady industry; he is frequently a squatter on other people's lands; 'he owns a rifle, a lot of children and dogs, a wife, and if he can read, a lawbook,' said a lawyer describing this character to me. 'He moves from place to place, as the humor seizes him, and is generally an injury to his neighbors. He will not work regularly; but he has a great tenacity of life, and is always ready for a lawsuit.'"[1]

The most significant agricultural development of the period was the expansion of wheat farming, especially in the great interior valleys of the Sacramento and the San Joaquin. The boom began in the late sixties and continued for two decades. From an agricultural standpoint, it probably surpassed anything else of its kind the state has ever known. Although much of the lower Sacramento and San Joaquin valleys was covered by Mexican land grants, farther back from the coast the federal government had inherited title to a princely empire. But within a few years many millions of acres of these public lands passed out of the possession of the government, to some degree into the hands of bona fide settlers, but mostly into the control of railroads, land monopolists, and large companies, such as that of Miller and Lux.

As the demand for California cereals increased, more of this land, formerly used for sheep or cattle, began to be planted to wheat and barley. Individual holdings in the grain regions sometimes embraced forty or fifty thousand acres; and from the time the virgin soil was broken up until the grain reached tidewater

[1] Charles Nordhoff: *California: For Health, Pleasure, and Residence* . . . (1873), p. 138.

at San Francisco Bay, where much of it was shipped abroad, every process was carried out on a true Brobdingnagian scale.[2] "A man will plough but a single furrow a day on his farm," wrote W. H. Bishop, a visitor to the state in 1872, "but this may be twenty miles long." Planting on such an immense scale necessitated the use of gang plows to prepare the ground; and the wheat was cut, threshed, and sacked all in a single operation.

"The ploughs, thirty-five in number," wrote Frank Norris in a memorable scene in his famous novel *The Octopus*, "each drawn by its team of ten, stretched in an interminable line, nearly a quarter of a mile in length. . . . They were arranged, as it were, *en echelon*, not in file—not one directly behind the other, but each succeeding plough its own width farther in the field than the one in front of it. Each of these ploughs held five shears, so that when the entire company was in motion, one hundred and seventy-five furrows were made at the same instant. At a distance, the ploughs resembled a great column of field artillery. Each driver was in his place, his glance alternating between his horses and the foreman nearest at hand. Other foremen, in their buggies or buckboards, were at intervals along the line, like battery lieutenants. . . ."[3]

Even in the midst of the wheat boom the movement to provide land for small farms in the San Joaquin Valley, develop irrigation, and diversify crops was rapidly going forward. In the early seventies the San Joaquin and Kings River Canal and Irrigation Company constructed a canal, forty miles long, fifty-two feet wide, and six feet deep, to provide water for irrigation. Other land and water companies undertook similar development programs, and presently vineyards, fruit orchards, and dairy farms began to encroach upon the wheat fields.

But the lot of the pioneer settler was still beset with difficulties. In addition to the usual vicissitudes of drought, wind, flood, and

---

[2] Many contemporary articles on California agriculture referred to a 50,-000-acre wheat ranch in Colusa County, owned by Dr. Hugh Glenn. Even larger ranches were to be found in the San Joaquin and Sacramento valleys.

[3] Frank Norris: *The Octopus* (1901), pp. 127–8.

the like, he had to contend with uncertain land titles, the pre-emption of his water by large landholders, trespassing cattle, arbitrary freight rates, loneliness, malaria, lack of easily available markets, inexperience in farming methods best suited to the land, and pests of many kinds, including grasshoppers, coyotes, go-phers, squirrels, and the long-legged, long-eared jack-rabbits that bred in the valley by the tens of thousands.

Finding it impossible to keep the rabbits in check by the use of guns and dogs, settlers often resorted to so-called rabbit drives, which, if properly conducted, were effective but altogether hor-rible in accomplishing their purpose.

Despite the planting of large areas to wheat and the develop-ment of small farming communities, cattle-raising continued as an essential industry in both the Sacramento and San Joaquin valleys. After the severe drought of the mid-sixties, most of the ranchers drove their cattle into the "High Sierras" as soon as the snow was sufficiently melted, and pastured them there on the mountain meadows until early fall. During those years the San Joaquin Valley became the seat of the fabulous domain of land, grass, and cattle developed by Henry Miller and Charles Lux. The outposts of that empire reached as far north as Oregon, as far south as Mexico, and as far east as the Rocky Mountains. It was said that Miller and Lux owned half a million acres and ran 100,000 head of cattle. Whatever the truth of the statistics, they were the largest landowners in California.

The repeal of the "no-fence" law in 1872 and the development of rail transportation gave great impetus to settlement and diver-sified farming in the valleys. But despite the railroad's invaluable contributions, its policy of exacting subsidies before it would build through certain towns, evading taxes, charging high freight rates, and refusing to dispose of its lands at the prices stipulated in the federal grants, created a deep-rooted hostility among the settlers that survived long after the causes themselves had been removed.[4]

_____

[4] The conflict between the ranchers and the railroad came to a climax in a pitched battle at a place called Mussel Slough, near the little town of Han-

In the field of California finance the era after the Civil War was one of frenzied speculation, reminiscent of the notorious South Sea debacle or of John Law's historic Mississippi Bubble. During the sixties the silver mines of the Washoe Valley in Nevada came into production on an immense scale. The output fluctuated widely, however, since the mines would often run out of fabulous bonanza into long stretches of barren rock. Such sudden and violent extremes, combined with the passionate gambling spirit inherited from the days of '49, turned the San Francisco Stock Exchange, on which the shares, or "feet," of more than a hundred of the Nevada mines were listed, into an indescribable bedlam of speculation.

One of the largest and most powerful of the Washoe syndicates was composed of William C. Ralston, president of the Bank of California, William Sharon, manager of Ralston's extensive interests in Nevada, and Darius O. Mills, co-founder, with Ralston, of the Bank of California. For a decade, at least, Ralston was the most spectacular, and perhaps the most trusted, figure in San Francisco's business and financial life. He lived lavishly, gave generously, speculated on a grand scale, and initiated a dozen constructive enterprises in as many different fields. "In rapid succession his fertile brain projected and his superhuman energy put through the Mission Woolen Mills, the Kimball Carriage Factory, the Cornell Watch Factory, the West Coast Furniture Factory, the San Francisco Sugar Refinery, the Grand Hotel, the Palace Hotel, the Dry Dock at Hunter's Point, the Reclamation Works at Sherman Island, the Irrigating Works of the San Joaquin Valley, the Rincon Hill Cut, the extension of Montgomery street, and the California Theatre." [5]

In their operations in the Comstock Lode, near Virginia City,

---

ford. Of the eight men who actually participated in the affray, seven were killed and one was seriously wounded. A quarter of a century later Frank Norris built his novel *The Octopus* about this bloody tragedy of the San Joaquin.

[5] Quoted in Ira B. Cross: *Financing an Empire* (1927), Vol. I, p. 402.

Nevada, Ralston and his associates soon found a formidable rival in Adolph Sutro, a practical-minded dreamer who proposed to construct an enormous tunnel, or adit, to drain the lower levels of the lode and thus open the silver deposits that could not be reached by ordinary methods because of the flooded condition of the mines. Somewhat later a third group, representing the un-usual combination of two mining men, John W. Mackay and James Fair, and two saloonkeepers, James C. Flood and William S. O'Brien, also acquired valuable holdings on the Comstock. About the same time John P. Jones and Alvinza Hayward bought up the stock of the Nevada Mill and Mining Company and opened a noted mine called the Crown Point.

In the spring of 1873 Fair's syndicate tapped one of the richest ore bodies of the lode—a vein more than fifty feet wide that many miners estimated would yield at least half a billion dollars in silver. A few months later Sutro completed his huge adit, and the increased yield thus effected made the Washoe mines the largest silver-producing properties in the world. Speculation in San Francisco knew no bounds. Everyone—banker, barkeeper, housewife, schoolteacher, prostitute, clerk, laborer, hostler, doc-tor, lawyer, barber, merchant—contracted the fever. Shares, re-acting to a hundred wild-flying rumors that reached the city, rose to fantastic heights or fell to corresponding depths in a single week. Speculation went to such mad extremes that a few shrewd men even undertook to float stock in a fictitious diamond mine, supposedly located in the wilds of the Rocky Mountains. Thou-sands of dollars' worth of low-grade, uncut stones, purchased in London, were salted throughout the property; mining experts sent out to examine the field were cleverly hoodwinked; and the whole enterprise was cloaked in an air of profound secrecy to make it more alluring. Ralston and a number of other important San Francisco businessmen were drawn into the project and became so genuinely excited that they prepared to take the field over, lock, stock, and barrel. Only the revelation of the fraud by Clar-ence King, who some years before had acquired first-hand geological knowledge of the region, prevented the swindle from becoming what might well have been the most costly fraud of its kind in all American history.[6]

About four hundred million dollars were poured into mining development or speculation during the hectic days of the Comstock Lode, making it almost impossible, for nearly twenty years, to secure necessary capital for the development of the state's great agricultural resources or for other constructive purposes. From a financial and business standpoint, the state was thus clearly riding for a fall. The disaster occurred in the panic of 1874–5.

Following a time lag which at that time was a normal feature of the state's business life, the financial depression that paralyzed the Eastern states in 1873 reached California approximately a year later. About the same time the Comstock bonanza began to taper off; and the resultant state-wide business stagnation forced one bank after another to close its doors. On August 26, 1875, a run began on the supposedly impregnable Bank of California. As the panic spread, an enormous crowd of frenzied depositors began to mill about the bank. "From his window Ralston could see that California Street was as wild and tumultuous as a wind-tossed sea. Waves of humanity swept up the stairs and swirled about the doors. Like drowning men, people clung to balustrade and window-frame. Inch by inch they fought for right of way, hurling their bodies into any opening breech. Now and then, heavy fists, like great combers, bore down on plate-glass windows as if they would smash a way into the interior by violence. At the doors, wild men, papers fluttering overhead, threw each other ruthlessly aside and tried to trample one another under foot. Among the white faces Ralston noted laborers; pale women with children trailing at their skirts; and policemen trying to keep lines in order. In the crowd he could recognize many friends—

---

[6] The story is told in Asbury Harpending: *The Great Diamond Hoax,* ed. by James H. Wilkins (San Francisco: The J. H. Barry Company; 1913)

friends whose confidence in the bank had never been shaken." [7]

The collapse of the Bank of California, followed by the suicide or accidental death of Ralston, started a melancholy procession of similar failures. Nearly all the banks of San Francisco suspended operations; three in Los Angeles followed suit; all over the state the springs of credit and business began to run dry. Widespread unemployment added to the general distress. The situation was aggravated, both actually and psychologically, by the presence in the state of thousands of Chinese coolies, most of whom had been imported to construct the Central Pacific Railroad. "Crocker's Pets," as they were called, had been sufficiently unpopular even when they were building the railroad in the depths of the Sierra Nevada Mountains. When they swarmed back from the construction camps to compete with unskilled labor in the cities, and with ranch hands and truck gardeners in the rural districts, dislike turned to hatred; and hatred soon found expression in mob violence and persecution.

Perplexing enough in its complicated economic aspects, the Chinese question was rendered tenfold more difficult of solution by race prejudice, political opportunism, and demagoguery. The people of California, in the position of householders on an exposed beach watching the rising tide of an illimitable sea, saw themselves engulfed by the unrestricted flow of Chinese immigration. The danger was there, imminent and real; but it should have been met with reason, justice, and common sense instead of by ignorance, hysteria, and the worst forms of political propaganda.

As already indicated, the prejudice built up against the Chinese during the mining era grew more sullen and widespread with the use of coolie labor by the "Big Four." The Burlingame

---

[7] George D. Lyman: *Ralston's Ring* (1937), pp. 294–5. J. Ross Browne, vigorous critic of California banks, railroads, and monopolies, said of Ralston that he was "impatient of restraint, confident of his powers, inspired by a noble ambition to make San Francisco the Queen City of the western world." *Overland Monthly*, Vol. XV, p. 348.

Treaty of 1868 added fresh fuel to the flames by extending the principle of "free immigration and emigration" to the vast millions of the Chinese Empire. Under direction of the famous socio-economic organizations known as the Six Companies, which worked in close co-operation with steamship lines interested in the revenue possibilities of mass immigration, and with corporations seeking an unrestricted supply of cheap labor, as many as twenty thousand coolies were sometimes imported into California in a single year; and the number promised to expand indefinitely as time went on.

Working for a few cents an hour from early morning till late at night, thriving under a low standard of living; stoical, inarticulate, given to strange customs, worshipping strange gods, and rendered politically impotent by the denial of the ballot, the Chinese coolie became the convenient scapegoat for a score of economic and social ills with which the state was then afflicted. Popular enmity, rising to the pitch of mob hysteria, frequently expressed itself in the wholesale destruction of property, shameful cruelties, and wanton murder. The massacre of at least twenty-two Chinese in a riot in Los Angeles in 1871 represented the climax of such disgraceful barbarity; but similar incidents on a smaller scale besmirched the records of nearly every California city of the time. By the mid-seventies anti-Chinese agitation had assumed the proportions of mass hysteria; and the phrase: "The Chinese Must Go," was the trademark of the movement.

One of the most serious aspects of the Chinese question was the conflict between federal and state jurisdiction—a conflict settled in the case of the Chinese in 1882 by an amendment to the Burlingame Treaty that effactually closed the doors to coolie immigration—but one that was destined to break out in even more violent form when, a quarter of a century later, California attempted by state legislation to deal with the influx of the Japanese.

To the widespread unrest aroused by the presence of the Chinese, the California land situation added another fruitful source of social instability and discontent. Many of the huge Spanish-

Mexican ranchos still remained; railroad lands were being withheld from the market, sold with little regard to the maximum prices stipulated in the federal grants, or acquired in large blocks by so-called land monopolists. Enormous tracts of federal and state lands, supposedly set aside for the benefit of bona fide settlers, had also fallen, by fair means or foul, into the hands of the same land monopolists and wealthy speculators. The discontent thus engendered laid the foundation for some violence and provided excuse for the depredations of railroad bandits such as Evans and Sonntag, who kept the San Joaquin Valley in a state of excitement in the late 1880's.

Not all large landholdings, however, were economically unsound or socially reprehensible. Much California land was still useful only for sheep or cattle ranges. Without water, in a land of "sun-burned rivers" and little rain, it was impossible to convert such large areas into small farms or open them for settlement; and the initiation of irrigation on an extensive scale required a large outlay of capital, the development of engineering techniques, and in many cases prolonged and expensive litigation to obtain the necessary water rights. Confusion and uncertainty in land titles, a vicious legacy of the Spanish-Mexican grants and the federal Land Act of 1851, also deterred the break-up of large landholdings.

The chief weight of the general property tax, principal source of revenue for both state and county governments, rested upon land. Here, again, there was great popular discontent because the railroads, speculators, and large individual landholders found many ways, including low assessments, outright evasions, and legal technicalities, to escape their full share of the tax. For years James McClatchy of the *Sacramento Bee* served as the leader of a vigorous crusade to lay a much heavier tax upon the large ranchos, railroad grants, and lands in the hands of speculators, and thus break up the so-called land monopoly.

Henry George's *Progress and Poverty*, with its fetish of the single tax—a book that owed much of its inspiration to the Sacramento editor—was in part the outgrowth of the conditions just described. George believed that land constituted the basis of all wealth, and that most important tax problems could be solved by having only one type of tax, a levy on land and its value increase. But thousands of Californians who declined to go to the extreme lengths favored by Henry George advocated drastic reforms in the system of land taxation. "The only remedy we can suggest," said the San Francisco *Chronicle*, "is to tax these lands for the full value of what they would be worth in the possession of farmers. . . . The Board of Supervisors and the local Assessor should run roads, build stone culverts and bridges, erect schoolhouses and tax—tax heavily; tax to their full value. If one man or a half dozen men are ambitious to own a county let them pay for it."

The unrest and discontent among the agricultural population found tangible expression in the establishment of branches of the nationwide Patrons of Husbandry, an organization which for a time attained extensive popularity and effected some of the economic and social reforms most badly needed. The organization was secret in membership, nominally nonpolitical in character, and worked largely through regional units, or clubs called granges.

The Patrons of Husbandry were catholic in the objects of their crusade. They directed their attack against prohibitive freight rates and other railroad abuses; excessive commission fees; great landholdings; extortionate interest charges; oppressive taxes; wasteful and ignorant methods of agriculture; high prices of farm necessities, including implements, jute bags, and general merchandise; pre-emption of water by large landowners; and the numerous flourishing monopolies in the state. Though belittled and ridiculed, the organization played an important role in attacking deep-seated economic evils, shaping public opinion, and furnishing a medium through which the small farmers and hardpressed settlers could make their grievances articulate.

Discontent and unrest among the laboring classes found much more direct, violent, and spectacular expression than that to which the farming groups resorted. Prolonged and widespread unemployment, coupled with a conspicuous lack of social responsibility on the part of large users of labor, created an acute situation in some of the larger cities (especially in San Francisco, where, as early as 1867, there were nearly thirty labor or trade unions) and led to frequent outbursts of lawlessness and rioting. By 1877 it was estimated that thirty thousand men in San Francisco alone were out of work, and bread lines had become a normal feature of the city's daily life.

As the months passed, the situation grew progressively worse; and on July 23, aroused by the reports of railroad and labor riots in Philadelphia, a mass meeting of the unemployed culminated in a violent anti-Chinese demonstration and in threats, scarcely less violent, against the millionaires on Nob Hill. Rioting broke out on a large scale and continued almost unchecked for two days. Fearing that the regularly constituted authorities could not cope with the situation, and that consequently the city would be given over to pillage or made the victim of incendiary fires, a body of citizens, headed by W. T. Coleman of Vigilante fame, assumed the responsibility of restoring order, appointed a Committee of Safety, and organized a semi-military force of five or six thousand men.

Under instructions from the Secretary of War the Committee was furnished with arms from the United States arsenal at Benicia; the Secretary of the Navy ordered several vessels to stand by in the harbor to render whatever aid might be required; and Coleman equipped some fifteen hundred volunteers with hickory pick handles and sent them, accompanied by three hundred mounted guards, to patrol the streets. After considerable damage had been done both to persons and property, but fortunately without precipitating a pitched battle, the "Pick-handle Brigade" gained control of the situation and quickly brought the city back to normal.

A few months after the violent outburst in San Francisco certain militant leaders, determined to carry the fight for labor reform into the field of politics, organized the so-called Workingmen's Party. The conservative elements of the state looked upon the movement as radical, subversive, and revolutionary. Yet, aside from a violent anti-Chinese plank, the measures advocated by the party are now almost universally accepted as desirable features of our economic and political life. They included the eight-hour day; popular election of United States senators; state regulation of banks, railroads, and other corporations; tax reform; compulsory education; and an improved monetary system. The language in which the party leaders advocated their reforms, however, was often intemperate and ill-considered.

At the head of the Workingmen's Party stood Denis Kearney, an Irishman by birth. Each Sunday afternoon thousands of workingmen were accustomed to assemble on the sand lots opposite the City Hall in San Francisco. In such an environment Denis Kearney, orator, born politician, fighter, and demagogue, was at his best. With his ready wit, coarse humor, belligerent manner, and vituperative language, he played almost at will upon the emotions and prejudices of the crowd; and had he actually believed as much in direct action as his words implied, both San Francisco and the state as a whole might well have been exposed to the horror of mob insurrection.

After about a year of meteoric success Kearney either lost or voluntarily surrendered his hold on the Workingmen's Party and quickly disappeared from public view. It is difficult to evaluate his effect upon the politics or social conditions of the time. To some degree he opened the eyes of the complacent, both to the economic distress and social evils of the day and to the explosive danger of a society so full of poverty and unemployment. But there is no objective standard by which to measure his influence, and contemporary opinion was too violently prejudiced on one side or the other to serve as a safe guide.

Believing, with some reason, that many of their ills were due to the failings and shortcomings of the state government, the people finally sought relief in a new constitution. The delegates elected to draft the document met from September 28, 1878 to March 3, 1879. The convention was composed of a hundred and fifty-two members, fifty-one of whom belonged to the Workingmen's Party, seventy-eight to a fusion or non-partisan movement, and the remainder to various smaller political groups, including the People's Independent Party, known in popular parlance as the "Dolly Vardens" because of its "heterogeneous constitution, parti-colored complexion, and unusual make-up."

Though many extreme and impractical resolutions were proposed in the convention, only a few radical measures were actually adopted; and the constitution as finally drafted was a compromise measure unexpectedly moderate on the whole in its provisions and general tone.

In addition to various clauses aimed at the Chinese, the document sought to provide a remedy for the most pronounced grievances of the people by creating a State Board of Equalization (to ensure equity in taxation), establishing a more uniform system of land assessment, defining railroads as common carriers, outlawing combinations or agreements to hinder competition, and setting up a State Board of Railroad Commissioners with power to regulate the rates of public utilities and prohibit illegal discriminations.

In its more fundamental aspects the constitutional convention was thus obviously a meeting-ground of two antagonistic political philosophies—the semi-laissez-faire conception of society, later idealized under the term "rugged individualism," and the rapidly spreading doctrine of rigid government control. The Workingmen's Party and similar liberal-radical groups criticized the constitution as inadequate and ultra-conservative, or damned it as at best a timid, milk-and-water measure. The big corporations, banks, city merchants, and wealthier classes generally denounced it, on the other hand, as socialistic, confiscatory, and full of crackpot ideas.

Opposition to the constitution, represented by outspoken extremists of both sides, was thus so powerful that when the document came before the people for ratification, out of a total vote of approximately 145,000 it obtained a majority of less than 8 per cent. A "New Constitution" party, which proclaimed ratification a signal victory over the "banded cohorts of capital," was immediately formed to enact legislation to make the constitution effective. But the good people of California, who hopefully put their trust in the new instrument of government, soon discovered that they were leaning on a broken reed.

For a decade or more after the constitution went into effect, the platforms of all the political parties in the state—Democratic, Republican, Independent, Workingmen's, Temperance—continued to denounce the great landholdings, unequal taxation, public-utility monopolies, and confiscatory freight rates. In the popular mind, at least, the political organization developed by Huntington and his associates, and in later years universally known as the Southern Pacific Machine, continued to be the real government of the state. It was not until the late nineties, indeed, that the Southern Pacific interests suffered their first major defeats. In 1894 a three-year fight began in Congress over an attempt to scale down the Central Pacific's huge obligations to the federal government, or to remit them altogether. Leading the opposition to Huntington's campaign were Adolph Sutro (builder of the Comstock adit and generous benefactor of San Francisco), and the son of another Nevada mining millionaire, William Randolph Hearst, who parlayed his father's fortune into control of a large segment of the American press.

In Ambrose Bierce, whose pen was thrice dipped in gall, and Homer Davenport, California's greatest cartoonist, Hearst found the ideal pair to pierce the joints in Huntington's long-invulnerable armor. As the opposition to his bill increased, Huntington went to such desperate lengths to influence Congress that the New York *Evening Post* finally declared: "The most pitiable and at the same time the most disgusting spectacle that now offends the national capital is the Huntington lobby. The list of paid lobbyists and attorneys now numbers twenty-eight, and their brazen attempts to influence Congress to pass the Pacific Railroad Refunding Bill have become the disgrace of the session." [8] Despite all his resources and generalship, however, Huntington was unable to force the measure through Congress; and in the end the railroad paid the full amount of its indebtedness to the government.

---

[8] Glenn Chesney Quiett: *They Built the West* (1934), p. 245.

In the long-drawn-out struggle over the construction of a deep-water harbor in southern California, Huntington suffered his second major backset. The choice lay between Santa Monica, over whose waterfront the Southern Pacific held exclusive control, and San Pedro, the long-established port of entry for Los Angeles. Supporting San Pedro for the necessary federal appropriations were many of the leading businessmen of Los Angeles, represented by the young but already lusty Chamber of Commerce, under the direction of the crusading idealist Charles Dwight Willard; Harrison Gray Otis, militant and uncompromising editor of the Los Angeles *Times;* certain railway interests naturally hostile to the Southern Pacific; and one of the ablest representatives California has ever had in Washington, Senator Stephen M. White.

Against such a formidable alliance Huntington pitted all the resources of the Southern Pacific system and his own superlative experience in political manipulation. The nominal questions involved in the choice between the two ports were chiefly of a technical or an engineering character. But from a contemporary point of view, the controversy symbolized something far deeper and more significant. The real issue was whether the Southern Pacific Railroad should continue to dictate the California policies of the federal government, use Congress and the War Department to secure its coveted monopoly on deep-water transportation, and set itself up as the arbiter of the economic development of the state. The struggle continued with varying fortunes for six years and ended in a complete triumph for the advocates of the free harbor.

Early one morning in August 1900, a year after construction actually began on the breakwater at San Pedro, Collis P. Huntington, sole survivor of the "Big Four," and personification both of the great virtues and of the great vices of his age, reached the end of his long and imperious career. After his death the political machine with which his name had so long been associated began to fall apart. According to spokesmen for the Southern Pacific, this dissolution was wholly voluntary, and the railroad directors welcomed the opportunity to withdraw from all political activity and devote their energies exclusively to the business interests of the company.

But the leaders of the Lincoln-Roosevelt League, who initiated the historic reform movement in state politics in 1907, offered a very different explanation. They boasted that they had "kicked the Southern Pacific out of politics," forcibly redeemed the state from its long era of bondage, and left the railroad politically as impotent as Bunyan's stricken giant who could only sit at the mouth of his cave, grinning at pilgrims as they went by and biting his nails because he could not come at them.

CHAPTER 17. The Flood Tide of
Immigration

I N THE mid-eighties an immense publicity campaign, sponsored by railroads, steamship lines, business organizations,
land companies, and chambers of commerce, spread the fame of
California throughout the United States, and into almost every
corner of the civilized world. Pamphlets and booklets describing
the country's climate and natural resources in language not always
sober or restrained, and setting forth the opportunities available
to settlers, tourists, investors, and others, were distributed by the
tens of thousands.

Through the Commissioner of Immigration, the state itself gave
effective support to the publicity campaign and provided valuable information to prospective and actual settlers alike. "The
California Immigrant Union was founded in October, 1869, by a
group of outstanding citizens, 'for the purpose of Encouraging Immigration to the State of California.' It maintained an office on
California Street in San Francisco, and offered itself as a clearing-
house for information on state lands, showing special interest in
the formation and settlement of colony groups. Its leaders included both old and new settlers. There was an honorary committee headed by George Newton Booth and numbering on its roster
such names as Leland Stanford and Jesse Livermore, while Mark
Hopkins and Peter Spreckels were members of the board; William T. Coleman, of vigilante fame, was the first president. The
Union had a general agent at San Francisco, and others at Copen-
hagen, Hamburg, and Bremen. There was also a travelling agent
in Germany, and a general agent for the Eastern states." [1]

Almost as effective as the highly organized advertising campaign of a public or semi-public nature was the stream of letters

[1] Glenn S. Dumke: *The Boom of the Eighties in Southern California*
(1944), p. 203.

that flowed back from California to the home states. Travelers and tourists, returning to the dingy cities and prosaic towns of the East and Middle West, ever afterwards looked back on California through a golden mist of sunshine, roses, and orange blossoms, and forgot the dust and intolerable heat of the ride across the desert, the boredom of endless rainy days, the penetrating chill of rooms innocent of stoves and fireplaces, the poor hotels, ill-cooked meals, and all the other discomforts of a new, raw land.

As portrayed by Charles Nordhoff and others who wrote at the behest of the railroads, overland travel to California was a pure delight. Compared to "the fierce and rapid rush of an Eastern lightning express," which traveled at the rate of forty miles an hour, the twenty-two-mile clip of the transcontinental lines was "what a gentle and easy amble is to a rough and jolting trot." [2]

To complete the picture, Nordhoff described California as a country in which the hotels were "clean, the beds good, the food abundant and almost always well cooked, and the charges moderate." But a somewhat greater descriptive writer than Nordhoff, a mortally ill wanderer from Scotland named Robert Louis Stevenson, wrote otherwise both of the overland journey and of the so-called "two-bit" hotels of the state, with "the tablecloth checked red and white, the plague of flies, the wire hencoops over the dishes, the great variety and invariable vileness of the food, and the rough, coatless men devouring it in silence." So, too, Stevenson's picture of the hot, crowded, squalid emigrant train crawling across the plains offered a striking contrast to the idealized version of transcontinental travel penned so delightfully by Nordhoff.

But whether in Pullman and palace cars or in comfortless emigrant trains, settlers, tourists, and visitors came in increasing thousands to California, until the influx reached flood proportions. In 1885 more than fifty thousand potential homeseekers visited the state. Two years later, when the Atchison, Topeka, & Santa Fe

---

[2] Nordhoff: *California*, p. 25.

Railroad completed its transcontinental line to Los Angeles, the number of visitors more than doubled.

The opening of the new road marked the beginning of a rate war almost unparalleled in the history of transportation. Fares from Mississippi Valley points to California were reduced, first by one road, then by the other, until for a brief time the rate from Kansas City to Los Angeles was only a dollar. The rush to buy tickets at such bargain prices was enormous.

"Great crowds of people congregated yesterday at the railroad ticket offices," said the Los Angeles *Express* of March 7, 1886, "and the merry war continued with tickets at one's own price. At 9 A.M. the California Southern posted the following bulletin: 'Whoopla! First-class to Kansas City, Deming and El Paso, $15; third-class, $10; Chicago and St. Louis, $17 and $15; New York, $30 and $27.' The Union Pacific retaliated with: 'Down she goes. Lower! Lower!! Lowest!!! Kansas City, $12 and $10; Chicago and St. Louis, $17 and $15; New York, $30 and $27.' The Southern Pacific cut its rates to Chicago to $17 and $15 and later posted a price of $1 to Kansas City, raising later to $10 and $8 with $15 and $13 to Chicago and $28 and $25 to New York. Later the California Southern dropped its prices to Kansas City to $3 and Chicago $7, which the Southern Pacific met with a price of $2 to Kansas City."

As the rate war progressed, the floodgates of publicity were opened even wider. Newspapers, books, brochures, magazines, lectures, and private letters, all added to the deluge. Voluntary promotional organizations, called "state societies," made extensive use of letters and articles in home-town papers to advertise southern California.

The colony method of settlement was used by the Illinois Association; the California Colony of Indiana and the San Gabriel Orange Grove Association, developers of Pasadena; the American Colony that founded Long Beach; and a dozen other similar organizations. The plan was "singularly well adapted to conditions of life in southern California."

As a result of the endless and ingenious publicity lavished on

California, and the consequent influx of thousands of settlers, tourists, and sightseers, the stage was set for the wildest, most spectacular real-estate boom the state has ever known. Centering in southern California, it affected city lands, farm lands, and wastelands alike. Towns were laid out on cattle ranges, sheep ranches, deserts, mountains, and sand hills. Lots were sold in town sites no human eye had ever seen; and investors stood in line to buy business frontages in cities that are still as tenuous and insubstantial as the air.

"The methods of some of these promoters, or 'Escrow Indians,' as they were popularly called, elicited highly uncomplimentary opinions. Guinn states that they were, for the most part, 'fellows who had left their consciences (that is, if they had any to leave) on the other side of the Rockies. These professionals had learned the tricks of their trade in the boom cities of the west when that great wave of immigration which began moving after the close of the war was sweeping westward from the Mississippi River to the shores of the Pacific. These came here not to build up the country, but to make money, honestly, if they could not make it any other way. It is needless to say they made it the other way.'

"Their confident attitude, their suave talk, and their ingratiating manners made otherwise intelligent people gullible. The *Times* classified the newcomers as 'dudes, loafers, paupers, those who expect to astonish the natives, those who are afraid to pull off their coats, cheap politicians, business scrubs, impecunious clerks, lawyers, and doctors.' Nefarious practices, such as hanging oranges on Joshua trees, and then selling desert lots as citrus groves to 'greenhorns,' did not add to their popularity." ³

The boom finally reached such fantastic proportions that Charles Dudley Warner sarcastically remarked: "If the present expectations of transferring half-frozen Eastern and Northern people there by the railway companies and landowners are half realized, Southern California in its whole extent will soon present the appearance of a mass meeting, each individual fighting for a

---

³ Dumke, *op. cit.*, p. 201.

lot and for his perpendicular section of climate." Another commentator wrote: "The average eastern mind conceives of California as a small tract of land situated in and about Los Angeles."

The southern California real-estate boom reached its climax in 1887, hesitated momentarily, then completely collapsed. For a time, like a man who has indulged in a prolonged debauch, the country lay exhausted and befuddled. But the constructive forces, of which the boom was merely an exuberant, undisciplined expression, had laid the secure foundations for a new economic era.

Between 1880 and 1890 the state's population rose from 517,-000 to 1,200,000. For the most part the newcomers were of thrifty, substantial, self-reliant stock, "the bone and sinew of the nation," as the San Francisco *Call* somewhat floridly remarked, "the flower of the American people." They brought with them the decent morals and customs of middle-class Americans, a large amount of capital, and a ready capacity to adapt themselves to the conditions and opportunities of the new land.

Throughout much of the state, indeed, the period marked the development of the third stage in California's agricultural evolution. First had come the pastoral century of grass and cattle; then, for the great inland valleys, at least, the days of the immense grain fields; and lastly, wherever water could be obtained, the era of intensive and diversified farming. Between 1870 and 1890 a series of booms in agricultural products, as well as in real estate, swept over the state. "Silk and cotton furnished the most spectacular examples of such excitement. Starting in an obscure way, the idea that California could be developed into one of the major silk-producing centers of the world rapidly grew into an obsession. At least a score of companies were formed to engage in the venture; newspapers and magazines were filled with articles on the subject; millions of silkworms and larvæ were imported from France and Japan; hundreds of acres were planted to mulberry trees; and the state legislature offered liberal bounties to encourage the experiment."

The boom in cotton during the nineteenth century, at least, never reached the exaggerated proportions to which the silk enthusiasts pushed their campaign; but hundreds of acres, extending from Merced in the north to Riverside in the south, were planted to the crop. Even the city of Los Angeles boasted a plantation of eighty acres. The tract lay north of Jefferson and west of Figueroa, and when the crop matured "the bursting bolls whitened the fields like the snows of winter." The California Cotton Growers and Manufacturers Association acquired ten thousand acres near Bakersfield to plant to cotton. But because of the Association's inability to secure local labor to harvest the crop and the desertion of a Negro colony imported from the South, "the cotton crop went to grass and the cotton growers went into bankruptcy." After the boom died down, cotton was raised in California only in a desultory way until shortly before the outbreak of the first World War. Interestingly enough, since that time the state has become one of the largest cotton-growing centers in the Union.

The cultivation of the navel orange, escaping the fate of the silk and cotton booms, became the most distinctive agricultural development of California during the closing part of the century. The citrus industry had been on a commercial footing in southern California since the early sixties, and by 1875 there were nearly a hundred thousand trees within the state. About five million oranges were shipped annually to San Francisco from the Los Angeles basin; and orchards in full bearing sometimes yielded a profit running as high as a thousand dollars an acre.

Nearly all the early orchards were planted to so-called seedling stock, the original of which came from the trees about the old Franciscan missions. In 1873, however, L. C. Tibbetts of Riverside planted two orange trees of a seedless variety which had been sent from Brazil to the Department of Agriculture in Washington. The Brazilian orange, called the Washington Navel, was so superior in looks, taste, and marketability, and the trees proved so well adapted to California soil and climate, that hundreds of acres were budded over or planted to the new variety. With the opening of the Santa Fe Railroad "there was a veritable boom in orange planting. Some of the returns from these orchards were almost incredible, as much as $3,000 from one acre having been reported, and $800 to $1,000 being no uncommon yield. Of course an industry that would pay such profits was eagerly sought. Land suitable for orchards advanced rapidly in value; other lands advanced collaterally, and it became profitable to subdue them to this purpose. Land companies, irrigation companies, and planting companies were organized with sufficient capital to carry out their schemes, and the whole extent of the country benefited. Unfortunately, the technical demands of the citrus industry were sometimes beyond the abilities of those who entered it, and in some cases the enthusiastic amateur found only bankruptcy instead of the leisure, livelihood, and romance he was looking for.

In 1886 the ranchers and farmers of California were thrown into consternation by a decision of the state Supreme Court upholding the old English common-law doctrine of riparian water rights, and giving to landowners whose property bordered rivers and watercourses the prior use of the waters of such streams. The decision added to the confusion already existing in the irrigation laws of the state, and in most cases benefited the large landowner at the expense of the small farmer. The state irrigation convention, meeting in San Francisco in May, gloomily declared that the application of the doctrine of riparian rights to California would result in a general collapse of agriculture and the ruin of thousands of farmers.

In addition to his many other problems and discouragements, the rancher found himself at the mercy of the railroad, the commission merchant, and the fluctuations of a market over which he had no shadow of control. Learning from costly experience that it was impossible to fight such an alliance single-handed, especially in the lean years of the early nineties when "thousands of statements came from eastern commission houses showing, in red ink, that the fruit consigned to them had been disposed of for less than the amount of the freight and handling charges," citrus-growers of southern California began to form neighborhood exchanges, or associations, through which they could co-operate in solving their common problems. In 1893, under the inspiration of

T. H. B. Chamblin of Pachappa and Riverside, appropriately called the "father of the Exchange," a convention of fruit-growers met in Los Angeles and adopted a plan of district associations which, that same year, resulted in the formation of a sort of federated union among the local exchanges, called the Southern California Fruit Exchange. The organization proved of incalculable benefit to the California citrus ranchers and as the California Fruit Growers Exchange developed into a pattern for agricultural co-operative enterprises throughout the world.

By 1900, according to the federal census reports, the annual value of California farm products was in excess of a hundred and thirty million dollars; and the state's extraordinary progress in agriculture and her seemingly limitless resources had become the monotonous theme song of real-estate promoters, public and semi-public advertising, and the individual California booster. Thanks to climatic conditions, a wide choice of soils, and the substitution of irrigation for variable and capricious rainfall, California's agricultural products were as diversified as her physiography. From her ranches, farms, and ranges came horses, cattle, sheep, wheat, barley, sugar beets, wine, brandy, raisins, oranges, lemons, alfalfa, dairy products, figs, prunes, peaches, other deciduous fruits, almonds, walnuts, poultry, and an endless list of other products.

But though agriculture and land settlement played the major role in California's development between 1880 and the turn of the century, the foundation for the industrial development that has since revolutionized the state's economic and social life was also being laid during those decades. By 1900 "there were 12,500 manufacturing plants in the state, representing an increase of 70% for the decade; capital invested in industrial enterprises was placed at $205,000,000 as against $147,000,000 ten years before; and manufactured products were valued at $303,000,000 or $90,-000,000 more than in 1890. The industries with a minimum annual output of $10,000,000 . . . named in order of importance, were as follows: Sugar and molasses refineries; lumber mills; slaughtering and meat-packing plants; flour-and-grist mills; fruit and vegetable canneries; foundries and machine shops; clothing factories; and printing and publishing establishments." [4]

Two industries, both of which originated prior to 1885, played an especially important part in California's later economic development. In 1882 a Canadian named George Chaffey, who combined a fruitful imagination with unusual engineering ability, initiated an extensive irrigation and land-subdivision enterprise on a part of the old Rancho Cucamonga, a few miles west of San Bernardino. In connection with his water system Chaffey installed a small hydroelectric plant—a little-noticed experiment out of which sprang one of the greatest of modern California industries. Ten years after Chaffey's pioneer development at Etiwanda, the San Antonio Light and Power Company began the transmission of electricity for commercial purposes from a power plant in San Antonio Canyon, north of the present town of Claremont. About the same time the Redlands Electric and Power Company built a station on Mill Creek, in the San Bernardino Mountains; and a year or two later the San Gabriel Light and Power Company erected a much larger plant at the mouth of the San Gabriel Canyon, near Azusa.

These pioneer ventures on the small rivers of southern California prepared the way for exploiting the enormous water power of the Sierra Nevada Mountains. Within a generation after the installation of Chaffey's plant, the streams that Smith, Walker, Ogden, Young, and other Mountain Men once trapped for beaver had been harnessed by modern engineering skill and made to produce electric power for factories, transportation systems, and thousands of homes and farms throughout the state.

In the immense petroleum deposits that underlay so much of her surface, California found another and even greater source of fuel, wealth, and power. Long before the coming of Europeans, the Indians of California used asphaltum, which they obtained from widely distributed oil seepages, to weatherproof their huts,

---

[4] Robert G. Cleland and Osgood Hardy: *March of Industry* (1929), p. 138.

calk their canoes, and make many of their artifacts. The Spanish-Californians, in turn, roofed their adobe houses and sometimes made sidewalks with the same material.

In the mid-fifties Andrés Pico discovered small quantities of petroleum in Pico Canyon (north of the San Fernando Mission), collected the heavy oil in shallow pits as it exuded from the sandy shale, and refined it in a crude still. About the same time a little illuminating oil was produced from the crude petroleum exudations found here and there along the coast between Santa Barbara and Ventura.

The development of petroleum in Pennsylvania, after Colonel Drake's historic discovery at Titusville, started a wave of prospecting in California. In February 1860, the Los Angeles *Star* reported that a San Francisco capitalist was about to establish a "Kerosine Manufactory," for the production of "kerosine," or oil of coal tar, from the abundant supplies of bitumen near Los Angeles. "If the enterprise succeeds," the editor added, "it will be of great moment to our community." For once, at least, a Los Angeles editor's prophecy was to prove a marvel of understatement!

A few years later California had her first oil boom. In many widely separated areas, from Petrolia, in Humboldt County, to the Workman-Rowland Rancho of La Puente, near Los Angeles, speculators were preparing "to embark on the enterprise of penetrating the earth for streams of pure kerosine"; while promoters, speculators, and swindlers were mulcting the public by means of fly-by-night companies, runaway stock markets, and hundred-to-one-shot wildcat wells.

The California Petroleum Company, for example, advertised that it had "Twenty natural oil wells of the largest size," on a tract of land in Santa Barbara County. The property was modestly valued at ten million dollars; and "the spring marked number one on the map" was said to have "144,500,000 gallons of oil actually in sight." The prospectus then pointed out that the development of only ten successful wells on the property would bring the company an annual revenue of nearly five and a half million dollars!

By 1865, when actual production was estimated to be between

forty and fifty thousand gallons, the petroleum boom died down, and pessimists predicted that the industry would never be revived; first, because there was not enough oil in California for commercial production; and, second, because nobody wanted petroleum, or could make profitable use of it, anyway.

But despite such gloomy forebodings the industry managed to survive. The Pioneer Oil Company, organized by a group of prominent Los Angeles citizens, including Phineas Banning, W. S. Hancock, John G. Downey, and B. D. Wilson, undertook to produce oil on a portion of the old pueblo lands, as well as on near-by ranches. Development in Ventura County was carried on by Colonel Thomas Scott of the Pennsylvania Railroad and his able representative, Thomas R. Bard.

Wells at that time were put down with spring-pole rigs, and seldom reached a depth of more than two or three hundred feet. Steam was first used in drilling in 1887. By that time the industry could boast an annual production of nearly sixteen thousand barrels, a few small refineries, and a brisk trade in asphalt (used chiefly for roofs and sidewalks), illuminating oil, and lubricants.

The eighties and nineties witnessed the rise of the petroleum industry to a place of increasing significance in the state's economic life. Instead of a handful of shallow wells, yielding a few hundred gallons of heavy oil a day, persistent wildcatting, coupled with improvements both in apparatus and technique, opened a number of extensive, large producing areas. South of the Tehachapi, the list included the Newhall, Summerland, Fullerton, and Los Angeles–Salt Lake fields; and several small producing districts in Ventura County.

In the late nineties pioneer drillers began to tap the upper strata of the rich deposits of the San Joaquin Valley; and by the opening of the century the Coalinga, McKittrick, Sunset, and Kern River fields had all been discovered. The state was then producing about four million barrels of petroleum annually, and the industry had found an entirely new and ever expanding market in the use of oil for fuel in locomotives and for other heating purposes.

California's economic development during the nineties was broken by several periods of acute depression. Many localities, slowly recovering from the collapse of the real-estate boom of the eighties, were crippled even more severely by the panic of 1893. The failure of the Riverside Banking Company touched off disastrous runs on banks throughout the state and forced financial and mercantile houses of all kinds to close their doors.

Bread lines were opened in the larger cities; public works were authorized by state and local governments to furnish jobs for the army of unemployed; and private citizens were called upon to feed a multitude of hungry and often desperate men, who wandered over the state vainly seeking to find work. In 1894 local units of the celebrated "Coxey's Army" appeared in various parts of California, ostensibly bound for the Capitol in Washington. The "Army" lived rather bountifully off the country through which it passed, and caused a measure of apprehension in the communities along its line of march; but when the ragged company reached the edge of the forbidding Colorado desert, the enthusiasm of many of the crusaders dried up, and they decided to return to the inviting fleshpots and more delectable climate of California.

The disastrous Pullman strike of 1894 also had unfortunate repercussions in many parts of California, paralyzing railroads, causing heavy losses to shippers of perishable goods, bringing additional woes to the farmers, and leading to serious riots and bloodshed in some of the railroad centers. The state's economic ills were greatly accentuated by three years of devastating drought that ruined ranchers and stockmen and caused acute water shortages in many towns and cities.

By the turn of the century, however, the years of depression were almost forgotten, and California faced the coming of a new era, full of confidence and enthusiasm. In five eventful decades, following the Treaty of Guadalupe Hidalgo, the state had developed so rapidly and progressed so far that the days of the ranchos and missions, the stirring events of '49, the period of readjustment after the Gold Rush, and the life of isolation before the coming of the railroad seemed to belong to a distant, almost legendary age.

During that short half-century the march of civilization had changed the frontier from a reality into a tradition; it had converted the waste places into populous cities and transformed cattle and sheep pastures into highly cultivated farms; it had subdued the wilderness and planted an empire by the Western sea. At the beginning of the twentieth century California in truth had become of age—"For the Lord thy God bringeth thee into good land, a land of brooks of water, of fountains and springs, flowing forth out of valleys and hills; a land of wheat and barley, and vines and fig trees and pomegranates; a land of olive trees and honey; a land wherein thou shalt eat bread without scarceness, thou shalt not lack anything in it."

CHAPTER 18. A Preface to California
Literature

ON JUNE 15, 1846, William B. Ide, one of the leaders of the
historic Bear Flag Revolt, issued a proclamation inviting
"all peaceable and good citizens of California" to unite in establishing a republican form of government which should assure civil
and religious liberty, "encourage virtue and literature," and "leave
unshackled by fetters Agriculture, Commerce, and Mechanism."
The proclamation, though couched in peculiar if not grotesque
English, illustrated the fixed, almost universal determination of
the pioneer American settlers of California to perpetuate their
Anglo-Saxon culture, religion, and political traditions on the remote wilderness frontier.

Even before the Gold Rush, California had produced literature
of fair quality. Mention has already been made of the voyage of
the *Lelia Byrd* and the travel account which she partly inspired,
Richard J. Cleveland's *A Narrative of Voyages and Commercial
Enterprises* (1842) which was an outstanding contribution to
knowledge of the American merchant marine in the days of its
glory and of trade contacts with the Pacific Coast. James Ohio
Pattie, fur trader and blazer of the Gila trail to California, wrote
in his *Personal Narrative* (1831) an account of frontier adventure
which contained so much melodrama that it warranted the attention of an editor, the Reverend Timothy Flint, who prepared the
manuscript for publication.

Then, at the top of the literary scale, appeared Richard Henry
Dana's *Two Years Before the Mast* (1840). Dana came from an
intellectual New England family. Having a serious case of mea-
sles during his attendance at Harvard which affected his eye-
sight, he determined to build himself up physically by signing on
as a common seaman aboard the brig *Pilgrim* in 1834. The *Pilgrim*,
fortunately for historians, was engaged in the hide and tallow

trade along the California coast, and Dana participated in this business for sixteen months, enough to give him an authoritative view both of the commerce and the country. His account of the voyage and his descriptions of the land he visited reflected his Harvard training and the literary interests of his family. It is a beautifully written volume, as worthy a contribution to the field of American literature as it is a valuable historical document.

The hide and tallow trade produced another worthwhile volume in Alfred Robinson's *Life in California* (1846). Robinson was an agent for Bryant and Sturgis, merchants engaged in the trade, and he married into the de la Guerra family. His account of California and its citizens during the days of the missions is detailed, sympathetic, and colorful.

The Gold Rush itself, with its immense polyglot, chaotic immigration, gave rise to many striking contrasts and interesting anomalies. The San Francisco of saloons, brothels, gambling houses, crime, lawlessness, vigilance committees, and riotous extravagance was also the San Francisco that founded an Academy of Science, established distinguished public libraries, supported scores of printing and publishing establishments, issued more newspapers than London, and gave birth to at least five magazines of definite literary merit.

This cultural flowering in the boisterous metropolis of the Gold Rush was due to the presence of three congenial elements. In the first place, many of the Argonauts were well-read, well-educated men, and a surprisingly large number had previously had extensive experience as journalists and writers. According to Franklin Walker, wealth and leisure, both the product of the fabulous treasure-chest of the Sierra Nevada Mountains, supplied a second necessary ingredient in the development of California's early literary culture. The life of the period itself, a curious fusion of hardship, drama, humor, tragedy, change, and contrast furnished the third essential element.

Four writers of special note appeared during the decade that began with the Gold Rush. Under the pen name of "Old Block," Alonzo Delano, a forty-niner with a monumental nose and a penchant for misfortune, wrote with realism, wit, and understanding of mines, miners, and the pathos and humor of the diggings. Delano is chiefly remembered for a series of articles in the *Pacific News,* published in book form under the title, *Chips from the Old Block,* and *Old Block's Sketch Book;* and for an authentic account of the Gold Rush called *Life on the Plains and among the Diggings.*

A second writer of distinction during the fifties was Louisa Amelia Knapp Smith, "a small, fair, golden-haired blue-stocking from New England." This "dainty adventurer with a sturdy soul," wrote under the pen name of Dame Shirley. For vividness and charm, "Dame Shirley's" descriptions of the mines have never been surpassed.

Lieutenant George H. Derby today is merely a name in the archives of the United States Navy. But John Phoenix, Derby's alter ego, was California's favorite wit, punster, satirist, and perpetrator of extravagant and preposterous hoaxes from the time of his arrival on the coast in 1849 until he left seven years later to build lighthouses on the Gulf and subsequently die of the effects of sunstroke. Derby enriched American humor by the *Squibob Papers* and *Phœnixiana.*

John Rollin Ridge was a Cherokee Cavalier. His father, a full-blooded Cherokee, was a man of wealth and culture, and his mother, Sarah Northrup Ridge, the daughter of a New England schoolteacher, "dressed in silk every day" and had a retinue of seventeen personal servants. After the Cherokees removed to the Indian lands beyond the Mississippi, John Rollin's father and grandfather were both assassinated by a rival tribal faction, and the boy grew to manhood dominated by his people's traditional thirst for revenge.

After participating in the blood feud that cost his father's life, Ridge fled to California, where he remained, an exile from the Cherokee Nation, until his death of a brain malady in Grass Valley in 1867. During his years in California, Ridge wrote the life of the famous bandit, Joaquin Murrieta; published numerous poems and verse under the name of "Yellow Bird"; and after

Lincoln's election became one of the best-known of the pro-Confederate newspaper editors in the northern part of the state.

During the interval between the Gold Rush and the close of the Civil War numerous literary magazines appeared on the California horizon, climbed with varying success toward the zenith, and eventually plunged into bankruptcy and oblivion. Some of these journals, such as the *Golden Era, Hutchings' California Magazine,* the *Pioneer,* and *Hesperian,* were nearly equal in quality to contemporary Eastern journals and testified to both the educational background of their editors and the discriminating literary taste of the California reading public.

The most distinguished of all California magazines, the *Overland Monthly,* made its appearance in July 1868. According to the caption on the first page, the *Overland* was "Devoted to the Development of the Country," and the economic historian still turns with gratitude to the many scholarly articles on California sheep-raising, orange culture, irrigation, mining, Chinese labor, and a score of kindred subjects which appeared in successive numbers of this distinguished journal.

But the lasting significance of the *Overland* rests not so much upon its contributions to our knowledge of the social and economic aspects of the state's development as upon the literary quality of the stories, poems, and articles that it brought to its readers and preserved for subsequent generations. The Golden Age of California letters was created by authors whose names appeared in the table of contents of the first numbers of the celebrated *Overland.* Francis Bret Harte served as editor of the magazine during its first and most distinguished years and also enriched its columns by a score of poems and such popular tales as "The Luck of Roaring Camp," "Tennessee's Partner," and "The Outcasts of Poker Flat."

Bret Harte owes whatever measure of literary renown his name enjoys to the Gold Rush and the California it created. His tales of the Sierra mining camps are well done and widely read; but when, all too eagerly, he shook the dust of California from his feet and hastened east to edit the *Atlantic,* he left his creative ability and popularity behind. Thereafter his talent traveled on halting feet, or, as he wrote to his wife and children from London: "I grind out the old tunes on the old organ, and gather up the coppers." Indirectly, by his influence upon such authors as Mark Twain, Ina Coolbrith, and others of the Golden Age, Harte perhaps contributed as much to California literature as through the medium of his own writings.

Charles Warren Stoddard, Prentice Mulford, Bayard Taylor, Bishop Kip, first Episcopal Bishop of California, Ina Coolbrith, the one authentic poet laureate of the state, and Henry George, sponsor of the theory of the Single Tax, were all members of the *Overland* fellowship.

Sometime seaman, steward, prospector, typesetter, day laborer, filibusterer, newspaper reporter, journalist, pamphleteer, economic theorist, social crusader, Henry George acquired his greatest fame as the author of *Progress and Poverty*, by long odds the most widely and persistently read book on an economic subject yet written in the United States.

Later writers for the *Overland* included Joaquin (or Cincinnatus Heine) Miller, John Muir, Clarence King, and Stephen Powers. Powers was an ethnologist of note who walked from Raleigh, North Carolina, to San Francisco in 1868, and wrote vivid descriptions of people, places, and experiences, under the curious pen name of "Mr. Socrates Hyacinth."

An occasional contributor to the *Overland*, and now the foremost name in the Golden Age of California letters, was an obscure journalist, unsuccessful prospector, mining-stock speculator, and semi-vagabond named Samuel Clemens. In the robust life of Virginia City, then virtually a part of California, and later in San Francisco, to which he inevitably found his way from the rough trails and rougher experiences of the Nevada silver mines, Mark Twain's genius found both the freedom and inspiration necessary for its gorgeous flowering. His immortal humor, his vivid power of description, his sure knowledge of human nature, his contempt for quackery and humbug, all bear the stamp of the Far West of the post-Gold-Rush days. *Roughing It* and *The Celebrated Jump-*

ing Frog of Calaveras County are typical products of Samuel Clemens's Nevada-California life; but the influence of those days and of his unconventional life in "the land of the large and charitable air" is stamped upon all his lasting literary works.

Mark Twain's humor is the humor of the West, a contrasting mixture of gross exaggeration and supreme understatement, at once "whimsical and bombastic," a product of the elemental democracy of the Nevada mining camps and the untrammeled tolerance and individuality of the San Francisco in which Mark sojourned for a few brief years. It was in the West of the pre-railroad era that Mark Twain learned "to make the common people laugh." [1]

Joaquin Miller, though read much less today than either Mark Twain or Bret Harte, had a large following three quarters of a century ago. He was an eccentric extrovert, with unlimited enthusiasm, who resorted to the baldest, most extravagant publicity stunts to attract attention. Walker says that at his first meal in San Francisco he ordered only a toothpick and a glass of water. In London he attended fashionable dinners dressed in the typical miner's outfit—sombrero, red flannel shirt, coarse pantaloons, cowhide boots; and sometimes a war-whoop marked his entrance into a drawing-room. Such outlandish mannerisms, Miller explained, helped to sell his poetry and "tickled the duchesses."

Late in the eighties Miller brought a tract of land, which he named "The Hights," in the hills overlooking Oakland. There he built monuments to Moses, John C. Frémont, and Robert Browning and erected a funeral pyre for himself. But with all his peculiarities and conceit, Miller was a true lover of California, and his best-known book of poems, *Songs of the Sierras,* still merits a place in American verse.

The California mountains provided the inspiration for many other writers of this early period. Clarence King, a man of un-

---

[1] One would have to stretch the possessive instinct too far to claim a place for Robert Louis Stevenson on the list of California authors. His stay in the state was altogether too brief and casual and the California influence on his writings too imperceptible to justify such presumption.

usual versatility who later organized the United States Geological Survey, put all nature-lovers deeply in his debt by a small volume entitled *Mountaineering in the Sierra Nevada*. In one of his chapters a heavy snowstorm in the Yosemite Valley is broken by this interlude of beauty:

The luminous cloud-bank in the east rolled from the last Sierra crest, leaving the whole chain of peaks in broad light, each rocky crest strongly red, the newly fallen snow marbling them over with a soft, deep rose; and, wherever a cañon carved itself down their rocky fronts, its course was traceable by a shadowy band of blue. The middle distance glowed with a tint of golden yellow; the broken heights along the cañon-brinks and edges of the cliff in front were of an intense spotless white. Far below us the cloud stratum melted away, revealing the floor of the valley, whose russet and emerald and brown and red burned in the broad evening sun. It was a marvellous piece of contrasted lights,—the distance so pure, so soft in its rosy warmth, so cool in the depth of its shadowy blue; the foreground strong in fiery orange, or sparkling in absolute whiteness. I enjoyed, too, looking up at the pure unclouded sky, which now wore an aspect of intense serenity. For half an hour nature seemed in entire repose; not a breath of wind stirred the white snow-laden shafts of the trees; not a sound of animate creature, or the most distant reverberation of waterfall reached us; no film of vapour moved across the tranquil sapphire sky; absolute quiet reigned until a loud roar proceeding from Capitan turned our eyes in that direction. From the round, domelike cap of its summit there moved down an avalanche, gathering volume and swiftness as it rushed to the brink, and then, leaping out two or three hundred feet into space, fell, slowly filtering down through the lighted air, like a silver cloud, until within a thousand feet of the earth it floated into the shadow of the cliff and sank to the ground as a faint blue mist.[2]

William H. Brewer, a noted scientist whose name is borne by one of the highest of the Sierra peaks, wrote a series of extraordinary letters describing life and scenes in California during the early sixties. The letters were published in 1930 under the title: *Up and Down California in 1860–1864*, and the book promises to

---

[2] *Mountaineering in the Sierra Nevada* (1872), p. 163.

become almost as much of a classic in its field as Dana's *Two Years before the Mast*. Brewer's skill in description is illustrated by his picture of a drought-cursed ranch in the wind-swept valley of the San Joaquin:

As we cross the summit the Sierra Nevada should be in view, with its sharp outline and cool snows; but not so—we look out on the dry plain, which becomes more indistinct and finally fades away into the hazy air, shutting out like a veil all that lies beyond. The wind blows heavily over the pass, and we descend to the San Luis Ranch. The wind is so high that we can build no fire, so we cook in the dirty kitchen. Dust fills the air—often we cannot see fifty yards in any direction—it covers everything. We cook our dinner, but before it can be eaten we cannot tell its color because of the dirt that settles on it. Our food is gritty between our teeth, and as we drink out our cups of tea we find a deposit of fine sand in the bottom. Dirt, dirt, dirt—eyes full, face dirty, whole person feeling dirty and gritty.

All around the house it looks desolate. Where there were green pastures when we camped here two years ago, now all is dry, dusty, bare ground. Three hundred cattle have died by the miserable water hole back of the house, where we get water to drink, and their stench pollutes the air.

This ranch contains eleven square leagues, or over seventy-six square miles. In its better days it had ten thousand head of cattle, besides the horses needed to manage them. Later it became a sheep ranch, and two years ago, when we camped here, it fed sixteen thousand sheep besides some few thousand cattle. Now, owing to the drought, there is no feed for cattle, and not over one thousand sheep, if that, can be kept through the summer. The last of the cattle, about one thousand head, were lately sold for $1,500, or only $1.50 each! Such is the effect of the drought on one ranch.[3]

Though many others wrote of the California mountains, the name of John Muir is probably the most beloved among the devotees of the great Sierra Nevada range. Of Scotch Covenanter ancestry, with heather in him, as he said, and a solution of bog juices in his veins, this "wiry young man with auburn hair," who

---

[3] William H. Brewer: *Up and Down California, 1860–1864*, pp. 508–9.

memorized the New Testament from St. Matthew to Revelation, seemed to feel neither cold, heat, hunger, nor fatigue. He would live for a week in the mountains on raisins, bread, and tea, and often slept without blankets at the highest altitudes, content to lie between deep snowbanks in the lee of some granite boulder, even when the nights crackled with cold and the water froze in the rivulets.

Muir made himself an authority on the geology and botany of the Sierra; but his fame rests primarily on his passionate love of the grandeur and silence and wild beauty of the great range, on his ability to awaken that love in other hearts, and on his successful crusade to save the forests for future generations.

In addition to a score of magazine articles, Muir wrote at least ten books, including *The Mountains of California, The Yosemite,* and *My First Summer in the Sierra.* Muir Woods, near Mill Valley, and the Muir Trail, between the Yosemite and Mount Whitney, are fitting memorials to one who taught the people of California to appreciate their heritage of forests and mountains and virgin solitudes. Muir's facility of description is seen in the following typical passage:

Looking eastward from the summit of the Pacheco Pass one shining morning, a landscape was displayed that after all my wanderings still appears as the most beautiful I have ever beheld. At my feet lay the Great Central Valley of California, level and flowery, like a lake of pure sunshine, forty or fifty miles wide, five hundred miles long, one rich furred garden of yellow *Compositæ.* And from the eastern boundary of this vast golden flower-bed rose the mighty Sierra, miles in height, and so gloriously colored and so radiant, it seemed not clothed with light, but wholly composed of it, like the wall of some celestial city. Along the top and extending a good way down, was a rich pearl-gray belt of snow; below it a belt of blue and dark purple, marking the extension of the forests; and stretching along the base of the range a broad belt of rose-purple; all these colors, from the blue sky to the yellow valley smoothly blending as they do in a rainbow, making a wall of light ineffably fine. Then it seemed to me that the Sierra should be called, not the Nevada or Snowy Range, but the Range of Light. And after ten years of wandering and wondering in the heart of it, rejoicing in its glorious floods of light, the white beams of the morning streaming through the passes, the noonday radiance on the crystal rocks, the flush of the alpenglow, and the irised spray of countless waterfalls, it still seems above all others the Range of Light.[4]

The contrast between John Muir and Ambrose Bierce, his contemporary, is as striking as the contrast between the shining mountains Muir so joyously described and the dead, poisonous, strangely fascinating salt pools of Death Valley. Like Edgar Allan Poe, Ambrose Bierce is popularly known today for his tales of mystery and horror. But to his contemporaries he was primarily a journalist whose biting phrases and bitter sarcasm lacerated his victim's feelings and too often despoiled his reputation. If living today, Bierce would stand unchallenged as the nation's most famous, effective, and dreaded columnist. More than any other journalist of his generation, Bierce filled the role of gadfly, and while one writer styles him "the bitterest American that ever lived," another says: "if his name lives, it is within the range of probabilities that it will be as a tradition of wit, courage, and decency." [5]

Bierce reached California in the late sixties and made his journalistic debut as the "Town Crier" in the San Francisco *News Letter*. A few months later he became editor of the journal and served in that capacity for four years. Next he went to London, to become both an extreme Anglophile and, to some degree, a frustrated snob. Returning to San Francisco, determined, as he said, "to purify journalism in this town by instructing such writers as it is worth while to instruct, and assassinating those that it is not," Bierce contributed his vitriolic columns first to the *Wasp* and later to the *Argonaut,* journals that then had both originality and influence. He was feared profoundly, and with good cause; he was hated venomously, and was popularly known as "the wickedest man in San Francisco."

In 1887 Bierce began to write a column called "Prattle" for the editorial page of Hearst's *Examiner*. His association with Hearst

---

[4] John Muir: *The Yosemite* (1912), pp. 5–6.
[5] Carey McWilliams: *Ambrose Bierce* (1929), p. 335.

continued from 1887 to 1913, and his caustic pen played a large part in defeating Collis P. Huntington's attempt to pass the Central Pacific refunding bill in Congress in the mid-nineties. In addition to his political contributions, Bierce established his reputation as the foremost American writer of his time in the literature of mystery, horror, and suspense. He became, in his own eyes at least, "the literary dictator" of the Pacific coast, and profoundly influenced such writers as Ina Coolbrith, Edwin Markham, George Sterling, and Joaquin Miller. Perhaps his best known work is *The Cynic's Word Book* (1906) later republished (1911) as *The Devil's Dictionary.*

Bierce's death is still surrounded by mystery and speculation. Old, frustrated, and disillusioned, he left San Francisco in 1913 to join the Mexican outlaw Pancho Villa, and disappeared in the wild no-man's land of northern Mexico. There, whether before a firing squad or in some less violent fashion, he escaped into the "good, kind darkness" he sought so earnestly and long. Bierce's philosophy was embodied in two sentences: "Do not write about ignoble persons"; "Do not trust humanity without collateral security; it will play you some scurvy trick."

The last quarter of the nineteenth century witnessed the rise of a school of California historians who found the chronicles of the state a treasure-house of almost inexhaustible richness and variety and rendered invaluable service to all subsequent writers in the field.

Theodore H. Hittell, a San Francisco lawyer, was the initial member of the group. He brought to his task remarkable capacity for research, sound and discriminating judgment, and an unusual measure of literary skill. His four-volume *History of California* is consequently a standard reference work for the scholar and the best-written comprehensive history of the state yet to appear in print.

While Hittell was still in the ground-breaking stage of his important work, a fellow San Franciscan, Hubert Howe Bancroft, merchant, bookseller, and publisher, embarked upon a literary venture that far exceeded in objective and magnitude any similar undertaking of any other American writer. Gathering together a monumental collection of books, pamphlets, manuscripts, and official documents, Bancroft organized a corps of clerks, secretaries, and obscure authors to compile and write a series of histories of the Pacific coast. This "factory system of production" yielded thirty-nine large volumes, seven of which relate specifically to California. As literature, the books that bear Bancroft's name are inferior; as history, they violate many of the canons of sound scholarship; as reference and source books they remain the starting-point of all subsequent histories of the state.

Like Hittell and Bancroft, but on a much less ambitious scale, Charles Howard Shinn, who wrote of the mines and miners of the Gold Rush with understanding born of personal experience, and Josiah Royce, who interpreted society more as philosopher and moralist than as historian, made lasting contributions to the social and economic history of the beginnings of the state.

About the time of these historians, California literature began to sound a note of protest against the economic ills and social callousness of the day. Henry George's *Progress and Poverty*, as already noted, offered the single tax as the one great panacea for society's innumerable evils and maladjustments.

The deplorable condition of the California Indians, the tragic victims of society's conspicuous injustice and neglect, provided the motive of Helen Hunt Jackson's widely read *Ramona*. The novel is not great literature, and no charity of judgment can make it such, but the lapse of more than half a century has not extinguished its popularity nor retired it from the list of California classics. Mrs. Jackson came of an academic family and first visited California in 1872, where she gathered material for a series of descriptive sketches. She married a Colorado businessman and became interested in the plight of the American Indian and his relations with the government. Indignant at what she had discovered, she published *A Century of Dishonor* in 1881, which was an indictment of federal Indian policy. She returned to California to do some magazine articles, and there became interested specifically in the California Indian. The result was a novel, *Ramona*, which, like Harriet Beecher Stowe's *Uncle Tom's Cabin*, was not a literary highlight, but became a best-seller because of its overdone theme. She painted her picture with broad strokes, peopling her pages with stereotypes, and the social accuracy of her portrayal was not high. Yet the book struck a responsive chord in the hearts of the American people, and even today the Ramona Pageant at Hemet and "Ramona's Marriage Place" at San Diego remind Californians of the impact of Mrs. Jackson's work.

In 1899 a California writer, who as a boy had lived on a farm, worked in a blacksmith shop, and herded cattle and sheep, voiced his warning against society's "immemorial infamies, perfidious wrongs." The writer was Edwin Markham; the protest was called "The Man with the Hoe"; the poem was destined for immortality. Translated into some forty languages and reprinted in over fifty thousand newspapers, Markham's prophetic verses far exceeded all other California poems in popularity and influence. "Lincoln," next to "The Man with the Hoe" Markham's chief contribution to American literature, was fittingly chosen for the dedication of the immortal Lincoln Memorial in Washington.

The close of the century marked the beginning of the tragically brief literary career of Frank Norris, one of the most promising of California novelists. In contrast with Edwin Markham, who knew only the narrow horizons of a poor country boyhood, Norris enjoyed educational and cultural opportunities of exceptional scope. Son of a prosperous Chicago jeweler and a mother who was both teacher and actress, he studied art in Paris and London and afterward attended Harvard and the University of California. In the mid-nineties he went to South Africa to represent the San Francisco *Chronicle* and fell into the hands of the Boers when Dr. Jameson made his ill-timed raid.

In 1898 and 1899 Norris wrote three novels—*Moran of the Lady Letty*, *McTeague*, and *Blix*—which attracted national attention. These were followed by *The Octopus*, the first of three carefully planned works in which Norris proposed to write the epic story of California wheat. *The Octopus* describes the wheat boom in the San Joaquin Valley during the disturbed seventies and tells the story of the struggle between the settlers and the Southern Pacific Railroad, which culminated in the historic and bloody gun battle of Mussel Slough. *The Pit,* Norris's second contribution to the trilogy, was published posthumously in 1903. The volume is built around the speculation, intrigue, and ruthless competition that characterized the wheat market before the government undertook to restrain its most vicious practices, in the days when neither the law of God nor that of man materially inconvenienced the activities of the Chicago Board of Trade. In *The Wolf,* the last of the contemplated series, Norris proposed to portray the want, tragedy, and cruelty that brutalize and destroy the masses in a famine-stricken country. In the hands of the gifted and maturing writer, the potentialities of such a novel were enormous; but death prematurely intervened before Norris was able to bring his purpose to fruition. Many of today's literary critics consider *McTeague* his best novel.

Three years before Norris ushered in a new era in California literature with *The Octopus,* an unknown writer named Jack London sold his first story to the *Overland Monthly* for five dollars. When he began his literary career, London, like Shakespeare's famous contemporary Robert Greene, was "young in years but old in wickedness." Born in 1876 of an illegitimate union, London became "a figure impossible save in the California of the opening decade of the twentieth century. His family, both sides of it, was of old American stock; English adventurers with a dash of Puritanism, Welsh settlers in New Jersey, Teutonic refugees in Pennsylvania, the most restless soul of a restless age." [6]

London grew to manhood a rebel in both philosophy and action against the precepts and restraints of conventional society—an Ishmaelite of the stews and waterfront, whose hand was against every man as every man's hand was against him. While attending grammar school in Oakland, the boy delivered newspapers, rode an ice wagon, and worked in a bowling alley and a cannery.

---

[6] Fred Lewis Pattee: *Side-Lights on American Literature* (1922), p. 102.

At fourteen his boon companions were a runaway sailor and a drunken harpooner on an opium-smuggling yacht in San Francisco Bay.

At fifteen London mated with a girl as lawless and reckless as himself, and the two became known as the "Queen and Prince of the Oyster Pirates." During the next few years the young vagabond served as deputy in the fish patrol, worked in a jute mill, lived as tramp, sealer, able-bodied seaman, and boat puller, and served a brief jail or prison sentence. His experiences, especially as a hobo, brought him, in his own words, into "the pit, the abyss, the human cesspool, the shambles, and the charnel house of our civilization."

Determined to obtain an education, London studied nineteen hours a day to pass the University of California entrance examinations; but after spending part of a year in the uncongenial atmosphere of the campus and lecture room, the new recruit left the university, restless and dissatisfied, to train himself as a novelist and story-writer. The following summer he joined the mad rush to the Klondike; and there the cold, savage realism of the north gave him material for his first literary triumphs.

"An Odyssey of the North," which appeared in the *Atlantic Monthly* in 1900, marked London's real beginning as an author. During the following sixteen years he wrote nineteen complete novels, one hundred and fifty-two stories, three plays, and eight sociological or autobiographical volumes. In his writings London has appropriately been called a stark realist, a brutal exponent of the "cult of the primitive," and a "master of swift and vivid action and adventure"; or, as another critic says, "Everything in his life watered and fertilized the wild individualism that was his birthright." [7] Restless, untamed warped and scarred in spirit by a boyhood denied all tenderness and decency and beauty, self-confident or conceited far beyond the capacity of normal men, harassed by a demon within and forever tormented by the world of poverty and injustice and inequality without, "not once in his

---

[7] *Ibid.*, p. 102.

forty-one years did Jack London look on life with quiet eyes, nor did he ever know the meaning of tranquil happiness." [8]

London was both a teller of tales and a passionate social crusader. His *Call of the Wild* and *The Sea Wolf* unquestionably rank with the greatest of American stories; but it is possible that the influence of his social writings will establish his fame more securely in the tumultuous realm of modern world history than among the literary figures of his own land.

While Jack London was burning himself out in feverish writing and unbridled dissipation, many lesser authors, some of whom at times skirted the edge of genius, were enriching the literary tradition of the state. This list included Mary Austin, sometime resident of the mountain-girt Owens Valley, the artists' village of Carmel, a lonely convent in Italy, New York City, and the ancient Spanish capital of Santa Fe, New Mexico, who ran almost the full gamut of the literary scale. A mystic, transcendentalist, and militant feminist, Mrs. Austin turned her prolific pen to novels, poetry, social and political essays, and nature writing. Much of her product, the verbose expression of "arrogant faith in her own intuitions," was abstract, difficult to read, and of little philosophical or literary value. But when she wrote of nature, Mary Austin passed into a different realm. There she employed a keen faculty of observation and "a spiritual perception which placed her in the tradition of Thoreau and John Muir." She became, in Edwin Markham's phrase, "the exquisite interpreter of the desert and the Indian." "Without glorification, with frugal epithet," he continues, "she makes her shepherd, her prospector, her derelict men and women stand out sharply individualized, human, important. Her own poetry of desert and mesa and her transcription of Indian poetry, are also of the spirit and substance of far places." [9]

Margaret Collier Graham was a member of the family which subdivided the Lake Elsinore region, and she may be the one who

---

[8] Joseph Noel: *Footloose in Arcadia* (1940), p. 266.

[9] Edwin Markham: *Songs and Stories* (1929), p. 17. The published works of Mary Austin include thirty-two volumes and over two hundred magazine articles.

named the town of Wildomar from the names of the family partners, William Collier, Donald Graham, and Margaret Graham. She wrote short stories and conducted a column for the *Land of Sunshine* entitled "The Angle of Reflection." Her work was gentle, highly polished, and reflective of the rural life of southern California during the 1890's and its effect upon the character of typical settlers. Her stories appeared regularly in *Harper's* and *The Atlantic Monthly* and were later published under the titles *Stories of the Foot-hills* (1895) and *The Wizard's Daughter and Other Stories* (1905). Never widely popular, Mrs. Graham nevertheless contributed a gentle finesse and a literary gloss to California writing which helped to mark its developing maturity.

CHAPTER 19. Turn of the Century

JOHN BIDWELL, the moving spirit in the historic emigrant
company of 1841, lived nearly sixty useful and distinguished
years in the land of his adoption. When he arrived, there was a
thin line of pueblos and ranchos along the coast, and Sutter's
newly established fort on the Sacramento, but California itself
was a vast wilderness, a "wild, wide wasteland," of almost terrifying distances and unexplored solitudes. The country's few Spanish-Mexican inhabitants were an unsophisticated people of simple
customs and pastoral habits, who limited their economic activities to cattle-raising and bartered hides and tallow for merchandise of foreign manufacture. When he died, in the spring of
1900, the American frontier had long since disappeared, the "Far
West" was only a nostalgic tradition, and the thinly inhabited
Mexican province of his adventurous youth had become a great
American commonwealth, boasting a population of 1,500,000, ri-
valing the wealthiest of other states in agricultural production
and variety of natural resources, and confounding even the most
sanguine of the prophets by the rapidity of its development.

With typical California enthusiasm, the annual report of the
San Francisco Chamber of Commerce at the beginning of the
new century listed some of the tangible evidences of this material
progress: annual exports and imports, $76,000,000; gold pro-
duction, $15,000,000; wheat and barley crops, 30,000,000 and 20,-
000,000 bushels respectively; orange and lemon shipments, 24,000
cars; wines and brandies, 18,000,000 gallons; petroleum, 9,000,000
barrels. Three great railroads then linked California with the
Mississippi Valley; and, according to the London *Telegraph*, the
$20,000,000 recently set aside for the foundation and endowment
of Stanford University represented a benefaction for education
"unparalleled for magnitude in the history of mankind."

John Bidwell's life in California, as already suggested, spanned
the unbelievable gulf between the Mexican cattle frontier of the

primitive 1840's and the amazing California that greeted the opening of the new century. But the incredible changes Bidwell witnessed in the half century between the Treaty of Guadalupe Hidalgo and the close of the Spanish-American War were actually surpassed by the even more incredible changes that took place in California between Bidwell's death and the opening of the second World War.

In 1900 it was evident that California was entering upon a new era. The hesitancy and depression of the mid-nineties were over. Population was steadily increasing. Bank clearings had risen seventy-four per cent in three years. The state's basic industries—agriculture, manufacturing, shipping, lumbering, and mining—were expanding in both variety and volume. A rapidly growing demand for petroleum was stimulated in part by the use of fuel oil by the railroads, and the continued discovery of new fields in central and southern California promised to add another major industry to the state's prodigal resources. Similarly the success of a few tentative experiments gave weight to the prediction that hydroelectric power would eventually provide at least a partial substitute for California's basic lack of coal.

The awakening of the Far East, the annexation of Hawaii, and the acquisition of the Philippines during the closing years of the nineteenth century, opened unprecedented opportunities for the expansion of California shipping and Pacific trade. The Panama Canal, construction of which was finally begun in 1903, promised to benefit the state almost as much as the opening of railroad traffic had benefited it in 1869. Southern California felt the stimulus of the development of Imperial Valley, the assurance of the Owens River aqueduct, the beginning of the deep-water harbor at San Pedro, the revolution in local transportation brought about by the radiating lines of Henry E. Huntington's Pacific Electric Railway, and the inauguration of direct traffic with the Great Basin by means of Senator W. A. Clark's Los Angeles, San Pedro & Salt Lake Railroad.

Interestingly enough, four of the most revolutionary factors in the development of modern California were looked upon as passing fads or little more than scientific curiosities at the opening of the century. In 1896 Marconi took out his first English patent for wireless telegraphy. As late as 1903 the motion-picture industry was represented in California by a glorified Los Angeles peep show, known as Tally's Phonograph and Vitascope Parlor. In December 1903, the *Virginia Pilot* described the epic flight of the Wright brothers at Kitty Hawk, North Carolina; and in the same year an automobile made the first motor trip across the continent. It is impossible to conceive of the California we know today without the radio, motion picture, automobile, and airplane. But what prophet, gazing down the decades from the vantage point of 1900, could foresee the revolutionary effect that these four inventions would exert upon the future he was seeking to envision?

Within the state itself, at the turn of the century, the political, economic, and cultural center of gravity seemed permanently fixed in San Francisco, and the supremacy in those fields which the northern city had enjoyed for fifty years promised to remain as unchallenged in the future as it had been in the past. According to the federal census, San Francisco then had a population of 342,000 and ranked as the ninth city in size in the United States. Los Angeles, her nearest competitor, had only 103,000 inhabitants and stood twenty-sixth among American cities.

The contrast in tradition, psychology, and prestige between the two communities, furthermore, was even more marked than their disparity in population and economic importance. Los Angeles, half city, half sprawling, overgrown town, though no longer dubbed the Queen of the Cow Counties, had not yet acquired true metropolitan stature, maturity, or self-assurance; and her chief resources—climate, oranges, tourists, and a few newly opened oil fields—were scarcely adequate foundation upon which to contemplate the erection of a great city.

San Francisco, on the other hand, "the future seat and center of the world's commerce," had long since become cosmopolitan, urbane, world-renowned. Writers pointed out that China's patient and industrious four hundred millions, the vast reaches of Siberia, even then on the eve of a great awakening, and the island empire of Japan were ready and waiting to become the city's "peaceful spoils." If London, in half a century, had increased her population from a million and a half to five millions, asked one San Francisco enthusiast, "what shall not be done by this young giant of the West in whose veins the best blood of all the finest races in the world commingles?"

Unfortunately, along with her many outstanding advantages, San Francisco had inherited a few equally notable liabilities. Chief of these was a tradition of corrupt politics that originated in the days of the Gold Rush, found dramatic expression in the Vigilance Committees of 1851 and 1856, and culminated a generation later in the shameful rule of the "Blind Boss," Chris Buckley. A few years after Buckley's death a new regime even more efficient and spectacular in its prostitution of the city's government came into power in San Francisco. The city's dominant position in the state made its political humiliation the West Coast counterpart of New York's infamous Tweed Ring.

In 1898 James D. Phelan was elected Mayor of San Francisco. Phelan was wealthy, socially prominent, and highly respected. During his administration the people adopted a charter that gave the Mayor almost autocratic powers, permitted the city to own and operate public utilities, made municipal franchises subject to the initiative and referendum, and vested legislative control in a board of eighteen supervisors.

The voter's faith in the efficacy of the new charter to provide a panacea for the city's ills was naïvely optimistic, and the era of good government proved disappointingly shortlived. Beginning in 1900 a series of ugly labor disputes disrupted the industrial and business life of the city and at times paralyzed all shipping in the harbor. The farmers of northern California were especially hard hit by the resultant embargo on the movement of crops and developed a community of interest with the San Francisco employers against the demands and practices of organized labor.

The struggle between capital and labor organizations reached a climax during the summer of 1901 when the powerful Employers' Association, uncompromisingly hostile to organized labor, determined to break the unions' control in San Francisco and engaged in a war to the finish with the combination of waterfront unions known as the City Front Federation. The ensuing struggle degenerated into a brutal dog-eat-dog affair in which both labor and capital sought to destroy each other, regardless of the effect of the conflict upon either themselves or the community at large. In the end the Employers' Association broke the strike and successfully maintained the principle of the open shop for its members. This result was achieved primarily by the use of a huge war chest and Mayor Phelan's active suppression of violence by means of the San Francisco police.

The defeated labor unions deeply resented Phelan's attitude and bitterly complained "of the shooting and clubbing of strikers, the wholesale arrests of hundreds of inoffensive men, the surrender of the entire police force to the Employers' Association, the employment of special policemen, and the call of Police Commissioner Newhall for the National Guard." On the basis of these charges, the unions determined to organize their own political party and gain control of the city government.

The Union Labor Party, as the new organization was named, lacked the support of some of the more powerful branches of organized labor, notably those in the building trades, but in the November election it placed its candidate, a former professional musician named Eugene E. Schmitz, in the mayor's office. Schmitz succeeded himself two years later and won the election again in 1905 by a still larger majority.

During the new regime, politics in San Francisco reached an all-time high-water mark for venality and corruption. Schmitz was called "the smallest man mentally and the meanest man morally that ever occupied the Mayor's chair." For five years the city's real overlord was Abraham Ruef, a shrewd, capable, unscrupulous attorney, whom a writer in *Harper's Weekly* described as "a very little lawyer with curly black hair, shifty black eyes, an excellent mind, great political ambition, and boundless avarice." [1] Speaking even more bluntly, according to its custom, the Los Angeles *Times* said that Ruef was "as watchful of his acts as a prowling coyote, and as skillful at covering up his tracks as a prowling Indian." [2]

The Ruef-Schmitz combination began the prostitution of the city government as soon as Schmitz came into power. In a short time the tie-up between the mayor's office and the underworld became notorious; and during Schmitz's second administration a grand jury reported "that every branch of the executive department was honeycombed with corruption." After the overwhelming victory of the Union Labor Party in the election of 1905, the machine threw restraint to the winds and proceeded to exact tribute from reputable business houses and corporations as well as from all other usual sources of graft in a dishonestly governed city.

In earlier years, when political conditions became intolerable, San Francisco had been in the habit of forming vigilance committees, which acted either within or without the law as circumstances required, to give the city a thorough house-cleaning. Something of this nature was perhaps in the minds of the three men who finally initiated an all-out attack on the Ruef-Schmitz machine. The triumvirate was composed of Fremont Older, the pugnacious and publicity-minded editor of the San Francisco *Bulletin;* Rudolph Spreckels, member of an old California family and wealthy businessman and landowner in his own right; and James D. Phelan, the distinguished Mayor who preceded Schmitz. Older succeeded in enlisting the militant support of President Theodore Roosevelt and through his good offices obtained the services of William J. Burns, a detective of rising fame in the United States Secret Service, and of Francis J. Heney, an attorney who was then concluding the government's successful prosecution of certain notorious timber-land frauds in the Northwest.

---

[1] William Inglis: "For the Kingdom of California," *Harper's Weekly,* May 23, 1908.
[2] Issue of November 22, 1908.

Before the graft investigation could be fully launched, however, the earthquake and fire of April 18, 1906, laid waste a large part of San Francisco and threw the normal life of the city into temporary chaos. In the midst of the disaster Schmitz displayed unexpected initiative and leadership, but when the emergency was over, he and Ruef resumed their corrupt activities and found still larger opportunities for graft in the rehabilitation and restoration of the stricken city.

Public-service corporations became a special object of the grafters' solicitude. Fortunately for the cause of decency and good government, however, the San Francisco election of 1905 brought at least one honest man into office. By a strange oversight, Ruef permitted William H. Langdon, a former superintendent of schools, to become district attorney. Using Langdon as the spearhead of the movement, the reform committee first began an investigation of the brazenly corrupt city government and instituted a series of raids upon gambling centers, slot-machines, and notorious houses of prostitution, that served to reveal to some degree the extent and variety of the tribute the machine was exacting from the underworld.

But these preliminary attacks failed to reach the major sources of graft or seriously threaten the power of the Ruef-Schmitz regime; and it was not until October, 1906, that Heney and Burns were able to begin their well-financed and carefully planned effort to clean up San Francisco's Augean stables.

The investigation was almost blocked at the start by one of Ruef's clever and characteristically unprincipled maneuvers, a barefaced attempt to usurp the district attorney's office and play the role of prosecutor in the investigation of his own acts. This plot excited the indignation of the decent people of San Francisco and awoke many of them for the first time to the shameful state into which the city had fallen. Popular resentment was further aroused by a reign of crime and violence that swept over the city when the saloons, which had been closed after the earthquake and fire, were prematurely allowed to resume business.

The summoning of a new grand jury on November 7, 1906,

marked what might be called the official beginning of the graft prosecution. With little waste of time, the new grand jury indicted Ruef and Schmitz for extorting payments for "legal services" from the city's brothels. Schmitz, as already stated, was then in Europe and thus beyond the jurisdiction of the California courts; and before the day set for trial, Ruef secreted himself in a roadhouse known as the Trocadero, a few miles from the center of San Francisco. There a special officer appointed by the court took him into custody when the sheriff professed inability to find his hiding-place. The arrest of their leader left Ruef's followers badly frightened, and when Burns trapped three of the supervisers in an open and flagrant case of bribery, the corrupt political machine rapidly fell apart.

Under the state's promise to recommend immunity, eighteen of the supervisors confessed the wholesale acceptance of bribes, not only from the organized activities of the underworld but on a still larger scale from public utilities and other corporations doing business in the city.

The graft investigation now took on a new complexion. "In the first moment of attack on municipal corruption, when it was simply a case of putting into jail Abe Ruef, the boss at the head of the system of robbery, Eugene E. Schmitz, the mayor who played figure-head for Ruef, and, perhaps, some of the Supervisors who took bribes to give away public utilities," wrote Will Irwin, "Spreckels, the financier, Heney, the prosecutor, and Burns, the detective, had the 'united decency' of the city behind them. From the time when they went beyond these smaller fry and reached up, not for the men who took the bribes but for the pillars of finance who gave them or sanctioned their giving, they faced a powerful opposition from the forces that govern business in San Francisco." [3]

On the basis of the testimony of the guilty supervisors and other evidence produced by the district attorney's office, the grand jury indicted responsible officers of some of the largest corporations in

---

[3] "They Who Strike in the Dark," *American Magazine*, Vol. LXVII, p. 564.

San Francisco. The list included the Pacific States Telephone & Telegraph Company, the Home Telephone Company, the Pacific Gas & Electric Company, the Parkside Realty Company, and —most important of all—the powerful traction company known as the United Railroads. The trials of the indicted men revealed to the full the weaknesses of our judicial procedure. Both sides spent money lavishly and used every device known to the practice of criminal law to accomplish their purpose.

Next to the trials of Ruef and Schmitz, public interest centered chiefly on the case of Patrick Calhoun, president of the United Railroads, and Tirey L. Ford, the company's chief counsel. The criminal charges against Calhoun were based chiefly on the bribery of Ruef, Schmitz, and the members of the board of supervisors to grant the United Railroads an overhead trolley franchise. The wholesale reconstruction of the city after the 1906 earthquake offered a new opportunity for the advocates of an underground system to press their claims for a franchise, but the board of supervisors closed the issue by abruptly granting an overhead concession to the United Railroads. Evidence subsequently unearthed showed that the traction company used at least $200,000 to obtain the franchise.

As previously indicated, the indictment and trial of Calhoun and his prominent business associates proved the turning-point in the graft investigation. Up to that time the crusaders' program had enjoyed popular approval; thereafter it became the object of one of the most effective, highly organized campaigns of discrediting propaganda the state has ever known. Hearst's *Examiner,* the San Francisco *Chronicle,* the Los Angeles *Times,* and subsidized newspapers far removed from the scene of the trials attacked Heney, Burns, and the other sponsors of the prosecution with unrestrained hostility. Older, Phelan, and Spreckels felt even more keenly the sting of social ostracism and severed friendships. Calhoun was cast in the role of martyr and portrayed as an outstanding hero because his imported professional strikebreakers won a bloody victory over the employees of the United Railroads.

As the trials proceeded, there were repeated charges of intimidation, bribery, subornation of perjury, and violence. The house of the prosecution's chief witness was blown up with dynamite. Fremont Older was kidnapped by the use of a questionable warrant and carried as far south as Santa Barbara. Francis Heney was shot in open court by an ex-convict named Haas whose criminal record Heney had dramatically and perhaps unnecessarily revealed as a means of disqualifying him for service on the jury. Heney escaped death by a hair's breadth, and Haas was either murdered in his cell to keep him from being questioned by the prosecution or committed suicide.

The shooting of Heney, the most dramatic incident in the long and spectacular graft trials, occurred on November 13, 1908. The incident, followed by the death of Haas, threw the city into a violent uproar and led to a demand for a Citizen's or Vigilance Committee similar to those of 1851 and 1856.

A great mass meeting, presided over by Dr. Edward R. Taylor, a reform mayor elected in the spring of 1907, summed up the tense popular feeling and voiced the indignation of thousands of outraged citizens against the attorneys, business leaders, and newspaper editors who were charged with uniting to discredit the prosecution and defeat the ends of justice.

Following Heney's forced withdrawal from the trial, two San Francisco attorneys, Matt I. Sullivan and Hiram W. Johnson, were selected to continue the graft prosecution. Ruef was convicted and sentenced to fourteen years in the penitentiary; but after months of evasion and delay the trial of Pat Calhoun ended in a divided jury, and from then on, the graft prosecution steadily lost ground. The trials, in truth, had lasted too long; justice had become impotent through the lapse of time. The public had grown tired of the crusade; the city's business "was being hurt by the publicity"; the man in the street had begun to question the good faith of the crusaders; and even liberal publications like the New York *Nation,* which spoke of the "thievery and political corruption of the United Railways," neutralized their comments by an equally strong condemnation of the prosecution.

In the municipal election of 1909 Langdon refused to run again for district attorney, Heney received the Democratic nomination, and Charles M. Fickert became the candidate of the Republican and Union-Labor parties. The election of Fickert as district attorney, and of P. H. McCarthy, the Union-Labor candidate, as mayor, to all intents and purposes ended the graft trials, though the last of the indictments against Calhoun was not dismissed until 1912.

Those who believed in the impartial administration of justice and the punishment of men who fouled the springs of government observed the San Francisco graft prosecutions with growing cynicism and disillusionment. Nearly four hundred indictments resulted in the conviction of only four defendants. Three of the four were freed on appeal to higher courts. Eugene Schmitz was saved from the penitentiary by the most specious of technicalities. Ruef alone was sent to prison—a trifling sop to justice for which the chance absence from the state of one of the California Supreme Court justices was alone responsible!

Undoubtedly the San Francisco graft prosecution, though almost barren of tangible results, helped to discourage subsequent instances of a similar nature and profoundly influenced the political uprising in California that led to the triumph of reform under the Lincoln-Roosevelt League and the Progressive Party.[4] But one may well question whether these gains offset the cynical disbelief in the majesty of the law and the even-handed administration of justice that came to infect the rank and file of the citizens.

As Governor George C. Pardee pointed out in his second biennial message to the legislature, the integrity and independence of the whole judicial system were rapidly passing under popular suspicion and the people were coming to look upon the courts as mere sieves through whose meshes men of wealth and influence could easily escape. Yet it is of interest to note that both Judge Frank H. Dunne and Judge William P. Lawlor, who presided over the graft trials and vainly sought to prevent the ham-

---

[4] In 1907 a corrupt municipal administration in Los Angeles led to the recall of Mayor A. C. Harper and the election of George Alexander in his place.

stringing of justice, were reelected to office, in 1909 and 1912 respectively, and that Judge Lawlor, who bitterly denounced Calhoun in open court and opposed the dismissal of the indictments against him, was later elected to the State Supreme Court by an overwhelming popular vote.

CHAPTER 20. The Era of Reform

THE CORRUPTION in civic government revealed by the San Francisco and Los Angeles graft investigations represented in aggravated form the general state of California politics at the turn of the century. Such political debasement was not peculiar to California, but, outwardly at least, the state seemed to be more subservient to its machine-controlled bosses than were other American commonwealths.

In the early 20th century the Southern Pacific machine, so carefully organized in the early days of the railroads by Collis P. Huntington and his colleagues of the "Big Four," was functioning close to maximum efficiency. Its influence affected every branch of politics, its activities extended to the remotest corners of the state, and its arrogance and disregard for public welfare were an intolerable offense to every principle of democratic government. As Charles Edward Russell said, the machine not only "dominated the government of California, it was the government and all the branches thereof."

Collis P. Huntington, last and most powerful of the Big Four, died in August 1900. The following February the Union Pacific Railroad acquired a large block of Southern Pacific stock from Huntington's estate and by subsequent purchases gained a working control of the California lines. The transfer did not affect the railroad's political activities or change the character of the former Huntington machine, for E. H. Harriman, who controlled the Union Pacific, was not the man to overlook such an important asset as the Southern Pacific's political organization or to use it less efficiently than his predecessor.

The Southern Pacific's domination of state politics was strikingly shown in the Republican state convention that met at Santa Cruz in September 1906. In 1896, with the close of Governor James H. Budd's administration, the Democratic Party went into a prolonged eclipse in state politics and failed to send another governor to Sacramento for upwards of forty years. At the time of the Santa Cruz convention, however, the party still remained a dangerous threat, though stand-pat Republican leaders felt secure enough in their position to disregard the growing signs of popular rebellion, even among their own followers, and continue their alliance with the Southern Pacific machine.

George C. Pardee, of Oakland, whose term as chief executive was about to expire, was the logical and most popular candidate for the Republican nomination; but he was opposed by the Southern Pacific Railroad and other large corporations because he had shown increasing signs of opposition to the practices by which such companies too often destroyed or crippled weaker competitors. The Standard Oil Company, rapidly building up a monopoly in California, as elsewhere, by obtaining special tariffs and rebates from the railroads, and by depriving its rivals of profitable markets, was one of the Governor's favorite targets.

Pardee, who had built up a strong personal following during his administration, was opposed by two rival candidates in the Santa Cruz convention. Abe Ruef, not yet seriously discredited by the graft scandals, brought forward J. O. Hayes, of San Francisco, solely for purposes of a "buy-off"; and the Southern Pacific retainers supported Congressman James N. Gillett of Humboldt County, Harriman's choice for governor. William F. Herrin, boss of the Southern Pacific machine and nominally a Democrat (though not inaptly called the "boss of the Republican Party"), did not attend the convention; but Judge J. W. McKinley, of Los Angeles, chairman of the gathering, ably represented the Southern Pacific interests.

In the opening days of the convention Pardee seemed assured of the nomination; but the railroad faction in the Republican Party, distrusting the Governor's independent attitude, successfully blocked his election. A coalition of Ruef's followers and Gillett's supporters defeated Pardee and threw the nomination to Gillett. The details of the bargain between the disreputable San Francisco boss and the Southern Pacific interests have never been revealed; but the San Francisco *Call* openly charged that

Herrin paid Ruef twenty thousand dollars in gold for the vote of the San Francisco delegation, and Ruef later testified that he received substantially that amount for throwing his support to Gillett.

Yet despite the triumph of the reactionary Republicans in forcing Gillett's nomination, all was not well in the party. The rank and file of the voters were either frankly disgusted or openly rebellious.

Herrin had not anticipated any serious revolt in the Republican ranks against Gillett and consequently took no steps to select delegates to the Democratic convention, which soon met in Sacramento. An actual majority of the gathering was thus free to take advantage of the threatened split in the Republican Party and nominate a man who would be acceptable to the anti-railroad faction.

Discarding the slate prepared by Herrin, the Democratic convention consequently nominated Theodore A. Bell, a young attorney from Napa. Bell was an able, independent, public-spirited citizen, and the discontent in the Republican ranks afforded him an even chance for election. But his campaign was successfully sabotaged by William Randolph Hearst through the organization of the so-called "Independence League" and the nomination for governor of William H. Langdon, the district attorney of San Francisco, whose contributions to the city's graft investigations had already made his name widely known throughout the state. The Democratic convention branded the Independence League a political machine, "created by William Randolph Hearst for his own political preferment"; and Bell characterized Hearst as the arch-enemy of good government in California.

In the ensuing election Gillett received approximately 125,000 votes; Bell, 117,000; Langdon, 45,000; and Lewis, the Socialist candidate, 16,000. The results justified the bitter Democratic contention that Hearst's nomination and support of Langdon cost Bell the election.

If popular criticism may be relied upon, either the legislature that assembled at the capital after the Santa Cruz convention was one of the worst in the history of the state, or else the public had at last shaken off some of its traditional apathy and developed a sudden sensitivity to the vices and shortcomings of the "esteemed and puissant statesmen by the muddy Sacramento."

Evidences of machine-controlled politics and petty graft were everywhere. According to the Fresno *Republican,* the assembly required eighty-three doorkeepers to guard three doors opening into one narrow corridor, and appointed "stenographers" who could neither read nor write. Not to be outdone, some of the members of the senate appointed women of dubious reputation to serve as committee clerks and allowed them free access to the senate chamber. The legislature also had "great hordes of appointees on the payroll who did not even stay in Sacramento, but discounted their whole season's pay and went back to San Francisco to carouse on it." Mayor Glasscock of Oakland reputedly summed up the situation with the remark: "You couldn't pass the Lord's Prayer in this legislature without money."

The liberal newspapers' condemnation of the proceedings at Sacramento found no echo, however, in the Governor's office, and Gillett characterized the 1907 legislature as "one of the best that ever met in the state capital."

The demoralization of California politics, so clearly revealed by the Santa Cruz convention, the San Francisco graft trials, and the corruption at Sacramento, prepared the way for a state-wide reform movement that proved little short of revolutionary, both in character and in scope.

Revolt against the long-continued rule of party dictatorships and machine control was in the air. Successful in his war against the Republican stalwarts, Robert La Follette had given the "Wisconsin idea" a leading place in liberal thought. In New Hampshire, Winston Churchill, with a crusader's approach, was urging a return to the old virtues of honesty, democracy, and righteousness in public life. The "muckraking" journalists were adding one sensational exposé to another, and though the American public was shrewd enough to question the purity of motive of many of the writers, it could not be blind to the sordid picture of American politics these articles revealed. California, in undertaking to set up a new political regime, was thus anticipating the great current of national reform that ushered in the second decade of the century. But as yet the progressive crusade was little more than a stirring in the public conscience. Political control by machine methods, as already emphasized, was even more inflexible in California than in most other states, and the organization subsequently formed under the name of the Lincoln-Roosevelt League thus in a measure became the spearhead of the progressive movement throughout the United States.

The effort to overthrow the long-established dictatorship of the old-line Republican Party in California was begun by two newspaper editors, Edward A. Dickson of the Los Angeles *Express*, and Chester H. Rowell of the Fresno *Republican*. Both men had watched the Southern Pacific machine in action at Santa Cruz and Sacramento and had felt the disgust, outrage, and smarting sense of helplessness all honest men experience when democracy is subverted by political bosses, pressure groups, and special interests of any kind.

With the adjournment of the discredited legislature of 1907, Dickson and Rowell undertook to canvass the state to see if public sentiment could be aroused to break down the power of the machine and lift California politics to a self-respecting level.

The logical nucleus for such a state-wide crusade was already at hand in the form of a nonpartisan organization that had carried through a reform program in the Los Angeles municipal election of 1906 with surprising success. This movement had been initiated by Edward A. Dickson of the Los Angeles *Express*, along with Russ Avery, Marshall Stimson, and Meyer Lissner.

Early in May 1907, Dickson sent up a trial balloon in the form of a personal letter to a number of Republican newspaper editors and other party representatives opposed to the machine, inviting them to attend a conference in Los Angeles to consider the feasibility of inaugurating a general campaign to enable the people of California to regain control of the state government and obtain "their political and economical independence." Participants in the campaign, Dickson bluntly added, must not be too sanguine of victory, prematurely discouraged by lack of immediate success, or unwilling to carry on a long, tough fight.

Responses to the invitation were unexpectedly gratifying, both in number and in sincerity of purpose. Fifteen men, including eight newspaper editors or publishers and four attorneys, attended the conference at Los Angeles on May 21. S. C. Graham, an independent oil-producer, was elected chairman of the group, and A. J. Pillsbury, editor of the Sacramento *Union*, served as secretary. After a general discussion of campaign methods and objectives, the Los Angeles conference agreed to sponsor a much larger gathering in Oakland to effect a permanent organization and launch the formal campaign.

The convention met at Oakland on August 1 in the old Metropole Hotel. The members represented nearly every section of the state and commanded the respect of the various communities and sections from which they came. With unusual unanimity and dispatch, the conference created a formal political organization, called the Lincoln-Roosevelt League, with Frank R. Devlin as president and Chester H. Rowell as secretary, and adopted the following platform:

The emancipation of the Republican party in California from domination by the political bureau of the Southern Pacific Railroad Comany and allied interests, and the reorganization of the state committee to that end.

The selection of delegates to the next Republican National Convention pledged to the nomination of Theodore Roosevelt for President, or should his nomination for any reason become impossible, then to vote for the candidate known to be truly committed to, and identified with, his policies, and to oppose the nomination of any reactionary styled "safe and sane" by the great corporate interests.

The election of a free, honest and capable legislature, truly representative of the common interest of the people of California.

The pledging of all delegates to conventions against the iniquitous practice of "trading" whereby political bosses effect nominations by bargain and sale, and the enactment of legislation penalizing such practices.

The enactment by the next legislature of such laws as will give voters an advisory voice in the election of United States Senators until such time as an amendment to the national constitution shall make that voice direct and absolute, which amendment we favor.

The pledging of candidates for the legislature to the enactment of such primary election law as shall afford the party voter a direct voice in the selection of party candidates.[1]

Almost from the outset the movement took on the character of a crusade. Ridiculed at first by the powerful standpat metropolitan newspapers, notably the San Francisco *Chronicle* and the Los Angeles *Times,* the League gradually developed such strength that the regular party leaders, no longer the masters of legislatures and conventions, eventually found themselves outmaneuvered, outgeneraled, and outfought.

Under the joint direction of Rowell and Dickson, the League built up an organization that far surpassed the powerful old-line political machine in thoroughness, adroitness, efficiency, and ruthlessness. These newspaper men capitalized on their newspaper contacts and experience to dramatize the League's crusade and keep its activities constantly before the people of California. A majority of the state's independent newspapers supported the League with something akin to religious fervor; and since radio broadcasting was then unknown and the press almost monopolized the formation of public opinion, such patronage was of incalculable value.

In 1908 the League won its first major skirmish—a mayoralty election in Sacramento—and came within striking distance of gaining control of the Republican state convention and dictating the choice of delegates to the National Convention at Chicago. Two years later, following the state-wide adoption of the direct primary in place of the long-established system of nominations

---

[1] J. Gregg Layne: "The Lincoln-Roosevelt League," Historical Society of Southern California *Quarterly,* September 1943, p. 90.

by party convention, the League entered the campaign with unity, confidence, clear-cut objectives, and a carefully devised strategy that contrasted strikingly with the division and confusion into which, by that time, the Republican machine had fallen.

In a surprisingly brief time the League made extraordinary progress. Practically all of Los Angeles County, two thirds of San Francisco, and most of Alameda County were under its control, and it seated its candidate, Clinton L. White, in the office of Mayor of Sacramento. In 1908 one of its candidates, former Lieutenant Governor Jacob Neff, successfully challenged the long-dominant machine by defeating Harrison Gray Otis to become one of the four delegates at large to the Republican National Convention at Chicago.

As the state prepared for the elections of 1910, the Lincoln-Roosevelt League was thus a recognized power in California politics and had become strong enough to enter a full ticket in the Republican primary. Herrin, at last thrown on the defensive and shorn of his domineering self-confidence, abandoned Gillett and attempted to rally the machine behind Alden Anderson, Lieutenant Governor of the state during Pardee's administration.

While this shift was taking place, Charles F. Curry, Secretary of State in Gillett's cabinet and long an obedient member of the Southern Pacific's political organization, suddenly added to the confusion by announcing that he too proposed to run for governor and expected the backing of the railroad. The situation was further complicated by the decision of Phil Stanton, speaker of the assembly and influential citizen of Orange County, to throw his hat into the ring and likewise make a bid for the railroad's support. Finally, to add further zest to what had already become a Kilkenny row, State Engineer Ellery announced his candidacy for the nomination, thus presenting the distracted Herrin with four avowed candidates for the machine's backing.

The Lincoln-Roosevelt League viewed Herrin's troubles with studied satisfaction. It was obvious that if all four candidates could be persuaded to remain in the race, the League was virtually assured of a victory at the primaries, and Rowell and Dick-

Los Angeles in the Early 1850's.

San Francisco in 1856, from an oil painting in the Huntington Library. This was the decade of

the city's most spectacular growth. Eight short
years earlier it had been only a tiny village.

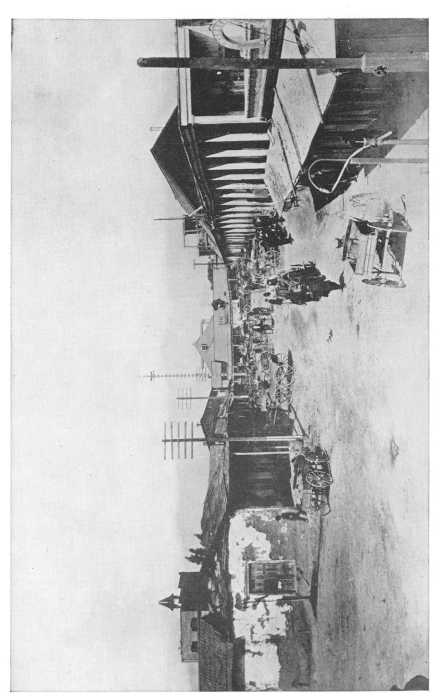

"Nigger Alley" during the Civil War period—a street lined by drinking dens and running off the Los Angeles Plaza. A center of hoodlumism in the city.

Collis P. Huntington, one of the "Big Four" who built
the Central Pacific Railroad, and its chief lobbyist.

Capture of John Sonntag, famous San Joaquin Valley bandit and train robber. He and his partner, Evans, kept authorities at bay for many weeks during their depredations of the 1880's.

The Raymond Hotel in Pasadena, one of the "boom" hotels of the 1880's which attracted tourists and settlers to southern California.

The great San Francisco fire. Following the earthquake of 1906, it did more damage and destroyed more property than the quake itself.

son adroitly directed their state-wide publicity program to that end.

The Lincoln-Roosevelt leaders assembled in San Francisco early in 1910 to select a full ticket for the coming election. After giving careful consideration to the names of several desirable candidates for the governorship, they finally agreed upon Hiram W. Johnson, one of the lawyers who had successfully prosecuted Abe Ruef after Francis J. Heney, badly wounded by the would-be assassin's bullet, had retired from the case. Albert J. Wallace, of Los Angeles, was nominated for lieutenant governor, and John D. Works, a former member of the state Supreme Court, was chosen to run for the United States Senate.

Johnson was then forty-four years old. Burton J. Kendrick described him as "rather handsome in appearance, with a round florid face topped by brown hair, rapid in his movements, with a gift for staccato oratory, and a fine aptitude in personal appeal and invective." Despite George Creel's remark that "he entered the campaign for governor with an effect of peevish martyrdom," the untried candidate proved militantly aggressive, fearless and domineering, catholic in his hatreds, skillful in keeping his name before the public—an almost ideal candidate for that particular time and occasion. Years later Senator Borah summarized one of the predominant traits of Johnson's character in the simple remark: "When a man opposes Johnson, he hates him."

Many of his loyal supporters, who freely sacrificed their own ambitions for his advancement, later found that the man's self-interest was too highly developed to leave much room for gratitude. Embittered by a fancied insult in the presidential campaign of 1916, he sulked like a lesser Achilles in his tent and let the candidate of his own party go down to defeat while he himself returned in triumph to the Senate. Still later, because of personal hatred for Woodrow Wilson, he became one of the Senators who blocked American entry into the League of Nations. Johnson's membership in the United States Senate, extending well over a quarter of a century, was marked by only two or three significant contributions to the public good; and thus in national politics, the only outstanding governor California has ever had played the role of an obstructionist and became each year more peevish, stubborn, and vindictive.

But these traits in Johnson's character were not evident in 1910, or at least they were not obvious to the voting public. Instead, the people saw in him only the fearless nominee of the Lincoln-Roosevelt League, the two-fisted champion of the common man, the California Roosevelt, the nemesis of the political machine.

Johnson conducted a memorable campaign. Touring the entire state by automobile, in a day when motor cars were still a novelty and paved roads the monopoly of large cities, he struck fire everywhere in the popular imagination, instilled in the supporters of his campaign the fervor of a holy war, and provided the aggressive, self-confident leadership necessary to the success of the reform movement and a victory for the Lincoln-Roosevelt League.

A political campaign in the early part of the century was as void of good taste and the amenities as a bare-fisted slugging match in the gay nineties. Following the Roosevelt pattern, Johnson attacked his opponents with a savage gusto that left no room for quarter or reconciliation on either side. He was shrewd enough to hold before the people a single, clear-cut, easily understood objective and refused to confuse the issue by a discussion of lesser matters.

With his battle cry: "Kick the Southern Pacific machine out of California politics," the League candidate traveled from one end of the state to the other, promising the throngs that poured out to hear him to hew Agag in pieces before the Lord, to redeem California from its long political bondage, and to destroy, once and for all, the Southern Pacific's influence in state and local government. Johnson's invective, as evidenced, for example, by his characterization of Harrison Gray Otis of the Los Angeles *Times* as "depraved, corrupt, crooked, putrescent," was cheered to the echo and he became the popular hero of the California progressive movement. But Johnson had no monopoly on political billingsgate, and his opponents responded in language equally pungent and insulting.

One of the most devastating features of the campaign publicity had its origin in an incident that occurred during the discredited Santa Cruz convention of 1906. After Gillett's nomination Frank McLaughlin, former chairman of the Republican State Central Committee, had staged a ratification dinner, inadvertently destined to become the most widely publicized social function in the history of the state, for a few of the "insiders."

By an inexplicable lapse of caution, McLaughlin permitted a reporter from the San Francisco *Call* to take a photograph of the dinner. The picture showed "Herrin's cabinet," as the group was later called, with Abe Ruef seated at the center of the table. Directly behind the San Francisco grafter stood Gillett, resting his hand on Ruef's shoulder in a companionable and familiar gesture.

In 1910 the publicity directors of the Lincoln-Roosevelt League used this photograph with telling effect to discredit the old-line Republicans. It was sent out under the caption: "The Shame of California," and appeared on billboards in every part of the state.

In the primary election Johnson received approximately 102,-000 votes. The remaining ballots, in round numbers, were as follows: Curry, 55,000; Anderson, 38,000; Stanton, 18,000; and Ellery, 2,000.

In the same primary Theodore Bell was nominated by the Democrats. In the general election, which took place on November 10, 1910, Johnson received approximately 177,000 votes to Bell's 155,000. Contrary to a rather widespread opinion, the election itself was not, like the Republican primary, a test between liberal and conservative, progressive and reactionary. The Democratic platform was as liberal in its political and social philosophy as that of Johnson, but the latter's violent, widely publicized attacks on the Southern Pacific machine turned the scale and won him the election.

Despite the prominence given to the Southern Pacific machine in the campaign, however, it is evident that the railroad organization had started to fall apart even before the election; and that, to change the figure, Johnson waged his dramatic crusade against a political ogre that had already begun to show signs of becoming impotent and palsied.

By that time the Southern Pacific management had learned that the company's political activities constituted a liability in money and goodwill, and were doubtless relieved to be rid of the costly and distasteful burden.

CHAPTER 21. The New Regime

THE ELECTION of Johnson as Governor and the triumph
of the Lincoln-Roosevelt League—a triumph that included
complete control of both the legislative and the executive branch
of the government—provided the prelude to the most important
era of political reform that California has ever known. The stat-
utes enacted by the new legislature embodied a long list of measures that the League had included in its organization platform in
1907 and gave California an advanced body of laws such as no
other commonwealth in the nation possessed at that time. Some
of the measures were designed to remedy specific evils and
abuses, while others involved fundamental changes in political
or economic philosophies.

Foremost on the reform schedule was a constitutional amendment providing for the principle of direct legislation through the
initiative, the referendum, and the recall. Nearly a decade before
the triumph of the Lincoln-Roosevelt League a small group of
enthusiasts had been able to introduce the principle of direct
legislation into a few California municipalities. The movement
owed its inception and financial support to Dr. John R. Haynes,
of Los Angeles, to whom that city's crying need for a new charter
during the opening years of the century offered the excuse for organizing the "Direct Legislation League of California."

To the great body of the electorate, the adoption of these measures represented the return of the government to popular control, a supreme triumph of the democratic principle, a pledge of
the long-awaited political millennium. To the extreme conservatives of both parties, however, the measures were anathema, the
crowning example of "freak" legislation, the beginning of the end
of the Republic. After the lapse of more than thirty years it is
obvious that the program of direct legislation, around which the
battle was fought between the conservatives and liberals with so
much sound and fury at the opening of the century, neither real-

ized the sanguine hopes and expectations of its ardent supporters nor justified the extravagant denunciations and despairing predictions of its opponents.

Other important measures adopted by the reform legislature included:

1. A number of humanitarian and social laws, such as those providing for old-age pensions, the abatement of commercialized vice, prohibition of child labor, reform of criminal procedure, restrictions on usury, pensions for schoolteachers, free textbooks for pupils in the public schools, and an act against racetrack gambling.

2. A number of labor laws including those establishing employer's liability, and a minimum wage and an eight-hour day for women.

3. Internal improvements, notably good roads and highways, flood control, reclamation, and forest, water, and power conservation.

4. Governmental measures, such as the extension of civil service throughout the state government; the establishment of a state board of control, with power to set up a state budget; the inauguration of an effective direct-primary law, with the corresponding elimination of boss-controlled conventions, and a provision for a nonpartisan judiciary.

5. Regulatory acts, including the extension of the authority of the State Railroad Commission over all public utilities, with power to fix rates and determine the character of service; a so-called "blue-sky law" to supervise promotional concerns and protect investors from unscrupulous stockjobbing companies; and a law governing weights and measures, primarily to prevent merchants from defrauding housewives and other consumers.

The creation, or rather revitalization, of the State Railroad Commission was one of the most important acts of the new legislature. In 1907 Governor Pardee had emphasized the uselessness and futility of the existing commission, a board which served neither the people nor the corporations and did no business because it had "no business to do." In the same message, as pre-

viously noted, Pardee also called attention to the use of rebates
by the Standard Oil Company, in connivance with the railroads,
to destroy independent oil operators and gain control of various
petroleum fields throughout the state.

The Wright Act of 1909 had given the impotent railroad body
a measure of authority, but the commission did not begin to function effectively until a constitutional amendment enabled the
legislature of 1911 to add greatly to the scope and the nature of
its powers. The new commission was given jurisdiction over all
other public utilities in the state as well as the railroads, and did
more business in two years than its predecessors had done since
1879.

The commission encountered strong and often stupid opposition from some of the more recalcitrant public utilities, notably
from the United Railroads of San Francisco; but on the whole the
public-service companies found it clearly to their advantage to
co-operate with the commission, and presently most of them came
to look upon it not as an enemy but as an invaluable protective
and stabilizing influence in the state's rapidly expanding business. "The Railroad Commission of the state of California," said
John A. Brittan, president of the Pacific Gas and Electric Company in 1914, "has done more in two years to inspire the investor
with confidence in California securities than all the gilt edge
promises of promoters in the years past." [1]

The triumph of the California reform program called forth extravagant praise on the one hand and even more violent condemnation on the other. Theodore Roosevelt looked upon it as
"the beginning of a new era in popular government . . . the
greatest advance ever made by any state for the betterment of
its people"; [2] and John W. Caughey speaks of it as "still the high
water mark in California's political achievement."

In contrast to such commendations, contemporary opposition
newspapers damned every act of the reform legislature as the
work of knaves or fools, and refused to admit that any good or

---

[1] *California Outlook*, June 13, 1914.
[2] Layne: "The Lincoln-Roosevelt League," p. 11.

salutary thing could come out of a government over which Hiram Johnson presided. The violent language in which these criticisms were expressed and the intolerant prejudice that lay behind them led thousands of independent voters to turn in disgust from the old party leaders to the new, and thus played directly into the hands of the astute insurgents. The following extract from the San Francisco *Chronicle* represents a typical example of the editorial hysteria of the time:

> *A Legislature of Progressive Cranks*
> It is Likely to Do Infinitely More Mischief Than a Legislature of Rascals Would Ever Attempt.

Nobody is attacking the moral character or good intentions of the majority of members of the present Legislature, but an honest Legislature whose ability to reason is destroyed by its imagination is more dangerous to society than a Legislature of felons. . . .

The number of tomfool bills is beyond computation. It is proposed to regulate the dress of school children; to forbid the sale of ice cream on Sundays; to "recall" judiciary decisions; to pay everybody's political campaign expenses; to fine citizens who fail to vote; to hire an "expert" to draw a pure paint law; to promote education in "social science" over the head of the University; to create a high-salaried "welfare commission"; to "investigate wages"; to remove property qualifications for "jurors"; to "establish industrial courts"; to "subject appointive officials to the recall"; "to regulate the newspapers"—and about everybody and everything else.[3]

The Progressive newspapers replied in kind to such attacks, and a journalistic free-for-all ensued that set a state record for tirade and billingsgate. In Los Angeles, especially, the long-standing personal feud between Harrison Gray Otis of the *Times* and E. T. Earl of the *Express* degenerated into a prolonged editorial squabble, offensive to dignity and good taste and extremely boring to the hapless public.[4]

---

[3] Franklin Hichborn: *California Legislature of 1913*, pp. 126–7.

[4] The controversy was all the more tiresome because it contained so little humor. On one occasion, however, a writer in the *Times* varied the monotony. Describing the various floats in one of the colorful Fiestas of the time,

By its outstanding victory in the primary election of 1910, the Lincoln-Roosevelt League, which had originated as a movement within the Republican Party, became the dominant wing of that party and retained the control and management of the Republican organization for four years. The League thus, in effect, became the Republican Party of California, with such leaders as Chester H. Rowell, former Governor George C. Pardee, Governor Hiram Johnson, Meyer Lissner, Edward A. Dickson, Marshall Stimson, Robert N. Bulla, Irving Martin, Marshall Hale, and Congressman William Kent serving on its executive councils.

Following the split at Chicago in 1912, Governor Johnson and many of his followers withdrew from the Republican Party and organized a Progressive Party in California, affiliated with the newly formed national organization, and gave their enthusiastic support to the Roosevelt-Johnson ticket. In the campaign this group routed the old-line party members and took advantage of the opportunities created by the new election law to ride roughshod over their opponents.[5] Roosevelt's tour of California was one of the highlights of the Progressive campaign. At the Shrine Auditorium in Los Angeles he climaxed his speech with the famous challenge: "We stand at Armageddon and we battle for the Lord."

As a result of the bitter war between the Progressives and the Old Guard Republicans, and the virtual elimination of the Taft electors, Wilson succeeded in winning two of California's thirteen presidential votes in the election of 1912, and lost the state to Roosevelt by less than two hundred popular votes.[6] The results

---

the reporter passed over the entry that represented Earl's two papers with the single sentence: "The float was followed by the entire paid-up subscription of the Los Angeles *Evening Express* and the *Morning Tribune,* and he was very footsore and weary."

[5] In complete control of both the Progressive and the Republican Parties in California, the Roosevelt-Johnson supporters were able to place the same set of electors on the two tickets in the presidential primary and thus leave the Taft faction only the forlorn hope of a write-in ballot.

[6] The returns gave Roosevelt and Johnson, running on the Progressive and Republican tickets, 283,610 votes; Wilson, 283,436; and Taft (Republican) 3,914.

thus clearly foreshadowed the outcome of the fateful presidential contest of 1916.

Re-elected governor by a large majority in 1914, Johnson presented himself as a candidate for the United States Senate two years later. By that time the Progressives and Republicans were nominally reunited under the name of the Republican Party, but within California itself the old hatreds, animosities, and suspicions burned as fiercely as ever.

During the six years that had elapsed since the Lincoln-Roosevelt League first selected him to serve as its candidate for governor, Johnson had traveled a long way in the field of practical politics and had perfected a highly efficient, smooth-running political organization, compared to which, as a prominent Los Angeles attorney once said, the old-time Southern Pacific machine functioned "like a creaking jalopy."

In the senatorial election of 1916 Johnson needed the support of southern California. Owing to the death of the incumbent, John Eshelman, the lieutenant-governorship was then vacant, and Johnson and William D. Stephens, a Progressive Congressman from Los Angeles, entered into the following gentleman's agreement relative to the two offices:

Stephens was to resign from Congress and Johnson was to appoint him Lieutenant Governor, the understanding being that if Johnson won the senatorship he would resign as Governor and Stephens would automatically assume that office. Stephens was promised that as Governor he would have a new legislature to work with; he would have the backing of the powerful Lincoln-Roosevelt League, and, hence, would be practically certain of re-election to the governorship in the election that was to come two years later, in 1918. Thus, if Johnson were elected, the North would have the senatorship and the South would have the governorship.

Relying on such assurances, Stephens carried out his part of the bargain and resigned from Congress. Johnson appointed him Lieutenant Governor, as was agreed, and then went on to victory in the senatorial campaign. After his victory, there was only one more thing for him to do in order to carry out his end of the bargain, and that was to resign as Governor. No one expected him to do it immediately, but all Stephens' friends, who were also great admirers of Johnson, were sure that he would resign in a month or so, but December came and went—the newly elected 1917 legislature, the one that Stephens was supposed to be able to look to to help him in any program that he might have to carry out, met and organized, but Johnson did not resign.

Still Johnson continued to sit in the Governor's chair, and there he sat until President Wilson called a special session of Congress in March of 1917. Then Johnson, knowing that he could not be sworn in as a Senator unless he ceased to be Governor, resigned and went to the Senate and Stephens became Governor in the early part of March, 1917, after the second session of the legislature, succeeding the constitutional recess, had begun.[7]

Johnson's animosity toward Stephens, reflected in both the open and the under-cover efforts of his followers to discredit the new state administration, greatly handicapped Stephens in the governorship and in his campaigns of 1918 and 1922.

California's part in the presidential election of 1916 provided one of the most dramatic chapters in the history of American politics. Momentous events, both national and international, depended upon the results of the election, and Hiram Johnson determined the outcome.

Woodrow Wilson carried California by a popular vote of less than four thousand. That narrow margin profoundly affected the future of two great political parties, the fate of the United States, and the destiny of the world. Obviously, the slightest change in public opinion during the campaign would have wiped out Wilson's insignificant majority and placed his Republican rival in the White House. Hughes owed his defeat in California to five factors: a personality that aroused little enthusiasm among the voters; a deep-rooted feeling that his election would restore the reactionary leadership of the Republican Party in California; the alienation of the union-labor vote; a blunder of the first magni-

---

[7] The contributor, who prefers to remain anonymous, is a leading member of the California bar and speaks from first-hand knowledge.

tude on the part of the Old Guard, who, both to compensate for six long years of humiliation and to capitalize on their conspicuous influence with Hughes, deliberately ignored the former Progressive-Republican leaders and refused to allow them to have any real share in the conduct of the candidate's supposedly triumphant tour; and, finally, Governor Johnson, who, deliberately affronted by the conservative Republican leaders in California and inadvertently offended by the candidate himself, gave little more than lip service to the support of Hughes, and thus indirectly encouraged some of his followers to bolt the Republican ticket and vote for Wilson.

The details of the "incident" that changed the outcome of the election—and perhaps the fate of the world—have been the subject of repeated speculation and extreme partisan distortion. They are told here, for the first time, simply and dispassionately, by Edward A. Dickson, former publisher of the Los Angeles *Evening Express* and one of the two men to whom California is indebted for the origin of the progressive movement:

Sifted down to the cold facts, the story is one that began at the Oregon State line—and climaxed at the Long Beach hotel.

California that year had two members of the Republican National Committee—William H. Crocker, representing the regular, and Chester H. Rowell, representing the progressive wing of the Republican Party. The State Chairman was Francis V. Keesling, also a regular, and a long time political antagonist of Governor Johnson. All three of these men went north to the Oregon boundary to welcome Justice Hughes, the Republican nominee for President.

Rowell was accorded an opportunity to meet the Presidential candidate, but as soon as the formalities were over, according to reports, Crocker and Keesling took over and were closeted with Hughes during practically the entire trip to San Francisco. Rumor soon had it that Rowell had been snubbed, and a natural resentment quickly spread among the Johnson supporters.

A few days later—on a bright Sunday morning—Governor Johnson, who had been conducting his own campaign for United States Senator in the interior of the State, arrived at Long Beach, registering at the Virginia Hotel. Unbeknown to the Governor, Justice Hughes' southern schedule included a brief stop at the same hotel. A large gathering of the "regulars" was on hand to greet Hughes, and the presence of the Governor was obviously unwelcomed.

On Governor Johnson's invitation, I had accompanied him to Long Beach. Realizing that his presence would not be welcomed, Governor Johnson suggested that we retire to his apartment until after the departure of Mr. Hughes. We did so, and the two leaders did not meet.

During the afternoon, a telephone message from a Mr. Farnham, in charge of the Hughes Presidential party, was received by the Governor. Justice Hughes, Farnham explained, had just learned that Governor Johnson had been at the Virginia Hotel at the time of his own brief visit there. He extended the regrets of Justice Hughes, coupled with an invitation to the Governor to come to Pasadena for dinner that evening. Johnson was unable to accept this dinner invitation, but arrangements were made for conference with Farnham later in the evening.

Governor Johnson urged me to remain for the after-dinner conference, but feeling that a heart-to-heart talk between Johnson and Justice Hughes' secretary was necessary to remove existing irritation, I declined the invitation and returned to Los Angeles.

Governor Johnson was therefore alone when Mr. Farnham arrived, carrying the compliments of Justice Hughes. But Farnham was not alone. With him was State Chairman Keesling. It is doubtful if any other individual in all California could have aroused Johnson's peculiar form of political venom as effectively as the State Chairman.

Keesling's presence with Farnham immediately confirmed in the Governor's mind all the suspicions and rumors that had been accumulating since the Rowell-welcoming incident in the north. That Keesling should appear as a peace ambassador from Justice Hughes, constituted, in the Governor's mind, a deliberate and planned affront. He now became convinced that Hughes was knowingly permitting the presidential campaign in California to be used by his political adversaries to defeat him for the Republican nomination for Senator.

With cold courtesy, Governor Johnson received the greetings from Justice Hughes. With equal cold courtesy he asked that his greetings be carried to Hughes. That was all there was to the conference. But an "incident" had been created—an incident that cost the Republican Party the election.

On the following morning, Governor Johnson requested me to

come to Long Beach to confer on the happenings of the evening before. I endeavored to minimize the Keesling participation, arguing that Keesling probably had been requested by Hughes to accompany Secretary Farnham solely because of his position as State Chairman. I urged a friendly meeting with Hughes immediately so as to avoid a spread of rumors of a Johnson-Hughes feud. Johnson, however, was adamant, and determined to go forward with his own Senatorial campaign. Accordingly Hughes left the State without having met California's chief executive.

Governor Johnson, however, gave no outward indication that he was harboring a hurt feeling. In all of his speeches, he continued to laud Justice Hughes, and to urge his election. However, the Democrats, eager for any political mishap that might engender discord among Republicans, seized upon this phase of the Hughes trip, and vigorously fanned the flame by spreading stories that even went so far as to assert that the two distinguished leaders actually met in the hotel lobby and that Hughes had brusquely refused to shake hands with Johnson.

Had Justice Hughes been advised of the fact that the Governor of California was in residence at the hotel, customary amenities would have called for a visit by Hughes on the State's chief executive to pay his official respects. It is reasonably certain, however, that Hughes was not so advised, and that he came and departed in complete ignornace of Governor Johnson's presence at the hotel. There was, of course, no intentional slight on the part of Hughes, as was subsequently asserted.

Thousands of Republicans, however, were convinced by the riot of rumors that in some fashion or another their Governor had been subjected to an affront by Justice Hughes, and many switched to Wilson out of sheer resentment.

But for the unfortunate Virginia Hotel episode, Hughes would easily have carried California. With California's vote he would have been elected. With Hughes as President, instead of Woodrow Wilson, how might world events have been altered! [8]

The Old Guard Republicans laid the full responsibility for Hughes's defeat at Johnson's door. The latter returned the charge with interest, and for months the two California factions damned each other with passionate bitterness for the party's unnecessary defeat.

---

[8] Edward A. Dickson to Robert G. Cleland.

CHAPTER 22. "Dynamite"

ALTHOUGH the Progressive program included a noteworthy body of labor legislation, such as the eight-hour day for women and a workingman's compensation act, the era of political reform described in earlier chapters was marked by a succession of violent disputes between labor and capital that involved extensive destruction of property, serious loss of life, and the creation of prolonged and deep-seated ill feeling.

The opening years of the century witnessed a phenomenal increase in union membership—a sort of mass conversion of California workingmen to the principles of organized labor. "It is doubtful," says Professor Cross, "whether any other state in the Union has ever felt the ardor for organization that characterized the workers of California during the period 1899–1901. In 1902 the State Labor Commissioner reported that there were 495 labor organizations in California, 124 of which were in San Francisco, 68 in Los Angeles, 45 in Sacramento, 36 in Oakland, and the rest in other centers of population. . . ."[1]

San Francisco, then the one metropolis on the coast, was traditionally a city of labor controversies. A succession of strikes demoralized the city's business at the opening of the century, but the powerful Employers Association, supported by the National Association of Manufacturers and other kindred bodies, proved more than a match for the unions and temporarily checked the growth of the closed shop in San Francisco. In a few years, however, thanks in part to the Union Labor Party's control of the city government during the Ruef-Schmitz era, organized labor regained its position and converted San Francisco into the only closed-shop city in the United States.

The strike of the employees of the United Railroads in 1907 for

---

[1] Ira Brown Cross: *A History of the Labor Movement in California* (1935), p. 229. The author adds that the number of labor unions in California increased about 75 per cent between 1900 and 1902; membership expanded by 125 per cent; and the number of organized trades or vocations rose from 81 to 149.

a time almost paralyzed transportation in San Francisco. The men went out in May when the company refused to grant their demand for a modest increase in wages and the substitution of the eight- for the ten-hour day. The strike continued until September and resulted in the death of at least thirty-nine persons and the injury of more than seven hundred—a toll of dead and wounded far heavier than the combined casualties of the famed Bear Flag Revolt and the American conquest of California! Conservative newspapers throughout the state unsparingly condemned the unions, both for the strike itself and for the attendant violence and bloodshed.

But the other side of the picture was equally black. At the time of the strike Pat Calhoun, president of the United Railroads, was under indictment for bribery. His acquittal depended in part upon the support of public opinion. Members of the graft prosecution, labor sympathizers, and liberals generally accused the traction company's president of fomenting the walk-out to divert public attention from the graft trials and permit him to pose as the savior of the city by a dramatic defiance of the union and the wholesale use of thugs and gunmen to break the strike. One may add that the merits of the controversy were successfully obscured and the waters of truth badly muddied by the tactics and propaganda employed by both sides.

The history of the labor movement in San Francisco and Los Angeles offers a good example of the cliché that the contrasts between the two cities are much more obvious than their similarities. For half a century, except for short interludes, San Francisco recognized the dominant position of organized labor; while Los Angeles, thanks chiefly to the Los Angeles *Times,* and the close-knit Merchants and Manufacturers Association, an organization inseparable from the *Times* in origin, purpose, and opinion, remained the citadel of the open shop.

Until death dissolved the relationship in 1917, the *Times* was Harrison Gray Otis, and Harrison Gray Otis was the *Times.* For the city's growth and development during the early part of the century Los Angeles probably owed more to Otis, his son-in-law,

Harry Chandler, and the *Times* than to any other influence. By the same token, during Otis's lifetime, at least, no Los Angeles newspaper was so thoroughly hated as the *Times;* no Los Angeles citizen so wholeheartedly damned by his enemies as its irascible, pungent-speaking, white-goateed, unyielding, uncompromising editor.

Otis, in turn, hated as savagely as he himself was hated, and his hatred was catholic as well as violent. He hated Theodore Roosevelt and Hiram Johnson and the whole Progressive Party. He hated his rivals in the newspaper business, E. T. Earl and William Randolph Hearst. He hated free silver and free trade, state socialism and direct legislation. Most of all, he hated organized labor (unless it remained decently moribund) and the principle of the closed shop.

In 1890, eight years after Otis came into possession of the paper, the *Times'* printers struck for a continuation of the wages paid during the boom years of the preceding decade and for recognition of the typographical union and the closed shop. Otis thereupon declared a lifelong war upon organized labor and started a crusade to prevent the growth of labor unions in Los Angeles. To him the 1906 Republican state convention's declaration at Santa Cruz, "that organized labor is the true and only way in which the rights of labor can be safeguarded and protected," was a doctrine as pernicious and subversive as any villainy ever uttered by Karl Marx.

With radical labor infected by the virus of a class war and San Francisco committed to the principle of the closed shop, Los Angeles, the "scab city," became, far too literally, a battleground between militant labor leaders and the equally determined and militant champions of the open shop. About the middle of 1906, according to Cross,

the unions of San Francisco were warned by their employees that, unless they unionized Los Angeles and thus equalized wages and working conditions between the two cities, the open shop would be introduced in San Francisco.[2]

[2] Cross: *ibid.*, p. 282. According to Louis Adamic, the business leaders of

By June every metal trades plant in Los Angeles was involved in a strike, and both sides were making preparations to fight. In the ensuing struggle the individual employers served as shock troops for the Los Angeles Merchants and Manufacturers Association, the Los Angeles *Times,* the Chamber of Commerce, and the National Association of Manufacturers, which lent the local bodies its active support in the fight against the unions. The strikers, on their part, drew heavily for leadership and reinforcements upon the aggressive San Francisco unions and had the active backing of such powerful organizations as the International Molders Union and the International Association of Bridge and Structural Iron Workers.

Alarmed by the spread of the strike and the increasing violence and brutality on both sides, the Los Angeles city council acceded to the demands of the Merchants and Manufacturers Association and passed an ordinance designed to do away with picketing. The strikers immediately challenged the measure, and scores of arrests resulted from its violation. For some months the situation went from bad to worse, with neither side, in the bitterness of the conflict, showing much respect for law or the welfare of the general public.

At this juncture a group of extremists among the national labor leaders, who were already committed to a policy of terrorism, sent their agents to Los Angeles to bomb the plants and homes of the most conspicuous anti-labor figures. The dynamiting campaign was directed by the leading officials of the International Association of Bridge and Structural Iron Workers. The three men directly involved in the Los Angeles dynamitings were John J. McNamara, secretary of the International Association of Bridge and Structural Iron Workers, his brother, James B. McNamara, and Ortie McManigal, chief saboteur for the na-

---

San Francisco and the heads of the labor unions agreed that "it would be mutually beneficial to employers and union labor if the labor situation between San Francisco and Los Angeles were 'equalized.'" *Dynamite* (1931), p. 206.

tional movement, who later testified that he participated in twenty-one dynamiting jobs between June 1907, and April 1911. In the dynamitings in Los Angeles, J. J. McNamara selected the buildings to be destroyed and the other two prepared and planted the bombs.

The *Times* was naturally chosen as the first target by the dynamiters. In August 1910, J. B. McNamara met Olaf A. Tveitmoe, secretary of the Building Trades Council, in San Francisco. Tveitmoe, one of the most prominent labor leaders on the coast, had been appointed to the San Francisco board of supervisors by Eugene Schmitz in 1906. Later he was caught in the dragnet of the graft investigation and convicted; but on appeal his conviction was reversed, and his influence in union labor circles suffered as little from the bribery revelations as Pat Calhoun's position in the social and business life of San Francisco suffered from the same scandal.

According to McManigal's subsequent testimony, Tveitmoe instructed J. B. McNamara to proceed to Los Angeles and blow up the *Times*. Before leaving San Francisco, McNamara bought enough dynamite to wreck half the buildings in Los Angeles. Long immunity from arrest, however, had made him unbelievably careless, and in certain phases of the transaction he disregarded the most rudimentary precautions. Instead of buying ordinary dynamite, containing forty per cent nitroglycerin, a purchase that would be difficult to trace, McNamara stupidly went to the Giant Powder Company's factory at Point Pinole on San Pablo Bay and asked for several hundred pounds of ninety per cent nitroglycerin. The company could not fill such an unprecedented order, but after some argument agreed to make up five hundred pounds of an explosive known to the trade as "giant gelatin," containing eighty per cent nitroglycerin. Taking part of the explosives with him in a suitcase, McNamara left the main supply in a rented house in South San Francisco and boarded a Southern Pacific train for Los Angeles.

When he reached the city, McNamara found the *Times* housed

in a large brick building, trimmed with stone, on the northeast corner of First Street and Broadway. North of the *Times* Building proper, and separated from it by a narrow blind corridor, commonly called Ink Alley, stood the plant of the Times-Mirror Printing and Binding Company, another Otis enterprise.

As the name implied, Ink Alley was used as a storage place for the large quantities of ink required by the presses in both buildings. This, though highly inflammable, was kept in wooden barrels and shared space in the passage with great rolls of paper on which the *Times* was printed. Making little attempt at concealment, McNamara casually walked into Ink Alley on the night of September 30 and shoved a suitcase filled with twenty pounds of giant gelatin behind the barrels of ink, rolls of paper, and general litter that cluttered up the corridor.

The bomb's mechanism was set to go off at one o'clock in the morning, a time when, according to newspaper practice, only part of the force would be found in the building. The bomb actually exploded at seven minutes past the hour. The devastation caused by the blast, terrific enough in itself, was rendered even more appalling by roaring flames from broken gas mains and exploding barrels of ink.

Twenty-one of the *Times* employees were either killed outright or burned to death, for in an incredibly short time the rubble-choked rooms and hallways became blazing furnaces from which there was no possible escape, and to many of the hopelessly trapped victims death came as an indescribable mercy. A large number of other persons suffered major or minor injuries. General Otis was en route to Los Angeles from Mexico on the night of the disaster and so escaped injury. Harry Chandler, by mere chance, had left the building only a short time before the explosion.

An hour after the disaster, and without the benefit of any investigation, the officials of the *Times* decared that labor-union agents were responsible for the explosion. The statement began: "The Times Building was destroyed this morning by the enemies of industrial freedom by dynamite bombs and fire." It closed with the defiant note: "They can kill our men and wreck our buildings, but by the God above they cannot kill the *Times*." [3] As a counter-blast, spokesmen for labor declared that escaping gas rather than dynamite actually caused the explosion, and that the Otis-Chandler accusations against the unions were only thinly disguised attempts to divert public attention from their own criminal failure to replace the notoriously defective gas mains in the *Times* Building. Some labor partisans even declared that Otis himself planned the explosion to discredit the unions and damn the movement for the closed shop!

A few hours after the disaster Mayor George Alexander engaged William J. Burns, whose direction of the San Francisco graft cases had brought him nation-wide publicity, to take charge of the official investigation and bring the perpetrators of the crime to justice. The work of the investigators was greatly simplified by a mishap in J. B. McNamara's plans. After leaving the bomb in Ink Alley, the dynamiter planted a similar device under the window of the bedroom in which General Otis customarily slept, and a third bomb close to the house of Felix J. Zeehandelaar, secretary of the Merchants and Manufacturers Association. Each suitcase contained sixteen sticks of giant gelatin and the usual cheap alarm clock. Fortunately both bombs were discovered before they exploded. One, hurriedly taken to a vacant spot in Westlake Park, shattered plate-glass windows within a radius of two or three blocks when it went off; the other, which failed to explode, furnished a number of clues that revealed the source of the dynamite, and thus gave the detectives an opportunity to obtain excellent descriptions of its purchasers from the officials of the Giant Company's plant at Point Pinole.

Meanwhile, the dynamite conspiracy was actively renewed. After leaving the time bombs in Los Angeles the night of the *Times* explosion, J. B. McNamara took a train for San Francisco. There he spent four days with his fellow conspirators, and then went into hiding for two weeks at the home of J. E. Mumsey,

---

[3] October 1, 1910.

alias Jack Bright, business agent of the Bridgemen's local union, in Salt Lake. Highly nervous, and perhaps slightly deranged as a result of the *Times* disaster, McNamara later joined a hunting party, of which Ortie McManigal was a member, in the Wisconsin woods. As the days went by he became increasingly morose; and on one occasion, in a fit of despondency or suspicion, attempted to waylay and shoot McManigal.

In the meantime Burns had unraveled part of the story of the national dynamite conspiracy, and some of his detectives, disguised as deer-hunters, were able to fraternize with the members of the party and talk at length with McNamara when he was both drunk and garrulous.

Soon after the end of the hunting trip John J. McNamara sent McManigal to Los Angeles to take up the wholesale plan of sabotage that J. B. McNamara had begun. McManigal's orders included the destruction of the *Times* auxiliary printing plant, the Baker Iron Works, the Llewellyn Iron Works, and two buildings still under construction—the Hall of Records and the Alexandria Hotel.

With the intense excitement created by the destruction of the *Times,* rewards totaling a hundred thousand dollars for the apprehension and conviction of the perpetrators of the crime, and a ruthless investigation under way to bring the conspirators to justice, ordinary discretion and common sense called for at least a temporary cessation of dynamiting activities in Los Angeles.[4] But those whom the gods wish to destroy . . . !

Ortie McManigal reached Los Angeles on December 12 and registered at the Rosslyn Hotel under the name of F. F. McKee. He brought with him a large quantity of dynamite, a number of Tatoo Jr. alarm clocks, his favorite device for setting off the bombs, and the necessary fulminate of mercury caps. Caching the dynamite in the sandy bed of the Los Angeles River, near the North Broadway Street Bridge, the dynamiter improved his

---

[4] Included in the $100,000 rewards was one of $7,500 offered by Tveitmoe on behalf of the San Francisco Building Trades Council!

time by visiting the old San Gabriel Mission, Long Beach, and other centers of attraction, including the scene of the *Times* disaster. Furthermore, following his usual custom of sending his wife a souvenir from each city to which the dynamiting expeditions led, McManigal purchased two plumes from the Cawston Ostrich Farm in South Pasadena and mailed them to Mrs. McManigal.

McManigal later retrieved the explosives from the cache in the river bed and prepared three alarm-clock bombs, which he sought to plant in the Llewellyn Iron Works, at the corner of Redondo and North Main streets, the night before Christmas. While he was adjusting the mechanism, however, the detonating caps in two of the bombs exploded, painfully wounding him in the hand and leg.

McManigal angrily tossed the two defective bombs into some weeds and trash near the ironworks, where they were later found by the detectives and subsequently used as evidence in the trial, and planted the third machine in a little room that adjoined the main foundry. The bomb went off between eleven and twelve o'clock on Christmas Eve. The explosion tore out about forty feet of the front of the building and extensively damaged the interior of the plant, but fortunately caused no loss of life.

When the explosion occurred, McManigal was well on his way to San Francisco. There he met E. A. Clancy and other labor leaders, and on December 28 continued his journey to Chicago and Indianapolis to resume his routine work of bombing non-union structures in other cities.

Meanwhile Burns had accumulated a mass of evidence bearing both on the dynamitings in Los Angeles and on the nationwide conspiracy directed from the headquarters of the Association of Bridge and Structural Iron Workers in Indianapolis. In this investigation Herbert S. Hockin, former secretary of the international union, who claimed he had broken with the McNamaras because "they wanted to do a lot of killings," served as one of his chief undercover agents.

On the night of April 11, after completing a dynamiting job in Toledo, McManigal and J. B. McNamara registered at a hotel in Detroit, where they intended to set off five explosions. There operatives for the Burns Detective Agency took the conspirators into custody and, partly by force and partly by trickery, induced or compelled the two to accompany them to Chicago. Believing that his fellow dynamiters were about to adopt an every-man-for-himself policy, McManigal made a full confession.

Burns's agents next arrested John J. McNamara in Indianapolis. Then, without troubling to conform to the inconvenient law regarding extradition papers, the detectives secretly rushed the three captives under heavy guard to Los Angeles and lodged them in the county jail. The whole labor world united in angry protest against both the arrest of the union representatives and the violation of law by which their return to Los Angeles was effected. Warrants were sworn out for the officers making the arrests, a fund of $300,000 was raised by labor sympathizers for the defense of the McNamaras and McManigal, and Clarence Darrow, spokesman for the unions and reputedly one of the cleverest of the nation's criminal lawyers, was sent to Los Angeles to conduct the defense.

The case quickly became an international *cause célèbre*. The prosecution was conducted by John D. Fredericks, district attorney of Los Angeles County, and a number of his ablest deputies; serving with Darrow for the defense were Le Compte Davis, Joseph Scott, Ex-Judge Cyrus McNutt, and Job Harriman, Socialist candidate for mayor in the current election in Los Angeles.

The case was heard before Judge Walter Bordwell and began on October 11, 1911 with the trial of J. B. McNamara for the murder of Charles Haggarty, one of the twenty-one victims of the *Times* explosion. The trial immediately became a test of skill, shrewdness, maneuver and counter-maneuver, pressure by publicity and public opinion, manipulation, and possibly outright intimidation, bribery, and subornation of perjury. Excitement reached a new high in the judicial history of Los Angeles and feeling on both sides became so partisan and violent that after seven weeks and the examination of six hundred talesmen, the jury was still only two thirds complete.

Then, with tension near the breaking-point, the defense suddenly capitulated and brought the trial to an astounding, melodramatic end. James B. McNamara accepted responsibility for the destruction of the *Times* and J. J. McNamara pleaded guilty to conspiring to dynamite the Llewellyn Iron Works. The confession was a stunning triumph for the prosecution, an inglorious if not a dishonorable defeat for Clarence Darrow, and a cruel disillusionment to all honest and sincere supporters of organized labor throughout the nation.

Various explanations were offered for the McNamara confession, none of which was wholly conclusive, and after the lapse of more than thirty-five years some of the elements in the debacle still remain obscure. Lincoln Steffens, in his *Autobiography*, claims that a dictograph planted in Darrow's office made the defense counsel uncertain as to what information the prosecution actually possessed. In addition, shortly before the McNamaras pleaded guilty, Darrow was indicted for the bribery of a juror. Considering all the circumstances, Darrow probably followed the prudent course in having his clients plead guilty, both to keep them from being hanged and possibly also to protect himself in the case of the bribery indictment.

From the standpoint of the prosecution, the time element was fully as important in the settlement of the McNamara case as the actual conviction of the two brothers. A municipal election was scheduled in Los Angeles for December 5, 1911. Job Harriman, one of the attorneys for the defense, was running for mayor on the Socialist ticket and seemed certain of winning the election. To the *Times* and the other supporters of the open shop, a Socialist victory meant disaster. It was therefore infinitely better to compromise with the McNamaras, force them to plead guilty on the eve of the election, and thereby knock Harriman's chance for victory into a cocked hat, than to allow the trial to run its normal course, even though it brought the death penalty to the dynamiters in the end.

"Viewed fundamentally," said the *Times*, "the stupendous climax of the case was . . . the most consequential event that has occurred in this country since the close of the Civil War." Despite the exaggeration of the paper's exultant statement, the dramatic denouement of the McNamara case, when the whole courtroom "seemed to fly apart," unquestionably swept Job Harriman into oblivion, broke the backbone of the Socialist Party in the state, discredited Clarence Darrow, left Los Angeles the "Gibraltar of the open shop" for another thirty years, and dealt a crippling blow to organized labor in southern California.

McManigal, the prosecution's star witness in the trials, went to Honduras in 1915 or 1916 and lived there for a time under an assumed name. He then returned to Los Angeles as W. E. Mack and in 1932 became a watchman in the County Hall of Records. When he retired twelve years later, the Los Angeles County board of supervisors presented him with a scroll testifying to "the long, faithful, and efficient services rendered to the people of this County."

CHAPTER 23.   Durst and Mooney

THREE years after the bloody climax of the open-shop war in Los Angeles the California public was shocked by another labor tragedy. Unlike the *Times* disaster, this second incident had no connection with the activities of labor unions or the conflict in the industrial world. It involved migrant agricultural workers instead of urban employees, and sprang, in the main, out of living and working conditions of which the great mass of California citizens were naïvely unaware. The tragedy, usually spoken of as the Wheatland hop riots, occurred on a large ranch in the Sacramento Valley which belonged to a man named Richard Durst.

Labor conditions in general were unsatisfactory during the winter of 1913. San Francisco was considering the reestablishment of bread lines, and an eccentric character who styled himself "General" Kelley had organized an "Army" of some two thousand unemployed transients to carry on a campaign for relief or regular employment. Then, too, the Industrial Workers of the World, those bitter Ishmaelites whose hands were turned alike against capital and organized labor, had already boldly begun to spread their propaganda of sabotage, direct action, and the class war in small rural communities as well as in the larger cities.

Fresno and San Diego, attempting to suppress I.W.W. activities by ordinances that were patently in violation of the constitutional provision of free speech and by citizens' committees that bore more than a faint resemblance to the Coleman "Pick-handle Brigade" of the sand-lot riot days in San Francisco, found themselves unable to cope with the "Wobbly" hordes that flocked in by prearrangement from every section of the state as well as from other parts of the West. A hundred of these agitators were arrested in Fresno and even larger numbers in San Diego. The battle continued for eight months in the latter city and involved arrests, beatings, tar and feathers, and the ordeal of the gantlet, in which men in groups of six or eight were compelled to run between two lines of so-called vigilantes who "belabored them with clubs and black-snake whips."

According to most reports, the owner of the ranch on which the Wheatland tragedy took place was neither more mercenary nor more inhumane than his fellow Californians. He was a successful rancher who for years had used migrant labor to harvest his seasonal crops without giving much thought, one way or another, to the conditions under which his temporary employees ate, slept, and lived, or to any of the other human factors involved.

Prior to the opening of the hop season in 1913, Durst advertised extensively for pickers and, like many other advertisers, failed to adhere strictly to the truth. His notices called for more pickers than the ranch could use, implied that anyone who applied would receive steady employment, and promised higher wages than he actually proposed to pay. These misstatements, however, were not the chief cause of the ensuing riot.

The hop-pickers who came to the Durst ranch represented a medley of types and races. The unorganized multitude included Hindus, southern Europeans, native Americans, and representatives of various other nationalities. Among them were professional bindle stiffs, rootless itinerants, migrant laborers with homes and families who followed the crops during harvesting season, and ordinary American workingmen looking for the combination of a job and a vacation. Lastly there were members of the Industrial Workers of the World, whose chief mission in life was to foment violence and set one class against the other.

Twenty-eight hundred pickers were camped on a treeless hill which was part of the Durst ranch, the largest single employer of agricultural labor in the state. Some were in tents, some in topless squares of sacking or with piles of straw. Eight small toilets had been erected and four days' use had made them revoltingly filthy. No toilets had been allotted to women. There was no organization for sanitation, no garbage disposal. The temperature during the week of the riot had remained near 105 degrees and though the wells were a mile from where the men, women, and children were picking, and their bags could not be left for fear of theft of the hops, no water was sent into the fields. A lemonade wagon appeared at the end of the week, later found to be a concession granted to a cousin of the ranch owner. Local Wheatland stores were forbidden to send delivery wagons to the camp grounds. It developed in the state investigation that the owner of the ranch received half of the net profit earned by an alleged independent grocery store that had been granted the "grocery concession" and was located in the center of the camp ground.[1]

Taking advantage of a mass meeting that had been called to protest against such conditions, "Blackie" Ford, a skillful I.W.W. orator, brought the overwrought feelings of the workers dangerously near the explosive state with a highly dramatic condemnation of Durst and the whole capitalistic regime. At that moment, when the crowd was singing a hate-inspired I.W.W. song, the sheriff of Yuba County and a number of deputies drove up in automobiles.

Despite the tenseness of feeling, the massed workers had not yet degenerated into a mob; but when the sheriff attempted to arrest Ford, one of the excited deputies fired over the heads of the crowd. This started a riot, in which the infuriated men knocked the sheriff down, kicked him senseless, killed one of his deputies, and fatally shot the district attorney. Two of the workers, one a mere boy, also lost their lives in the melee, and many others suffered serious injuries. The surviving members of the posse soon fled from the scene, and no attempt was made to bring the camp under police control until the following day. Then a company of state troops, acting under orders from the Governor, took command of the situation.

The Wheatland hop riots led the state authorities to take drastic action against the I.W.W. as a subversive organization and to arrest, sometimes without even the form of legality, many of its members. Ford and one of his close associates named Herman

---

[1] Carleton H. Parker: *The Casual Laborer and Other Essays* (1920), pp. 6–7. Parker's official report to Governor Johnson and the State Commission of Immigration and Housing described conditions in much more loathsome detail. See the *California Outlook*, March 14, 1914.

Suhr were sentenced to life imprisonment, and several other leaders served long terms in the penitentiary.

Moving along more constructive lines, the state legislature established a Commission of Immigration and Housing, with Simon J. Lubin as chairman, and gave it authority to inspect agricultural labor camps, as well as city lodging houses, and to require employers to meet certain standards of comfort, decency, and sanitation. Definite improvement in the migrant-labor field was made under the new law, but many of the problems were too intricate and deep-rooted to be solved by simple legislative action; and in the jobless thirties California witnessed a return of the conditions that converted the Durst hop ranch into a place of filth, poverty, and blood.

Another violent episode in which the labor issue was injected occurred in the summer of 1916. On July 22 of that year the advocates of a strong national military policy sponsored a huge "Preparedness Day" parade in San Francisco. As the parade got under way, a bomb exploded at Steuart and Market streets, killing six persons, fatally wounding four, and more or less seriously injuring forty others. The weight of evidence indicated that the bomb was placed in a suitcase and set to go off at a given time; but there is some possibility that it may have been dropped from a roof or perhaps thrown out of a window.

Unfortunately, in the confusion and excitement following the blast, no adequate steps were taken to safeguard the evidence and some of it was destroyed by the milling crowds and even by the police themselves, so the exact nature of the explosion was never fully determined. Experts believed, however, that the bomb consisted of a piece of iron pipe, capable of holding about two quarts, and that it was filled with dynamite, or dynamite "soup," and loaded cartridges.

With the destruction of the Los Angeles *Times* still vividly in mind, San Francisco was naturally thrown into a fever of excitement and indignation. Large rewards were offered for the arrest of the criminal or criminals, the Law and Order Committee of the

Chamber of Commerce went into action, secret investigators were sent out to gather evidence, and the district attorney's office began to move against certain labor leaders on the assumption that the explosion was the work of radical union sympathizers.

Suspicion centered on an aggressive radical named Tom Mooney. For ten years Mooney had been at loggerheads with law. He had been one of J. B. McNamara's intimates when the latter passed through San Francisco on his way to Los Angeles to blow up the *Times* Building, sufficiently close to the Indianapolis dynamite conspirators to be included in the general indictment, a vigorous defender of the leaders of the I.W.W. who were arrested after the Wheatland riots, a friend of Emma Goldman and other anarchists, a contributor to an anarchist journal called the *Blast,* and the instigator of a threatened strike on the United Railroads.

Because of his aggressive part in fomenting and supporting strikes and his reputation for lawlessness, Mooney was a marked man with the businessmen's law-and-order committees and protective bureaus; and when the disastrous explosion of July 22 occurred and neither the motive nor the perpetrator was easily discovered, the advocates of the open shop raised a strong hue and cry against him and other left-wing labor leaders.

Openly aligning himself with this group, Charles Fickert, San Francisco's district attorney, ended his search for the murderers with the arrest of Mooney and his associates and virtually refused to examine any evidence that pointed to other suspects. In thus closing the door on a thorough and impartial investigation of the crime Fickert ignored at least one reasonable possibility that deserved the fullest consideration. The feeling between militarists and anti-militarists seemed as bitter as anything the nation had experienced since the outbreak of the Civil War. Pacifists, pro-Germans, a small group of Mexicans (violently incensed by General Pershing's invasion of Mexico in pursuit of Pancho Villa), and certain labor unions that looked on the parade as both a militaristic demonstration and a thinly disguised effort to bolster the open shop, were extremely vocal in their criticism of the whole Preparedness Day idea, including its sponsors, methods, and objectives.

On the morning of July 22, San Francisco newspapers were warned to expect an act of violent or spectacular protest. The communication, written in Roman script with an indelible pencil, contained a number of underscored words and a few repetitions. The first paragraph read as follows:

Editor: Our protests have been in vain in regards to this preparedness propaganda, so we are going to use a little direct action on the 22nd which will echo round the earth and show . . . that militarism cannot be forced on us and our children. . . . Things are going to happen to show that we will go to any extreme, the same as the controlling class, to preserve what little democracy we still have. Don't take this as a joke or you will be rudely awakened.

The writer then invited the members of the San Francisco Chamber of Commerce to march in a body "if they want to prove they are no cowards." The letter was signed "The Determined Exiles from Militaristic Government, Italy, Germany, United States, Italy, Russia." [2]

Similar threats were received at parade headquarters; but owing to the negligence, inefficiency, or indifference of the district attorney, who himself at first laid the blame for the explosion on some fanatic incited to violence by the tirades of the opponents of the parade, the source of these communications was never determined.

Ignoring the possibility that the bomb had been planted by a fanatic or a saboteur, Fickert took Warren K. Billings, one of Tom Mooney's close associates, into custody. A day or two afterward he arrested Mooney and his wife, Rena. Later he indicted two prominent labor-union leaders, Edward D. Nolan and Israel Weinberg.

Billings, with a prior criminal record, was summarily tried, convicted of murder in the second degree, and sentenced to life imprisonment. Facts later brought to light raised serious doubt as to

---

[2] The Los Angeles *Times*, July 23, 1916.

the validity of the evidence used against him. From an examination of official records one writer concludes that he "was convicted and sentenced to life imprisonment on the testimony of a drug addict, an ex-convict, a garrulous ex-prostitute with a police record, and an apparently irresponsible mother and daughter, later discredited." [3]

Mooney was convicted of first-degree murder and sentenced to be hanged. The verdict, in the light of what many regarded as inconclusive evidence, aroused intense resentment among union labor groups in the United States and even led to a popular demonstration before the American Embassy in Petrograd. Many thoughtful Americans, wholly without sympathy for Mooney's radical ideas, were nevertheless deeply concerned over the manner of his conviction and the possibility of a grave miscarriage of justice. Their doubts became even more disturbing when Fremont Older published a number of letters in the San Francisco *Bulletin,* showing that the testimony "which decided the case for the prosecution" was apparently perjured from beginning to end.

Eventually the Mooney case became so clouded over with prejudice, partisanship, face-saving, legal shibboleths, and technicalities that justice and truth became difficult to determine, although many investigators have since agreed that the conviction, in the light of the evidence, was probably unjust. The San Francisco Law and Order Committee denounced Older as an anarchist. Judge Franklin A. Griffin, who heard the Mooney trial, urged U. S. Webb, the Attorney General, to take necessary measures to have the case retried. Webb sought to carry out the recommendation, but the California Supreme Court refused to accede to the Attorney General's recommendation on the ground that the court could not go beyond the official record and admit new evidence, even though the defendant had been convicted on perjured testimony. One of the prosecution witnesses was tried for perjury and acquitted, but under the circumstances the verdict was a foregone conclusion.

---

[3] Lillian Symes: "Our American Dreyfus Case," *Harper's Magazine,* Vol. CLXII, p. 645.

When brought to trial, Rena Mooney was acquitted on substantially the same evidence that had brought the death sentence to her husband. A month later Alexander Berkman, an avowed anarchist, was indicted for first-degree murder as an accomplice in the explosion; but Berkman was then in New York and Governor Whitman refused to honor the extradition papers.

Billings's conviction was upheld by the California Supreme Court; but after several months in prison Edward Nolan, one of the five indicted suspects, was freed for lack of evidence. Finally a jury required only twenty minutes to acquit Weinberg, the last of the five original defendants.

In 1918 a Mediation Commission appointed by President Wilson threw further doubt on the credibility of the prosecution's testimony. But the California Supreme Court again found itself incapable of going outside the record, and upheld the death penalty against Mooney. In November the United States Supreme Court refused to review the case, and only the urgent request of President Wilson led Governor Stephens to commute Mooney's sentence to life imprisonment.

President Wilson's intervention sprang both out of a desire to conciliate union labor in connection with the Allied war effort and from his grave concern over the miscarriage of justice in the Mooney trial. After a full and confidential investigation of the case J. B. Densmore, Solicitor for the Department of Labor and later Director of Employment, made a lengthy report to President Wilson, in which he said in part:

The plain truth is, there is nothing about the cases to produce a feeling of confidence that the dignity and majesty of the law have been upheld.[4]

Reversing the usual procedure, interest in the Mooney-Billings "martyrdom" waxed instead of waned as the years passed. Petitions and appeals for pardon flooded the office of each new Cali-

---

[4] *The Mooney Case.* A Report to the Secretary of Labor by J. B. Densmore, Director General of Employment, San Francisco, November 1, 1918. House Documents, 66th Congress, 1st Session, Doc. 157, p. 4.

fornia Governor—none of whom took favorable action—and legal technicalities prevented the courts from granting the men a new trial.

In 1931 a subcommittee of the Hoover-appointed National Commission on Law Observance and Enforcement, commonly known as the Wickersham Commission, rendered an extensive report on the Mooney-Billings trials. The subcommittee's report was suppressed by the commission on the grounds that it was beyond the commission's province "to investigate individual cases with a view to making recommendations as to their disposition." The commission then added:

. . . With regard to the contentions concerning the recantation of testimony given on the trials of Mooney and Billings after the event, it is to be remarked that on a second hearing by the Supreme Court of California, on an application for pardon made by Billings, the witnesses concerned appeared in person at a public hearing by that court, where they were examined and cross-examined, after which the court, one justice alone dissenting, upon a thorough review of the testimony refused to recommend a pardon. Obviously, this commission could not undertake to review that action. This commission was not appointed to sit in review upon the judgment of the courts of any State. We may say further that the impropriety of any discussion of the case, had we power to review it, would arise from the fact that an application for a pardon for Mr. Mooney is now, as we have been advised, under consideration by the Governor of California.[5]

The conclusions of the suppressed report of the subcommittee were as follows: Police and prosecution never made any scientific attempt to find the guilty; their major efforts were devoted to locating evidence to convict the accused, and in their treatment of the latter the authorities behaved, in some instances, unlawfully. The techniques employed whereby witnesses "identified" the accused were slipshod and unfair, and evidence casting doubt on the veracity of prosecution testimony was deliberately withheld.

---

[5] National Commission on Law Observance and Enforcement: *Report on Lawlessness in Law Enforcement*, No. XI, p. 9.

Witnesses were carefully coached, and contradictory evidence studiously concealed. Finally, a campaign deliberately arranged to arouse public prejudice against the accused was carried on through the press, by intemperate arguments of prosecuting attorneys, and by propaganda even after the trials had concluded.[6]

Fifteen years after Mooney's arrest the judge before whom the case had been tried, the ten surviving jurors, the assistant district attorney who had prosecuted Billings, the chief of the detective bureau who had organized the evidence, and the district attorney of San Francisco petitioned the Governor to pardon the prisoners. Spontaneous contributions and highly organized solicitations placed thousands of dollars at the disposal of the directors of the movement to free the two men, until at last Mooney and Billings lost their character as individuals and were magnified, by worldwide propaganda, into impersonal symbols of what labor considered its age-old fight for justice and the rights of common men.

Mooney's pardon by Governor Culbert F. Olson in 1939 and Billings's release a few months later thus came as a definite anticlimax to the martyr's role the two men had been called upon to play. During their long years of imprisonment they had come to personify to millions of sympathizers throughout the world the alleged iniquity, oppression, and injustice that marked the capitalistic war against union labor and the closed shop. When the prisoners went free, the symbols lost their significance, the propaganda dwindled to a trickle and soon dried up. Mooney and Billings passed from the headlines of the world's press into the oblivion of very ordinary free men.

The San Francisco tragedy of July 22, 1916 included much more than a dastardly explosion with an appalling toll of innocent victims. Its aftermath involved grave charges of the prostitution of justice, a host of baffling legal technicalities that somehow defeated every effort to obtain a fair and impartial retrial for the defendants, a fog of doubt and uncertainty that still makes it impossible to arrive at a clear-cut opinion on many aspects of the case, a

---

[6] *The Mooney-Billings Report* (1932), pp. 242–3.

bitterness of feeling that ran like a fever through the body politic, and over twenty years of "martydom" for the two men whom the law had held guilty of the crime. From a realistic point of view, the conviction and long imprisonment of Mooney and Billings proved a godsend to the union labor leaders of California.

CHAPTER 24.   A Changing State

ALTHOUGH political upheavals and labor controversies added an element of drama to the early twentieth-century chronicles of California, economic and social developments were of more lasting and fundamental significance.

During the first twenty years of the century, California experienced a major economic revolution. Population rose from 1,486,-000 to 3,427,000, representing a gain of sixty per cent during the first decade and of approximately forty-four per cent from 1910 to 1920. Agricultural production increased in value from $106,000,-000 in 1899 to $612,000,000 in 1919; the state's mineral and petroleum output expanded from $29,000,000 to $202,000,000; and value of product of lumbering, fishing, and manufacturing increased from $90,000,000 to $714,000,000 during the same period. The total value of output of basic industries thus rose in twenty years from $226,000,000 to $1,528,000,000—a gain of close to seven hundred per cent.

The production represented by the above figures resulted both from a phenomenal expansion of enterprises—such as agriculture, lumbering, oil, mining, and various branches of manufactures—that were already firmly established in California at the beginning of the century, and from the rise of new industries, notably motion pictures, the generation of hydroelectric power, and the bewildering variety of activities to which the widespread use of the automobile gave rise.

It is safe to say that nothing ever influenced California life and society so spontaneously and profoundly as automotive transportation. As late as 1907 Governor Pardee's message to the legislature made no reference to the automobile, but spoke of the benefit of good roads in "the saving of money in horse flesh, harness, wagons, time, and draught power." The first paved highway in California, constructed especially for automotive traffic by the state, was built in 1912, and even as late as 1910 there were only about 36,000 motor vehicles registered in California. By that time, however, by voting $18,000,000 for a system of paved roads throughout the state, the people had already begun a policy of highway construction that made California a leader in the motor age. Despite the enormous cost of such a program, its benefits were so obvious that bond issues for new highways were voted thereafter fully as readily as bond issues for new schools.

The State Highways Act of 1909 authorized the Department of Engineering to map out a state highway system that would run "north and south through the State, traversing the Sacramento and San Joaquin Valleys and along the Pacific Coast, by the most direct and practicable routes, connecting the county seats of the several counties . . . and joining the centers of population. . . ."[1]

Before recommending the routes for the new roads the Department of Highways made a careful survey of the state. A description of the experiences of one of the commissioners provides a vivid commentary on the roads of that day:

We covered six thousand eight hundred fifty miles on our tours. We were kicked off mountain roads by mules, we were stuck in river fords, we slid around dangerous mountain grades, we broke our windshield and punched holes in the bottom of our gasoline tank on the rocks on the desert, and after we had covered the trunk lines and laterals of California from Oregon to Mexico we went back to Sacramento and drew the State Highway routes on a big map of the state.[2]

During the next decade the electors approved two additional state highway bond issues, one for $15,000,000 in 1916, the other for $40,000,000 three years later. Cities and counties incurred even larger obligations for local street or road construction during the same period. By 1920 there were over 604,000 registered automobiles in the state. California, indeed, became a state on wheels. The automobile broke down isolation, diffused population, en-

---

[1] California State Automobile Association and the Automobile Club of Southern California: *The State Highways of California* (1921), Vol. 1, p. 11.

[2] Rockwell D. Hunt and William S. Ament: *Oxcart to Airplane* (1929), pp. 206–7.

couraged rural and suburban life, relieved urban congestion, greatly increased the inflow of tourists, opened the mountains and deserts to endless throngs of visitors, made the beaches universal playgrounds, acquainted Californians with the beauty and varied resources of their own state, carried them far afield into other states, and radically affected styles, dress, customs, manners, culture, and morals.

The effect of the automobile upon California's economic development was even more revolutionary than on the state's social and cultural life. In addition to ushering in an entirely new era in transportation, it transformed the petroleum industry, greatly stimulated certain branches of manufactures, initiated an entirely new era of highway and bridge construction, and created innumerable subsidiary enterprises from which California profited even more than most of the other states.

A second great change in California's economic life resulted from the growth of industry and manufacturing. Two great themes run through this story, one the gradual coordination of California's industrial economy with that of the rest of the nation as isolation ended, and second the spectacular manner in which southern California first caught up with and then surpassed the northern counties.

Early California industry was small scale and adapted to frontier needs. Milling of lumber and grain, the processing of leather, and the manufacture of horse-drawn vehicles, notably by John Studebaker of Placerville, joined mining as important occupations. The Civil War force-fed still more the development of an indigenous industry, temporarily deprived of eastern sources of supply, and the boom period of the 1880's provided an optimism and an expanded market which led to further expansion.

Until the great earthquake and fire of 1906 San Francisco centered the state's manufacturing activities, but that event set back the bay area, and by the 1920's Los Angeles was the first manufacturing city in the state. This occurred despite the fact that World War I had relatively smaller effect in southern California than elsewhere. War industry, as such, did not affect southern counties markedly until World War II. By the 1930's California was engaged chiefly in petroleum production and refining, canning and preserving, fishing, lumber production, meat packing and slaughtering, and foundry and machine shop enterprises.

The second World War and its aftermath again changed the industrial scene. Now aircraft and its corollaries became important, textiles and garment manufacture made California a significant style center for the nation, automobile assembly expanded, and finally chemicals and electronic industries and research facilities grew rapidly. Throughout the entire period southern California remained a center of the entertainment industry, first with silent films, then "talkies," then radio and television.

While most of the earlier industries were California-owned, operated, and financed, many of the newer enterprises represented the westward expansion of large nationally known corporations whose management, control, and financing bore the imprimatur of Wall Street. Such companies, created by the economic penetration of Eastern capital and industry, not only greatly accelerated the movement toward state industrialization but drew California irrevocably into the current of national economic life and gave such problems as labor unions and the open shop a national rather than a local setting.

A third major contrast between the California of 1920 and the California of the early twentieth century resulted from a shift in population and economic initiative from northern to southern California. The line of demarcation between the two traditional divisions of the state is wholly arbitrary; but for convenience' sake it is usually drawn between Monterey, Fresno, Kings, and Mono counties on the north and San Luis Obispo, Kern, and Inyo counties on the south. In this division forty-seven counties are assigned to northern and eleven counties to southern California.

In 1900 the population of southern California was less than 350,000, in contrast with northern California's population of nearly 1,150,000. By 1910 the figures stood at 815,000 and 1,562,000 respectively. The census report of 1920 gave southern California 1,431,000 and northern California slightly less than 2,000,000. In

the relative growth of Los Angeles and San Francisco the transition was even more striking. From slightly over 100,000 in 1900,
the population of Los Angeles increased to 319,000 in 1910 and to
576,000 in 1920. San Francisco's population rose to 416,000 in 1910
and to 506,000 in 1920. The assessed valuation of San Francisco
(city and county) increased from $413,000,000 in 1901 to approxi-
mately $820,000,000 in 1920; during the same period that of Los
Angeles County rose from $103,000,000 to $1,276,000,000.

The disproportionate growth of southern California, in both
wealth and population, was due to a great variety of factors, chief
of which were the extraordinary expansion in agriculture, petroleum, hydroelectric power, and the motion-picture industry; the
construction of the Owens River aqueduct and the deep-water
harbor at San Pedro; climatic advantages; an abundance of readily accessible land suitable for subdivision; persistent advertising,
which at times became plain ballyhoo; installment sale of homes
and real estate; fewer labor controversies than in San Francisco,
and the nationwide reputation of Los Angeles as a city of the open
shop; a preponderance of good roads and automobiles; the indefatigable efforts of the Chamber of Commerce and other agencies
to make Los Angeles the largest city in the West; and the momentum of mass immigration, which began as far back as the real-
estate boom of the middle and late eighties.

If the truth must be told, Los Angeles suffered from an inferi-
ority complex, dating back to the days of the Gold Rush, which
made her, to compensate, a city of incorrigible boosters and led
her to move heaven and earth first to overtake and then outdis-
tance San Francisco—a city that, having long since arrived, was
not passionately concerned, like her southern rival, with the in-
cessant expansion of boundaries and the endless multiplication of
population. Yet for all her crassness, in the light of actual accomplishments, Los Angeles was perhaps justified in boasting of the
greatness of tomorrow with as much assurance as she boasted of
the quite incredible achievements of the past.

It was in this spirit of growing self-confidence that Los Angeles
undertook the construction of the Owens River aqueduct (the

subject of a later chapter) and the deep-water harbor at San Pedro. The latter undertaking, like the aqueduct, required a bold imagination and hard-headed foresight, for it involved the conversion of a region nature had designed for mud flats and sand dunes into one of the greatest man-made harbors of the world.

The undertaking presented some peculiarly difficult political as well as engineering problems. The first prerequisite was to gain access to the sea and bring the site of the proposed harbor under the jurisdiction of Los Angeles. Since the new harbor and its extensive tidelands lay within the corporate limits of San Pedro and Wilmington, some sixteen miles from the inland metropolis, it was necessary for Los Angeles to annex a narrow strip of territory extending from its southern boundary to the nearest limits of the seacoast cities. The delineation and annexation of this long "shoestring strip," in some places only a few hundred yards wide, was as pretty a piece of gerrymandering as California has ever witnessed.

But though this move brought Los Angeles to within a mile of tidewater, the harbor itself still lay outside its jurisdiction and the city could not legally undertake to develop it or finance any part of such operations. There was no law, however, that prevented an inland city from creating a harbor commission and drafting plans for the construction of a port. Accordingly, even though Los Angeles had neither harbor, access to salt water, nor ocean frontage, the city council passed an ordinance providing for a harbor commission, the Mayor appointed its three members, and the body proceeded to carry out its non-existing functions.

Under pressure from the Los Angeles Chamber of Commerce, Congress had already authorized the establishment of definite harbor lines in what was called the Wilmington Lagoon. The original bill, introduced by Senator Frank P. Flint, who owed his election to the Southern Pacific Railroad, gave the company a near monopoly of control over the proposed harbor. But the newspapers and civic organizations in Los Angeles protested so loudly that the measure was quickly amended to meet the public needs. The Los Angeles Harbor Commission then adopted the general plan of development to which the present port conforms; but the purchase or condemnation of private and corporation holdings, the settlement of adverse claims, and the acquisition of public lands necessary to complete the harbor required years of litigation and the enactment of a considerable body of favorable state and federal legislation.

Although California law made it impossible for one incorporated community to annex another, the California legislature enabled San Pedro and Wilmington to effect the necessary union with Los Angeles by passing an act permitting the "consolidation" of two or more cities. The "consolidation" elections took place in August 1909, and because of generous pledges from Los Angeles to voters of the smaller cities, the measure carried by large majorities. Most of these pre-election promises were kept, some were later ignored, and a few went unfulfilled because of legal obstacles.

With the major legal obstructions removed, Los Angeles went rapidly ahead with the physical development of the harbor, which nature itself had so niggardly endowed. The original breakwater, begun in 1899, was completed in 1910. When the Panama Canal was opened to commercial traffic in 1914, the dredging of the inner harbor was well advanced; a large number of docks, piers, and warehouses were already built; and Los Angeles had begun to publicize the port with her traditional enthusiasm.

During the fiscal year 1911–12, imports and exports amounted to nearly 2,500,000 tons, and rose to about 3,000,000 tons on the eve of the European war. Then, because of a shortage of ships, the business of the harbor abruptly declined. By 1920, however, shipping had risen to nearly 4,520,000 tons, and the development of the modern harbor was well under way.[3]

But even though Los Angeles thus possessed one of the world's largest ports, the city's population remained on the whole an inland people. They were not born to the tradition of the sea. Most

---

[3] Clarence H. Matson: *Building a World Gateway* (1945), *passim*. By 1939 Los Angeles and the federal government together had spent at least $60,-000,000 on the port and its annual commerce amounted to over 20,000,000 tons.

of them saw the ocean only a few times a year, and when they thought of it they thought in terms of holidays, vacations, and bathing-beauty contests. San Franciscans, by contrast, even though their harbor no longer completely dominated the state, were a sea-minded people. Their eyes looked out each day upon the historic waters of the great bay and through the Golden Gate; and when they thought of the sea, they thought instinctively of trade and ships and tropic ports.

Occupying a seemingly impregnable position as the first city on the Pacific coast, San Francisco watched the growth of southern California, and particularly of Los Angeles, during the early part of the century with a blend of indifference and tolerant superiority. Then, shortly after the end of the war, the bay metropolis woke to find herself outstripped by her upstart southern rival in population, building permits, and various other indices of prosperity.

San Francisco's lack of an aggressive booster spirit, as well as of a concerted, carefully fostered advertising program, testified to the difference in attitude and outlook of the state's two largest cities. For a time, at least, San Francisco was "not avid for mere numbers." Then, too, the topography of the Bay City was poorly adapted to the mushroom growth to which Los Angeles grew accustomed. The labor unrest and graft trials of the first decade furnished poor publicity for new industries or prospective settlers. And, finally, the effects of the devastating earthquake and fire of April 1906, proved a serious and protracted deterrent to the city's normal growth.

Earthquakes of damaging proportions have been a familiar California phenomenon from very early times. They plagued Portolá's exploring expedition of 1769 and even led one of the pious friars to name the Santa Ana River the River of the Sweet Name of Jesus of the Earthquakes. During the era of the missions many of the adobe-walled structures suffered serious damage from such temblors. San Francisco was periodically shaken by severe earth disturbances during the fifties and sixties of the nineteenth century, and in 1872 an earthquake of almost record-breaking intensity caused heavy loss of life and serious property damage among the settlements of the Owens Valley.[4]

Many of the worst disturbances were due to an ancient rift or earthquake fault that leaves the sea near the mouth of Alder Creek, above Point Arena in Mendocino County, and makes its way southward to the Mexican border. During the millions of years since it first split the land this rift has given rise to hundreds of thousands of earthquakes, great and small, and has suffered both a huge horizontal slip and an aggregate vertical displacement of over half a mile. The ancient break is known as the Portolá-Tomales or, more commonly, the San Andreas fault. From Alder Creek it closely parallels the coast, passes close by the Golden Gate, and extends to Chittenden, in the Pajaro Valley in Monterey County. From Chittenden the fault follows the axis of the Gabilan Mountains, runs through the so-called Carrizo Desert on the edge of the San Joaquin Valley, continues many miles along the slope of the Sierra Madre Mountains, and finally curves eastward past the San Bernardino and San Jacinto mountains to lose itself in the Colorado Desert not far from Yuma. The rift can thus be traced a total distance of some six hundred miles.

On the morning of April 18, 1906, the San Andreas fault yielded to the earth's accumulated pressure, as it had done innumerable times before. At approximately quarter past five on that disastrous morning the sleeping city of San Francisco was shaken to its foundations by a succession of violent earthquake shocks. Wide fissures opened in the ground; streets and sidewalks pitched and

---

[4] *The Earthquake History of the United States,* issued by the United States Coast and Geodetic Survey, lists the Tejon earthquake of 1857, that of Owens Valley in 1872, and the San Francisco quake of 1906 as "outstanding." On the Rossi-Forel scale all of these and the Imperial Valley earthquake of May 18, 1940 are given the maximum intensity, X. At least fifteen severe earthquakes were felt in California between 1906 and 1955. Heavy damage was done to life and property by earthquakes at San Jacinto and Hemet on April 21, 1918; at Santa Barbara on June 29, 1925; at Long Beach on March 10, 1933; in the Imperial Valley on May 18, 1940; and at Tehachapi and Bakersfield in 1953. The Long Beach earthquake is rated as the second most destructive shock ever to occur in the United States. It killed over 100 persons and caused property damage in excess of $40,000,000.

heaved like the waves of a troubled sea; office buildings were wrenched from their foundations and twisted around to face in entirely different directions; cheap brick structures were overthrown by the score; and fires of appalling intensity broke out in a hundred different places.

Bad as it was, the damage done by the earthquake in San Francisco later seemed inconsequential compared to the destruction wrought by the fires that sprang up throughout the stricken city. The main force of the earthquake, following the fault that crossed the entrance to the Golden Gate and reached the shore again at Mussel Beach, broke all the water mains entering San Francisco from the great reservoirs of Crystal Springs, San Andreas, and Pilarcito, thus leaving the city virtually without water to fight the overwhelming conflagration. An attempt to check the fire at Van Ness Avenue by the use of dynamite was seriously handicapped by lack of concerted effort and unfamiliarity with the use of explosives.

Thus virtually unrestrained, the fire burned continuously for three days and two nights. It spread over more than five hundred city blocks, an area four square miles in extent, and destroyed twenty-eight thousand buildings. Between four hundred and five hundred lives were reported lost in the earthquake and fire, though the actual number was probably far greater. According to Frank Leach, superintendent of the United States Mint in San Francisco, "every bank, every theatre, every hotel of importance, all newspaper offices, telegraph offices, libraries, municipal buildings, and nearly all the business houses in San Francisco were destroyed." [5]

Fortunately for the city, Mayor Schmitz acted with vigor and dispatch to meet the emergency, and federal troops from the Presidio assumed responsibility for the maintenance of order in the stricken areas. A special emergency body, called the Committee of Fifty, acted with the Mayor and virtually took over every function of the municipal government, including the or-

---

[5] *Recollections of a Newspaper Man* (1917), p. 352.

ganization and administration of relief. Schmitz issued a proclamation notifying the people that looters would be shot on sight; all
gas and electricity were shut off; and citizens were urged to remain at home from nightfall to daylight and exercise the greatest
caution against the spread of fire.

General Frederick Funston, a popular figure of the Spanish-
American War, was in command of the Army in the San Francisco
district and took personal charge of the troops in the stricken city.
The work of the Army, whether in dynamiting buildings, dealing
with citizens, suppressing looting, or administering measures of
relief, was highly praised by many responsible citizens, but condemned by others with equal vigor.

San Francisco, always ready to respond to others in distress,
now found the rest of humanity equally generous in its aid and
sympathy. When news of the earthquake reached the outside
world, doctors, nurses, food, medicines, blankets, clothing, and
supplies of all kinds began to flow at once toward the stricken
region. States, counties, cities, federal agencies, foreign governments and peoples, churches, lodges, organized charities, and
thousands of individuals joined in this spontaneous outpouring of
relief. All told, the contributions in cash and supplies for the tens
of thousands of refugees whom the disaster left homeless reached
the huge total for that day of fifteen million dollars.

At first food, medicine, clothing, and blankets were distributed
as individual need required; and thousands of families camped
out in parks, in vacant lots, and on the beach. In time, however,
the relief agencies constructed comfortable camps, with wooden-
floored tents or small wooden houses, hot and cold water, bath-
houses, public kitchens, and eating places. Sanitary regulations
were strictly enforced. Hundreds of sewing machines were distributed among the women, and thousands of dollars' worth of
tools were placed at the disposal of carpenters and mechanics. In
the administration of the large contributions of money and immense stories of supplies, Edward T. Devine, special representative of the American Red Cross, reported that none of the thousands of refugees suffered from lack of food, clothing, or shelter;

that no money was wasted, stolen, or misappropriated; and that complete harmony prevailed among the numerous agencies that sought to meet the distress of the unfortunate city.[6]

As in every major disaster in a great city, rape and looting on a small scale marred the heroism and sacrifice of the vast majority of the citizens. The human aspect of the disaster was described by Mary Austin:

South of Market, in the district known as the Mission, there were cheap man-traps folded in like pasteboard, and from these before the rip of the flames blotted out the sound, arose the thin, long scream of mortal agony.

Down on Market Street Wednesday morning, when the smoke from the burning blocks behind began to pour through the windows, we saw an Italian woman kneeling on the street corner praying quietly. Her cheap belongings were scattered beside her on the ground and the crowd trampled them; a child lay on a heap of clothes and bedding beside her, covered and very quiet. . . .

Not far from there, a day-old bride waited while her husband went back to the ruined hotel for some papers he had left, and the cornice fell on him; then a man who had known him, but not that he was married, came by and carried away the body and shipped it out of the city, so that for four days the bride did not know what had become of him.

There was a young man who, seeing a broken and dismantled grocery, meant no more than to save some food, for already the certainty of famine was upon the city—and was shot for looting. Then his women came and carried the body away, mother and betrothed, and laid it on the grass until space could be found for burial. They drew a handkerchief over its face, and sat quietly beside it without bitterness or weeping. It was all like this, broken bits of human tragedy, curiously unrelated, inconsequential, disrupted by the temblor, impossible to this day to gather up and compose into a proper picture.

The largeness of the event had the effect of reducing private sorrow to a mere pin prick and a point of time. . . . The will of the people was toward authority, and everywhere the tread of soldiery brought a relieved sense of things orderly and secure. . . .

---

[6] *Outlook*, December 1, 1906.

In the parks were the refugees huddled on the damp sod with insufficient bedding and less food and no water. They laughed. They had come out of their homes with scant possessions, often the least serviceable. They had lost business and clientage and tools, and they did not know if their friends had fared worse. Hot, stifling smoke billowed down upon them, cinders pattered like hail—and they laughed —not hysteria, but the laughter of unbroken courage.[7]

Although the loss of life and property were worse in San Francisco because of the fire and the congested population, the earthquake left extensive devastation in its train from Point Arena to Priest Valley, fifty miles beyond Chittenden on the line of the San Andreas rift. All the cities in the bay region suffered severely. Stanford University, then only about fifteen years old, lost many of its newly erected buildings. Virtually all brick buildings in Santa Rosa "collapsed like so many sand piles," and the earthquake and fire together destroyed twelve or thirteen business blocks in that city and took a toll of at least seventy lives. Similarly the Mission of San Juan Bautista, near Hollister, was almost destroyed. Bad though the earthquake was, irresponsible newspaper reports magnified its terrors tenfold.

The rebuilding of the devastated cities, particularly San Francisco, required courage, determination, and imagination of the highest order. Property destruction in San Francisco exceeded half a billion dollars, and thousands of people moved away either because of the housing shortage or from fear of a repetition of the disaster. It is a tribute to the spirit of the city that the work of rebuilding began before the flames subsided or the embers became cold. By April 1907, a year after the disaster, San Francisco building permits averaged two million dollars a week. The most sanguine estimated that five years, at the very minimum, would be required to restore the city; but the task, to all intents and purposes, was finished in less than half that time.

But despite the remarkable success achieved in the restoration and rebuilding of San Francisco and the other damaged cities in

[7] Mary Austin: "The Temblor," in *The California Earthquake of 1906*, edited by David Starr Jordan (1907), pp. 344–9.

the bay region, the effects of the earthquake were not wholly or immediately wiped out. Many who left the region did not return, business and capital were to some extent deflected to Los Angeles, and the fear of a repetition of the quake turned the flow of immigration from the East and Midwest even more definitely to southern California.

When the gates of the Panama-Pacific Exposition opened at San Francisco on February 20, 1915, however, almost no trace of the terrible holocaust that the city had suffered nine years before remained to greet the visitor; and the exposition, so magnificently conceived and so incomparably beautiful, fittingly symbolized the noble rebuilding of the devastated city and the courageous spirit of its people. Like San Francisco itself the exposition, despite the outbreak of the European war, was international as well as national in its genius. Twenty-five foreign governments and most of California's fellow states accepted invitations to be represented by buildings and exhibits.

Well might a lover of San Francisco write:

She has distinction, beauty, charm, and many lovers. One must envy the good fortune of those who are yet to come under her spell. When such a one comes for the first time to this glamorous city, he will learn to love her cool, gray beauty; he will delight in seeing her rise ghostlike on her high hills—an uneven, sawtoothed Whistler silhouette, dimly outlined against an indefinable sky. And sometime he will watch from a ferry at sunset these startling color-changes which turn the sky from flaming apricot to the blue and then to that cool, compassionate, all-encompassing gray which lays its mask over the city like a visible hush. At the Golden Gate he will see the sun lie low in a bed of cherry coals, flaming between black headlands. And then, suddenly, the city will be swallowed up in darkness, and all will vanish save the flashing jewel of Alcatraz, fantastic island castle of a pastry-cook's dream.[8]

The San Andreas Fault still has its restless moments. In March 1957 another stiff temblor, not as severe as the 1906 shake, jarred the city again, especially the southwestern sector. But no fire fol-

---

[8] Glenn C. Quiett: *They Built the West* (1934), p. 255.

lowed this slippage, and modern building construction kept damage to a minimum. The fault is there, however, lying like a quiescent serpent, clearly visible from the air in many parts of the state. Doubtless it will shift again, but this time San Francisco will be ready for it.

CHAPTER 25.   Prosperity and Cultural
Development

CALIFORNIA entered upon the postwar era in 1920 keyed
to a new pitch of extravagance and instability; and before
the economic crash of 1929, the southern part of the state, at least,
had gone more than a trifle mad. The war years had brought unprecedented prosperity to many classes in California—bankers,
farmers, oil producers, manufacturers, and skilled employees.
Agricultural production rose from $254,000,000 in 1914 to $612,-
000,000 in 1919. The output of mines and oil wells increased in
value during the same period from $94,000,000 to $202,000,000,
and manufactures expanded from $657,000,000 to $2,000,000,000.
Much of this new-found wealth originated in southern California,
and the stream was augmented by a flood of investment and
speculative capital from other parts of the country.

Before the mid-twenties southern California thus found itself in
the throes of a spectacular orgy of speculation—the boom of the
eighties fantastically expanded and set to the tempo of the jazz
age. Many factors accounted for this amazing era, including a
spontaneous determination on the part of some millions of Americans to enjoy a more attractive and less arduous way of life, the
development of cross-continent automobile traffic on a large scale,
the magic name and glamorous lure of Hollywood, enlarged opportunity for industry and industrial employment, high-pressure
publicity and advertising, a long-pent-up demand for new homes
and a huge reservoir of prospective home-seekers created by the
interruption of the normal flow of tourists to California during the
war, and a wild oil boom that accompanied the opening of one
new field after another, including three of the richest the state has
ever known.

The real-estate boom developed first. In four years, beginning
with 1921, the value of realty transfers in the city of Los Angeles

amounted to $2,777,000,000, and transactions elsewhere in southern California added another $700,000,000. In 1922 and 1923 the demand for real estate was so great that thousands of acres were subdivided and 140,000 new lots placed on the market. Building permits followed the same fantastic pattern: $28,000,000 in Los Angeles in 1919; $200,000,000 in 1923; $500,000,000 between 1923 and 1927. During much of the same period the city's population increased at the rate of a hundred thousand a year.

As the boom gained momentum, it swept everything before it. Grazing lands, grain fields, orchards, truck gardens, and chaparral-covered hillsides were subdivided and thrown on the market as fast as the necessary maps could be recorded. Vacant crossroads suddenly developed into important business centers; quiet villages woke to find their skylines broken by towering office buildings and spacious apartment houses; and almost overnight compact little communities changed into sprawling, hectic, metropolitan centers. Glendale, whose population in 1910 was only 2,700, became "the fastest growing city in the world" and by 1930 boasted 62,000 inhabitants. Between the census of 1920 and that of 1930 the population of Long Beach rose from 55,000 to 142,000. The phenomenal transformation in the status of these two cities had its counterpart in the growth of one community after another, until the population influx to southern California was characterized as "the largest internal migration in the history of the American people."

During this period much of the rare California landscape was shamefully disfigured by numerous cheap and shoddy promotion schemes, the abominable practice of dividing new tracts into miserable fifty-foot lots (thereby despoiling future generations of their proper heritage of earth and space), and a rash of square, flat-roofed, unlovely stucco houses, supposedly conforming to the Spanish-Mexican tradition, which covered the once attractive hillsides. Like the enterprising philistine that he was, the Los Angeles real-estate promoter, who thought primarily of quick and easy profits, subordinated beauty to utility and ridiculed the idea of letting æsthetic considerations interfere with the maximum gain to be derived from the subdivision and sale of the good earth. Despite these offenders, however, many of the new developments of the twenties showed a great advance in both architectural taste and landscape design over the poorly planned and badly correlated subdivisions of earlier years.

The methods employed by real-estate promoters and salesmen in the boom of the twenties were basically the same as those used by their predecessors forty years earlier. Florid advertisements rang the changes on climate, soil, scenery, population, agriculture, trade, manufacturing, automobile registration, bank clearings, unrivaled cultural advantages, the languorous charms of beach and desert resort, the glamour of Hollywood, southern California's amazing past and unimaginable future, and the general perfection of life available only to those who lived in the magic land.

W. W. Robinson, foremost of authorities on southern California land titles and real-estate activities, thus describes the methods used to attract the thousands of prospective settlers, investors, and speculators from among whom the actual purchasers finally emerged:

In Carthay Center, lots were sold on the strength of their being fourteen minutes from Pershing Square, the heart of Los Angeles, *by subway*. That subway is still a lovely dream. A mountain-top subdivision, "Rim of the World Park," with "cabin sites" at $150, was described as having "flower-dotted grass; mountain streams gliding between tall, cool pines; gentle balsam-spiced air; high, blue peaks near-by; a wisp of cloud in an azure sky." Quite true, but oh, how hard to get there! Beach clubs, golf clubs, trout clubs, lake clubs, salt-water swimming clubs, artists' clubs, all with fine club houses, extensive equipment and grounds, were organized daily. Full-page ads in the papers, with pictures of handsome structures, did the trick. If a bank clerk joined the Deauville Beach Club one day, the next morning on reading the *Examiner* he will regret that he had not joined the Gables Beach Club with its proposed taller building. . . .

The motion picture colony at Hollywood was drawn upon to furnish color and entertainment at tract "openings," in addition to bands, barbecues and lot lotteries. . . . On Sunday afternoons even Palos Verdes gave free programs of music, Spanish dancing, stunt flying, athletic contests, aquaplaning and yacht racing. The Hollywood Legion Band of forty-five pieces and Gary's Hotel Hollywood Orchestra aided, while boy scouts and G.A.R. members took part in flag-raisings. There was a Kiddies' Tent at Palos Verdes, on these important afternoons, with playground teachers, physicians and free toys. . . . When the guests climbed out of that bus a free lunch was served. They then were led into a tent for a snappy lecture, to clinch the travelogue and the good food. Afterward they were taken out to the long rows of salesmen's "closing" offices, tiny frame huts looking like confessionals. Here, one to a hut, they were destined to sign on the dotted line.[1]

The real-estate boom of the twenties, though spectacular and extravagant enough in itself in all conscience, was dwarfed in many particulars by the frenzied speculation in oil that accompanied the opening of half a dozen major fields in the so-called Los Angeles basin and two or three others elsewhere. A gasoline shortage resulting from the war, an unprecedented demand for petroleum created by the automobile and rapidly expanding industrial activity, and vastly improved methods of drilling, refining, and production led to a feverish search for new fields—a search that eventually proved so successful that it almost bankrupted the oil industry and badly demoralized the already unstable southern California public.

In 1919 the Standard Oil Company completed a discovery well at Huntington Beach. In 1921 the Shell Oil Company brought in a well on the prominent landmark, near the northern limits of Long Beach, known as Signal Hill. During the same year the Union Oil Company, making the novel experiment of drilling on a wide, level plain, struck oil on the Alphonzo E. Bell ranch at Santa Fe Springs, a few miles south of Whittier.[2] The three fields had several things in common: their potential capacity was enormous; the oil, produced under heavy gas pressure, was unusually light; and years before the discovery well was drilled, much of

---

[1] The Historical Society of Southern California *Quarterly*, March 1942, pp. 26–7, 30.

[2] The Elk Hills, Richfield, Torrance, Wheeler Ridge, Dominguez, Rosecrans, Inglewood, and Ventura fields were all opened between 1918 and 1925.

the oil-bearing land had been subdivided and sold in the form of town lots. The conditions were ideal for setting off a boom of staggering proportions. The state had no conservation restrictions worthy of the name and exercised little control over the sale of wildcat oil stocks. Money was available in unheard-of quantities, much of it brought into the state by new arrivals who had not yet had opportunity to invest it in more substantial ways.

The fever of speculation was sweeping over the whole nation as ruthlessly and universally as the influenza epidemic had swept over it a few years before; and stories of the fantastic fortunes derived from royalties in newly drilled wells received as wide publicity as the rumors of new silver discoveries had ever enjoyed in the hectic days of the Comstock. Promoters, speculators, outright swindlers, and a few bona fide independent oil operators who needed outside capital, quickly took advantage of this golden opportunity. No California generation had ever seen its equal before; none is ever likely to see its counterpart again.

Shrewd promoters organized companies, or "syndicates," leased or purchased small bits of land (in many cases scarcely large enough to permit the erection of a derrick) in or near one of the widely publicized fields, and sold interests or "units" in a prospective well. Theoretically the unit holder in such a company was entitled to his proportionate share of the profit from the venture after the cost of the land, drilling and production expense, promotional charges, overhead, and landowners' royalty had been deducted.

In some instances the fields were so prolific that the wells produced enough, even under these conditions, to return a dazzling profit to the gullible but lucky "investor" who risked his life savings in the gamble. But in the end the fortunate speculator, lured by the astute promoter to plunge more and more heavily into other wildcat ventures, usually awoke to find that his initial success was only the prelude to disaster. Meanwhile the army of "unit" salesmen played up the profits of his original speculation with all the skill of Hollywood publicity agents and thus anesthetized the common sense of other prospective victims.

Among the many fly-by-night promoters who found southern California a virgin hunting ground during the hectic twenties, a master of ballyhoo from the mid-continent oil fields named C. C. Julian enjoyed the most colorful and meteoric success. Julian was a genius in arousing the public's interest and capitalizing on its confidence, cupidity, and goodwill. By rare good luck he obtained a ten-acre lease some distance from the discovery well at Santa Fe Springs, erected a derrick, and began to drill. At the same time he started an advertising and sales campaign that struck the public fancy and aroused popular interest as nothing else of its kind, even among the southern California masters and connoisseurs of ballyhoo, had ever done before.

Julian employed newspaper advertisements almost exclusively for his publicity—one wonders what fabulous sums he might have extracted from the gullible, trusting, and avaricious public if the radio had then been available!—and appealed primarily to the Midwest farmers who flocked to California after the war. His advertisements, which usually began with the homely phrase: "Say Folks," showed a profound knowledge of the psychology of this cross-section of American society. He made his first appearance in the Los Angeles *Times* of June 19, 1922, with the announcement in bold headlines: "C. C. Julian Breaks into Santa Fe Springs the Gusher Field of America." Thereafter, with much the same avidity with which they waited for the Sunday comic page or the newest scandal in Hollywood, the southern California public daily looked forward to Julian's slangy, unorthodox, egotistical, ungrammatical wheedlings, promises, and warnings. His enterprises later came under grand jury investigation, and he was discredited.

As a result of the discovery of the great bonanza fields and their frenzied exploitation, California's petroleum production rose from 103,000,000 barrels in 1920 to 263,000,000 in 1923. Of that amount Santa Fe Springs produced 80,000,000 barrels; Long Beach, 69,-000,000; and Huntington Beach, 34,000,000. At one time the daily output of Santa Fe Springs was over 330,000 barrels and that of Signal Hill close to 245,000. Between 1920 and 1926 California wells yielded approximately 1,300,000,000 barrels of petroleum, and for a time threw the oil industry of the United States completely out of gear because of this overproduction.

While the real-estate and oil booms were in progress, the industrialization of California proceeded at an accelerated rate, and by 1925 Los Angeles had become one of the largest manufacturing cities in the United States. During these years the motion-picture industry expanded like one of its own fantastic creations, and entered in 1926 upon an era of new magnitude and variety with the introduction of sound pictures. As explained elsewhere, Los Angeles harbor also came into its own at this time, and cargo shipments increased nearly eight times, in both tonnage and value, between 1920 and 1930. Petroleum, lumber, and cotton figured most prominently in this expansion.

The phenomenal increase of wealth and population during the postwar period necessarily reflected itself in every phase of California's economic life. Lumber felt the stimulus of the great real-estate boom, and a new era in the development of hydroelectric energy was stimulated by growing public demand. In 1900 the total capacity of the plants in California was less than 31,000 kilowatt hours; by 1925 the state's hydroelectric companies were producing over forty times that amount of power.[3] In 1946 production was approximately 2,500,000 horsepower.

Geography, distance, and geological conditions confronted the California electrical industry with a variety of intricate technical problems, such as the transmission of huge power loads over previously prohibitive distances, and provided it with engineering tasks of the first magnitude. One such enterprise, to cite a typical example, required the erection of a huge dam at the lower end of Lake Almanor in Plumas County and the creation of an immense artificial lake, capable of storing 1,300,000 acre-feet of water. The lake supplied a year-round flow for the operation of a number of the Great Western Power Company's important hydroelectric plants on the Feather River.

---

[3] In 1927 the Southern California Edison Company reported the following distribution of its output: agriculture, 14%; industry, 33%; lighting and cooking, 11%; railways, 16%; resale to municipalities, 21%.

By means of the so-called "hook-up" arrangement, sponsored especially by the State Railroad Commission, the transmission lines of all the major power companies of California can be joined into one common system to meet an emergency created by drought, war, or other disaster. Under this arrangement, which was given its initial test in the drought of 1924, surplus power generated in southern Oregon can be sent as far south as the Mexican border.

As in the case of other public utilities, the State Railroad Commission regulates electric power rates, service, and the issuance of securities. In the matter of rates, the commission protects the consumer against extortionate charges, but permits the companies a fair return on capital investment.

California's remarkable economic expansion after World War I reflected itself in the field of banking and finance as well as in industry, trade, and population. Early in the century California banks had been called upon to face two serious crises—the San Francisco earthquake and fire of 1906 and the nationwide depression of the following year. The widespread financial panic of 1907, which followed close on the heels of the San Francisco crisis, led to the temporary or permanent suspension of some thirty California state banks, chief of which was the California Safe Deposit and Trust Company of San Francisco, with liabilities of over $9,000,000. Partly as a result of the panic and the subsequent bank failures, comprehensive banking legislation was passed in 1909 to supersede the long outmoded act of 1878.

The prosperous postwar decade witnessed a number of fundamental changes in the California banking system. Bank deposits increased from $1,890,000,000 in 1920 to over $3,000,000,000 in 1930. More and more the banking field came to be dominated by a few large institutions, most of which were the product of mergers and consolidations. Under the aggressive and at times ruthless leadership of the Bank of Italy (now the Bank of America) the system of branch banking spread through the state and absorbed most of the small local banks. During this era of the state's revolutionary economic growth large amounts of Eastern capital poured into California for speculation and investment, and California bankers developed a much more cosmopolitan point of view. Despite the growth of southern California, San Francisco remained the financial capital of the state.

The opening decades of the twentieth century witnessed cultural changes in California comparable to those that took place in industry, agriculture, and finance. The influence of churches upon the state's intellectual and spiritual development was as powerful as it was quiet and unspectacular. California was born in the noble tradition of Franciscan zeal and religious devotion. After the American occupation, churches were considered as necessary as schools and newspapers for the welfare of the frontier settlers. By 1900 there were 674,000 Protestant communicants and Catholics in California out of a total population of a little less than 1,500,000. In 1940 the population of California was nearly 7,000,000. Church membership had risen to over 2,000,000, and denominational rivalries were no longer a major factor among the historic Protestant denominations. Every city had its church buildings of dignity and beauty. In every town and rural area the church fulfilled its age-old mission of ministering to the hunger and thirst of man's eternal spirit; at the same time it fought a never ending battle for civic righteousness and served as the center of the community's social and intellectual life.

Loyal to the American tradition of education from the time of the framing of their first constitution, which provided both for a system of free public schools and a state university, Californians came to look upon state-supported education as an indispensable cultural inheritance, the chief bulwark of their society, institutions, and democratic way of life. The public school system, with its grammar schools, high schools, and teacher training, or state normal, schools, was well established and generously supported out of public funds many years before the close of the century. But the developments in education since 1900 have outdistanced not only the maximum accomplishments but the fondest dreams of the crusaders for the public school system of that older generation.

In 1900, as elsewhere remarked, the state had a population of approximately 1,500,000. Primary and secondary school enrollment was then 272,000, and the total annual appropriation for such schools, from state, county, and municipal funds, came to $7,289,-243. In 1940, when California's population had risen to about 7,000,000, there were over 1,900,000 pupils enrolled in the state's public school system, and the annual expenditure came to approximately $200,000,000.

A number of major changes were also made in the organiza- of the state school system. As early as 1907 the legislature made possible the establishment of public junior colleges, and within another decade such institutions were an important feature of the California educational program and an integral part of the plan to furnish opportunity, at public expense, for an educational experience that extended from kindergarten through the professional school. The more advanced state college took the place of the old normal school as a center of teacher training. The first "normal school" was established in San Francisco in 1862 and later moved to San José, where it became San José State College. Other normal schools were founded, and went through the same metamorphosis, until the present state college system includes twelve institutions, some emphasizing liberal arts, some agriculture, some teacher training. Accredited private colleges and universities were also authorized to issue teachers' credentials for California schools.

In the field of higher education California owes a great debt both to the state-supported university and to the privately endowed university and college. The University of California, oldest and largest of the universities, was chartered on March 23, 1868. The University of Southern California, a Methodist Episcopal Church foundation, was established in 1879 as the result of the donation of a tract of land in the southwestern part of Los Angeles by "a Jew, a Catholic, and a Protestant." The university had difficult sledding after the boom of the eighties and did not enter upon its phenomenal era of large student enrollment and athletic triumphs until after World War I. Stanford, youngest of the three major universities, was founded as a memorial to the only son of

Senator and Mrs. Leland Stanford. The cornerstone of its first building was laid in 1887, and its resources and endowment made it incomparably the richest educational institution in the world at the time of its foundation.

After 1918 California universities, like those of other states, underwent phenomenal expansion, and each developed according to its chosen objectives and fundamental philosophy. Each has its own traditions, history, and individuality, but lack of space precludes the detailed discussion that these matters almost irresistibly invite.

All but one or two California colleges owed their foundation directly or indirectly to the church. The College of the Pacific, earlier called the University of the Pacific, was established at San Jose by the Methodist Episcopal Church in 1851. Before 1870 the Catholics had established six colleges, including Santa Clara, St. Ignatius (now San Francisco University), the College of the Holy Name, St. Mary's, and Loyola. Mills College was founded in 1871 by Dr. Cyrus T. Mills, a former missionary in Hawaii, who taught the students "to spell correctly, to read naturally, to write legibly, and to converse intelligently," and who provided in his deed of gift that the college should be a Christian but nonsectarian institution.

In 1887 a group of Presbyterian ministers and laymen chartered an institution of higher learning, now known as Occidental College, in Los Angeles. Pomona College was founded by New England Congregationalists a few months later. Whittier College was established by the Friends in the early nineties, and in 1909 Redlands University was opened by the Baptists. Sectarianism never played an important part in the life of the colleges of Protestant foundation; and early in the century many of them, by agreement with their respective churches, gave up all organic denominational connection. In most of them, however, the religious tradition still remained a vital part of the institution's philosophy and life.

In 1906, under the direction of Dr. George Ellery Hale, astronomer, professor, and inventor of the spectroheliograph, the Carnegie Foundation established a world-famous observatory, with a one-hundred-inch reflecting telescope, on the summit of Mount Wilson, overlooking Pasadena.[4] Sixteen years later, with the financial support of a group of southern California philanthropists, Robert A. Millikan and a company of distinguished scientists transformed Throop College of Technology (founded by Amos Throop in 1890 under the name of the Polytechnic Institute) into the California Institute of Technology, an institution destined in a few years to win world renown as a center of scientific education and research.

The contributions of the California Institute and of the Mount Wilson Observatory were so outstanding that the Rockefeller Foundation in 1928 provided the necessary funds to erect a giant two-hundred-inch telescope on Mount Palomar, in San Diego County, thereby making southern California the chief center of astronomical research in the world. The Mount Palomar undertaking, like the Mount Wilson Observatory, the California Institute of Technology, and later the Huntington Library and Art Gallery and the Pasadena Civic Center were all in part the dream and creation of Dr. Hale.

In 1919 the state established a branch of the University of California at Los Angeles. The institution was later located on a large campus in the new district known as Westwood and in 1927, under the name of the University of California at Los Angeles, became co-ordinate with the parent university at Berkeley. Increased enrollment rapidly placed it in the rank of great American universities.

During the mid-twenties, as part of a carefully conceived plan of introducing the English concept of college-university organization into American education, President James A. Blaisdell of Pomona College, at Claremont, initiated a movement that led to the establishment of Scripps College, a women's college of limited enrollment, and the Claremont Colleges, a graduate school stressing the humanities, to work in close co-operation with Pomona.

---

[4] The Lick Observatory on Mount Hamilton, directed by the University of California, was the first of the state's large astronomical observatories.

California's cultural advance was reflected by its libraries, museums, and art galleries as well as by its colleges and universities. In 1919 Stanford University became the seat of the Hoover Library of War, Revolution, and Peace, established by the future President of the United States, which became the repository of thousands of books, reports, government documents, and manuscripts (a large part of which relate to World Wars I and II) and rapidly grew into one of the world's chief centers of research in modern diplomatic, political, social, and economic history.

Unique among the libraries of California, and in some respects among the libraries of the world, the Huntington Library and Art Gallery was the gift of Henry E. Huntington, nephew of the railroad-builder Collis P. Huntington, to the people of California. Huntington's interests, however, were not scattered or heterogeneous, like those of Adolf Sutro, who founded the amazing Sutro Library in San Francisco, but lay almost wholly in the field of Anglo-Saxon history, literature, and culture. In addition to the library, art gallery, and two-hundred-acre estate, Huntington left an endowment for the bequest which now exceeds thirteen million dollars.

Comparable in importance, from another standpoint, to such magnificent research libraries as the Huntington, Hoover, and Bancroft foundations are the State Library at Sacramento and the large municipal libraries of San Francisco and Los Angeles. The growth of library facilities in small towns and rural communities throughout the state also constitutes a form of educational and cultural leaven of incalculable value in the body politic. County libraries, for example, that maintain units in thinly populated regions offer opportunities to the isolated settlers that were utterly unattainable—indeed, almost undreamed of—a generation ago.

The theater came to California with the Gold Rush and flourished along with opera and vaudeville, especially in San Francisco, until a list of the artists who played to capacity houses, as John Caughey remarks, "would be a roll call of the generation's celebrities: Melba, Homer, Caruso, Alice Nielsen, Nat Goodwin, Lillian Russell, Julia Marlowe, Otis Skinner, DeWolf Hopper, Sarah Bernhardt, Weber and Fields." Subsequently the theater barely survived the onslaught of that bewildering contradiction of art, industry, science, and ballyhoo called Hollywood. Today California supports the legitimate stage in a few of the largest cities with commendable enthusiasm and finds outlet for genuine interest in pageantry and drama in such community institutions as Hemet's *Ramona,* the Bohemian Grove plays, the Community Playhouse of Pasadena, and the Pilgrimage Play of Los Angeles.

As already suggested, San Francisco long ago established the rich tradition of supporting the best in music the nation had to offer. According to one writer: "No American theater did so much to popularize opera as the Tivoli." In 1879 Gilbert and Sullivan's *Pinafore* ran there for eighty-four consecutive nights. For twenty-six years thereafter the Tivoli "gave 12 months of opera each year, never closing its doors." Alice Nielsen rose to fame from the Tivoli chorus, and Tetrazzini first came to the notice of the music-loving public when she sang the role of Gilda in *Rigoletto* on the Tivoli stage in 1905. The San Francisco Symphony, the San Francisco Opera Company, the San Francisco String Quartet, and popular choral and orchestra performances testify to the permanency of the city's musical tradition and the warm appreciation of its citizens for musical excellence.

Los Angeles, though badly handicapped by the lack of an adequate opera house, established its widely known symphony orchestra in 1919 and a few years later created the great outdoor amphitheater, the Hollywood Bowl, where concerts, plays, ballets, and "Symphonies under the Stars" attract nightly audiences running into the thousands and rival in popularity the football games in the Los Angeles Coliseum. As Hollywood gathered to itself authors and writers of all kinds, so it brought to its studios composers, conductors, and great concert artists. It thus supplied a large and varied reservoir for radio broadcasting companies, until, between radio and motion pictures, Los Angeles more and more became the musical rival of New York.

California architecture, like that of the rest of the English-speaking world, suffered from the artistic blight of the Victorian age. One looks at the photographs of the wealthy California homes of half a century and more ago with a certain horrible fascination, for to most architects of that day a house was merely a framework on which to hang as many gables, cornices, pillars, towers, cupolas, arches, and other gingerbread adornments as imagination could conceive and ingenuity find room for. The real-estate and building boom that followed World War I led to the construction of large numbers of cheap, unlovely homes, but when this period ended, California readily adopted the new architectural philosophy that sought to harmonize utility and comfort with grace of construction and beauty of design.

Architects also became aware that virtually any style, provided the architecture itself was sound and right, would harmonize with the diversified and accommodating California landscape. Lovers of beauty long ago discovered that flowers, shrubbery, and trees would make even the rough, redwood, boxlike houses of the semi-frontier days pleasing to the eye, and as wealth increased and taste grew more refined and discriminating, the landscape gardener became almost as important as the architect.

The Panama-Pacific Exposition in San Francisco, with its well-designed buildings in a superlatively beautiful setting, and the Panama-California Exposition at Balboa Park in San Diego gave strong impetus to the erection of public buildings worthy of the cities of a great commonwealth.

The Civic Center of San Francisco, with its marble City Hall, Public Library, State Building, and Civic Auditorium, and, to a still more marked degree, the curving grace of the great bridges that span the bay, are part of California's successful search for beauty in concrete, stone, and steel.[5] The San Francisco–Oakland Bay Bridge, completed in 1936, is four and a half miles long and ranks first in size and cost among the bridges of the world. The Golden Gate Bridge, completed in 1937, is the largest, highest

[5] The buildings listed above were erected after the disaster of 1906, or in connection with the Panama-Pacific Exposition.

single-span suspension bridge ever built. Its two towers are 746 feet high, and the bridge itself is suspended 266 feet above the water.

Los Angeles also gave thought to the dignity and beauty of its public buildings. The towering City Hall, Union Railroad Station, and numerous state, county, and federal public buildings grouped around the long-fought-for civic center bear witness to the success of this quest. Oakland, San Diego, Pasadena, Santa Barbara, and other California cities, large and small, have successfully attained the same ends. San Francisco's financial district and Wilshire Boulevard in Los Angeles are evidence that the architectural evolution is proceeding in California's industrial and commercial centers as well as in the field of private homes and public buildings.

Despite a more or less extended residence in the state of such landscape artists as Albert Bierstadt, Thomas Moran, William Keith, Maynard Dixon, Hanson Putoff, Alson Clark, William Ritsche, and William Wendt; sculptors such as Douglas Tilden and Arthur Putnam; portrait painters such as Seymour Thomas and Arthur Cahill; modern painters such as Millard Sheets, Barse Miller, Phil Dyke, McDonald Wright, and Dan Lutz, the prophecy of the development of a distinct and distinguished field of California art has not yet been fulfilled. It is appropriate to add, however, that "today there are so many artists in California, working in such a profusion of styles and aims, that the State has become one of the leading centers of art activity in the Nation."

Colonies that render valuable service to California art and the fellowship of artists flourish at Laguna, Carmel, and Santa Barbara. Important art galleries, represented by the M. H. de Young Memorial Museum in Golden Gate Park, the California Palace of the Legion of Honor in Lincoln Park, and the San Francisco Museum of Art, are available in San Francisco. The Museum of History, Science, and Art in Los Angeles, the Fine Arts Gallery in Balboa Park in San Diego, and the Henry E. Huntington Art Gallery in San Marino serve the needs of southern California. The Crocker Art Gallery in Sacramento was one of the earliest in the state. The Golden Gate International Exposition of 1939 contributed to the education and appreciation of the California public in the field of art as its predecessor, the Panama-Pacific Exposition, had done a quarter of a century before.

City-planning, though still in its infancy on the Pacific coast, has already given evidence of the incalculable benefit of wide automobile freeways, the reorganization of ugly, congested metropolitan districts, and the elimination of tenements and slum areas.

CHAPTER 26. Bread without Scarceness

THE ANNUAL value of California farm products at the be-
beginning of the century amounted to approximately $106,-
000,000. Forty years later the figure had risen to nearly $900,000,-
000. This increase in four decades was due to a great variety of
factors, some of which were in no sense peculiar to California but
constituted an integral part of the nation's general economic and
technological progress.

Transportation in its various branches furnished an obvious example of this truth. The extension of railroad facilities, faster
schedules, ventilated and refrigerated cars, cheaper freight rates,
improvements in cargo vessels, paved highways, automobiles, and
the development of the immense and widely ramified trucking
business, all played a major role in California's rapid agricultural
expansion.

In similar fashion, agriculture profited enormously from the
revolution that took place in the state's banking and financial position during the forty years in question. The change was evident in
the lowering of interest rates on farm mortgages and in the willing-
ness of large banks and insurance companies to lend money on
California farms. In California, as elsewhere, this ample supply
of capital in many instances changed farming from a precarious,
hand-to-mouth existence into a highly organized, largely mech-
anized business. California agriculture was also profoundly affected by the revolution in diet and taste the modern era brought
about in the United States.

In addition to such extraneous influences as transportation, financing, advertising, markets, and the like, there were numerous
factors of major importance within the industry itself that accounted for the phenomenal expansion of California agricultural
production after 1900. One of these was the development of irrigation. It is not necessary to describe in detail the evolution of
this all-important branch of California agriculture from the early

use of nearby streams and springs to the huge developments represented by the Metropolitan Water District of Southern California or the still larger undertaking officially known as the Central Valley Water Project in the Sacramento and San Joaquin valleys. Wells, storage and flood-control reservoirs, canals, spreading grounds, check dams, forest and brush conservation, and the development of hydroelectric power were all part of California's twentieth-century irrigation program. Many of the enterprises were privately financed; some were undertaken by co-operative or mutual irrigation companies; but the most extensive resulted from state or federal action.

An immense amount of litigation arose from disputed and uncertain water rights; and as late as 1913 the State Conservation Commission pointedly remarked that as long as such titles remained unsettled, "the possessors of the largest purses can indefinitely harass and annoy those whose purses are not so long." The Wright Act of 1887, providing for the formation and bonding of irrigation districts, was the first California legislation that enabled the ranchers of a community to finance, construct, and operate an irrigation enterprise for their own use. Additional laws were enacted from time to time to simplify the organization of irrigation districts or make their operations more effective. In 1930 about four million acres were included in such districts.

In most irrigation matters the state operates through a branch of the Department of Public Works, called the Divison of Engineering and Irrigation. This body is called upon to investigate and report on proposed irrigation districts and their bond issues; to supervise expenditure of funds from approved bond issues and inspect the work of irrigation districts; to collect data, make surveys, and form plans for the reclamation of the Sacramento and San Joaquin rivers; to pass on plans and specifications for the construction of dams unless the dam is a municipal or public-utility enterprise; to rectify river channels and provide for the control of floods.

In 1921 the legislature appropriated $200,000 to enable the Division of Engineering and Irrigation to prepare a complete inventory of all the waters within the state's boundaries and an estimate of the future needs of water for ultimate development that would secure the greatest public service from the state's water supply. With this fund, augmented by contributions from non-government sources and by additional appropriations from the state, a co-ordinated plan was devised for the development of the waters in the major geographic divisions of the state.

The development of new sources of water supply was accompanied by many experiments in methods of irrigation. On citrus ranches, for example, the trend was from the basin to the furrow, and from the furrow to the sprinkler. According to the federal census report of 1950, more than 6,500,000 acres of the state's agricultural lands were under irrigation, in contrast to only 1,500-000 in 1900. The completion of still more ambitious irrigation projects now in progress will transform millions of additional acres of waste, pasture, and grain lands into diversified farms.

One of the most important factors in the development of twentieth-century California agriculture was the introduction of new crops, such as grapefruit, dates, and avocados. The return to crops, such as cotton and rice, that were once tried experimentally and then abandoned proved even more profitable. Experimenters such as Luther Burbank in Santa Rosa added to the list of novelties in agriculture.

Despite the fact that there was no good reason why rice should not be grown in California, it was not until 1910, or a little later, that the grain was first planted on a large scale in the lower Sacramento Valley. Here it did so extraordinarily well that within a few years California had become one of the leading rice-producing states of the Union. From a production of 70,000 bushels in 1912 the California rice crop rose to a maximum of 9,000,000 bushels in 1919. In recent years the annual yield has been maintained at about the same level. The average production per acre is consistently higher in California than in any other state and in 1950 reached 72.5 bushels per acre. As a recent writer remarked, "Comment seems baffled by a product which increased ten thousandfold in a decade. It is too sudden and too great to be either fully understood or appreciated."

Although the state had undergone an extensive cotton boom in the decade after the Civil War, the crop was not raised again in California on a commercial scale until 1910. In that year 9,000 acres were harvested and the yield was a little over 6,000 bales. World War I greatly stimulated the interest in cotton planting in California, and between 1916 and 1920 the average planting was 90,000 acres a year, with an average yield of 48,000 bales. A decline then ensued for a number of years, but between 1926 and 1930 planting exceeded 217,000 acres annually and production rose to an average of 183,000 bales a year. As the result of the war demand, the yield was increased to 325,000 bales in 1944.

Cotton can be grown in many parts of California but almost the entire production now comes from the San Joaquin valley. The alcala, a medium-short-staple variety, comprises virtually the entire crop, and the grade of California cotton, thanks to climatic advantages and a longer staple, runs higher than the average grade throughout the United States. The cotton fields of the San Joaquin and Imperial valleys were one of the major reasons for the location of large automobile tire factories in southern California.

The citrus industry is the most widely publicized branch of California agriculture. The state in recent years has produced about sixty per cent of the oranges grown in the United States. It has a virtual monopoly of domestic lemon production, but ranks only third or fourth, depending on the season, in the output of grapefruit. In 1951 the orange crop, confined almost wholly to the Valencia and Washington Navel varieties, reached a total of approximately 38,300,000 boxes; lemons, chiefly the Eureka and Lisbon varieties, yielded about 12,800,000 boxes; and grapefruit totalled 1,150,000 boxes.[1]

The principal orange-producing counties are Orange, Los An-

---

[1] Lemons and grapefruit are grown almost exclusively in southern California, but orange culture reaches as far north as Tehama County.

geles, San Bernardino, Tulare, Riverside, Ventura, and San Diego. Ventura, Los Angeles, Orange, San Diego, and Santa Barbara counties furnish the bulk of the lemon crop. Grapefruit, of a sort, can be grown in many sections of California, but the largest acreage is in Imperial County, where the climate produces fruit of an exceptionally fine quality.

The success of the citrus industry in California was due in large part to the development of the highly efficient co-operative organization known as the California Fruit Growers Exchange; to the constant and intelligent effort of the growers to combat the many enemies and hazards to which the industry is exposed; and to the application of the same methods, organization, and technical skill that have proved so successful in other branches of American industry and business to this particular branch of agriculture.

According to C. C. Teague, sometimes spoken of as the father of co-operative marketing in California, the California Fruit Growers Exchange is

a federated democracy in the purest sense of the word, with a clearly defined channel of representation running from the individual grower to the central organization. The foundation of the Exchange is the 201 local packing associations comprising over 14,500 individual citrus growers throughout California and Arizona. . . . Each local association is governed by a board of directors elected from its membership list and each association is independently operated from an administrative standpoint.[2]

The two hundred or more local packing associations are organized into twenty-five district exchanges, and over these, in turn, stands the California Fruit Growers Exchange. Though marketing constitutes the primary business of the Exchange, three subsidiary corporations are included in the Exchange system: the California Fruit Growers Supply Company, the Exchange Orange Products Company, and the Exchange Lemon Products Company.

The California Fruit Growers Supply Company was organized in 1907 as a direct result of the threatened lumber shortage that

---

[2] Charles Collins Teague: *Fifty Years a Rancher* (1944), p. 82.

followed the San Francisco earthquake and fire the year before. By the acquisition of large holdings of timber lands in northern California and the operation of its own mills the organization is able to furnish box material and other lumber products to the growers at reasonable cost. But the Supply Company's activities reach into many other fields as well, and today it furnishes a great variety of additional items, including tissue wraps, nails, box labels, fertilizers, orchard heaters, and budwood.

The Exchange Orange and Lemon Products companies were organized to provide profitable outlets for cull and surplus fruit. Both companies carry on a highly organized program of laboratory and scientific research in the by-products of citrus fruits. At the present time juices, juice concentrates, citric acid, oil, and pectin constitute the most important of these by-products.

In addition to the functions already mentioned, the Fruit Growers Exchange, its subsidiaries, and the local packing houses carry on a multitude of activities, including picking, hauling, packing, inspection, pest control (usually by fumigation, dusting, or spraying), research, advertising, claims adjustments, transportation, and marketing.

Citrus culture, like all forms of agriculture, is a respectable game of chance. In this case, however, the stakes run much higher than in almost any other type of farming. During the past half century thousands of incompetent, unlucky, or inexperienced investors failed in this battle. Lifetime savings were lost, and the roseate hopes and dreams ended in financial disaster and tragic disappointment. Those who succeeded in the industry, on the other hand, enjoyed a degree of comfort, prosperity, and culture that bore little resemblance to the restrictions and hardships of the traditional farmer's life. In a certain sense the California citrus ranchers thus constituted almost a separate agricultural class, a phenomenon in American society interesting and significant enough to warrant more extensive and detailed study.

Owing in part to a certain romantic implication, grape culture, like orange ranching, brought California its most distinctive reputation as an agricultural state. Indeed, in some respects the growth of the table and raisin grape industry after 1900 constitutes the most remarkable aspect of California agriculture. From a yield in 1900 of only 12,000 tons, the production of table grapes rose to 163,000 tons in 1920, and 385,000 tons in 1928. Following a similar pattern, the output of raisin grapes increased from 47,000 tons in 1900 to 177,000 tons in 1920, and 321,000 tons in 1928. Juice grapes rose from 310,000 tons in 1920 to 472,000 tons in 1928.

The huge increase in both table- and raisin-grape production during the highly inflated prices of World War I resulted in serious loss to the growers. Thousands of acres were planted to vineyards when grape and raisin prices were at a maximum, and the additional production so completely demoralized the market that large numbers of ranchers who had overextended their holdings lost their ranches and homes through foreclosures. Between 1919 and 1923 the price of raisins fell from $235 to $45 a ton; and, in the space of a few years more, table grapes lost two thirds of their former market value. For a time the whole grape industry, especially in the San Joaquin Valley, was thus so thoroughly demoralized that only drastic curtailment and reorganization could save it from complete disaster.

The effect of the depression upon co-operative marketing among the raisin-growers, who had followed the lead of the citrus industry and formed an association known as the Sun Maid Raisin Growers of California, was especially unfortunate. In general the plans of organization, purpose, and method of the raisin-growers' co-operative were similar to those of the California Fruit Growers Exchange. The successful operation of such an enterprise, however, depends on the ability of a large majority of the growers to co-operate effectively over a long period of time. In the lean years after World War I the management of the Sun Maid Raisin Growers came under severe criticism, many growers withdrew from the organization, and the association found it difficult to keep its former dominant position in the industry.[3]

---

[3] Co-operative marketing has been established, with varying degrees of success, among the growers of nearly all kinds of deciduous fruits in California. But as one rancher remarked, when the plan was in its infancy, "You

The San Joaquin Valley is the great grape-producing center of California. In 1930 it contained over half the vineyards of the entire state, which then had about 675,000 acres planted to grapes and produced nearly ninety per cent of the grape crop of the United States.

Wine grapes have been grown in California since the beginning of the mission era. Soon after the Gold Rush a number of European varieties were planted in various areas, largely through the efforts of Arpad Haraszthy, and in 1870 a boom in grape lands swept the state. Plantings ran as high as 25,000,000 vines, and some vineyards reportedly sold for $2,000 an acre. The boom was checked by the appearance of the destructive French phylloxera; but by 1900 the industry was thoroughly re-established. The state was then producing about 19,000,000 gallons of wine, or over eighty per cent of the national output.

National prohibition caused a serious temporary disarrangement of the wine industry, but in a few years California growers found a ready market in the East for all the wine grapes they were able to produce, and the vineyardists planted an enormous acreage to varieties that bore a heavy crop, produced a good ordinary wine, and were capable of standing the long shipment to the East. By the end of prohibition such shipments represented three times the total wine-grape production of 1920.

Wine grapes can be grown in many sections of the state, but the chief producing centers are found in the Central Valley region, immediately east of San Francisco Bay; farther south in the San Joaquin Valley; and in San Bernardino County, where the 5,000-acre Italian, or Guasti, vineyard is advertised as the largest in the world. Napa Valley has the reputation of producing the choicest wines in the state.

Beginning about 1900, the development of Imperial Valley, a huge segment of the Colorado Desert in the extreme southeastern part of California, added a romantic and highly important chapter

can get one third of the growers together in an organization; they can get another third to join; but no power outside the Almighty can draw the other third in."

to the state's agricultural history. Before the introduction of water from the Colorado River, the region constituted an immense, waterless, unspeakably formidable desert. To change this wilderness into one of the richest, most prolific agricultural areas in the world required time, faith, courage, tenacity of purpose, engineering genius, the expenditure of large amounts of capital, and unfettered imagination.

A century ago Dr. Oliver M. Wozencraft, a physician who came to the valley from San Francisco, and William P. Blake, later to win international recognition as geologist and mining engineer, suggested the feasibility of diverting water from the Colorado River to irrigate the region. Wozencraft did not stop with the suggestion, but spent the remaining forty years of his life vainly seeking to win the financial and political support necessary to make his dream a reality. After his death three men of a younger generation—Charles Robinson Rockwood, Anthony H. Heber, and George Chaffey—overcame a succession of discouraging legal, financial, and engineering obstacles to divert a portion of the flow of the Colorado and begin the recreation of the valley by irrigation.

The work was carried on by means of a corporation, organized chiefly by Heber and Rockwood in 1896, called the California Development Company. The company operated on a hand-to-mouth basis and was involved in serious financial difficulties when Chaffey, ignorant of the true state of affairs, became its operating head. Because of these entanglements and the resultant friction with his associates, Chaffey sold out his interests in the company in 1902 and surrendered the management, with its involved engineering and construction problems, to less competent successors.

Meanwhile the valley passed through the initial stages of an extensive boom. A number of towns, such as Imperial, Calexico, El Centro, and Holtville, were laid out; by 1903 some fifty thousand acres were under cultivation; and at the close of 1904, three times that amount of land had been wholly or in part reclaimed from the desert.

Life in the valley during those early years was marked by frontier simplicity and hardships. Tents and brush huts were more common than houses. Candles or kerosense lamps took the place of electric lights. Settlers in the newly established communities learned again to live without schools, churches, doctors, nurses, hospitals, newspapers, and hotels. Wind, flash floods, and mud of an inconceivable tenacity and stickiness added to the settlers' discomfort in winter, and the intense heat of the long summers turned the valley into a purgatory for the inexperienced and unacclimated. The land yielded unbelievably, in both variety and abundance, but crops were occasionally damaged and even ruined by killing frosts, hard, unseasonable rains, or insufficient water for irrigation. Even the wild ducks, coming to the valley in immense flocks, sometimes destroyed lettuce and grain fields as thoroughly as a plague of locusts.

But these inconveniences and misfortunes sank into insignificance compared with the overwhelming disaster that threatened the valley in the summer of 1905. The intake of the main canal of the California Development Company, which brought the water from the Colorado River into Imperial Valley, was originally located at Pilot Knob, not many miles from Yuma. From this point, because of the line of huge, shifting sand dunes west of the Colorado, the canal ran south, parallel to the river, crossed the international boundary line, and continued four miles into Mexico until it reached the dry bed of a stream called the Alamo. Then, after following the channel of this stream for a few miles, the canal turned back across the border and entered the Imperial Valley.

The flow of the Colorado is determined chiefly by the snowfall in the Rocky Mountains. In 1904 the spring run-off was unusually low and the ranches of the valley suffered a serious water shortage. This was aggravated by a partial stoppage of the main diversion canal by an accumulation of silt. The situation was further complicated by a quarrel between the Water Users' Association, an organization of ranchers formed at the suggestion of representatives of the United States Reclamation Service, and the California Development Company. Additional mischief was done by an ill-timed and grossly erroneous report issued by the Department of Agriculture which discredited the valley's future development because of the excessive alkalinity of the soil. The report temporarily curtailed the sale of land and brought the Development Company close to the verge of disaster. The War Department then entered the picture by declaring that the lower Colorado was a navigable stream under its jurisdiction and challenging the validity of the withdrawal of water for irrigation. The Reclamation Service next filed on four million miners' inches of the "unappropriated" waters of the Colorado; and a measure to authorize the federal government to buy out the California Development Company was blocked in Washington.

These multiplied political and financial difficulties, coupled with the threat of a serious water shortage because of the silting up of the canal and an inadequate flow of water through the gate at Hanlon Heading, led A. H. Heber, president of the Development Company, to negotiate a contract with the Mexican government to tap the Colorado River below the international line. In return for this concession the company agreed to permit the use of fifty per cent of the water on Mexican land. Most of the territory for which this water was available was held under a concession from the government by a Mexican citizen named Andrade, who later sold a substantial part of the grant to General Otis of the Los Angeles *Times.*

In September 1904, Charles Rockwood, chief engineer for the Development Company, made a 3,300-foot cut below the international line to divert the water from the Colorado River into the main Imperial canal. Unfortunately the Mexican government delayed approval of the company's plans for a gate to control the flow of water through this cut until the river got out of control and did irreparable harm.

In February 1905, the first of five great floods swept down the Colorado. All attempts to close the new intake proved futile, and by the end of June a stream fifteen feet deep, carrying 14,000 second-feet of water, was flowing through the ancient channel of a wash or arroyo called New River into the Salton Sea. By the time the summer floods had subsided in October, nearly the whole flow of the Colorado River, abandoning its old course to the gulf, was emptying into this inland sink, and the rapidly rising waters of the new lake were encroaching upon near-by farm lands and the Southern Pacific Railroad's main line to New Orleans. The situation indeed was desperate, for unless the river could be turned back into its former channel, most of the Imperial Valley was doomed to become again a vast inland sea such as it had once been in the ancient past.

Unable to cope with the menace to the valley, the California Development Company surrendered the task of harnessing the rebellious Colorado to the Southern Pacific and in effect turned over the company's entire management and affairs to the railroad. Epes Randolph, E. H. Harriman's chief lieutenant in the Southwest, assumed the presidency of the Development Company, and H. T. Cory, his assistant, later took Rockwood's place as chief engineer. Even with the resources of the railroad thrown into the battle, the Colorado refused to resume its way to the gulf, and its defiant waters destroyed every device with which the railroad engineers sought to restrain them.

As against a normal volume of from 5,000 to 7,000 second-feet, the Colorado in March 1906 twice carried a flow of 70,000 second-feet, and the run-off in June was nearly 50 per cent larger than even the great March flood. By that time the intake into New River was over half a mile wide, and week after week the whole flow of the swollen river poured into Salton Sea.

Failing to induce the federal government to assume responsibility for the task, the Southern Pacific made a final herculean effort to close the break. In two weeks nearly three thousand flatcars loaded with rock, clay, and gravel were dumped into the swirling waters, and on November 4, 1906, the flow through the main breach was temporarily checked. But a month later a flood poured into the Colorado from the Gila River, threatened to reopen the gap to the Salton Sea, and forced the railroad company to renew the long and costly struggle. The battle ended successfully in February 1907. The valley thereafter enjoyed an uneasy peace until the construction of Hoover Dam, more than a quarter of a century later, removed the ever recurring danger of flood and brought permanent security to those who had lived so long at the uncertain mercy of the great river.[4]

Financial difficulties, hopelessly magnified by the long fight against the Colorado, forced the California Development Company into bankruptcy. From 1909 to 1916 the management of the company was largely in the hands of W. H. Holabird, of Los Angeles, who served as receiver for the company's assets in the United States. Despite much criticism and innumerable controversies, Holabird developed the property of the company, accumulated surplus funds for the creditors, and supplied the ranchers with water at the low rate of fifty cents per acre-foot. The properties of the California Development Company were finally acquired by the Imperial Irrigation District, a municipal organization formed under the California Irrigation District Act and having as broad powers within its own field as those of a city or county government.

The growth of the Imperial Valley added greatly to the value and variety of California agricultural products. The expansion of railway service and the construction of a network of automobile highways furnished the transportation facilities prerequisite to all large-scale agricultural development. Richness of soil assured abundant yields, and the valley's mild winter climate brought crops to market weeks or even months before they ripened in other sections of the country.

The chief agricultural products of the valley are tomatoes, melons, lettuce, alfalfa, dates, grapefruit, grapes, and livestock.[5] During the brief harvesting season of such perishable crops as melons, tomatoes, and lettuce, when a few days, or even a few hours, may determine the fate of thousands of crates of produce,

---

[4] The Southern Pacific sought to collect $3,000,000 from the federal government for its fight against the Colorado. In 1930 it received about one third of this amount.

[5] Coachella Valley, the northern end of Imperial Valley, supplies a large part of the dates grown for commercial purposes in the United States and contains the widely famous resort known as Palm Springs.

the valley lives in a state of feverish activity and shipments reach gargantuan proportions.

Much of the farm land in the valley is held in large blocks by corporations or wealthy individuals. Prior to 1940, ranchers relied chiefly on Mexican labor, though they also employed Hindus, Negroes, Filipinos, and Japanese. Negroes came into the valley, when cotton was first planted, in response to advertisements inserted in leading Southern newspapers offering cheap transportation and high wages to pickers and field hands.

In the spring of 1928 a strike among Mexican pickers threatened the Imperial melon-growers with the loss of most of their crop and led local authorities to use extra-constitutional methods in dealing with the strikers. An even more serious strike in 1934 involved eight thousand lettuce-pickers and caused serious rioting and bloodshed.

The wide variety of agricultural products raised commercially in California makes it impossible to include a description of other individual crops. Even an alphabetical list of the state's farm products fills a formidable space, and runs from alfalfa, almonds, and apples, to walnuts, wheat, and wool. For variety and fertility, the lands of California are almost unmatched in the nation.

CHAPTER 27. Rivers of Water

CALIFORNIANS learned very early in their experience that
water was the indispensable prerequisite for the growth of
crops, industry, and population. The development, conservation,
and distribution of water have therefore been the most elemental
of all the state's economic and social problems. They touch the
life of every community, of every farm, of every industry, of
every household. "Water is life" is a hard reality as well as a
threadbare aphorism.

Without attempting to explore the subject as a whole, the following pages give a brief account of four recent triumphs in man's
ceaseless struggle to prevent California from reverting to the
desert as nature seemingly intended her to do. It is a sobering
thought that only to the degree we balk or change that ancient
plan will California's civilization and prosperity endure.

With characteristic temerity Los Angeles made the first noteworthy attempt to overcome nature's limitations on the city's
growth, by tapping a distant water-shed. The task involved the
construction of a 232-mile aqueduct from Los Angeles to the
lower reaches of the Owens River, on the eastern side of the Sierra
Nevada Mountains. The proposed route lay through the Mojave
Desert and across equally desolate mountain ranges. Even today
the task would be considered a major financial and engineering
accomplishment; when it was undertaken in 1905 it presented
problems of an almost unprecedented character and magnitude.

The idea of using the water of the Owens River originated with
a former city engineer and mayor of Los Angeles named Fred
Eaton, who recognized that the rapid growth of Los Angeles after
1885 and the constantly expanding immigration to southern California would soon place an impossible drain upon the city's very
limited water resources. Under the pueblo grant of 1781 Los Angeles was entitled to the flow of the river for which the city was
named. This right, according to subsequent court decisions, in-

cluded both the small surface trickle to which the river was reduced during a large part of the year, and the immense natural reservoirs that underlay the river's drainage basin in the San Fernando Valley. It was obvious, however, that even this age-old supply would not be sufficient to meet the ultimate needs of the growing city, an unpleasant reality made all the more evident by the serious decline of all southern California water tables during a protracted drought in the mid-nineties.

Eaton, who had an intimate knowledge of the water resources of southern California, including those of the Sierra Nevada, convinced William Mulholland, chief engineer of the municipal water department, that the Owens River offered the only possible solution to the city's problem. From that time on, Mulholland became the chief figure in the drama of the aqueduct and the Owens Valley. Meanwhile Eaton filed a claim in his own name on a large part of the surplus flow of the river, as well as on reservoir, dam, and power sites in the valley.

The Owens River, discovered by Joe Walker on his return from Monterey to Salt Lake in 1833, rises south of Mono Basin in the Sierra Nevada Mountains and flows down the valley formed by the White and Inyo mountain ranges on the east and the Sierra Nevada on the west. Except for a brief headlong plunge into a canyon called the "Gorge," the stream follows a leisurely course through green meadows and lava-strewn barrens until it reaches the alkaline sink called Owens Lake.

Prospectors, who came into the valley in the early sixties, found that the region was well adapted to grazing and offered limited areas suitable for more intensive cultivation. In the course of time these pioneer settlers "pushed back the disputing sands," became cattlemen and farmers, and established the four small towns of Lone Pine, Independence, Big Pine, and Bishop. In later years an occasional mining rush brought temporary prosperity, lawlessness, and fame to certain parts of the valley.

For a few years the settlers lived in peril of Indians and lawless whites, and in 1872 a great earthquake brought ruin and desolation to settlements in the lower end of the valley. In places the temblor was so violent, indeed, that it seemed to shake the very foundations of the Sierra and sway the summits of the giant granite peaks. Eyewitnesses described how huge rocks and roaring avalanches plunged down the sides of the sheer crags and granite walls to fill the valley with deafening reverberations and, by the friction thus engendered, turned night into a weird and ghastly day. At the opening of the century the Owens Valley was still a semi-frontier mining, cattle, and ranching community. Its people were clannish, sturdily rooted, deeply attached alike to the age-old mountains in whose shadow they lived and to their independent way of life.

Mulholland, after extensive studies of this region and of routes from it to Los Angeles, announced to a small group of responsible Los Angeles citizens that the aqueduct could be built for approximately $24,000,000. The Los Angeles Water Board accepted Mulholland's recommendations, and in July 1905 the Los Angeles *Times* announced the city's plan to build the aqueduct. Two months later the voters overwhelmingly approved a bond issue for $1,500,000 to take over the Eaton options and meet other preliminary expenses. In 1907, after a board of three nationally known engineers had passed on Mulholland's report, approved it with only a few minor changes, and estimated that the aqueduct could be completed in five years, the citizens of Los Angeles— perhaps with more temerity than prudence—voted an additional bond issue of $23,000,000 to finance the undertaking. In the light of present-day expenditures the sum seems small enough; but measured by the standards of that time, it laid a staggering load on a city so small and financially limited as Los Angeles. The debt was justified only by necessity.

Actual construction of the aqueduct was begun in 1908. By that time the city had acquired some seventy thousand acres of land in the lower and more arid portions of the Owens Valley and obtained the backing of Congress, the Roosevelt administration, and the Department of the Interior for its ambitious venture. It had also begun its tragic encroachment, necessary though it may have been, upon the rights and interests of the Owens Valley settlers.

The actual construction of the aqueduct was worthy of the best traditions of American engineering and a striking example of the success of a properly directed municipal enterprise. The details of the task are thus described by Don J. Kinsey in *The Romance of Water and Power:*

Under the leadership of Mulholland, an army of 5,000 men labored through blazing desert summers and freezing mountain winters for five long years to complete the most gigantic and difficult engineering project theretofore ever undertaken by an American city.

Before the aqueduct itself could be constructed, it had been necessary for the builders to conquer and tame a vast and well-nigh inaccessible wilderness. A railroad 120 miles long must be constructed to carry thousands of tons of heavy machinery and supplies. More than 500 miles of highways and trails must be opened to reach the line of the aqueduct with materials and men. To provide for the necessity of water in the desert, a complete pipe line system was laid out to carry on construction work and supply workers. There were no established lines of communication and, therefore, hundreds of miles of telegraph and telephone wires were strung to connect the fifty-seven division camps erected to house men and supplies.

Construction of the aqueduct itself presented hundreds of engineering difficulties, apparently insurmountable, but ultimately and invariably solved. From its intake in Owens Valley, the aqueduct pushed its way southward through mountain barriers, crossed scores of wide and precipitous canyons and burrowed under the blistering sands of the Mojave Desert.

When completed, the aqueduct included 142 separate tunnels aggregating 53 miles in length, 12 miles of inverted steel siphons varying in diameter from 7 to 11 feet, 24 miles of open unlined conduit, 39 miles of open cement lined conduit, and 97 miles of covered conduit. Additional miles were taken up by three large reservoirs, the largest of these, the Haiwee Reservoir, being capable of storing more than twenty billion gallons of water.

The aqueduct was completed within the estimated cost, in somewhat less than the five years allotted to the task, and without the unsavory evidences or suspicions of graft so common to most large municipal enterprises. The water was released into the San

Fernando reservoir in November 1913, in the presence of some forty thousand spectators, as the climax of a two-day civic celebration. The one really noteworthy speech of the occasion was Mulholland's laconic remark as the foaming water roared down the spillway: "There it is, take it."

The sources of the Owens River are several thousand feet above the altitude of Los Angeles, and the aqueduct thus provided opportunity for the development of an enormous amount of hydroelectric energy. The city proposed not only to build its own power plants for this purpose but also to distribute the electricity as a municipal enterprise. The plan met with powerful and persistent opposition, but beginning in 1916 with a single generating plant in San Francisquito Canyon, the Bureau of Power and Light rapidly expanded its production facilities, effected a sharp reduction in both domestic and industrial rates, and in 1922 acquired that part of the distributing system of the Southern California Edison Company that lay within the city limits. This gave the bureau a potential monopoly of the city's electrical market and made it one of the important factors in the light and power business of the nation.[1]

Though unquestionably the salvation of Los Angeles, the aqueduct unfortunately resulted in a grim, long-drawn-out feud between the city and the Owens Valley residents. When Los Angeles first applied for the surplus flow of the river, the settlers offered no particular opposition, though W. A. Chalfant, editor of the *Inyo Register,* headlined the announcement of the aqueduct plan: "Los Angeles Plots Destruction.—Would Take Owens River, Lay Lands Waste, Ruin Peoples, Homes and Communities."[2]

It was not until the early twenties, indeed, that the conflict of interests between the valley and the city first became acute. Al-

---

[1] The Bureau of Power and Light, a division of the Department of Water and Power, to which the development of municipal power was entrusted, was presided over for many years by Dr. John R. Haynes, a wealthy physician who carried on a determined crusade for the initiative, referendum, and recall during the early part of the century and eventually gave up the practice of medicine to devote his full time to the cure of the ills of the body politic.

[2] August 3, 1905.

ready in possession of nearly one hundred thousand acres of arid valley land, in 1923 Los Angeles began its much-criticized policy of buying up irrigated Owens Valley ranches to obtain both the surface and underground water rights such properties possessed. The water was then added to the flow of the aqueduct, while the ranches themselves were allowed to revert to desert. From the standpoint of the settlers, the city's new policy spelled disaster. The little oases they and their fathers had established became indistinguishable from the waste lands around them; and in place of the homesteads and farms of an earlier day, the traveler saw only a succession of parched, uncultivated fields; orchards withered and dead; ditches choked with sand and brush—a valley "made waste and desolate, a land abandoned to ruin."

By sharply reducing the number of ranchers and farmers in the valley, the city's policy also seriously curtailed the merchants' patronage and thus reacted as disastrously upon the towns as upon the rural areas; and the eventual prosperity that came from the city's own large-scale operations and the greatly increased flow of travel into and through the valley afforded poor consolation to the tradesmen and merchants who had gone bankrupt or perhaps moved away from the valley in the interim.

By 1924 the conflict between the valley residents and the city was in full swing. The settlers were bitterly critical of Mulholland and repeatedly charged that his refusal to build the storage reservoir in Long Valley was responsible for the lack of water that set the valley and the city at loggerheads. According to the editor of the *Inyo Register,* the accepted spokesman for a majority of the settlers, Mulholland blocked the construction of the dam both to prevent Fred Eaton and W. D. Longyear, another Los Angeles ranch-owner in Long Valley, from forcing the city to pay excessive indemnity for their holdings, and because of his "consuming and destructive hatred for Owens Valley."

One of the most galling aspects of the situation from the standpoint of the valley settlers was the use of a large part of the water carried by the aqueduct for the irrigation of farming lands in the San Fernando Valley. Prior to the completion of the aqueduct much of the land in the latter valley was suitable only for grazing or dry farming, but in 1910 a syndicate, called the Los Angeles Suburban Home Company, organized by the Otis-Chandler interests, purchased the 47,000-acre holdings of I. N. Van Nuys, brought about the annexation of the land to Los Angeles, and later used the water of the aqueduct for both irrigation and domestic purposes. Settlers by the thousands moved into the valley, grain fields gave place to diversified farms, towns sprang up and prospered, and the holdings of the syndicate increased in value by thirty-, sixty-, and a hundred-fold.[3]

Violence was interjected into the controversy between Los Angeles and the Owens Valley residents in the spring of 1924 when a small charge of dynamite was set off against the wall of the aqueduct, not far from the town of Lone Pine. The explosion did little actual damage and apparently was designed either to serve as a warning to the city or merely to bring the controversy to the attention of the outside world.

In October of that year the Los Angeles Board of Public Service Commissioners submitted a proposal to the Owens Valley residents that involved the reservation of thirty thousand acres in the upper part of the valley for agricultural purposes, but valley property-holders offered to come to terms with the city only if the latter would advance $5,400,000 as reparations for the shrinkage in property values in the four valley towns; purchase all land and water rights in the valley (thereby automatically liquidating any claims for damages against the city) for $12,000,000; or agree to set up a board of arbitration with power to determine the values of urban and rural lands and fix the compensation the city should pay to the owners of such properties. This counter-offer, like the city's original proposal, died aborning.

In the meantime, on November 16, 1924, an organized band of valley residents seized a large spillway in the rough, tortuous

---

[3] Much of the water used for irrigation in the San Fernando Valley lands percolated down into the underground reservoirs and thus remained available for domestic or industrial use in Los Angeles.

Alabama Hills south of Independence, raised the aqueduct gates, and allowed the water to run to waste on the floor of the valley. This committee held the spillway for four days and restored the water to the aqueduct only upon formal assurance from the Los Angeles Clearing House Association that it would use its best efforts to bring about an equitable settlement of the valley's grievances.

The Alabama Hills incident brought the controversy between Los Angeles and Owens Valley into the full floodlight of national publicity, and was the prelude to a period of dangerous tension between Los Angeles and the Owens Valley settlers. In 1926 and again more extensively in 1927 a series of dynamite explosions destroyed many of the city's newly drilled wells, damaged a number of power houses, and blew out different sections of the aqueduct.

The quarrel was rapidly developing to the point of serious bloodshed when a sudden domestic catastrophe overwhelmed the valley settlers and left them stunned, leaderless, and beaten. The tragedy was caused by the defalcation and failure of N. N. and M. G. Watterson. The two brothers were not only the dominant figures in the valley's long fight against the city, but occupied a position of trust and leadership among the settlers probably unequaled in any other community in California. They were active in all the industries of the valley—mining, ranching, lumbering, and stock-raising; but above all, through control of the Inyo County and First National banks in Bishop, and of branch banks in the other three communities, they were the trusted financial custodians and counselors for the entire valley.

Unfortunately, while the Wattersons were waging the settlers' fight against the city and seeking sincerely, one may still believe, to develop the resources of the valley, they were playing fast and loose with the banks' funds and juggling their accounts into hopeless confusion. On August 4, 1927 the incredulous citizens of Bishop read the following notice on the doors of the Inyo County and First National banks:

We find it necessary to close our banks in the Owens Valley. The
result has been brought about by the great four years of destructive
work carried on by the city of Los Angeles.

N. N. Watterson, President of the Inyo County Bank
M. G. Watterson, Cashier [4]

The machinations of the city of Los Angeles, though certainly
not without effect upon the fortunes of the Wattersons, were at
best only a minor cause in the brothers' failure. An investigation
by Will C. Wood, state superintendent of banks, showed that the
bank shortage exceeded two million dollars and that most of the
depositors' money had been lost in mining speculations. The Wattersons, after indictment for nearly every possible violation of the
state's banking laws, were convicted on thirty-six counts and sentenced to long terms in the penitentiary.

This debacle bankrupted many of the settlers and left the valley
no longer able to carry on its long-drawn-out fight against the city.
Fortunately the Los Angeles Department of Water and Power was
able to provide work for many of the impoverished ranchers and
townspeople on the various projects it then had under way and
thus in some measure relieved the widespread and acute distress
that blanketed the valley.

About this time the collapse of a large dam that Mulholland
had constructed in San Francisquito Canyon, not far from the
little town of Saugus, released a huge flood of water down the
Santa Clara Valley and caused one of the greatest disasters in the
history of southern California. The dam was 600 feet long, 180
feet high, and impounded 38,000 acre-feet of water. Just before
midnight on March 12, 1928, the structure suddenly gave way
and, in the words of C. C. Teague,

the entire volume of water was at once released and swept through
the Santa Clara Valley to the sea, a course of about 65 miles. For
some distance below the dam the wall of water was at least 60 feet
high and even when the flood reached Santa Paula, 50 miles below the

---

[4] *Inyo Register*, August 4, 1927.

dam, the crest was 25 feet above the normal level of the stream. The flood carried before it a terrific mass of debris—trees, telegraph poles, bridges, railway tracks, fences, buildings—in fact anything and everything movable that lay in its path. Three hundred and eighty-five lives were lost; 1,240 homes were either completely destroyed or badly damaged; 7,900 acres of land were flooded, and damage of every kind and degree was done to farms and orchards.[5]

The dam had been inspected by Mulholland and H. A. Van Norman, who later succeeded Mulholland, only a few hours before the disaster occurred. Mulholland courageously accepted sole responsibility, however, for failure to note the precarious condition of the structure.

Property damage entailed by the flood ran into the millions of dollars, and the loss of life approached the toll of San Francisco's terrible disaster of 1906. Rumor immediately ascribed the collapse of the dam to sabotage, but an official investigation showed that the structure collapsed because the bed-rock foundation was weak and badly faulted.

The restoration of the losses suffered by the ranchers and townspeople of the Santa Clara Valley, and the settlement of the many costly and involved claims for damages against Los Angeles, represent what is probably a unique chapter in the history of major American disasters. A fair, amicable, and common-sense procedure was adopted for assessing the complicated damages and paying the huge claims to which the disaster gave rise. Los Angeles paid the awards, and none of the claimants brought suit against the city.

But the city suffered seriously, both tangibly and intangibly, from the unfavorable publicity aroused by the Owens Valley conflict. Many newspapers in the state criticized the city's methods, accused its officials of following "smart" business tactics, and even warned Arizona to remember the "ravishing of Owens Valley" in the negotiations then taking place over Hoover Dam and the use of the water of the Colorado River.

---

[5] *Fifty Years a Rancher,* p. 184.

With the growth of population and manufacturing, San Francisco, like Los Angeles, was compelled to go far afield to find an adequate supply of water. As early as 1901 Mayor Phelan filed upon the water of the Tuolumne River, some twenty miles above the Yosemite Valley, for the use of the city, and though the application was then denied, in 1908 Secretary James R. Garfield of the Department of the Interior authorized San Francisco to acquire a number of sites for storage reservoirs along the course of the Tuolumne, in the magnificent Hetch Hetchy Valley.

Garfield's action was the signal for a violent attack, led by the distinguished naturalist John Muir, upon San Francisco's proposed "spoilation" of the Hetch Hetchy. The issue was finally taken up by Congress, and in 1913 the Raker Act granted perpetual water rights on some 420,000 acres of the public domain to San Francisco. Eighteen additional years elapsed, however, before the cold, clear waters of the Tuolumne were actually diverted from the deep canyons of the Sierra Nevada into the homes and factories of San Francisco.

The San Francisco–Hetch Hetchy aqueduct was finally completed in 1931. It is approximately 186 miles long, and can provide water for nearly 4,000,000 people. In contrast to the $25,-000,000 that represented the cost of the Owens River aqueduct, the San Francisco enterprise involved an expenditure of over $80,000,000 for the aqueduct itself and an additional outlay of $41,000,000 for the Spring Valley Water Company's distributing system.

By the time the San Francisco aqueduct was completed, the gigantic task of harnessing the Colorado River, controlling its floods, distributing its surplus water, and generating the electricity that was to open a new economic era in the Southwest was well under way. The Colorado has been described as "one of the most terrifying influences for wholesale destruction in the United States." Its flow varies from 2,000 to 200,000 cubic feet per second, and each year it carries enough silt in its turbid waters to cover 100,000 acres a foot deep. In the river's lower reaches its bed is actually higher than the surrounding country, and its flood waters thus became a perennial threat to the ranches and towns of the Imperial Valley.

The story of the Colorado in its relation to Imperial Valley has been summarized in Chapter 25. After World War I, the control of the Colorado became the major engineering and conservation problem of the Southwest. A comprehensive plan finally emerged that called for the erection of one or more huge dams across the river, both to prevent recurring floods and to provide an immense supply of water for irrigation, the generation of enough hydro-electric power to revolutionize industry and transportation in the Southwest, and the construction of a canal running wholly through American territory into the Imperial Valley.

Between 1918 and 1922 the United States Reclamation Service, the Southern California Edison Company, and a number of individuals made preliminary investigations of possible dam and reservoir sites along the river; and in 1920 the Kinkaid Act instructed the Secretary of the Interior to make a survey of the Colorado and embody the findings in a report to Congress. The work was done by Arthur Powell Davis, chief of the Reclamation Service, and Frank C. Weymouth, the bureau's chief engineer.[6] The material obtained by the survey was embodied in the so-called Fall-Davis Report of 1922 and became the basis for the proceedings and legislation leading to the construction of Hoover Dam.

The year 1922 witnessed two further developments in the Colorado River program. In its long journey from the northern Rocky Mountains to the Gulf of California the Colorado and its important tributaries pass through the territory of seven states; and while most of the river's course lies within the United States, its lower reaches and outlet are under Mexican jurisdiction. The use and control of its waters, as emphasized in the *Report on the Problems of the Colorado Basin*, thus require both interstate and international agreements.

The concurrence of the representatives of seven states was

---

[6] Arthur Powell Davis was the nephew of John W. Powell, whose historic trip down the river in 1869 became a landmark in Colorado exploration.

brought about through the good offices of Herbert Hoover, Secretary of Commerce, and chairman of the Colorado River Commission. The formal agreement, officially known as the Colorado River Compact, was signed in the Ben-Hur Room of the Palace of Governors at Santa Fe, New Mexico, on November 24, 1922.[7]

Under the compact, the participating states were divided into those of the upper Colorado basin—Wyoming, Utah, Colorado, and New Mexico—and those of the lower basin—Arizona, California, and Nevada. Each division was allocated 7,500,000 acre-feet of water, while an additional million acre-feet were assigned to the lower-basin states until 1963.

In the meantime a bill for the construction of a dam in Boulder Canyon, introduced by Congressman Phil D. Swing of San Bernardino, had begun its long and tortuous course through the House and Senate. The measure immediately encountered strong and skillfully directed opposition. Army engineers had an honest difference of opinion as to the most desirable location for the dam; electric power companies fought the measure, both openly and by undercover methods; and the state of Arizona adopted a suspicious and hostile attitude toward California and proved a major obstacle to the bill's early passage. In defense of the proposed site in Boulder Canyon, the Reclamation Bureau issued the following report:

> There are 8 possible dam sites at which power may be developed below Grand Canyon; namely, Parker, Mohave Valley, Bulls Head, Boulder Canyon, Devils Slide, Spencer Canyon, Bridge Canyon, and Diamond Creek, studies of each of which sites have been made by our engineers. . . . The final results of these studies demonstrate conclusively that for power development as for flood control and irrigation storage the most feasible development on the lower river under existing conditions is the construction of a single large reservoir at Boulder Canyon.[8]

---

[7] The document was signed on the lap board on which General Lew Wallace wrote most of his manuscripts. The Arizona legislature refused to approve the compact, but two years later it went into effect on the basis of ratification by the other six states.

[8] *Report on the Problems of the Colorado River Basin*, p. 14.

Hoover Dam, photograph by Edward Weston. This massive structure controls the flow of the Colorado River and diverts it to the use of the entire Southwest.

The Sheer Walls of the Colorado, photograph by Claude Dudley. Such forbidding arid terrain presented a real challenge to explorers and settlers of the Southwest and California.

The Los Angeles Freeway system, one of the most complicated and extensive ever built, is that city's answer to the growing traffic problem.

Oil refining remains an important part of California's twentieth-century industrial development.

Hiram Johnson championed Boulder Dam in the upper House; but it was not until December 21, 1928 that the measure, now appropriately known as the Swing-Johnson bill, survived a prolonged filibuster in the Senate to obtain congressional approval and receive the President's signature.[9]

On July 3, 1930, President Hoover signed a deficiency appropriation bill that contained an item of $10,660,000 for preliminary construction work on the Boulder Dam project. Four days later Secretary of the Interior Ray Lyman Wilbur wired Elwood Mead, Commissioner of Reclamation: "You are directed to commence construction on Boulder Dam today." On September 17 the work was formally initiated by a ceremony in Las Vegas, Nevada, reminiscent of the completion of the Pacific Railroad at Promontory Point, Utah, sixty-one years before. Actual construction of the dam began in February 1931.

Boulder (now Hoover) Dam represents the type of accomplishment, epic both in conception and execution, in which American engineering traditionally excels. The dam, a great arc between primeval walls of volcanic rock, was bigger than anything of its kind man had ever built before, and involved engineering, supply, health, and transportation problems of such magnitude and complexity that no single company was willing to assume the risk. The work was accordingly undertaken by a corporation representing a combination of six large construction firms and appropriately named the Six Companies. The dam was completed on March 1, 1936, approximately five years after the work started.

The dam is 1,282 feet long, 727 feet high (or almost half again as high as the Washington Monument), 660 feet thick at the base and 45 feet thick at the top, massive enough to withstand a water pressure of 45,000 pounds to the square foot, and capable

---

[9] The official title of the measure was "The Boulder Canyon Project Act." The dam is actually located in Black Canyon, twenty miles downstream from Boulder Canyon. On September 17, 1930 Secretary Wilbur issued an official order naming the dam Hoover Dam, but the name was not recognized by Congress.

of impounding 30,500,000 acre-feet of water. The lake thus formed, the largest man ever made, was appropriately named in honor of Dr. Elwood Mead, one of the West's most constructive benefactors, who died a few months before the dam was finished.

Electric power generated at Hoover Dam, and distributed chiefly by the Bureau of Power and Light of Los Angeles and the Southern California Edison Company, plays a vital role in the industrial, mining, and urban development of the Southwest and is an essential factor in the operation of the Metropolitan Water District of Southern California.

The All-American Canal, which constitutes an integral feature of the Hoover Dam project and provides for the irrigation of the Imperial Valley, is in fact a huge man-made river—80 miles long, 220 feet wide, and 25 feet deep. It leaves the Colorado at Laguna Dam, above Yuma, drops down almost to the international boundary, and closely parallels that line to a point some ten miles west of Calexico. Over half a million additional acres in the Imperial and Coachella valleys in 1955 were under irrigation by the canal.

In 1923, long before the Swing-Johnson bill was assured of favorable congressional action, the city of Los Angeles began to look to the Colorado River for possible relief in the water shortage that drought, the postwar boom, and the Owens Valley controversy threatened to create. Upon Mulholland's recommendation, a survey was made of the feasibility of constructing an aqueduct from the Colorado to Los Angeles, and in the summer of 1924, the city filed on 1,500 cubic second-feet of the Colorado flow.

For various reasons, including the almost prohibitive expense and the fact that the water supply of many other fast-growing southern California cities was even more precarious than that of Los Angeles, it seemed unwise for the latter city to assume sole responsibility for the construction of the proposed Colorado River aqueduct. Accordingly, on February 15, 1928, following the removal of certain legal barriers by the state legislature, the board of directors of the city of Pasadena adopted an ordinance declaring that "public necessity and convenience require the organization and incorporation of a metropolitan water district." The cities of Anaheim, Beverly Hills, Burbank, Colton, Glendale, Los Angeles, Pasadena, San Bernardino, San Marino, Santa Ana, and Santa Monica joined the district, and a board was created to plan, finance, build, and operate an aqueduct from the Colorado River. San Bernardino and Colton subsequently withdrew from the organization, but Compton, Fullerton, Long Beach, and Torrance came in to take their places.[1]

In November 1930, the general manager of the district submitted a report to the Board of Directors recommending the construction of a diversion dam across the Colorado, near the town of Parker, approximately 155 miles below Hoover Dam. About a year later the voters of the Metropolitan District, by an overwhelming majority, authorized a bond issue of $220,000,000 for the construction of the aqueduct and dam. The latter, Parker Dam, less than a tenth as high as the great structure in Black Canyon, has been called "the most beautiful dam in the world."

From Parker Dam to the huge Cajalco Reservoir, or Lake Mathews, near Riverside, where the Metropolitan aqueduct itself ends and the distributing system begins, the water is carried across 242 miles of almost unbroken desert, through 55 miles of huge covered conduits, 62 miles of concrete-lined canals, 29 miles of siphons, and 29 separate tunnels. All but one of the tunnels, which vary in length from 338 feet to 18.3 miles, are sixteen feet both in width and height. Great pumps, driven by electric power generated both at Hoover Dam and along the aqueduct, lift a billion gallons of water a day a total of over 1,600 feet, from one level to another; and a large filtration and softening plant near Pomona purifies the water and reduces its alkali and borax content. Supplementing the local water sources, the Metropolitan aqueduct now supplies an area of 2,200 square miles and an estimated population of over 4,500,000.

Other California cities have solved similar difficult water prob-

[1] The coastal Municipal Water District was admitted in 1942 and the city of San Diego in 1946.

lems. San Diego, through the construction of dams and reservoirs in the upper reaches of its underground rivers, has laid the foundation for urban growth to an extent completely undreamed of by its pioneers. Increasing population confronts the city with the need to explore new and more distant water sources.

The latest of the great irrigation, power, flood-control, and reclamation enterprises undertaken in California is situated in the vast inland empire drained by the Sacramento and San Joaquin rivers. Officially known as the Central Valley Water Project, the plan primarily involves the conservation and revolutionary redistribution of the flow of the San Joaquin and Sacramento rivers. Under the plan the lower San Joaquin Valley will be irrigated by water from the Sacramento River so that most of the flow of the San Joaquin River can then be used on the inadequately watered lands south of Fresno. This adjustment is possible because the Sacramento Valley, which receives twice as much rainfall as the San Joaquin, contains only about one third of the 2,000,000 acres of irrigable land in the great inland basin.

The Central Valley Water Project is also designed to end the disastrous floods that have periodically inundated hundreds of square miles, especially in the Sacramento Valley, to prevent the encroachment of salt water on the rich delta lands near the bay, to generate an enormous amount of cheap power, and even to restore the once active water traffic on the two rivers.

The Central Valley Project consists basically of two large dams, Shasta on the Sacramento and Friant on the San Joaquin, both completed during the 1940's. In addition, a network of canals spreads the water to areas of greatest need. The Delta Cross Channel, completed in 1951, carries Sacramento water to the lower San Joaquin; the Contra Costa Canal takes it to the upper reaches of San Francisco Bay, while the Delta-Mendota (opened 1951), the Madera (opened 1944), and the Friant-Kern (opened 1949) canals water the San Joaquin Valley.

Friant dam is capable of storing half a million acre-feet of water. At the northern end of the Sacramento Valley, Shasta Dam impounds over 4,500,000 acre-feet of water and ranks as one of the major structures of its kind in the world. Because of the magnitude of the undertaking and the risk involved, it was built, following the pattern set in the case of Boulder Dam, by an organization called Pacific Constructors, Inc., composed of seventeen different construction companies.

In her account of the Shasta Dam, Viola P. May writes:

Shasta Dam is the "key" structure of the Central Valley Project— its out-standing and most important unit.

Everything about this project is "super." With Friant, Shasta will help store 70% as much water as all other 618 dams in California combined.[2]

The canals, when fully completed, will total some 350 miles.

Like every other enterprise of its kind in California, the Central Valley Water Project had to face much opposition. Fathered in 1933 by a state bond issue of $170,000,000, adopted by Congress as a federal reclamation project in 1937, and claimed, in some measure, by the War Department under its power to deal with navigable streams, the program has suffered both from uncertain and divided authority and from a conflict between the proponents of federal supervision and the advocates of state control.

The question of the generation and distribution of hydroelectric power has been a major source of conflict. One group favored both the generation and distribution of power by the government; the other advocated the sale of power to private corporations (in this case the Pacific Gas and Electric Company) for ultimate distribution to the farms, homes, and cities of the valleys. The Reclamation Bureau's policy of restricting the use of water to farms of a maximum of 160 acres also became a major controversial issue.

---

[2] *Shasta Dam and Its Builders* (1945), pp. 13–14.

CHAPTER 28.   The Confused Decade

IN CALIFORNIA, as elsewhere in the nation, the prosperity
of the twenties came to an abrupt and gloomy end in the autumn of 1929. Ironically enough, the only Californian who ever
occupied the White House had barely assumed office when the
catastrophe overtook the country. The ten years that followed
the debacle on Wall Street constitute a strangely confused and
unsettled decade for California, a decade of tragedy and widespread despair, of fear, bewilderment, and hesitation, of tinseled
hopes, of illogical experiments, and of leadership, sometimes
blind and deluded, sometimes shrewdly mercenary, that eventually brought bitter disappointment to hundreds of thousands of
misguided followers and at times threatened the state with out-
and-out disaster.

The state's prolonged economic and political confusion was the
result of the nationwide depression and unrest, accentuated by
a number of powerful local factors peculiar to California. When
the country went into its economic tailspin the California government, under James Rolph, Jr., was both extravagant and ineffec-
tual and had long since lost the confidence of the people. The
ineptness of the state executive was symptomatic, in the popular
mind, of what had come to be looked upon as stuffed-shirt leadership in the economic and business world as well as in politics.
Even before the failures, bankruptcies, and defalcations that followed in the wake of the stock market crash of 1929, many thousands of Californians had lost a large part of their savings in real-
estate speculation and wildcat oil ventures in the hectic booms of
the twenties.

The ranks of these self-impoverished unfortunates were now
swelled to a great host by wholesale losses and failures, running
into the hundreds of millions of dollars, for which the small investor had no responsibility and over which he could exercise no
shadow of control. One of the leading banks of Los Angeles lost

prestige and reputation because some of its officers were decoyed into a stock-rigging scheme, known as the Julian Oil Company scandal, by a smooth and utterly unscrupulous promoter, who, with his associates, reportedly fleeced 40,000 investors out of nearly $150,000,000. The president of a leading San Francisco bank ran into even greater difficulties with the law. The forced reorganization of California's largest insurance company, the bankruptcy of an important Los Angeles oil company and the conviction of its spectacularly extravagant officials, the collapse of bonds and other securities recommended by supposedly reputable brokers and investment houses, and the failure of numerous large building and loan associations not only brought economic ruin to tens of thousands of small investors but also destroyed the public's confidence in the integrity and wisdom of its long-accepted leaders.

As the depression continued, the bankrupt, disillusioned, and jobless turned with understandable if misplaced bitterness against the existing political and economic order, which most of them had formerly supported, and aligned themselves in bewildered desperation with any new movement, no matter how crack-brained or chimerical, that promised to restore prosperity and hope. At the end of the summer of 1934 more than 1,250,000 Californians, seventy per cent of whom lived in southern California, were on relief.

Certain traits of California society, especially evident in Los Angeles, also accounted in part for the widespread acceptance of unorthodox and often fantastic remedies for the depression. After the first World War hundreds of thousands of new settlers, chiefly from the farming states of the Middle West, came to California either to retire or to establish themselves in small lines of business in a less rigorous environment. Most of these newcomers chose to live in southern California. They bought houses and small tracts of land on the installment plan and usually sold their newly acquired homes at the first attractive offer. Many of them opened hot-dog stands, owned small "poultry ranches," operated filling stations, or worked as agents and salesmen. The condition soon gave rise to a large shallow-rooted element that had neither economic nor cultural stability and lacked capacity to use the abundant leisure at their disposal either for their own profit or the good of the community.

In a society so diverse in objectives, so lacking in cohesion and unity of character, the quack, the charlatan, the prophet of a new cult, the advocate of a new school of healing, the spokesman for the spectacular and bizarre, whatever its nature or purpose, seldom found it necessary to search the highways and hedges to obtain a following. The field of religion furnished a typical but by no means an exclusive example of this erraticism.

In a recent classified directory the Southern California Telephone Company listed twenty-six major religious denominations in Los Angeles. The list included Adventist, Assemblies of God, Foursquare Gospel (Angelus Temple), Latter-day Saints, Nazarene, Pentecostal, and Spiritualist as well as Catholic, Jewish, Congregational, Episcopalian, Presbyterian, and the other long-established Protestant denominations.

Under the heading "Churches—Various Denominations," the directory listed at least one hundred separate organizations, including Buddhist temples, Russian Orthodox churches, the Church of St. Albans, Nuptial Feast Ecclesia, Psychosomatic Institute, Self-Realization Fellowship, Institute of the Cosmos, Firebrands for Jesus, and Infinite Science Church. The names of many other "churches of various denominations," such as Aeonian Institute of Higher Thought, Agabeg Occult Church, Church of Atoraxia, Ancient Mystical Order of Melchizedek, First Assembly Church of the First Born of the United Sons of the Almighty, Spiritual Science Church of the Master, Special Rose Light Circle, and Nothing Impossible, do not appear in the directory.

Aimee Semple McPherson was an extraordinary person, and she showed unusual acumen when, out of all the cities of the land, she selected Los Angeles to be the center of her preaching, the seat of Angelus Temple, the citadel of the Foursquare Gospel. Los Angeles was the best possible choice, for no other city possessed, at least in anything like the same degree, the congenial elements so necessary for Mrs. McPherson's flamboyant methods.

It is not necessary here to analyze, praise, or disparage her success. Aimee and her Temple are embedded in perpetuity in the tradition of Los Angeles. Her followers, many of whom beyond all shadow of doubt were benefited by her ministry, believed in her and her gospel with fanatical sincerity. Her seizure of the public mind and attention reduced Hollywood agents to envious and impotent despair. The depths of the ocean and the waste places of the desert were her hiding-places; and if she scandalized sedate citizens by her disappearance and the miracle of her return, a compliant district attorney willingly overlooked the incident that featured the mysterious kidnapping of the most talked-of figure in Los Angeles. But year after year "Sister Aimee" filled the Temple, multiplied her converts, helped the sick and needy, supplied a social outlet for the lonely and uprooted, rescued the perishing, gathered in the money, and preached and publicized the Foursquare Gospel.

Conceding that, on the whole, Angelus Temple was a constructive force, various explanations may be offered for such separatist tendencies in southern California's religious life and for the curious religious cults and vagaries that flourished in Los Angeles with such remarkable abandon. A large element in the population, coming from a background of strong church affiliation and early religious training, severed their denominational connections when they started for California, but they could not so easily rid themselves of the deep-seated craving for some form of worship and religious expression. Many of the cults were thinly veneered rackets, in some cases enriching the clever organizers and propagandists literally by the millions of dollars.

Next to religion, politics offered the most fruitful field for fraudulent or blind leadership. To put the matter bluntly, the freeborn California voter, with no money in the bank and insufficient income to support his family, wanted something more than freedom of speech and worship and the press. He wanted a job and the opportunity to work and a living wage and a pension in old age. When conservative statesmen and economists gave him no hope, he turned to the sorcerers, soothsayers, and magicians for an economic miracle. Some of those who offered him a panacea were desperately sincere; others were political opportunists; a few were unmitigated rogues.

Technocracy, the first of the major movements to promise to California a new prosperity and a foretaste of the millennium, was a strange mixture, so far as the layman is qualified to judge, of scientific principles, mumbo-jumbo, and skillful publicity. The advocates of the new doctrine proposed to place the organization and operation of government in the hands of skilled engineers and technicians. Profit and the price system were to be eliminated. The full resources of inventions, machines, and scientific discoveries were to be devoted to the satisfaction of human wants; and under the new system, with modern means of production, the Technocrats proposed to limit employment to those between twenty-five and forty-five years of age and to establish a work-year of 132 hours. Under this plan the American people were promised a standard of living twice as high as they enjoyed in 1929. According to the Technocratic doctrine, physical wealth was not truly measurable in terms of labor, goods, or money, but only in terms of energy; and while energy appeared in many forms, all of these in turn could be measured in units of work or of heat, namely the erg, the joule, and the calorie.

Technocracy originated at Columbia University at the close of World War I as a serious study of the proposition that all civilization is founded on physical energy. A group of distinguished scholars, including Thorstein Veblen and Charles R. Steinmetz, were among the original sponsors of the study; but in the early thirties Technocracy became an organized "cause," an avowed crusade against the existing economic and social order. Howard Scott, an engineer who initiated the discussion of the energy theory at Columbia, became the champion of the new movement and used the depression, the rising tide of unemployment, and the threat of society's ultimate collapse as a means of directing nationwide attention to himself and his revolutionary doctrine. Under Scott's leadership Technocracy quickly attained widespread popularity in California.

A number of factors made California the nation's chief center of Technocracy. As already intimated, the people of the state, especially during the depression, were quick to support new movements and worship strange gods. Technocracy not only pledged itself to afford relief from poverty and unemployment, but promised that science, whose worship was then a universal cult in California, would itself perform the miracle. Finally, in E. Manchester Boddy, owner and editor of the Los Angeles *Daily News*, Technocracy found both an enthusiastic champion and an effective mouthpiece.

Boddy's editorials on Technocracy won a large following from among the mechanics, small tradesmen, and lower-paid white collar workers who then made up the bulk of the *Daily News* constituency. Centers of Technocracy were established in scores of neighborhoods and communities, meetings were held at frequent intervals, a considerable amount of money was collected to finance the crusade, an extensive educational and propaganda program was inaugurated, and Howard Scott the distinguished engineer became Howard Scott the infallible prophet and savior of society.

Pismo Beach claimed to be the semiofficial headquarters of the movement in California, but its chief strength lay in Los Angeles and other southern California communities. Many years after the depression, a few of the faithful still gathered in their neighborhood assemblies.

Even before Technocracy ceased to occupy the center of the stage, a new organization, called the Utopian Society, rose to dispute its place for popularity in California. The Utopian Society has been described as a strange "goulash of Technocracy, State Socialism, Ku Klux Klan, Populism, Fascism, Evangelism, and Voodoo." [1] It grew from a noble tradition of like societies in California, ranging from Thomas Lake Harris's Fountain Grove

---

[1] Quoted in Oliver Carlson: *A Mirror for Californians* (1941), p. 286.

colony in Santa Rosa to Madame Tingley's Theosophical center at Point Loma, and including such communal set-ups as Icaria Speranza on the Russian River, the Kaweah Cooperative Commonwealth, and Llano del Rio in the Antelope Valley, backed by Socialist Job Harriman.

According to Oliver Carlson, the original Utopians were an exbanker, a promoter, and a former stock salesman for the notorious Julian Petroleum Corporation. From an insignificant beginning in July 1933, the movement spread so rapidly that less than a year later thirty thousand people crowded into the Hollywood Bowl to attend a meeting of the society, and twenty thousand additional devotees were turned away. At the height of its popularity the Utopian Society had fully half a million members, and no auditorium in Los Angeles was large enough to accommodate the crowds who sought to attend its meetings.

The secret of the movement's brief but phenomenal popularity lay in its repudiation of the old economic order, its promise, through the "arithmetic of plenty," of a fanciful world of leisure and abundance, and its appeal to the American penchant for secret societies and symbolic ritual. The new Utopian convert was first introduced to the ritual and doctrines of the society in a small group called a "cycle." Here he underwent a secret initiation, received a number, and witnessed the "mysteries"—a modern version of the old morality plays that was used to spread the teachings of Utopia to immature minds. Each convert was encouraged to become a missionary; and as long as the spell lasted, the movement spread like one of the popular religious revivals of the last century. It ran its course, however, in less than two years, and by 1935 the Utopian Society was as outmoded as a model-T Ford.

Both Technocracy and the Utopian plan failed to develop into major political movements; but in 1934 a great popular crusade undertook to effect far-reaching economic and social reforms by direct government action. The movement was led by the widely read, ardently admired, oft-damned Socialist author Upton Sinclair.

Sinclair had risen to fame in 1906 with the publication of *The Jungle*, a sensational but unanswerable attack upon the unspeakable health and working conditions in the Chicago meat-packing industry. The book had an immense sale and its revelations were largely responsible for the enactment of congressional legislation requiring federal inspection of the slaughtering and handling of meat. Sinclair was given top rank among the muckraking journalists of Theodore Roosevelt's stormy time, and became one of the most prolific and widely read American authors of that or any other generation. A militant reformer, by both temperament and conviction, Sinclair poured forth an endless stream of novels, plays, and tracts exposing abuses, attacking individuals and organizations, and advocating radical changes in the existing economic and social order. For years prominent in the Socialist Party in the United States, he made the tenets of the party both a political philosophy and a religion.

But the distress, unemployment, and widespread economic paralysis in California after 1931 gave Sinclair the motive and opportunity for a daring political adventure. Convinced that the Socialist Party could never capture the state government, Sinclair agreed to register as a Democrat and seek the governorship on that ticket in the election of 1934.

The move was well timed and shrewdly calculated. The Democratic Party, defeated in every gubernatorial election since 1896, lacked prestige, leadership, and unity, but the triumph of Franklin Roosevelt in 1932 and the hypnotic popularity of the New Deal revived the long dormant hopes of California Democrats and promised to restore the party's rule in Sacramento. Sinclair had every reason to believe that he could capture the leadership of the badly divided Democratic Party, draw into it the great army of the discontented and rebellious, win the primary nomination and later the governorship, and then initiate a program of semi-socialistic measures to overcome the depression and restore prosperity.

His chances of success were greatly enhanced by the temporary but complete collapse of Republican leadership in national affairs—a phenomenon in American political history that still awaits adequate explanation. The mediocre character of Republican leadership in the state was well personified by Governor Frank Merriam, "an affable, rather ponderous old gentleman with few strong convictions," and a conservative do-nothing attitude toward the depression that was neither calculated to win votes nor restore confidence.

Sinclair's announcement of his candidacy for the Democratic nomination aroused some resentment among the Socialists, a measure of protest from conservative Democrats, and only apathetic concern on the part of the Republicans. In a short time, however, the storm broke in overwhelming fury and the campaign developed into the bitterest political struggle the state has ever witnessed.

Sinclair started his campaign with a pamphlet entitled *I, Governor of California and How I Ended Poverty; A True Story of the Future.* The pamphlet outlined twelve interrelated measures by which Sinclair promised to "end poverty in California." The promise became an imperative, and the initial letters of the slogan gave the movement its arresting name. To the slogan Sinclair added the emblem of a golden bee, and the motto: "I Produce, I Defend." The Democratic candidate's twelve-point program included the establishment of state land colonies, state operation of idle factories, "production for use" instead of "production for profit," state distribution of farm and industrial products, the issuance of scrip to finance the new state undertakings, a radical shift of the tax burden to public utilities and the incomes and estates of persons of large means, a modified form of the single tax, and provision for a pension of fifty dollars a month for those economically dependent because of old age, physical incapacity, or widowhood.

Soon after starting his campaign Sinclair formed an organization called the End Poverty League. From a very unpretentious beginning the League quickly developed into an efficient agency for publicizing the Epic doctrines, enlisting recruits, and carrying on the many other activities of the campaign. Much of the work was done by voluntary workers, for the Epic movement was poorly financed—a weakness that probably led to ultimate defeat —and had to rely in the main upon income from the sale of Sinclair's *I, Governor* . . . and other pamphlets, "voluntary dues" from members of the League, and the contributions of a few wealthy adherents.

Old-line Democrats and many supporters of the New Deal vigorously opposed Sinclair's bid for leadership. George Creel, director of propaganda in the first World War, had the support of the regular, or McAdoo, wing of the party in the primary; and Justus Wardell, a Democratic wheel-horse from San Francisco, carried the backing of the Isadore Dockweiler faction. Four other candidates entered the race for the Democratic nomination, but none of these was a serious contender.

The state primary election was held on August 28, 1934. Up to the beginning of summer the Republicans treated Sinclair as a troublesome crackpot, capable of fomenting dangerous ideas but too visionary, inexperienced, and politically obscure to prove a serious rival in the election. However, the results of the primary amazed California as well as the nation. In round numbers, the votes were as follows: Sinclair, Democrat, 436,000; George Creel, Democrat, 288,000; Frank Merriam, Republican, 336,000; C. C. Young, Republican, 331,000; John R. Quinn, Republican, 153,000; Raymond Haight, Progressive, 88,000.

Between the August primaries and the election in November, California witnessed the most confused and critical political battle in her career. Sinclair's followers were desperately sincere and determined, but they lacked both money and political experience. Propaganda on both sides became exaggerated and hysterical, and that against Sinclair passed far beyond the bounds of decency and fair play. He was pictured as "an Anarchist, a free-lover, an agent of Moscow, a Communist, an anti-Christ." [2] He was condemned as a "sinister pacifist," a millionaire, a vegetarian, and a believer in telepathy. Certain leaders of the motion-picture

[2] Lillian Symes: "California: There She Stands," *Harper's Magazine*, Vol. CLXX, pp. 367–8.

industry used the immense influence of camera and screen for election propaganda, and even resorted to falsification to make it more effective.

Sinclair was greatly disappointed by the attitude of the Socialists, many of whom denounced him as a deserter and opportunist. President Roosevelt's noncommittal attitude and the failure of most of the leaders of the New Deal to give him unqualified support also cost Sinclair many Democratic votes. In part Sinclair also owed his defeat to a last-minute attack by the Democratic leader, George Creel, and to a division in the ranks of the moderate liberals, many of whom chose to support Raymond Haight, the Progressive candidate, who had no shadow of chance to win the election, rather than to vote for Sinclair. In the November election the vote ran: Merriam, 1,138,620; Sinclair, 879,557; Haight, 302,519.

The excitement created by the Epic campaign to some degree obscured the dark labor situation in the mid-thirties and the general strike of trade-unionists in San Francisco, which ultimately involved over a hundred thousand men. The strike began on May 9, 1934, after government efforts to mediate the differences between the International Longshoremen's Association and the shipowners broke down. The controversy, involving wages, hours, control of hiring halls, a coastwide agreement, and one or two other points, quickly spread to other unions on the waterfront, and by May 15 ocean shipping was either tied up completely or seriously crippled by a coastwide strike which involved an unusual amount of violence and bloodshed.

The refusal of the members of the Teamsters' Union to move cargoes handled by strikebreakers paralyzed all shipping in San Francisco, and when industrial associations attempted to use strikebreakers to move the cargoes under police protection, "trucks were overturned; some were burned; goods were dumped into the street; police and pickets clashed; a riot occurred. Tear gas and pistols were met with cobblestones and brickbats. Two union men were killed; more than a hundred were seriously wounded; other hundreds were injured. A few days later, 10,000 union men marched in the funeral procession of their slain comrades." [3]

Rioting ceased when the Governor sent five thousand members of the National Guard to San Francisco to protect state property; but a general strike was called for July 16, causing an immediate run on stores, markets, and filling stations, and throwing the bay region into a near panic. By July 31, however, most of the unions and employers had compromised their difficulties or agreed to submit them to arbitration. The most troublesome and persistent issue, that of the control of hiring halls, was settled on October 12.

Out of this series of events rose Harry Bridges, destined to be as controversial a character in California labor history as Mooney or the McNamaras. During the depression, Bridges seized control of the longshoremen and led them into the C.I.O. when that group split from the A.F. of L. The seamen, however, stayed with the latter, and this divided allegiance on the part of two closely-related labor forces led to a series of jurisdictional disputes which served to lose much public support for both groups. Bridges, however, continued his leadership and rose to a position of power which gave him much authority over Pacific coast maritime business and, especially, the trade and shipping between California and Hawaii. Concurrent with his rise to power was the increasing popular suspicion that his politics took him too far to the left, and he was repeatedly accused of following the "Communist line" or of being a Communist himself. For twenty years his influence remained unshaken, and at this writing he is still a powerful force along the Embarcadero and by the Matson docks near the Aloha Tower.

---

[3] Ira Cross: *History of the Labor Movement* (1935), p. 257.

CHAPTER 29. False Prophets and False Hopes

WITH the defeat of Sinclair, the Epic movement lost its hold upon the hopes and imagination of the distressed masses and disappeared as a major political factor. But the ferment in California only grew more violent. As a plague-stricken community turns in desperation to the quack and the charlatan when orthodox remedies prove futile, so multitudes now turned to the proponents of one unorthodox remedy after another to find a cure for their grievous social maladies. No one knows how many hundreds of thousands and even millions of dollars the people of California paid during the years of uncertainty and distress to the self-appointed healers of the body politic for the privilege of living for a time in a world of unreality and delusion and false hope.

In the fall of 1934, while the success or failure of the Epic movement was still to be determined at the polls, Dr. Francis E. Townsend, of Long Beach, a retired physician who had turned to the sale of real estate for a precarious livelihood, suddenly occupied the spotlight as the sponsor of a fully-guaranteed-or-your-money-back plan both to restore prosperity to the nation and to provide pensions for all citizens over sixty years of age.

The movement, though officially entitled Old-Age Revolving Pensions, Ltd., was universally known as the "Townsend Old Age Pension Plan." Under his widely publicized, economically preposterous, and highly seductive scheme, Townsend proposed to levy a federal sales tax of two per cent on all the nation's business. From the funds thus obtained the government would pay a monthly pension of two hundred dollars to every citizen who had reached the age of sixty. These payments were to be made in federal scrip and each recipient was required to spend the entire two hundred dollars within the allotted thirty-day period. According to Townsend's theory, the forced circulation of the huge benefit payments would ensure the recipients a comfortable or even luxurious standard of living and provide a never failing market for the nation's industries and farms.

Though every honest and intelligent economist, businessman, banker, and statesman pointed out the fallacies of Townsend's proposal, the plan spread like wildfire and soon numbered its followers by the tens of thousands. Describing its meteoric success, Oliver Carlson wrote:

While Sinclair had been offering the unemployed a chance to work hard and create a new world, Townsend had begun offering the old folks a chance to do nothing to get $200 a month. Sinclair denounced the Townsend Plan; he was defeated. Republican Governor Merriam, himself a Long Beach man and an ex-Iowan, endorsed the Townsend Plan; he was elected. From then on Townsendism overflowed the borders of the Golden State, and the good doctor was off to the races. Townsend Clubs sprang up like oil derricks in the Signal Hill "strike." A weekly newspaper was launched and disciples snatched it off the presses. From everywhere in California, queries on how to organize a club poured into Long Beach. . . .

Outside the boundaries of California the Townsend movement had comparatively little effect except by indirection. In California, however, the Townsend movement sowed the dragon seed that brought forth a succession of proposed experiments even more fantastic, dangerous, and mercenary than the parent scheme itself. A certain notoriety-seeker named Robert Noble, whom the government convicted of sedition during the war, devised the first of the glamorous plans to win public recognition. The scheme originally involved the payment of a pension of twenty-five dollars every Monday to all citizens over fifty years of age; but two shrewd brothers, named Willis and Lawrence Allen, took the idea in hand, revamped some of its features to add to its publicity value, and put it out under the name "Thirty-Dollars-Every-Thursday Plan."

The scheme called for an amendment to the state constitution; the issuance every Thursday of thirty one-dollar "state warrants" to all unemployed persons over fifty years of age; the imposition of a stamp tax of two cents a week on each warrant; the establishment of a state "warrant" bank, financed by a $20,000,-000 bond issue and the sale of $52,000,000 worth of stock to the California public; the payment of all forms of state taxes in such scrip or warrants; and the imposition of a new three per cent gross income tax on all persons, firms, and corporations doing business or living in the state.

Since it was obviously out of the question to conduct a campaign under the impossible slogan of "Thirty-Dollars-Every-Thursday Plan," the promoters sought a name that would appeal in brevity and everyday familiarity to the mass of voters. One day, in addressing a group of campaign workers, a speaker promised that before the ensuing election the pension movement would become as familiar to the California voters as ham and eggs. The phrase was immediately seized upon as an answer to the quest for an inspired catchword, and the campaign for the millennium was conducted under that incongruous slogan.

The pension plan came before the voters as an initiative measure in the election of 1938, and, thanks to an intensive campaign of advertising and ballyhoo, polled 1,143,676 votes out of a total of 3,611,416! This phenomenal—and unexpected—support by the California electorate, and the huge sums collected in dues and contributions, gave the avid promoters of "Ham and Eggs" a golden opportunity to exploit the plan by a new initiative measure.

The Ham and Eggs campaign of 1939 marked the end of California's prolonged sojourn in the valley of economic and political confusion. The original measure was the brain child of a sincere but erratic social reformer, or self-styled "engineer economist," named Roy G. Owens. In 1936 Owens drafted a measure called "The Righteous Government Act" (later entitled the "Economic Adjustment Act"), which he proposed to present to the voters with the following preamble:

A BILL

In obedience to righteousness (right-use-ness) justice, truth, science,
   mathematics, and "The Constitution of the United States"
Written and Presented for the study and approval of every sincere
   and open-minded citizen of the U. S. A.—whether from school,
   pulpit, press, business, professional, legislature, lawyer or layman,
   who believes in "the Constitutional" and Scientific way out of
   our economic distress!

Furthermore, by giving dictatorial powers, subject only to the
control of the voters of the state by initiative action, to the administrator of the Thursday warrant act, the plan was a thinly veiled
attempt, as dangerous as any threat a state has faced since the
days of Reconstruction, to deliver California over into the hands
of sinister and designing men.

The campaign for Ham and Eggs was carefully organized and
shrewdly carried out. It depended for publicity upon radio programs, a large money-making journal called *National Ham and
Eggs*, a vast corps of voluntary propagandists, neighborhood
gatherings, huge mass meetings, and free barbecues and enter-
tainments. The following extract from a Ham and Eggs broadcast
illustrates the general tenor of such propaganda:

We must know that we cannot break up this bankers racket,—we
must realize that we cannot change our rotten and corrupt and dis-
honest money system without a battle. We are fighting the greatest
racket in the world. And the fight that they are giving us only shows
that we are prodding in a tender spot,—and they can't take it.

Keep your dues paid up, fellow members. If they are paid for the
month of April, then pay them for the month of May. Pay a dollar on
your dues, if you can, so that we can take the money now. We are in
the heat of battle. Support your organization like you have never done
before.

Really now, fellow members, get out your membership card tonight. And that little envelope. And send some money to your Association to help us fight these great battles. I know that you will, because
we all have confidence in each other. Get out that envelope tonight,
won't you? And send something to help. . . .

And by all means send in that One Dollar and get your name on the subscribers' list for National Ham and Eggs.[1]

The Ham and Eggs campaign organization was remarkably thorough. The total force, almost wholly made up of volunteer workers, ran close to 110,000 persons.[2] *National Ham and Eggs*, the official newspaper of the movement, had a paid circulation of 100,000 copies. One radio speaker claimed that nearly 80,000 persons attended the party's Fourth of July celebration. Dues-paying members numbered over 330,000 in July, 1939, new members were added at the rate of 4,500 to 5,000 a week, and 600 organization meetings a month were not uncommon.

As the summer wore on, the growing threat of the Ham and Eggs amendment to the economic stability and political well-being of the state became more and more evident and served to consolidate widely variant groups and individuals into a determined opposition. Harry Chandler and Upton Sinclair for once saw eye to eye; President Roosevelt called the plan "fantastic"; twenty ranking officers of virtually every major woman's organization in the state opposed it.

A hundred and thirty-eight economists from California university and college faculties advocated the principal of old-age pensions but condemned the Ham and Eggs amendment on the grounds that it would lead to dangerous inflation, prove unworkable, and soon collapse, thus doing untold harm to those whom it was supposed to benefit, that it would seriously impair the credit of state, county, and municipal governments, even perhaps to the point of bankruptcy, and that it would delegate powers of a dictatorial nature to the administrators of the proposed measure.

The widespread opposition to Ham and Eggs was finally concentrated in an efficient political organization called California Citizens against 30 Thursday. One branch of the organization had its headquarters in San Francisco, the other in Los Angeles. James C. Sheppard, an attorney prominent in southern California

---

[1] Radio broadcast, April 20, 1939, Station KMTR.
[2] Radio broadcast, April 20, 1939.

Democratic circles, directed the activities of the Citizens against 30 Thursday. The organization carried on a huge publicity campaign, making use of large numbers of mass meetings, tons of literature, hundreds of volunteer speakers, and a constant stream of radio broadcasts, as an effective counter-offensive to the extensive Ham and Eggs propaganda.

Governor Culbert L. Olson was counted upon to support the initiative because in the campaign of 1938 both he and Sheridan Downey, then running for lieutenant governor, had endorsed the Ham and Eggs proposal. Partly as a result of his support of the Ham and Eggs measure in 1938, Olson had soundly defeated his Republican opponent, Frank Merriam, "pictured on billposters as rather sheepishly protecting small cottages from the advances of mobs armed with red flags and sizzling bombs." The Lieutenant Governor, Sheridan Downey, "a weathervane so delicately set to the winds of doctrine that he responded to the first faint sigh of any political disturbance," had also shown his facile ability to leap at a moment's warning from a waning to a waxing popular movement by leaving the ranks of the Townsendites in 1938 to align himself with the Allen brothers.

With Olson and Downey both friendly to the cause of Ham and Eggs, the supporters of the measure expected the Governor to call the special initiative election early in August, when enthusiasm and contributions were at a maximum and the opposition still lacked cohesion and momentum.[3]

But Olson, for reasons of his own, underwent a change of heart between the fall of 1938 and the summer of the next year, and when a delegation of Ham and Eggs supporters requested a favorable date for the election, they found him evasive in his attitude toward the pension. The delegation did return, however, with what they regarded as Olson's pledge that the election would be held at a time satisfactory to the backers of the movement.

---

[3] Manchester Boddy and other keen judges of California public opinion believe the measure would have carried if it had come before the voters in August.

Accordingly, when the Governor later refused to call the election for early August but set it for November, the wrath of the Ham and Eggs crusaders boiled over and they vociferously protested that they had been betrayed by one of their own household. Their feelings were further outraged by Olson's pre-election statement that the passage of the Ham and Eggs amendment would retard rather than aid the state's progress toward a better economic order.

The election was held on November 7, 1939. Out of a total vote of approximately 2,975,000, the initiative measure received only 993,000, only a slightly larger percentage than its predecessor had obtained in 1938. The defeat proved a death blow to the hopes of old-age-pension promoters for a revival of Ham and Eggs, or any other comparable money-making, politico-economic mumbo-jumbo; and though the Allen brothers and their associates tried to whip up the spirit and enthusiasm of the multitude who had followed the mirage for five years, they met with no response. California had emerged from the strangest, most perilous decade of the state's domestic life.

CHAPTER 30. Aliens and Nomads

D URING the confused years of the depression and the Uto-
pias, California was also forced to deal with the so-called
"Okie invasion," a social and economic phenomenon of baffling
complexity and discouraging magnitude. This was not the state's
first experience, however, with the troublesome problem of immigration. An earlier generation had crusaded and rioted against
the Chinese. Between 1900 and 1930 the conflict had shifted to
the Japanese and, to some degree, to the Mexicans.

Japanese immigration, so long an explosive issue in California,
was an inseparable feature of the state's early twentieth-century
agricultural economy. After 1902 over 10,000 Japanese sometimes
entered the state in a single year, and by 1910 the Japanese population had risen to over 40,000.

Unlike the Chinese of the previous generation, against whom
there had been such violent agitation in the sixties and seventies,
the Japanese who came to California after 1900 were shrewd,
self-assertive, and aggressively ambitious. They were not content
to remain farm laborers, but rapidly acquired control of large
blocks of fertile land for themselves, either by rental or outright purchase. The Japanese acquired almost a monopoly of the
berry, potato, flower, and truck markets of California. In the
cities they were equally alert and aggressive, opening banks, restaurants, hotels, and small stores. They became doctors, dentists,
and lawyers, served in large numbers as gardeners and domestics,
and controlled much of the commercial fishing industry along
the coast.

The rising tide of Japanese influence was not accepted with
equanimity by a large element in California, and various strong,
well-organized bodies made determined efforts to restrain it by
agitation, adverse publicity, and legislation. In May 1900, a mass
meeting in San Francisco petitioned Congress to re-enact the
Chinese exclusion law and include the Japanese in its provisions.

Five years later the San Francisco *Chronicle* conducted a vigorous campaign against the Japanese, and San Francisco labor leaders organized the Oriental Exclusion League to oppose further immigration of Japanese and Korean nationals into the United States.

A few months later the San Francisco Board of Education created an international incident by announcing a plan of segregated education for all Chinese and Japanese children. Asserting that the act discriminated against its citizens and violated well-established treaty rights, the Japanese government lodged a formal protest against the measure with the State Department in Washington, and President Roosevelt was forced to use both the pressure of his office and his personal influence to induce the school board to rescind its action.

In September 1906, the Republican state convention adopted a resolution favoring the exclusion of the Japanese and all other Asiatics from the United States. The Los Angeles *Times,* which heartily endorsed most of the other acts of the convention, severely criticized the party's provision against the Japanese. "In the first place, California needs the Japanese," said the editor. "She needs them in the fields, on the ranches, in the orchards, and in the households of the commonwealth throughout its whole length and breadth. . . . In the second place the utterances of the convention serve as a gratuitous and unwise insult to a friendly nation with which we are at peace and with which we desire to do business. . . ." [1]

By 1907, California had a Japanese population of over 30,000. In that year, acting under authorization from Congress, the President issued an executive order excluding from the United States Japanese and Korean laborers who had received passports to enter Mexico, Canada, or Hawaii.

The mounting hostility to Japanese immigration, especially in California, and the growing tension between the Japanese and American governments, chiefly as a result of state and local anti-Japanese legislation, led to the adoption of what proved to be a

[1] September 7, 1906.

highly controversial and unsatisfactory compromise known as the Gentlemen's Agreement. Under the terms of the agreement, the Nipponese government undertook to restrict the issuance of passports to the United States to specifically limited groups of Japanese citizens. These included former residents of the United States, parents, wives, or children of such residents, owners of farms, and a few others.

From the standpoint of the anti-Japanese elements in California, the Gentlemen's Agreement failed signally and notoriously in its purpose. Aside from large-scale smuggling of Japanese into the United States, especially from Mexico, thousands of Japanese found their way into California by bland evasions and convenient subterfuges or through loopholes that the agreement did not cover. Exclusionists were especially severe in their criticism of the custom of so-called "picture-bride" marriages, under which hundreds of young Japanese women annually reached California to become in time the mothers of large families. By 1920, when the issuance of passports to picture-brides was discontinued by the Japanese government, the Japanese population of California had risen to 72,000, a gain of about eighty per cent in ten years. During the same period the state's white population increased only 22.4 per cent.

Meantime, except for an interval during World War I when the United States and Japan were waging a common war against the Central Powers, anti-Japanese agitation in California steadily increased. The California State Grange, the American Federation of Labor, and the Native Sons and Native Daughters of the Golden West were particularly active in such opposition. The issue reached a major climax in 1913 when the state legislature, by a vote of 35 to 2 in the senate and of 73 to 9 in the assembly, passed the Anti-Alien Land Act, which prohibited Japanese ownership or tenancy of agricultural land in California. The measure, sometimes called the Webb Act in honor of U. S. Webb, who was then the state Attorney General, was opposed, partly for economic reasons and partly because of its possible effect upon American-Japanese relations, by many civic and religious bodies and by such newspapers as the San Francisco *Chronicle,* the *Argonaut,* and the Los Angeles *Times.* The action of the California legislature led the Japanese government to issue three spirited protests, calling the measure "unfair, inequitable, discriminating, prejudicial to the rights of the Japanese in California, inconsistent with the treaty of 1911, and opposed to the spirit of amity existing between the two nations." [2]

The possible threat of war in Europe, combined with the chaotic internal situation in Mexico and the growing tension between that country and the United States, made the timing of the California law particularly inopportune from the standpoint of our own national government. President Wilson accordingly sent William Jennings Bryan, his Secretary of State, to confer with Governor Hiram Johnson and some of the key members of the legislature in Sacramento. Except to add to Johnson's political prestige in California and give the Governor an opportunity of thumbing his nose at a President and a Cabinet member whom he cordially disliked, Bryan's visit accomplished nothing. Asserting that eight states and the District of Columbia already had laws similar to the one enacted in California, Johnson refused to accede to the request of the federal government and signed the bill.

The California Alien Land Act, like the Gentlemen's Agreement, readily lent itself to violation and evasion, and many American landowners worked with the Japanese to devise ways and means of defeating the purpose of the law. At the close of 1919 individual Japanese and Japanese corporations owned or leased a total of 535,000 acres in the choicest agricultural regions of the state. The Japanese then produced from eighty to ninety per cent of the strawberries, celery, asparagus, and tomatoes grown in California and received an annual gross income of over sixty-seven million dollars from their farming operations. [3]

By a three-to-one popular vote in 1920, California adopted an

---

[2] Thomas A. Bailey: "California, Japan, and the Alien Land Legislation of 1913," *Pacific Historical Review,* Vol. I, pp. 47–8.

[3] *California and the Oriental,* Report of the State Board of Control (1922), pp. 50–1.

initiative measure designed to stop the loopholes in the Land Act of 1913. Three years later the state legislature amended the act to make it still more drastic. The constitutionality of the state's anti-alien land legislation, though repeatedly challenged, was upheld both by the California and the United States Supreme courts.

Recognizing the growing seriousness and complexity of the Japanese penetration of the state, Governor William D. Stephens, a liberal and able executive, finally addressed a comprehensive summary of the situation to Bainbridge Colby, who served as Secretary of State during the closing months of the Wilson administration. The report, dated June 19, 1920, represented in the main the point of view of a majority of the thoughtful Californians of that time. Stephens wrote:

. . . this problem of ours is not an insignificant or temporary one. It is not factious. It has no origin in narrow race prejudice or rancor or hostility. It is, however, a solemn problem affecting our entire Occidental civilization. It has nothing to do with any pretensions of race superiority, but has vitally to do with race dissimilarity and unassimilability.

But with all this the people of California are determined to repress a developing Japanese community within our midst. They are determined to exhaust every power in their keeping to maintain this state for its own people. . . .[4]

California's experience with the Gentlemen's Agreement and state alien land legislation led representatives of the anti-Japanese movement to demand a federal Japanese exclusion law as drastic as the Chinese Exclusion Act of the early eighties. Though such a measure was vigorously opposed in Congress by conservative and liberal organizations alike, the Immigration Act of 1924 denied Japan the status of a quota nation and virtually shut off all entrance of Japanese nationals into the United States.

The measure, on the basis of which Japanese apologists in 1941 explained in part the attack on Pearl Harbor, freed California from the immediate danger of further large-scale Japanese im-

---

[4] *Ibid.*, pp. 9–10.

migration, but offered no solution to the problems growing out of the prolific birthrate of the Japanese already in the state. The constitutional provision that makes any person born or naturalized in the United States a citizen thereof placed the issue definitely beyond the control of anti-Japanese crusaders. By 1940 California had a Japanese population of approximately 94,000. Some 37,000 Japanese lived in Los Angeles County, and the rest were about equally divided among Sacramento, Alameda, San Francisco, San Joaquin, and Fresno. "Little Tokyo," the Japanese quarter of Los Angeles, lying between First and Third streets east of Main, had close to 24,000 residents. The Japanese population of San Francisco was slightly over 5,000.

By this time nearly sixty-five per cent of the California Japanese were American citizens, or Nisei, but though they rapidly and very thoroughly absorbed the language, customs, education, and culture of their fellow citizens of Anglo-Saxon ancestry, a formidable gulf still separated the two races, even before Pearl Harbor.

Far outnumbering the Japanese population of California, but more readily accepted in most communities, Mexican immigrants poured into the state by the trainload during World War I to meet the demand for unskilled labor. With the end of the conflict, thousands of the workers returned to Mexico, but other thousands elected to remain permanently in California. Most of the newcomers settled in the Los Angeles metropolitan area, and by 1925 that former Spanish pueblo had become, next to Mexico City itself, the largest Mexican community in the world. Unfortunately, no concerted attack was made upon the problems of housing, wages, standards of living, education, and assimilation presented by the influx of such a large and less advanced population into our complex society.

The Mexicans furnished unskilled labor for railroads, construction jobs, and factories, and comprised the largest body of California's casual agricultural workers. By 1930, at least 250,000 Mexicans were living in the state, thus providing a great reservoir of labor upon which California farmers habitually drew.

The typical Mexican had his limitations, but these were far out-weighed by his superior qualities in other fields. According to a fact-finding committee appointed by Governor C. C. Young in 1928 to report on the problem of Mexican immigration into California, the Mexican "does tasks that white workers will not or cannot do. He works under climatic and working conditions, such as excessive heat, dust, and temporary employment . . . that are often too trying for white workers. He will work in gangs. He will work under direction, taking orders."

The Mexican made an excellent seasonal worker. He liked to travel, found the standards and conditions of camp life fully as good as those to which he was normally accustomed, and looked upon the four or six months of itinerant work as a welcome outing in which all the members of the household might share. Many families returned year after year to the same ranches and occupied camp sites to which they had first been assigned a generation before. Here in the evening the campfires spread their cheerful glow; laughter and music brought back memories of the California of the nostalgic and irrecoverable past; and life, for the moment at least, was moderately pleasant.

The other side of the picture was not so attractive. Even before the depression, the ignorance, lack of organization, and docility of the Mexicans invited injustice and exploitation; and during the thirties they suffered, like the Okies and all other casual laborers, from the twin evils of low wages and lack of employment.

The strike of 1928 among the melon-pickers of Imperial Valley brought the Mexican labor issue sharply to a head. In March of that year the so-called Confederation of Mexican Labor Unions (*Confederación de Uniones Obreras Mexicanas*) was formed in Los Angeles. One of the announced purposes of the organization was to restrict Mexican immigration into the United States and at the same time to arrange for the repatriation of Mexicans already here. The Confederation, denying that it had any intention of serving as a center of labor agitation, also proposed to unify the Mexican laborers in the United States, put them on an equal footing with American workers, furnish protection against exploitation by employment agencies, commissary stores, and employers, encourage cultural development, afford free legal advice, and provide funds for the destitute.

From 4,500 to 5,000 male workers were needed in the spring of 1928 to harvest the cantaloupe crop in Imperial Valley. Most of these workers were hired by Mexican labor agents whose contracts with the growers freed the latter from the responsibility of dealing directly with the individual employee and left the worker more or less subject to the honesty and good faith of the labor contractor.

At the beginning of the season an organization of pickers, called La Union de Trabajadores del Valle, demanded an increase in wages, elimination of some of the most glaring abuses under the contract system, and certain minor concessions from the growers. Many of the pickers went on strike when these demands were refused. The strike was perfectly timed to cause the maximum of consternation among the growers and confronted them with a clear decision; either to make the stipulated concessions to the pickers, or to take whatever drastic steps were necessary to break the strike. The growers chose the latter course. The sheriff appointed forty deputies, threw a number of strikers into jail for "disturbing the peace," and even arrested a number of labor leaders whom the district attorney had invited to confer with him on a peaceful method of settling the controversy. After a period of tenseness, thinly veiled disregard of constitutional guarantees by local authorities, and the intervention of the California State Department of Industrial Relations, the growers agreed to a more equitable picking agreement, the charges against most of the Mexican laborers were dismissed, the pickers went back to work, and the cantaloupe crop was saved.

To the unemployment, bankruptcies, and widespread lack of confidence from which the state suffered in the early years of the depression, the migration of tens of thousands of evacuees from the Dust Bowl area of the Plains States added a new source of poverty, labor unrest, and confusion during the mid-thirties. Behind this sudden shift of population lay one of the oldest of all factors in human history—the necessity of leaving a region ravaged by drought to seek a more productive land.

During the early thirties a prolonged cycle of dry years turned large areas of the Western prairie states into a waste land, covered by smothering, wind-blown dust, far more desolate and forbidding than the great reaches of the Colorado or Mojave deserts. In many parts of this graphically named Dust Bowl, agriculture, grazing, and the existence of human life itself became impossible. In other sections, machinery and large-scale farming forced tenants and sharecroppers, often woefully backward and improvident even under normal conditions and now reduced to the barest subsistence levels by the nationwide depression, to leave the region and migrate to other parts of the country.

Great hordes of these dispossessed Dust Bowl farmers turned to California as the land of hope and opportunity. The number of transient immigrants who came into California from impoverished Western and Southern states during the depressed thirties is somewhat problematical. According to one estimate, 285,000 refugees, "in need of manual employment," passed through the plant quarantine stations along the state's eastern border between January 1935, and January 1939, and a total of 350,000 emigrees entered the state between 1930 and the end of the decade.

The effect of this large immigration on California farm labor was almost revolutionary. The influx was composed of native white Americans, not foreign interlopers. They came by families rather than as individuals, and perhaps for that reason most of them preferred to stay permanently in one region rather than to move from place to place. Before the close of the decade the influx was so great that California agriculture found it utterly impossible to absorb the new arrivals.

It has already been pointed out that the seasonal variation in the labor demand of California agriculture is enormous. During the peak months—that is, from May to October or November—California farms require from 100,000 to 250,000 more employees than during the remainder of the year. This situation necessarily creates a large, unstable labor population even under normal conditions, and the so-called Okie and Arkie influx added further poverty-stricken thousands to the large migrant group the state was already seeking to absorb.

"The migrants are familiar enough to anyone who has traveled much through California's interior," said a writer in *Fortune* in April 1939.

On the roads, where you can see them in numbers, they take on a kind of patchwork pattern. They come along in wheezy old cars with the father or one of the older boys driving. The mother and the younger children sit in back; and around them, crammed inside and over-flowing to the running boards, the front and rear bumpers, the top and sides, they carry along everything they own. A galvanized iron washtub is tied to the rear, a dirty, patched tent lashed to a fender. There is a cast-iron stove, a mattress, some boxes full of old dishes, extra clothing, and a few staple groceries like flour, lard, and potatoes. You see, at odd angles, the protruding handle of a broom, part of a paint-flaked bedstead, perhaps even an old phonograph or radio. You notice the faces of the people in these cars. There is worry, but also something more: they are the faces of people afraid of hunger; completely dispossessed, certain only of being harried along when their immediate usefulness is over. As one boy said, "When they need us they call us migrants. When we've picked their crop, we're bums and we got to get out."

The unprecedented influx of this moneyless, unskilled horde came at the worst possible time for California. Agriculture, of all kinds and in every section, was nearly prostrate. It was manifestly impossible, when agriculture itself was in such a desperate plight, for California farmers to absorb the enormous number of surplus migrants that poured into the state during the thirties.

The average family income of the migrant farm laborer was approximately four hundred dollars a year, or about half the amount state authorities considered necessary for a subsistence living-standard. On some large farms the migrants were housed in camps provided by the owner. These varied greatly in comfort, facilities, and cleanliness; but because of overcrowding and the owner's reluctance or inability to provide necessary funds for enlargement and upkeep, most of the camps eventually became unfit for human habitation. A description of one such camp appeared in the report of the State Relief Administration for 1936:

In Imperial County, many families were found camping out by the side of the irrigation ditches, with little or no shelter. One such family consisted of the father, mother, and eight children. The father hoped there would be some work in the valley later in the year. The mother had tuberculosis and pellagra and it was because of her health that the family came to California. One of the children had active tuberculosis. The family had no home but a 1921 Ford. The mother was trying to chop some wood for the fire. . . . A meat and vegetable stew was being cooked in a large, rusty tin can over a grate supported by four other cans. A cupboard and a table had been constructed of boxes. There were no toilet facilities, Nature's needs being attended to behind bushes. Some water was brought from the ice plant in El Centro for drinking purposes, but for cooking and washing, water from the irrigation ditches was used. The family had been sleeping on the ground. The blankets were kept during the daytime in the car. There was no possible shelter.

Many of the families camping along the irrigation ditches were using the ditchwater for drinking purposes as well as using the side of the ditch as a toilet. In February a child from one of these families was taken to the County Hospital with spinal meningitis. There had been no quarantine and the other members of the family were mixing with their neighbors. Children dressed in rags, their hands encrusted with dirt, complexions pasty white, their teeth quite rotted, were observed in these camps.

Acting through the Farm Security Administration, the federal government at last established both permanent and mobile camps for the benefit of the migrant workers. The federal camps were equipped with well-floored tents, sanitary toilets, communal laundry tubs, cooking facilities, showers, a nursery, an assembly hall, a health clinic, and an isolation center. Under the supervision of an employee of the Farm Security Administration, the migrants ran and maintained the camp. Each occupant paid a weekly communal benefit fee of ten cents, either in work or cash. Each camp also contained from twenty to fifty comfortable but cheaply constructed frame houses for permanently employed, specially selected tenants. Each house was surrounded by enough good land for a large garden and rented for approximately eight dollars a month.

Unfortunately California's agricultural labor problem in the thirties was complicated by widespread, subconscious, easily excited fear. Many factors were responsible for this peculiar state of mind. So far as the conservative farming element of California was concerned, the economic collapse of 1929 and the failure of the administration either to foresee or to check the depression undermined self-confidence and morale.

The philosophy and vast-scale experiments of the New Deal angered and frightened the farm-owners still worse. They came to believe that Communism and Soviet Russia, either openly or in a hundred clever disguises, only waited the opportunity to destroy private property, individual initiative, free enterprise, and the American Republic itself. In this frame of mind, the farmers even went so far as to appose the labor camps built and directed by the federal government for the benefit of the migrant laborers, on the questionable ground that they were "hotbeds of radicalism." [5] This feeling was in part, however, the product of actual experience, under totally different circumstances, which the ranchers had passed through in former years.

In 1931 Communist agitators attempted to organize fruit-pickers in various sections of the state and even used force and intimidation to bring the workers into line. During 1933 and 1934 the left-wing Cannery and Agricultural Workers' Industrial Union organized a succession of nearly fifty strikes, involving fifty thousand workers in such crops as peas, lettuce, peaches, apricots, and cotton.

A strike on the Balfour, Guthrie ranch, northeast of Mount Diablo, led to drastic action by the peace officers and landowners. Some two hundred strikers were driven into a cattle pen and later escorted out of the country by armed guards. Eight union leaders

[5] Frank J. Taylor: "California's Grapes of Wrath," *Forum*, Vol. CX, p. 237.

were convicted of treason under a law against criminal syndical-
ism that was ostensibly passed as a war measure by the California
legislature in 1919 and thereafter allowed to remain on the statute
books as a weapon against Communism and the I.W.W. philosophy of sabotage. Three years later the appellate court reversed all
eight of the convictions.[6]

The conservative agriculture organization known as the Associated Farmers was the chief leader of the "anti-red," "anti-Com-
munist," "anti-radical," "anti-labor-union" crusade. California is a
state of large agricultural landholdings, and the type of crops and
method of farming give these large properties the semblance of
what Carey McWilliams aptly calls "Factories in the Fields"; or,
as another writer remarks, "California's agriculture is not 'farming'
in the traditional sense. It is industry as much as lumbering and
oil are industries."[7]

Although the Associated Farmers rendered many valuable services to large and small growers alike, the organization had many
critics, even among influential landowners; and its general labor
policy, at least during the thirites, was so much more reactionary
than constructive that even *Fortune*, the businessman's magazine,
felt called upon to censure its activities and methods.

From labor's point of view, the Associated Farmers is a thinly camou-
flaged strikebreaking agency. To the big grower, it is a strong-arm
defense against the menace of Communist agitation.[8]

Steinbeck's *Grapes of Wrath*, the *Uncle Tom's Cabin* of the California Okie, focused the nation's attention upon the tragic plight of

---

[6] Some 350 persons, mostly members of the I.W.W., were arrested under
the act and 93 were convicted. The trial and conviction of Miss Char-
lotte Anita Whitney, a woman of distinguished family and reputation, became a *cause célèbre*.

[7] About one half of the state's agricultural production comes from only ten
per cent of its farms. The following figures throw further light on the subject: 20 million acres are held in farms of 1,000 acres or over; 9 million in
farms of 1,000 to 5,000 acres; 3 million in farms of 5,000 to 10,000 acres;
and 8 million in farms of 10,000 acres and over. The largest ranches, however, are mostly unirrigated grazing lands.

[8] *Fortune*, April 1939.

the uprooted migrant families; but the book, like Harriet Beecher Stowe's powerful nation-dividing classic, was after all a novel rather than a careful sociological study; it was fiction, not history; and it dealt with word-pictures and emotions rather than with an intricate, many-sided economic problem.

Less widely known than Steinbeck's masterpiece, but even more unpopular with the large California landowners, Carey Mc-Williams's *Factories in the Fields* went back to Henry George's oversimplified explanation of California's land plight and offered the breakup of the great ranches as the only possible solution for the state's chronic agricultural labor problem.

Meantime the Joads, the Jacksons, the Smiths, and the Robinsons continued to arrive. As previously emphasized, they were not outlanders and foreigners like the Hindus, Mexicans, and Japanese. They were Americans of English extraction, who became, indeed, the sorry "poor white trash" that constitutes one of the major human tragedies in so many of our Southern states.

"You know you can't feed a family o' six on forty-five cents a day," said one of the Okies to an inquiring journalist. "It ain' my fault, is it? Jees, I worked hard since I was a kid. I allus done what I thought war right, and I think I know right from wrong. I allus tried to teach my kids right from wrong. But I'm beginnin' to wonder. I don't know what to do. There's nothing back in Oklahoma for us to go to now and there's nothing here. Somehow somethin' don't seem right—I want to work and I can't—I want to bring up my kids decent. You been to college, Mister, maybe you can explain it to me." [9]

These desperate conditions were relieved only with the stimulus to industry and agriculture, the demand for labor, and the rise in wages that returned to California and the entire nation with the terrible approach of war.

---

[9] *Fortune*, April 1939.

CHAPTER 31.   Vanity Fair

SANDWICHED in between the announcement of a special
sale of Indian curios and the space daily devoted to Cawston's South Pasadena Ostrich Farm, the following brief ad-
vertisement appeared on the front page of the Los Angeles
Times of April 16, 1902:

ELECTRIC THEATER   262 S. Main   Off Third St.
NEW PLACE OF AMUSEMENT
Up to Date High Class Moving Picture Entertainment Especially for
Ladies and Children. See the capture of Biddle Brothers, New York
in a blizzard and many other interesting and exciting scenes. An
hour's amusement and genuine fun for
10 Cents Admission
Evenings 7:30 to 10:30

In this unspectacular fashion, thanks to T. W. Tally, owner of
the Electric Theater, the California public was informed of the
genesis of one of the most amazing innovations of our amazing
generation—an innovation that was at once an art, an industry,
and a revolutionary force.

To recount the story of the tentative beginnings of the cinema
industry outside California does not fall within the province of
this volume except to note that the eleven thousand feet of pictures of the Corbett-Fitzsimmons championship fight at Carson
City, Nevada, on March 17, 1897, provided the first "national
sensation" in the history of the films. Sigmund Lubin, a dealer in
optical goods in Philadelphia, furnished an interesting sequel to
the authorized picture. According to Terry Ramsaye, Lubin used
an "outlaw" camera and employed "two freight handlers to re-
enact the fight, blow by blow and round by round" as he found it
described in the newspapers. He then "released" the picture un-

der the imposing and technically veracious title of *The Great Corbett-Fitzsimmons Fight* (*In Counterpart*).[1]

By 1903, motion pictures had become a recognized form of entertainment for the low-income masses in many large American cities, and the profits made by penny arcades, "nickelodeons," and the cheap vaudeville houses that displayed the first crude films led to a rapid development of the business and radical improvements both in production and in exhibition facilities.[2] A few years later the industry had outgrown the age of swaddling clothes, and half a dozen companies were engaged in a rough-and-tumble fight over the rapidly increasing flow of nickels and dimes into the picture theaters.

In 1901 two pioneer companies, Biograph and the Thomas A. Edison Company of New Jersey, which held many of the basic motion-picture patents, formed ten of the largest competing companies—chief of which were Lubin, Vitagraph, Selig, Essanay, Pathé, and Melies—into a tight monopoly called the Motion Pictures Patents Company, and sought to collect substantial royalties from all other producing organizations.[3] A five-year war, which recognized neither rules nor amenities, at once broke out between the so-called independents and the trust. According to several popular versions, this war was directly responsible for the establishment of Hollywood as the world's motion-picture capital. As the story goes, most of the independent producers, including such subsequently dominant figures as Carl Laemmle, Jesse Lasky, Adolph Zukor, Cecil B. de Mille, and Samuel Goldwyn, used cameras that infringed the Edison patents. It was consequently necessary for them to operate close enough to Mexico to be able to spirit their bootleg equipment across the international line where it would escape the jurisdiction of American courts and the danger of confiscation whenever the minions of the law,

---

[1] Terry Ramsaye: "The Motion Picture," *American Academy of Political Science,* November, 1926, p. 1.

[2] Six years before Tally opened his electric theater in Los Angeles, motion pictures had been shown in Koster and Bial's Music Hall in New York.

[3] The trust distributed its pictures through the General Film Company.

egged on by the attorneys of the Patents Company, became too inquisitive and meddlesome. "The minor makers of pictures," said Terry Ramsaye, "were more marked by their fleetness of foot in the evasion of process servers than in any other ability."

Driven from his Chicago studio in the war of "suits and injunctions, raids and riots," William Selig fled to Los Angeles and there completed *The Count of Monte Cristo,* the first commercial film produced in California. Under the name of the Nestor Film Company the Horsly brothers of New Jersey leased the old Blondeau Tavern and its barn at Sunset and Gower streets and produced Hollywood's first picture, *The Law of the Range.* Thus the outlaw film-producers, like the cattle rustlers of an earlier generation, located their closely guarded studios in Hollywood. But despite this wealth of evidence, one may still assume that Hollywood owed its supremacy in the motion-picture world to more lasting if less spectacular advantages than convenient proximity to the Mexican border.

As late as 1913, major studios were located in New York, Chicago, Philadelphia, San Diego, Santa Barbara, and Oakland, as well as in Los Angeles, Hollywood, and Santa Monica. But powerful factors were tending to concentrate the industry more and more within the wide area now generally called Hollywood, and before the end of another decade southern California enjoyed a virtual monopoly in the production of American-made pictures. This supremacy was due in the main to such obvious factors as climate, sunlight (especially in the days before the development of artificial lighting), the advantage of an early start, cheap production costs, excellent transportation facilities, and proximity to an almost unlimited variety of topography and scene.

With some exceptions, the pioneers in motion pictures, the men who rode with the industry to undreamed-of wealth and transient notoriety, represented the triumph of the commonplace. One of the most powerful figures in the industry was originally a peddler of spectacles, another ran a traveling minstrel show, a third was a garment worker, a fourth served as train newsboy,

a fifth was a bouncer at an amusement park, a sixth was a cowboy, two were bookmakers put out of business by the law against
race-track betting, and the four brothers whose family name is
attached to one of the largest of all the companies were the sons
of a Polish-born, Midwest butcher.[4]

Rosten says in his penetrating description of Hollywood:

The men who built the motion picture industry (Fox, Laemmle,
Zukor, Selig, Loew, Goldwyn, Lasky, Warner, Mayer) were not
drawn from the supposedly farsighted ranks of American business.
They came, instead, from the marginal and shabby zones of enterprise,
from vaudeville, nickelodeon parlors, theatrical agencies, flea circuses,
petty trade. They were tough-minded, hardworking, aggressive men
—rude in manner, quick in their hunches, with an instinct for ballyhoo
and a genius for showmanship.[5]

Further along in his volume Rosten adds:

The producers who emerged from the infancy of the film industry
were hard-driving, competent, and versatile. They had to be. The
first producers . . . took an active part in every department of
movie making. They raised money, borrowed cameras, and rented
"studio space." They thought up plots and wrote subtitles; they
created characters; they invented gadgets; they painted sets and set
up lights. They sometimes developed their own film and generally
edited their reels. They ran the entire threadbare business of making
mutilated images which moved jerkily on imperfect film, and they
sold their product to penny arcades and nickelodeon parlors. These
men were artisans as well as businessmen, craftsmen as well as promoters. They had to be. They combined the talents of bankers and
circus barkers. They possessed immense drive, resourcefulness, and an
almost maniacal capacity for work.[6]

The profits of many of the early picture companies were utterly

---

[4] Benjamin B. Hampton: *A History of the Movies* (1931), p. 177.

[5] Leo C. Rosten: *Hollywood: the Movie Colony, the Movie Makers*
(1941), pp. 67–8. I am greatly indebted to the publishers, Harcourt, Brace
Company, as well as to the author, for permission to quote both the above
paragraph and other extensive passages from this volume.

[6] Ibid., pp. 244–5.

fantastic. Kalem started in 1905 with a cash investment of $600; by 1908 the company was making $5,000 a week. In 1913 Jesse L. Lasky, Samuel Goldfish (better known as Samuel Goldwyn), and Cecil B. de Mille rented a barn at Sunset and Vine and pooled their resources of $6,000 to produce *The Squaw Man*. In three years their $6,000 had expanded to a capital of $4,000,000. From "total assets of Clara Kimball Young, a shoe string, boundless ingenuity, and unlimited self-assurance," Selznick enjoyed an equally spectacular and meteoric rise. Within little more than a decade the industry that had begun as a novelty in cheap peep shows and nickelodeons was responsible for a commerce of over half a billion dollars a year; and the center of that industry was already securely fixed in the immediate environs of Los Angeles.

The story of the triumph of individual stars and producers and the success of individual pictures during those formative years also reads like an incredible fairy-tale. In 1910 an actress named Gladys Smith, unknown even in the profession of the stage beyond a narrow and mediocre circle, was receiving a few dollars a week from Mack Sennett's recently organized Keystone Company. Three years later, known to half the world as Mary Pickford, the "Sweetheart of the Movies," the same actress was commanding $1,000 a day and an estimated income from her own pictures of at least $1,000,000 a year!

In 1913 an unknown English actor named Charlie Chaplin, one of two brothers who had been left as young boys in a London poorhouse by a sick and penniless mother, came to the United States with a second-rate theatrical company. The Keystone Company offered Chaplin $150 a week. Before the close of the year this "modern Don Quixote," "the one unforgettable actor of the screen," was drawing a salary of $1,250 a week; a little later he was receiving $10,000 a week and a bonus of $150,000 a year.

Born of an impoverished Kentucky family, son of a former Confederate colonel whose voice won him the nickname of "Thunder Jake"—poet, author, playwright, actor, inventor, sentimentalist—David Wark Griffith became the financial and artistic wizard of the screen, and left his name as one of the few permanent and authentic traditions of Hollywood. Griffith produced *The Clansman,* under the title of *The Birth of a Nation,* at a cost of $100,000. The venture ushered in a new era in motion pictures and in fifteen years yielded a gross return of $18,000,000.

As "admission fees to motion picture theaters all over the world were funnelled into Hollywood," the industry entered upon an era of exaggerated profits, preposterous salaries, soaring production costs, amazing expansion, and general extravagance that relegated the wildest California real-estate and oil booms to the level of sober business enterprises. Mergers and combinations, which involved both major producing and distributing companies, became the order of the day. Competition, whether for markets or in the field of personnel, followed the grim old rule: Let him take who has the power, and let him keep who can.

The cost of Griffith's masterpiece, *The Birth of a Nation,* was multiplied many times over even in the production of mediocre films, and such pictures as the *King of Kings* and *Ben-Hur* required an outlay of from $2,500,000 to nearly $5,000,000. Producing companies built enormous studios, one of which Carl Laemmle not inappropriately christened Universal City, which were in effect self-contained factories; and the affiliated distributing companies erected or leased hundreds of elaborate theaters both in this country and abroad. Instead of the original five- and ten-cent admission charge, exhibitors raised their prices to correspond to the minimum charges made by the legitimate theaters.

Capital for the expanding motion-picture industry came originally from private sources; later on some of the leading California banks took an active part in financing individual companies. William Randolph Hearst became interested in the industry. According to Rosten, Hearst later "bought stock in Metro-Goldwyn-Mayer which released the Hearst Movietone newsreels; organized Cosmopolitan Pictures to produce Marion Davies's films; and made deals for the distribution of the pictures, first with Metro-Goldwyn-Mayer and then with Warner Brothers." [7]

---

[7] Ibid., pp. 204–5.

But though Los Angeles could legitimately claim to be the motion-picture capital of the world, the industry, like most other great enterprises in the United States, eventually outgrew the restricted supply of local capital and turned to Wall Street to satisfy its constantly expanding needs. In the fall of 1919 Kuhn, Loeb & Company took the initiative in underwriting an issue of ten million dollars of preferred stock in Famous Players–Lasky Corporation. At that time both the common and preferred issues of this company, as well as the stock of Loew's, Pathé, and Fox, were listed on the New York Stock Exchange. Motion pictures had come to be recognized as "big business" in a large way. By 1926 it was estimated that Edison's original outlay of $24,000 in the process of inventing motion pictures had resulted in an investment in motion-picture studios, theaters, and auxiliary enterprises that ran from a billion and a half to two billion dollars; and California, as the center of the industry, profited in a hundred different ways from this investment.[8]

In 1926 the introduction of sound recording revolutionized the motion-picture industry. In two years or a little more, the silent films, which were at the very height of their popularity in the mid-twenties, were reduced by sound pictures to the status of the horse-drawn carriage and the kerosene lamp.

This abrupt collapse of the silent films brought devastation to many parts of Hollywood. Screen favorites who enjoyed worldwide fame and commanded fabulous salaries disappeared in a few months from public notice and returned to the drab obscurity out of which either their own talents or those of ingenious publicity agents had originally lifted them. During the transition period most of the large producing companies were forced to resort to drastic expedients to remain solvent. Sound pictures, on the other hand, proved the salvation of one of the largest companies and in one year turned a recurring annual deficit of many millions into a profit of $17,000,000.[9]

The use of sound thus revolutionized motion pictures both as

---

[8] Hampton: *A History of the Movies,* p. 362.
[9] Ibid., p. 387.

an industry and as an art. Because of their commanding position in the field of radio and sound, such great corporations as the American Telephone and Telegraph Company, Western Electric, Radio Corporation of America, Westinghouse, National Broadcasting Company, and General Electric intimately identified themselves with the venture and became dominant factors in the new era upon which motion pictures now entered.

The striking progress in writing, acting, and directing that followed the introduction of sound pictures was accompanied by corresponding improvements in chemistry, engineering, architecture, and other branches of the sciences and arts on which the films depended. The use of color films also added greatly to the beauty and charm of the new pictures.

The economic importance of motion pictures to California, and especially to Los Angeles, was almost incalculable. In 1939, according to the California State Chamber of Commerce, production costs in Los Angeles County studios amounted to nearly $216,000,000, or eighty-seven per cent of the total of these expenditures in the United States. Over 31,000 persons were employed in the industry, and wages and salaries reached the large total of $133,000,000.

But these figures told only a small part of the story. Innumerable industries in and about Los Angeles were dependent upon the motion-picture business for a market. Stores, restaurants, hotels, night clubs, resorts, automobile agencies, taxicabs, real-estate companies, builders, interior decorators, antique shops, jewelers, filling stations—these and an incalculable number of kindred enterprises, great and small, owed their existence to the patronage, publicity, and purchasing power of the endlessly ramified branches of the motion-picture world.

In similar fashion motion-picture profits and salaries furnished one of California's largest sources of investment funds. Capital that came out of Hollywood built office buildings, hotels, and apartment houses, as well as palatial residences; it drilled oil wells and opened race tracks; developed real-estate subdivisions, constructed factories, and flowed into the support of churches, colleges, foundations, hospitals, and other charities in a large but never very ostentatious stream.

The publicity value of motion pictures to California was also beyond calculation. The name Hollywood is probably more familiar in the far corners of the earth than that of London, Paris, or New York. Of the effects of such publicity upon the growth of Los Angeles twenty years ago, Hampton wrote:

Thus fortuitously was the fate of Los Angeles decided. In movie theaters everywhere people began to catch glimpses of streets filled with quaint little houses, of flower-filled patios, of palms and pepper trees, and eucalyptus. Stories were circulated of the everlasting summer, of the "bungalows" that could be rented so cheaply, of the romantic movie business that was a part of this enchanted town.[1]

The motion-picture industry also made Los Angeles one of the two or three leading style centers of the world. Thousands of buyers flock to Los Angeles each year, and as a result the city has become one of the foremost garment-producing centers of the nation and leads the world in both design and manufacture of sportswear.

More than any other factor, motion pictures were also responsible for making Los Angeles the radio and television capital of the west coast and a close rival to New York for leadership in the nation. The availability of world-famous motion-picture stars, an unequaled reservoir of writers and musicians, and a never ending flow of the great and near great to Hollywood are only a few of the influences that today make Los Angeles almost as well known in the field of radio and television as in the world of motion pictures.

In the realm of manners, morals, and taste the influence of Hollywood has been even more profound than in the field of economics. In these spheres one who attempts to evaluate the motion-picture industry is bewildered by the glaring contradictions, the hopeless jumble of good and bad, which constantly confuse one's judgment and demand adjustments in one's valuation. Too

---

[1] Ibid, pp. 79–80.

many films are tawdry, ostentatious, vapid—demoralizing alike to morals, taste, manners, and culture. And too many of the people who make and produce such films are like unto them. "Hollywood's wealth," says Rosten,

is first-generation wealth, possessed by people who have not inherited it, spent by people who have not been accustomed to handling it, earned as a reward for talent (or luck) rather than heritage. It is not surprising that the movie colony has not achieved stability or integration: it is too young, too new, and too uncertain. The people of the movie colony are characterized by showmanship, not breeding; glibness, not wisdom; audacity, not poise. Of Hollywood it might be written, as was written of the America of the 1880s, here is "a society that for the first time found its opportunities equal to its desires, a youthful society that accounted the world its oyster and wanted no restrictions laid on its will."[2]

Hollywood, as Dr. Louis B. Wright aptly says, is in raw crudity "the counterpart of some roaring mining camp of '49 without the mining camp's virility." Various motion-picture stars were involved in scandals that ranged all the way from unsavory divorces to suicide, rape, and murder; and even in the case of major crime in the inner circle of Hollywood, the law was consistently outwitted or reduced to impotency. A leading director was shot to death, a wealthy producer died under highly suspicious circumstances on board a yacht, a popular actress came to a violent end, but there were no arrests, no trials, no convictions.

To protect the industry against the outcry and ultimate censorship that such scandals and the production of indecent and vulgar pictures were bound to bring about, the industry organized the Motion Picture Producers and Distributors of America, chose Will H. Hays, Postmaster General in President Harding's Cabinet and a prominent Presbyterian layman, to serve as its head, and gave him almost dictatorial powers of censorship over all pictures produced by the members of the association. Hays, whose office was

---

[2] *Hollywood,* p. 57.

created in 1922, became the "czar" of the motion-picture industry, close to the climax of the so-called "jazz age," when the films were running dangerously amuck.

Considering the traditions of the industry and the complex problems of censorship involved, the Hays office brought a measure of restraint to films; but the battle was never ended, and in the early thirties pictures based on sex appeal and the activities of the underworld again began to flood the country. In 1934 the Catholic Church entered the struggle by organizing the Legion of Decency. Censorship, however, in all of its manifestations, has remained a knotty problem and the solutions applied to the motion picture industry have not provided the final answer.

The influence of motion pictures upon the standards, fashions, and attitudes of the American people became more marked with every decade. That influence, if we accept one evaluation, has reached into more lives and affected the thinking habits and customs of more people than "newspapers, religious institutions, and political governments." To a remarkable degree Hollywood has succeeded "in impressing its own vision of life on the world." As an analyst of American society remarks, adolescents (whether in years or intellectual development) find the motion picture a school as well as a place of entertainment:

They model themselves after movie stars; they repeat movie jokes and gestures; they learn the subtleties of free behaviour between the sexes; they develop surprisingly sophisticated manners; and they pattern their lives not on those of their parents, but on "the sharp figures on the silver screen which present gay and confident designs for living." [3]

Probably the most damning charge that can be brought against the motion-picture industry is its failure to realize the unlimited power at its disposal, its frequent prostitution of that power to useless and unworthy ends, and its occasional devotion to unworthy standards.

Hollywood, in a word, is old John Bunyan's town of Vanity,

---

[3] Rosten: *Hollywood*, pp. 366–7.

magnified to huge proportions, streamlined, fitted into the pattern of the present age—but still the town with the ancient Fair, as old, vain, and licentious as the human race itself—the Fair "wherein should be sold all sorts of vanity . . . as houses, lands, trades, places, honours, preferments, titles, countries, kingdoms, lusts, pleasures; and delights of all sorts—as harlots, wives, husbands, children, masters, servants, lives, blood, bodies, souls, silver, gold, pearls, precious stones, and what not."

But in the last analysis, when the full bill of particulars has been presented, the motion picture stands out as one of the supreme wonders of the modern age, a great force in the life and culture of the race, a medium that, with the possible exception of radio and television, has brought enjoyment and laughter, knowledge and enrichment, to more millions of people more widely diffused over the face of the earth than any other creation of our amazing era.

It is a far cry, indeed, from what William C. de Mille in 1911 characterized as a "cheap form of amusement," without a single redeeming feature, to Charles Laughton's *Ruggles of Red Gap,* the graphic, breath-taking heroism of the *Fighting Lady,* and the immortal fantasies of Walt Disney. A hundred years from now, when most of the productions of today have been forgotten, such a simple, universal character as Mickey Mouse may still survive as part of the motion picture's contribution to the folklore and tradition of the race.

Motion pictures are the property of the whole world and cannot be localized or monopolized by any one region or community. In that sense they are as universal as art, literature, and music. But because the industry established its physical habitation on such a large scale in metropolitan Los Angeles, the development of motion pictures means vastly more to California than to any other region.

Prophecies are rife at this writing that Hollywood is "on the way out," that the films themselves are a form of amusement rapidly being outdated. The sale of major studios to television producers supports this pessimism. But an area which has attracted so much creative talent very probably has the ability to adjust itself to changing circumstances and a new dominant medium, and many in the industry feel that Hollywood will continue its primacy as a thespic center.

CHAPTER 32. Recent California Literature

THE LITERATURE which California produced during the nineteenth century was tinged with the forcefulness of those who participated in the life about which they wrote. Mountain men, hide droghers, gold-rush journalists, travelers and nature lovers, and even the gadflies of social conscience had a close and sometimes astigmatic perspective of their themes and problems. More recently California writers have written with increased professional motivation, although there still appear examples of the earlier type.

Three more women gained varying degrees of literary recognition as the century turned. One of them, Kathleen Norris, achieved largely a commercial renown.

Differing from Mary Austin in background, temperament, outlook, philosophy, and literary style, Mrs. Norris began her productive career in 1910, soon after marrying Charles G. Norris, brother of Frank. Reputedly the highest-paid magazine writer in the United States and one of the nation's most consistent and prolific writers, she published nearly ninety novels, dealing chiefly with contemporary life, and writes in a style "smooth, seasoned, persuasive, and easy to assimilate."

Almost as prolific as Kathleen Norris and more deeply steeped in the color of California and especially in the local atmosphere of San Francisco than any of her contemporaries, Gertrude Atherton concerned herself much more with the drama and romance of California history than with its plebeian facts. Her range of subject matter was as wide as the unfenced ranges of the California cattle dons; but if, as an author, she earned notice, it was because she retold the simple tales and relived in her pages the idyllic life of the "splendid, idle" California rancho days.

In 1915, in a formal ceremony held at the Panama-Pacific Exposition in San Francisco in accordance with an act of the state legislature, Ina Coolbrith was officially recognized as the poet laureate of California. Niece of the Mormon prophet Joseph Smith, Ina Coolbrith came to California as a child in 1851 and lived in Los Angeles till the mid-sixties, when she moved to San Francisco. In 1868 Bret Harte invited her to become co-editor of the *Overland Monthly,* and she formed one of the small group that created California's golden literary age. After leaving the *Overland Monthly,* Miss Coolbrith served for more than thirty years as librarian in Oakland and San Francisco. Never a prolific writer, her collected verse, published in 1895 under the title of *Songs from the Golden Gate,* constitutes her chief claim to literary fame. In no sense a great poet, for she "piped but one silvery note, a wistful one in which unhappiness was temporarily submerged in pleasure over flowers, birds, and the wind," she had a devoted following.

Lincoln Steffens, product of the muckraking era, is difficult to catalogue or evaluate. With the exception of his *Autobiography,* his writings dealt almost wholly with the current scene and today have little value except to the student of American affairs. Though Steffens, as journalist and reporter, had few contemporary equals, his desire for the limelight led him to write much that had no depth but caught only the fancy of the moment. To his many admirers, however, he was the counterpart of Socrates, "a bold and humane pilgrim who so loved his fellowmen, that he was never able to condemn them," a man "without bitterness or negation" who spoke with the penetrating wisdom of an ancient prophet.

Steffens's two-volume *Autobiography,* published in 1931, is his enduring literary contribution. Writing of it in the New York *Times* a reviewer said: "These are extraordinary volumes in more ways than one—in the directness, intensity and at the same time the tolerance of the personality they reveal; in the wide range of the experiences they reveal into human nature; in their mingling of idealism with practicality."

Enormously popular during the years of his prime, now more than a quarter of a century ago, Stewart Edward White clothed the history of the state with a fitting garment of romance and wrote of its mountains and forests as one having both knowledge and affection. Charles F. Lummis, best known for his stories of New Mexico and California and as preserver and interpreter of the literature of the West while editor of the *Land of Sunshine* and *Out West*, is remembered almost as much for his eccentricities, defiance of conventions, and the foundation of the Southwest Museum in Los Angeles as for his literary legacy.

Upton Sinclair, faddist, passionate social reformer, source of an endless flow of tracts, plays, and novels, producer of best sellers or near-best sellers with almost monotonous regularity, is probably the most widely read California author of this or any other generation. Sinclair first came into prominence with the publication of *The Jungle* in 1906. Prior to that date he had issued at least five other novels under his own name, scores of "half-dime novels," dealing with West Point, for the "Starry Flag Library," and almost as many similar yarns relating to Annapolis for the "True Blue Library." Sinclair himself does not remember the names, contents, or number of these juvenile potboilers, some of which he turned out at the rate of almost one a week.

One compiler has listed twenty-four novels published under Sinclair's own name between 1901 and 1935; at least nine plays, probably half of which were not produced; sixteen non-fiction volumes that ranged all the way from *The Fasting Cure* to *Upton Sinclair Presents William Fox* and included extensive excursions into the subject of American schools, religion, business, journalism, literature, and mental telepathy; over thirty pamphlets; and nearly a hundred magazine articles, reviews, and poems.

Sinclair is still one of the most prolific authors of his time, and "his come-back as a novelist of enormous popularity" with the Lanny Budd books, after his unsuccessful excursion into politics, is one of the striking phenomena of the modern literary world. In an author's note to *A World to Win*, Sinclair wrote: "Up to the year 1938 there has been issued in European countries a total of 690 titles of the books of Upton Sinclair, and in India, China, and Japan a total of 57. The number of books cannot be estimated, but in Britain, Germany, and the Soviet Union the total was over seven millions." [1]

But despite such enormous contemporary popularity, the extent to which Sinclair's books will be read in the next generation is highly problematical.

Until the close of the first quarter of the century, when Robinson Jeffers began to rise to undisputed mastery, George Sterling was accepted in literary circles as California's foremost poet. Of seafaring ancestry, "handsome as a Roman faun," if Mary Austin were qualified to judge, wedded to action rather than thought, almost servile in his devotion to Ambrose Bierce, a lover of liquor and women, especially in later years, to an abnormal degree, Sterling practiced a philosophy best expressed in the words of his friend Robinson Jeffers: "Simply, out of this astonishing tangle of life, to choose pleasure and avoid pain, for ourselves and others."

Sterling wrote voluminously and at times superbly. But one biographer notes that he submitted over a hundred poems to the *Atlantic Monthly* and almost as many more to *Scribner's* and *Harper's* magazines before one of his manuscripts was accepted for publication. His verse has been described as "a steady flame of pure beauty"; and some of it, represented by a few lyrics and one or two "magnificent sonnets," is touched by an immortal quality.

One aspect of the character of California's greatest poet can be illustrated by an anecdote:

It was mid-morning in the high San Bernardino mountains. A thin film of ice had formed along the margin of the lake the night before, and small particles of frost still lingered on the north side of the giant pine trees. But the October sun was warm, and the blue-green water looked pleasantly inviting. From a giant rock that thrust its gray shoulder far out from the gravelly shore, four young men, naked as Pan, plunged headlong beneath the shining surface of the lake. The water was cold—deceptively, treacherously cold—so that three of the four swimmers came to the sur-

---

[1] *Dragon's Teeth* won the Pulitzer Prize in 1943, *World's End* was a Literary Guild selection, and *A World to Win* was both a Dollar Book Club and a Book Find Club selection. These were all "Lanny Budd" novels.

face gasping mightily for breath and desperately eager to regain the grateful warmth of the sun. The other member of the quartet, tall, well-muscled, and seemingly immune to the paralyzing cold, continued his leisurely swim in the deep waters of Big Bear Lake for upwards of half an hour.

The swimmer's name was Robinson Jeffers. I knew him as a reserved but congenial college mate, a good camping companion, a hard man to keep up with on the trail, and a poet, even then, of living beauty and haunting lines.

Today Robinson Jeffers rises above all other California poets, living or dead, as Saul towered of old head and shoulders above his brethren. Jeffers indeed is the one California writer who has "fully mastered the elements of great poetry, music, substance, imagination, emotion, expression and form," [2] and his lines are as sonorous as the wind-driven waves of Homer's far-sounding, infinite sea. Jeffers is the product of the classical tradition. Reading Greek at five years of age, he was nurtured on the Bible, the classics, the great writers of English prose and poetry, the beauty and mystery with which nature fills the world. That heritage reflects itself in all his poetry.

Jeffers's marriage and his life in Tor House, above the gray waters of the Pacific, are also part of the warp and woof of his poetry. "If ever a man and the spirit of a place had conspired for a mystical union, it is here," writes Benjamin de Casseres of the Carmel coast. "The portion of California—its hills, sea, blue lupin, golden poppies, sea-gulls, dirt roads, pines, firs, hawks, herons, and lighthouses . . . belongs as absolutely to Robinson Jeffers . . . as Wessex belongs to Thomas Hardy." [3]

Jeffers's poetry—the strongest of it—reflects his search for an answer to the mystery of the universe. Sex abnormality, the bald, repellent motif of his poems—"Cawdor," "The Roan Stallion," "The Women of Point Sur"—is in effect a symbolism of mankind itself—thwarted, perverted, inexorably tragic, driven by irresisti-

---

[2] Melba Berry Bennett: *Robinson Jeffers and the Sea* (1936), p. 79.

[3] Quoted in Lawrence Clark Powell's *An Introduction to Robinson Jeffers* (1932), p. 207.

ble forces to blind, catastrophic, inescapable doom. Jeffers has not solved the meaning of the universe, and his poetry represents a question unanswered, a search unfulfilled, a journey without an end. In his imagery, in his supreme mastery of words, where the influence of Homer and the King James Version is paramount, and in his compelling individuality of style, Jeffers has attained genuine greatness.

As Robinson Jeffers belongs to the redwoods and granite coast and giant breakers of Carmel, so John Steinbeck belongs to the fertile valleys and sandy plains and brown, wind-blown hills of the near-by Salinas Valley. Born in Salinas in 1902, the year Frank Norris died, Steinbeck enjoyed the advantages of a good family background and at least a desultory attendance at Stanford University. Much of the time, however, he sought the company of the rough, poorly educated, often brutalized and despised men, the hewers of wood and drawers of water, who furnish the unskilled labor upon which our civilization and society depend. So as boy and young man Steinbeck worked on a ranch in the Salinas Valley, served as deck hand on a freight boat, found a job with a New York newspaper, carried a hod in the building of Madison Square Garden, and spent some months as caretaker on an estate at Lake Tahoe.

When Steinbeck writes, he accordingly writes of the people and environment he knows; he describes what he has seen and, often, the experiences through which he himself has lived. His prose is hard, direct, and uninhibited. He writes of the offal of the fish cannery, the tragic squalor of the itinerant workers' camp, the obscenities and indecencies of the human race. But he also writes of the *paisanos* of Tortilla Flat, of social injustice and the even greater sin of social indifference, of loyalty and friendship between men—homeless, despised, unlovely men—whose devotion to one another surpasses the love of women and goes on blindly to the end. He is, as Harry Thornton Moore declares, "the poet of our dispossessed."

Steinbeck's most famous novel, *The Grapes of Wrath*, doubtless owed much of its popularity to well-nigh perfect timing. The book was published when the Okie invasion of California was in full spate. The public mind was thus thoroughly ripe for Steinbeck's earthy, plain-spoken, highly dramatized saga of the Joad family.

The Grapes of Wrath presented an overdrawn picture and encouraged greatly exaggerated generalizations from too few specific facts; and the bedeviled California farmers were justified in bitterly criticizing the book on those grounds. But the novel challenged a great social evil and aroused a people's conscience. It was not a factual, scientific treatise in sociology, but a protest on behalf of the unfortunate and dispossessed. Indeed, Steinbeck meant *The Grapes of Wrath* to be something bigger than an attack upon one particular form of social injustice, to go even beyond the dust bowl tragedy. "As far as social implications go," writes Moore of *The Grapes of Wrath*, "it is perhaps the most persuasively revolutionary novel published in America, and it is in the van of the proletarian movement in literature, without officially being a part of that movement." [4]

An airplane crash on a desolate Alaskan headland took from the common people of America a keen critic and an understanding advocate. Will Rogers, part Cherokee Indian, product of the Oklahoma short-grass range, sojourner in New York and Hollywood, was perhaps not truly great. But he had humor and insight, and courage to a superlative degree—and forthright honesty, which his countrymen admired in him most of all. Will Rogers's humor was but the expression of the spirit of the inner man— keen, incisive, swift to detect and puncture pompousness, hypocrisy, and sham—and he clothed it most effectively in the good, rough, homespun speech of the cowboy of the Oklahoma plains. He respected the wisdom of the common people and made their common sense articulate.

Because he dealt primarily with the swift-flowing current of contemporary life, the daily happenings that caught men's notice for a moment and then dissolved into oblivion, Will Rogers left little of literary value to posterity. But for a time his humor

---

[4] Harry Thornton Moore: *The Novels of John Steinbeck* (1939), p. 66.

burned with a bright and steady flame, so that its light showed us men and issues more nearly as they were.

Perhaps as a corollary of the motion-picture industry, which attracted writers to the West, California became a center of popular-fiction production on a scale which went far toward making the state a center of bourgeois culture. Most of these writers were not native Californians, but they lived in the state during the peak of their professional lives and certainly the work they turned out must be labeled "California" literature of a sort.

The most picturesque example of this clan was the author of *Tarzan*. Edgar Rice Burroughs had the advantage of a good education in the Midwest, but became a drifter, including among his range of vocations that of army officer, Sears Roebuck employee, policeman, cowboy, and advertising man. During this last experience, he became interested in "pulp" fiction, and wrote his first novel and, incidentally, his *chef d'oeuvre, Tarzan,* in 1914 for the modest sum of $400. It was shortly followed by *A Princess of Mars* (1917), another popular venture which carried on the tradition of Jules Verne and helped to start the present fad of scientific fiction. Other Tarzan and Martian stories followed in rapid succession, until by the close of World War II Burroughs had some fifty-five short novels to his credit. He invested in San Fernando Valley real estate, established the town of Tarzana, and counted his readers—partly through translated editions of his works—in the millions. He reached his peak of popularity during the 1920's and 1930's.

Zane Grey was also one of the most prolific popular authors. Born in 1875 in Ohio, he started life as a dentist and practiced for a time before embarking in 1904 on a literary career. By 1930 he had turned out forty-one books based on the theme of the American West and its conquest. Volumes like *The Thundering Herd* (1925) and *Tappan's Burro* (1923) stressed the beauties of nature, the qualities of manhood necessary to defeat the wilderness, and the unvarying purity of womanhood and its ability to uplift and inspire rugged frontier characters. One unkind critic has urged that anyone wishing to understand American literature should examine at least one volume written by Zane Grey—but that any one would do, as they vary little in plot and quality. This is not quite true, for Grey drew on his short experience as a professional baseball player to write some books for boys, and on his experience as a hunter and game-fisherman to pen a few excellent nature volumes. Whatever his weaknesses, Grey was one of the greatest western writers who ever lived, and his influence on the "western story" was large.

Zane Grey was emulated by scores of writers of "westerns," one of the best being Ernest Haycox, who lived in southern California and turned out excellent western novels, such as *Bugles in the Afternoon*, for book publishers and "slick" magazine editors. Frederick Faust ("Max Brand") was also a success in both print and film. Another style of popular fiction which experienced a renaissance partly stimulated by California production was the historical novel, one of the greatest commercial successes in this field being *Forever Amber*, by Kathleen Winsor, another Californian.

Perhaps the most versatile of the popular writers of this period was Harold Bell Wright. Born in New York state in 1872, Wright started life as a painter and decorator, graduated to landscape painting, and then became a minister of the Church of the Disciples. From 1897 to 1908 he held various pastorates in Missouri, Kansas, and California, his last call being to Redlands. Literary work then claimed his attention, and by 1930 he had published fourteen volumes. His major achievements were finished before 1920. "His women may slip and fall," said one critic, "though never flat." [5] The outstanding story credited to Wright was *The Winning of Barbara Worth*, based on the opening of the Imperial Valley and its water problems. This book attracted much attention to this new region and doubtless had an effect upon its rapid development.

Like Helen Hunt Jackson, Mrs. Gene Stratton Porter gained literary fame by clutching at America's heartstrings with novels

---

[5] Lawrence Clark Powell: *Land of Fiction* (Los Angeles: Dawson's Book Shop, 1952), v.

of overdone sentimentality. An Indianan, she engaged in editorial work before turning to fiction. Such books as *Freckles* and *A Girl of the Limberlost* gained her a wide following, and by the time of her death, in 1924 as a victim of the notorious southern California traffic, she had published nineteen books.

Of the four most popular "schools" of commercial fiction—westerns, science fantasy, historical romances, and mysteries—the last-named probably monopolized the efforts of more notable California authors than did the other three. One of the best was doubtless chagrined toward the end of his life to realize that his name would be better known as a writer of murder mysteries than as a serious scholar of the arts. Willard Huntington Wright was a Virginian, born in 1888, who was educated in part in southern California. A period at Harvard impressed him with the virtues of social polish, which he later caricatured to good effect in his stories, and he entered a career of editorial work and literary criticism. He was at various times editor of *Smart Set* magazine and music critic and art editor of the San Francisco *Bulletin*. He wrote a volume of poetry, a book on Nietzsche, and one on modern painting. Then, after his health failed, he turned by way of diversion and therapy to popular literature. *The Benson Murder Case,* starring a new literary sleuth, a polished, learned, wealthy idler named Philo Vance, was a success. He followed this achievement with a series of popular fictional murder "cases," writing under the pen name of S. S. Van Dine.

Other mystery writers have chosen California as their residence or locale. Raymond Chandler, in a series of ultra-realistic, hard-boiled, well-written mysteries, used modern Los Angeles as his scene. Erle Stanley Gardner, an attorney with some courtroom experience behind him, developed a plot formula featuring trial scenes and a dashing lawyer-hero named Perry Mason. Writing under the name of A. A. Fair, Gardner created other characters and other mystery series, and established a mass-production technique which proved so profitable that he purchased an estate back of San Diego and became a prime example of economic success in this field. Frank Gruber, a midwesterner who migrated to California, was a good example of the popular writer who combined rapid production of mystery and western novels with success as an author of motion-picture and television scripts.

Aside from the writers of formula fiction, the California of the 1950's presented hopeful signs of concentrated effort by authors interested in more serious approaches to literature. Just as the historian finds it difficult to gain genuine perspective when dealing with recent events, so does the literary critic experience trouble in attempting to select, out of a vast array, representative writers whose work is still in process of development. Some of those who have made an impact, however, deserve mention, even if proper adjudication of their role must await the appraisal of later generations.

Walter Van Tilburg Clark concentrated, in his three novels, on the American West, but not in the manner of Zane Grey. His first book, *The Ox-Bow Incident* (1940), gained him the most fame and showed him to be preoccupied with the local color of the West, but also with its effect on human mood and purpose. This story, made later into an excellent motion picture, deals with a lynching, but emphasizes the actual event less than the psychological problems it engenders. His pace was slow, his mastery of suspense undeniable, his writing facile and impressive. Clifton Fadiman acclaimed it "the year's finest first novel." In *The City of Trembling Leaves* (1945) he dealt with the problems of adolescence and artistic growth in a western city, and in *The Track of the Cat* (1949) he tackled the problem of evil in a symbolic manner. His other publications include a volume of short stories and one of poetry.

James M. Cain, another adopted son of California, began as a journalist and climaxed his career with several novels, three of which, *The Postman Always Rings Twice* (1934), *Serenade* (1937), and *Mildred Pierce* (1941), together with a novelette, *Double Indemnity* (1943), gained him literary recognition largely through highly successful motion-picture versions. Cain was a disciple of the "realistic" school, obviously patterned his style after Hemingway, and concentrated on unpleasant characters.

His writing has been called "barren and brutal," and has won both acclaim and strong criticism. Cain attracted another type of recognition when he concluded that his profits as an author from the motion-picture versions of his work were unfairly low, and he became a writer-politician, attempting to organize an "A.A.A.," an American Authors' Authority, aimed at defense of copyright and other authors' privileges, which won temporary support from the Screen Writers' Guild.

One of the most interesting literary figures of twentieth-century California was William Saroyan. Born in Fresno of Armenian parents, Saroyan capitalized on novelty in style and behavior to keep himself in the public eye. His first claim to fame, a short story entitled "Daring Young Man on the Flying Trapeze" (1934), launched him on a career which included writing both Hollywood scenarios and New York plays. Of his dramas, *My Heart's in the Highlands* (1939) and *The Time of Your Life* (1940) probably won him most recognition, while his most popular books included *My Name is Aram* (1940), *The Human Comedy* (1943), and *Adventures of Wesley Jackson* (1946). Arthur Foff has characterized Saroyan's work as being "wonderfully warm and human" during the best period. Saroyan appreciated to the full the public-relations value of offbeat behavior, and said of himself: "I am so innately great that, by comparison, others who believe they are great or act as if they believe they are great seem to me to be only pathetic, although occasionally charming." [6] He lived up to his principles by refusing to accept the Pulitzer Prize for Drama for *The Time of Your Life* on the ground that commerce should not patronize art.

One of the leading California women writers of this period was Jessamyn West. She was born in Indiana, but spent most of her life in California. Her education at Whittier College, a Quaker-founded institution, doubtless influenced her first volume, *The Friendly Persuasion* (1945), a story of Indiana Quakers of the Civil War period. In *The Witch Diggers* (1951) she again uti-

---

[6] Stanley J. Kunitz, ed.: *Twentieth Century Authors* (1st Supp.) (New York: The H. W. Wilson Company; 1955), p. 868.

lized an Indiana locale, this time for a more violent tale, and in *Cress Delehanty* (1953) she shifted her scene to California, where she told of a girl's problems in reaching maturity.

Another woman author was Kathryn Hulme. A native San Franciscan, her first book, *We Lived as Children* (1938), was largely autobiographical in nature, and her second, *The Wild Place* (1953), was also based on her experiences, this time as a United Nations worker with displaced persons in a Bavarian camp. This latter volume won the Atlantic Non-Fiction Award for 1953. She reached real popularity after her conversion to Catholicism with the publication of *The Nun's Story* (1956), a psychological treatment of convent life and of a woman who found the vows too heavy to be borne.

Just as Saroyan brought his Armenian folklore to the literary scene, so did John Fante depict the Italo-American and his problems in two novels, *Wait for the Spring, Bandini* (1938) and *Ask the Dust* (1939). The first told of an Italian mason and his family life in Colorado; the second dealt with the timeworn theme of a writer struggling for success in Los Angeles. *Dago Red* (1940) is largely a series of sketches. He was perhaps more widely known for his 1952 novel, *Full of Life,* a humorous and human account of a young married couple and their first child.

The faculty in creative writing and literature at San Francisco State College produced more than its fair share of California writers, both budding and established. Walter Van Tilburg Clark belongs in this "school," and Mark Harris and Arthur Foff produced volumes which have won their share of critical acclaim. Harris concentrated largely on baseball stories, but not of a strictly escapist nature. His *Bang the Drum Slowly* (1956) told of a baseball player suffering from Hodgkin's disease, and of his teammates' acceptance of and dealing with this fact. Away from sports, Harris contributed to the spate of "soldier's life" novels with *Something About a Soldier* (1957), which drew from one critic (William Hogan) the statement that he was "one of the most imaginative and talented young novelists in America." Arthur Foff, a third-generation San Franciscan, wrote of his home town in *Glorious in Another Day* (1947) and *North of Market* (1957). The first was characterized by Joseph Henry Jackson as "an admirable novel, simply and beautifully written," and the second was praised by Eudora Welty as "an extraordinary, haunting piece of work," and by Herbert Blau as "a major novel of uncompromising distinction." Both Foff and his wife, who writes under the name of Anton Fereva, are apparently rising stars in the literary firmament.

Other California colleges and universities have fostered and encouraged creative writers. Wallace Stegner of Stanford has done both fiction, *The Big Rock Candy Mountain* (1943), and nonfiction, *Beyond the Hundredth Meridian* (1954), a life of John Wesley Powell. Yvor Winters, also of Stanford, engaged in poetry and sharp literary criticism. Mark Schorer, of the University of California, wrote novels and criticism, and John Espey, of the University of California at Los Angeles, produced witty essays. Richard Armour, of Scripps College, ranked almost with Ogden Nash as a humorous versifier, and also turned out light prose, *It All Started with Eve* (1956), and other similar volumes.

Oscar Lewis belongs in a special category. Working in both fiction and nonfiction, his chief contributions centered in the latter, with such works as *The Big Four* (1938), a fascinating study of the builders of the Central Pacific Railroad, *Sea Routes to the Gold Fields* (1949), and *Bonanza Inn* (1939), the story of the Palace Hotel in San Francisco.

This list could be extended at length, but never without the risk of excluding some who have their strong adherents. Stephen Longstreet, who also wrote "whodunits" under the name of Paul Haggard, successfully combined a Hollywood career with novel writing. Hans Otto Storm merged an electrical engineer's responsibilities with the writing of, chiefly, novelettes. Theodore Bonnet, a San Franciscan who moved to Los Angeles, mixed newspaper work with fiction writing and emerged with the successful *Mudlark* (1949), a novel of the period of Disraeli. Niven Busch, like Longstreet, built a career on motion-picture writing, but also turned out such excellent items as *Duel in the Sun*

(1944). Other names could be mentioned, such as Jack Kerouac, Nevil Shute, and Eugene O'Neill—all of whom have been connected with California or its literary production in one way or another.

Two others almost defy classification. Aldous Huxley is primarily known as an English writer, yet his long residence in southern California, chiefly because it facilitated treatment of an eye ailment, involves him in this account. Mystic, critic, and essayist, he condescended to be influenced by the California scene long enough to turn out a novel about Los Angeles after a third world war, *Ape and Essence* (1948). Last, and almost indefinable as to influence or importance was Henry Miller. One-time resident of southern California after extended travels abroad, perennially poverty-stricken, Miller became the center of a little bohemian group near Big Sur. His work aroused constant question about censorship, propriety, and morality, but certain critics insisted he had something worth while to contribute. Future generations must decide.

The poetry of twentieth-century California brought out at least three names of interest, in addition to those already mentioned. Kenneth Rexroth, arch-radical and modernist, joined the San Francisco literary colony and turned out such volumes as *The Phoenix and the Tortoise* (1944) and *The Dragon and the Unicorn* (1952). He was granted the Shelley Memorial Award. Josephine Miles, of the faculty of the University of California, has done both poetry and criticism, and Kenneth Patchen, another member of the San Francisco school, has experimented, with Rexroth, in the combination of poetry and jazz.

From these brief treatments of California literature it can be seen that the state has fathered a literary development of no small proportions. Part of this must be attributed to the geographical and climatic attractions, which have lured producing authors to a new home. Part is due to the influence on cultural activity, however indirect, brought about by the centering of large segments of the entertainment industry in southern California. A portion is doubtless due to the inherent ability of any region to stimulate productivity and creativeness of its own. Whatever its causes, the literature of California is worth considering, and hopefully will attain greater heights as the social climate matures.

CHAPTER 33. California at Mid-Century

THE STORY of California to this point has told of the building of an empire, one whose current populousness and prosperity far exceed the most fanciful dreams of its pioneers. Yet, as the greatness of the state and its importance in the nation and the world have grown, its autonomy has diminished. No longer is it possible for the people of California to have adventures and experiences without finding their duplicates elsewhere; California's booms now reflect the fluctuations of the national business cycle; California politics are now inextricably interwoven with national partisanship. In earlier years an incident on the East Coast could be casually ignored by Californians, or, if they did react, it was only after a period of delay brought about by the primitive nervous system of an adolescent nation; today the stock market, congressional legislation, labor troubles in the steel belt, or an international incident in the Middle East all have immediate and jarring effects west of the Sierras. The three subjects requiring attention in mid-century California—war, boom, and politics—therefore must be considered as parts of a vastly greater whole. California during the twentieth century became a part of the nation and the world.

World War II had an impact upon California life which disproportionately exceeded the effect of World War I. The fact that World War II began, for this country, in the Pacific, the existence in California of an aircraft industry that was immediately called upon to help supply the free world's arsenal of weapons, and the presence in the state of thousands of persons of Japanese extraction, all combined to make California aware of this war as she had never been aware of any other.

California had long been conscious of her destiny as a Pacific state. Sea-otter hunters had established economic connection with the Far East, and during the Gold Rush ocean traffic between Honolulu and San Francisco almost reached the status of commuting. California had produced prophets who dwelt on this relation with the Far East; Homer Lea, an eccentric little hunchback who, like William Walker, was a frustrated military man, wrote in *The Valor of Ignorance* that both Japan and Russia would figure in California's and the United States's calculations before many years had passed. The ports of San Francisco and San Diego with their imposing naval bases made California a center of military activity, while the San Francisco military post office was the channel through which thousands of families maintained tenuous contact with their fighting men in the war against Japan.

One incident demonstrated that war in actuality was not far away. On the night of February 25, 1942, air-raid sirens screamed and the Los Angeles area went into an alert. As citizens of the Los Angeles basin huddled in the gloom and air-raid wardens paced from house to house, the chatter of anti-aircraft fire thudded from the coastal towns of Santa Monica and Ocean Park. Thousands watched shrieking tracers as they sped toward an unknown target high in the sky. Yet when the episode was over, no one knew exactly what had happened, whether hostile aircraft had actually invaded California, or whether, like so many other incidents, this was merely a false alarm. After the war the Japanese denied their culpability, but, in any case, California's proximity to the Pacific was brought forcibly home to her citizens, and the combat no longer seemed so distant.

The aircraft industry in California contributed magnificently to the war effort. Five major producers, Douglas, Lockheed, North American, Northrop, and Convair (formerly Consolidated Vultee), turned out many types of bombers, fighters, and interceptors, ranging from huge Flying Fortresses, which thundered over Germany and Japan on countless bombing raids, to wasp-like twin-fuselage P-38's, which darted through the skies in many combat zones.

Paralleling California's long-standing interest in the Far East, there was an equally respectable tradition of interest in aviation. Los Angeles first publicly demonstrated this in 1910, when a notable sporting meet was held at Dominguez Field. This event attracted some of the nation's greatest flyers—then considered to be little more than daredevils—and began the California press's attention to aviation matters. The 1910 meet was billed as the "first in America," and was staged over a ten-day period on an octagonal field one and a half miles in diameter. About 176,000 spectators attended and marveled, and the Army Signal Corps sent an observer. On the meet's first day, Glen Curtis made the first successful flight on the West Coast; he remained aloft for nearly two minutes and landed "at his own volition." On later days dirigibles were flown by aeronauts Roy Knabenshue and Lincoln Beachey, and a French aviator made a new altitude record—4,165 feet. Newspapers described the feelings of spectators in naïve and passionate phraseology; dire predictions were made about the utility of aircraft in wartime, and the day before the meet ended the Hague Tribunal's request to limit bombing from aircraft was given significant publicity. California therefore laid very early the foundations which later supported her wartime aircraft industry. Subsequent events, such as the flight of the *Graf Zeppelin*, Lindbergh's national tour, and the development of aircraft companies in the region kept public interest at a high pitch.

One of the earliest producers was the Douglas Aircraft Company, started by the famous aviator Glenn Martin, who spent his early years in Santa Ana. One of Martin's employees was Donald Douglas, an energetic Scot who accompanied his employer to New Jersey when Martin went to join the Wrights. Douglas returned to California in 1920 to start his own company, with the avowed objective of building a plane that would be able to span the continent nonstop. Douglas's initial activities were characterized by picturesque crudeness. He was said to have built his first plane in the back room of a barbershop and in a second-floor loft, from which completed parts had to be lowered to the ground in sections. He was encouraged by a $100,000 Navy torpedo-plane contract during World War I, and, needing money to fulfill this obligation, he obtained it with the aid of Bill Henry, then a *Los Angeles Times* reporter who was later to gain fame as a columnist and news commentator. Henry went to his employer, Harry Chandler, and induced him to invest in the project and to furnish a list of nine friends, who also subscribed.

When the arms race began which led eventually to World War II, Douglas found that his fortune was made. In 1939 he had two medium-sized plants, one at Santa Monica and another at El Segundo. But $69,000,000 in military orders forced him further to expand his facilities. He did so reluctantly—"We were shanghaied," was the way he described it—because of his conviction that war stimulus would be only temporary. But by 1943 he had plants in Santa Monica, El Segundo, Tulsa, Oklahoma City, Chicago, and Long Beach, in addition to more than one hundred auxiliary and repair establishments. In that year he hired 156,000 persons. The aircraft which gained him most fame were the A-20 (the Havoc), Flying Fortress bombers manufactured under lease from Boeing, C-47 and C-54 transports, the famed "workhorses" of the Air Force, and a Navy dive-bomber. Douglas's sales rose from $27,000,000 in 1939 to $1,061,000,000 in 1944, the peak of his wartime activity. At least one analyst has credited his organization with being "the cornerstone of American air-power."

Another "war-baby" was Consolidated Vultee, started by Gerard Vultee, a graduate of the California Institute of Technology. After working for Douglas, Northrop, and Lockheed, Vultee found himself unemployed during the depression, and founded his own concern, backed primarily by Errett Cord, a financier who was interested in American Airlines. Starting operations at Grand Central Air Terminal in Glendale, Vultee gradually expanded through foreign military orders, and eventually moved to Downey. Vultee was killed in a plane crash in 1938, and his company was acquired by a syndicate. Under the management of Richard Millar, the firm expanded tremendously, building two more plants and reaching a peak of $831,000,000 in orders in 1943. Subsequent reorganization merged the company with Consolidated Aircraft of San Diego, and, in financial alliance with General Dynamics, Convair joined the "big five" of California plane producers.

A third giant was Lockheed. Founded by two brothers, Allan and Malcolm Loughead (who later changed the spelling of their name to correspond with its pronunciation), the firm began turning out planes in 1916, including such famous ships as the Lockheed Vega, used by Wiley Post and Sir Hubert Wilkins, and the Sirius. The depression nearly drove Lockheed out of business, and the brothers were forced to sell out. Later, Robert Gross, an investment banker, bought the concern for $40,000—ironically enough, at the same time that Allan Loughead had raised $50,000 for the same purpose and was vainly trying to raise another $50,-000 on the assumption that that amount was too ridiculously low even for an initial offer. Gross turned Lockheed to transport production, and World War II stimulated gigantic and rapid growth.

Accompanying the expansion of the giants was a corresponding burgeoning of auxiliary enterprises manufacturing aircraft parts. Some observers thought that California was no place for the industry because of the state's lack of metal resources, its vulnerable geographical position, and its dependence on automobile transportation, which was severely curtailed during wartime. But the industry grew and prospered nevertheless. "But for the aircraft boom," said *Fortune*, "Los Angeles might have remained the stronghold of the open shop."

Another wartime industry of California was shipbuilding. The behemoth of this business was Henry Kaiser, noted for his construction of the San Francisco–Oakland Bay Bridge and participation in the Hoover Dam project. Kaiser controlled four shipyards, three of them in California: the Todd-California and Richmond yards at Richmond, the California Shipbuilding Corporation ("Calship") at Los Angeles, and the Oregon Shipbuilding Corporation at Portland. Kaiser-Todd was said to be the "General Motors of the shipbuilding world," and a large share of the awards granted by the Maritime Commission went to the organization. Kaiser-Todd was not the only shipbuilder in California; many others contributed their share to the victory of the merchant marine over Hitler's submarine campaign.

Other industries profited from wartime stimulus; metal products, machinery, textiles, and chemicals were among those encouraged, and the proportion of California's population living in cities and engaged in industrial production increased rapidly. By the time of World War II, California was no longer primarily an agricultural state.

A further wartime problem that afflicted California was the large population of Japanese extraction which had made a firm place for itself in the state's economy, controlled much of the truck farming and food supply, and congregated in both agricultural and urban colony groups, the largest of which was "Little Tokyo" in Los Angeles. This situation was of relatively recent origin. In 1880 there were less than 200 Japanese in the state, but between that date and 1924, when federal immigration laws excluded Oriental labor, more than 200,000 Japanese came into California. By 1940 there were 47,000 Japanese aliens and 80,000 American-born Japanese in the country, most of them living in the Pacific Coast states. During 1942 the Western Defense Command ordered all persons of Japanese extraction to leave certain critical Pacific Coast zones, including all of California, the western third of Washington and Oregon, and the southern quarter of Arizona. There was no stipulation at this time as to how they should go, and many voluntarily departed, choosing their own places of resettlement. However, the war spirit was at its highest, and evacuees who were willing to follow the order found it difficult to locate areas where they would be welcomed. By March 1942, the government realized that if the evacuation order were to be carried out, it would be necessary to provide places of refuge. As a result, "controlled mass evacuation" procedures were set up, which involved construction of "reception" and "assembly" centers, and finally barbed-wire-enclosed camps called "relocation centers." During 1942 more than 110,000 evacuees were moved to these relocation camps.

The problems that arose would have been complex under any circumstances, and were especially difficult during a period of war hysteria. Immediate questions came up, including a query as to why it was necessary to consider American-born Japanese (Nisei) in the same category as aliens, or why, indeed, there should be any difference in treatment between them and American-born Germans and Italians. Many Japanese had become entrepreneurs, and the resulting move not only affected their businesses, but sometimes utterly destroyed them, besides having violent effects on the California economy. Japanese children who had been brought up in American schools, spoke American slang, and considered themselves in every way American citizens were suddenly brought to the realization that there was a difference, with resulting bitterness. On the other side of the ledger, arguments supporting evacuation were largely based on intercepted radio messages which indicated that espionage bases existed in California, and that not all of the Issei (foreign-born) and Nisei were as loyal as they pretended.

Life in the great camps, including Manzanar and Tule Lake in California, constituted a sociological laboratory. Occupants divided themselves into two groups, one which accepted the necessity of the predicament and tried to make the best of it, and another, smaller, which rebelled at the treatment and bitterly opposed the camp administrations. Moreover, the American public, after the first flush of war fury had cooled, re-evaluated the evacuation project and demonstrated a sharply divided public opinion as to its necessity and merit.

In December 1944, the evacuation orders were rescinded, but by then, according to the most thorough analyst of the event,

one in three [Japanese] had migrated eastward from camps to American communities outside the exclusion areas or had entered the armed services, one in six was confined in a segregation center for the "disloyal," and the population remaining in relocation projects had dwindled to 62,000.[1]

---

[1] Dorothy Swaine Thomas: *The Salvage* (Berkeley: University of California Press; 1952), p. 5.

Tule Lake had become a center for the disaffected, and movement of the Japanese back to civilian occupations resulted in a pattern entirely different from the prewar demographic scene.

In addition to a brief baptism of fire, burgeoning war industry, and Japanese relocation problems, World War II gave California, along with the rest of the nation, an economic stimulus that swept the state to new pinnacles of prosperity, encouraged unbelievable population growth, and completely changed the manner of life and the aspect of the countryside. The postwar boom had two major characteristics—a tremendous upsurge in population growth and a continuation and intensification of the industrialization process which had started in the 1920's.

World War II encouraged people to come to California in hordes. Servicemen who had been stationed briefly in the state prior to departure for the Pacific theater of combat were impressed with climate and living conditions, and more than 300,-000 returned after the war to make their homes. Additional thousands were attracted to California by the prospect of jobs in defense plants—and they too stayed. Indirectly, the prosperity occasioned by the war enabled more Americans than ever before to travel for pleasure, and many of these went home merely to pack their household goods. California's population in 1940 totaled 6,907,387; in 1950 it was 10,586,223; in 1955 it was estimated to be 12,213,000. The war and its aftermath therefore nearly doubled the state's people, and settlers entered during this fifteen-year period at the average rate of more than 27,500 per month.

Said the *Los Angeles Times* (always alert for such information) in the 1955 "Midwinter Number":

If the entire population of Pittsburgh and Baltimore—1,755,000— were transported westward and settled within the Los Angeles metropolitan area you will have a fair estimate of our population increase between January 1, 1945, and January 1, 1955.

The impact of the migration [into the Los Angeles area] averaging nearly 500 new residents a day for ten years, makes even seasoned statisticians sit up and take notice.

The *Times* also concluded that only five American cities—New York, Chicago, Detroit, Philadelphia, and Los Angeles—exceeded the 1955 population of the San Gabriel Valley, formerly a pleasant agricultural region of small towns and orange groves. Growth during the postwar decade, expressed in percentages, of formerly small communities in southern California was astonishing:

Compton	148%
Downey	205%
Norwalk	258%
Pacoima	355%
Palos Verdes	288%
Torrance	320%
Van Nuys	239%
Westchester	267%

Not all small towns grew so rapidly, but the number that did served to fill in the open spaces in southern California, in the San Francisco Bay region, around Sacramento, and at certain spots in the Great Central Valley, so that what had formerly been waving wheat, thrifty cotton, or cool green orange groves now succumbed dustily to the bulldozer of the subdivider. In place of the varied "semitropical" crops which had been praised by Nordhoff and Ben Truman, there now sprang up rows and rows of "tract houses," most of which could be purchased by veterans on easy terms, and were. Some of these "developments" were attractive and architecturally in keeping with the terrain and climate; far too many, unfortunately, gave the appearance of sleazy construction and excessive sacrifice to economy measures.

It was estimated that the entire area of land between Los Angeles and San Diego (save, perhaps, for the Santa Margarita Ranch, a federal military reserve) would be completely filled in by new population within a quarter century, as would most of the land between Los Angeles and Santa Barbara on the north. The fringe of the desert just east of the mountains rimming the Los Angeles basin was already dotted with populous communities, new industry, and an entirely unforeseen year-round population, while the San Francisco peninsula was almost unbrokenly settled on the bay side, the Marin area was growing rapidly, and the northern, eastern, and southern shores of the bay were attracting their own throngs of permanent residents. Practically every town in California was growing, and growing fast.

As the people came, they found more and more to do, and most of this increased activity was in the form of urban industry. In 1940 there were 2,534,872 employed people in the state; ten years later the figure had risen to 3,902,000. By 1954 there were more than a million in manufacturing alone, with wholesale and retail trade, government operations, contract construction, and service occupations employing more thousands. The aircraft industry and its affiliates, food production, metal fabrication, apparel, printing and publishing, and petroleum production and refining were responsible for most of the activity. Despite these obvious gains, however, it was still possible for one expert to say in 1955:

When the industrial distribution of California's male workers in 1940 and 1950 is compared with that of workers in the United States and other states the general picture gained of California's industrial development is that of a state highly developed commercially and in the entertainment field, but lagging to a marked degree in manufacturing and the extraction of minerals as compared with the United States and the larger eastern states, and also a state in which agriculture is rapidly losing its status as a major industrial employer.[2]

The state's two major industrial complexes were centered in Los Angeles and San Francisco. Perhaps the most spectacular growth occurred in the south, with more than $1,600,000,000 invested in industrial expansion during the postwar decade. Ten years after V-J Day, one third of Los Angeles's investment capital was going into new or branch operations, two thirds into expansion and improvement of existing businesses. By the mid-1950's Los Angeles was the third largest industrial and marketing center of the United States, giving precedence only to New York and

[2] Warren S. Thompson: *Growth and Changes in California's Population* (Los Angeles: The Haynes Foundation; 1955), p. 134.

Chicago. Sources of relatively low-cost fuel and power accounted for some of this growth, but much of it was based flatly on the fact that many people liked to live in southern California. One of the fortunate developments was in the direction of industrial diversification. After a history characterized by reliance on a single, or at most two, economic activities (petroleum and, later, aircraft) southern California now enthusiastically went in for automotive construction, metal products, foodstuffs, building materials and supplies, chemicals, and electronic materials, relieving the fears of those who earlier had predicted that the Los Angeles economy would be based on newcomers' washing one another's cars. Aircraft and oil still maintained primacy, however. In 1954 there were 178,000 aircraft workers (down less than 100,000 from the wartime peak) in a plant area of thirty million square feet, involving twenty-eight per cent of the area's total manufacturing employment and twenty-nine per cent of the manufacturing payroll ($880,000,000 in 1954). The California oil business was second only to that of Texas, despite the lack of major discoveries since 1949.

Los Angeles paid for its industrial development in a spectacular manner. Having enjoyed a history of attracting immigrants from the East because of its climate, the city was dismayed to find that industrial development was in a fair way to end this reputation because of a single, obstreperous factor, "smog." Smog was the result of two things: a large population in the Los Angeles basin busy producing industrial, automotive, and household fumes, and an atmospheric condition which produced a cold air layer over a warm air layer, in which air movement was blocked by the mountain wall of the Sierra Madre, so that the fumes and atmospheric wastes lay heavily over the flatlands for days at a time. Many of these waste products were from petroleum combustion, and the resulting fumes, under photosynthesis, resulted in sulphur products which made the eyes water and irritated the lungs. Chemists analyzed smog sufficiently to be able to claim that the solution of the problem was largely a political one, and many concluded that filters on the exhaust pipes of private automobiles and control of fumes during delivery of raw gasoline would solve the worst of the problem, but these were expensive and difficult. Other California cities, particularly the east bay communities of the San Francisco region, also suffered occasionally from smog.

Ten years after the war the San Francisco region had a population of 3,000,000 in seventy-two incorporated cities. The area involved covered the shores of San Francisco Bay and measured about eighty by one hundred and fifty miles. The war brought $6,500,000,000 in contracts to the district, and postwar expansion centered in four industries: metals, food processing, petroleum, and chemicals. The 5,000 manufacturing plants produced an annual income of $6,500,000,000, and such industrial giants as Columbia-Geneva Steel at Pittsburg, C & H Sugar at Crockett, Standard Oil at Richmond, and Colgate-Palmolive-Peet at Berkeley welcomed a rapidly expanding population. San Francisco became a center for financial management and low-cost distribution. Communities in the bay region vied with those in southern California as the "fastest-growing" areas of the state.

Farming was not neglected. Still a major occupation of the Great Central Valley and tightly filling the gaps between subdivisions in the bay area and southern California, agriculture continued to carry the fame of the "semitropical" climate to all parts of the world. A million and a half bales of cotton, nearly forty million bushels of potatoes, forty-one million boxes of oranges, seventy-one million bushels of barley, fourteen million bags of rice, thirty-two million bushels of peaches, and two and a half million tons of grapes—this annual outpouring nearly gave the lie to those who insisted that California was becoming urban and industrial.

California was booming at a rate never before experienced. The eighties, the twenties—both paled into wan insignificance before the surge of economic activity that followed the war. And, if things continued to go well—always a debatable prospect— the end was not in sight. Economists of Occidental and Pomona colleges, working with the Committee for Economic Development, prophesied in 1955 that the Los Angeles metropolitan area alone would have to build a school every six days, including Saturdays and Sundays, until 1970, merely to keep up with population needs.[3] The future was bright; the chief problems those of learning how to cope with more people and prosperity.

Climate-minded, population-conscious, real-estate mad California has burst its breeches. In short, it is suffering from the worst case of economic growing pains in American history, and its civic and political leaders are not quite sure what's going to happen,[4]

said a national news magazine three years after the war ended. The state's leaders were not only unsure of the future, but were divided in opinion as to its benefits. Governor Warren announced: "We are getting the greatest population bargain of all time." When it was pointed out to him that newcomers were no longer middle-aged and elderly people with money, but chiefly young married people with debts, he said: "I would rather have the production of the best years of the young people now migrating to our state than the dollars the retired people earned elsewhere." [5] But Los Angeles's Mayor Fletcher Bowron was not as certain as Warren of the state's ability to solve its population problems. "Now don't go quoting me that I want people to stay away," he told a reporter in 1948. "But I do wish they wouldn't come in such numbers." [6]

The politics of California during this era of war and prosperity served to bring the state far more integrally into the national scene. One of the reasons for this was the career of Earl Warren, California's only three-term governor. Warren was the son of a poverty-stricken railroad worker in southern California, and his rise to prominence partook of the true Horatio Alger tradition. Working his way through the University of California Law School, Warren took a job as clerk of the state senate judiciary committee, then moved from that to membership on the staff of the district

---

[3] Southern California Research Council: *The Next Fifteen Years, 1955–1970* (1955), p. 40.

[4] "Crowded California," *Newsweek*, Oct. 11, 1948, pp. 36 f.

[5] Ibid.

[6] Ibid.

attorney of Alameda County. He rapidly rose to be district attorney and, like Theodore Roosevelt and Thomas Dewey in New York, quickly made a reputation for himself as a racketbuster. Criminals went to prison as a result of his work, and the municipal government of Oakland underwent some fundamental changes in personnel. While he was engaged in this task, Warren helped to bring about certain alterations in California criminal-court procedure in the direction of simplification and efficiency. His next step upward was to the attorney-generalship of the state. Here he continued his clean-up campaign, forcing the resignation of a county judge who had a record as a bribe-taker. His most spectacular achievement was a raid on gambling ships, belonging to notorious Tony Carnero, which operated off the southern California coast.

With this record behind him, together with his handsome presence, his personification of the legend of the self-made man, and his attractive personality, Warren was an easy choice for governor over Culbert Olson, whose Democratic administration had been discredited by vacillation and adherence to unworthy panaceas. Warren defeated Olson with a majority of 342,000 votes in 1942.

Warren's policies as governor proved to be liberal and progressive to the extent that many conservative Republicans eventually felt that he had betrayed his party. He was, however, keynoter at the Republican national convention of 1944, and ran in both 1948 and 1952 for the presidential nomination as a Republican favorite-son candidate. In California politics, however, he made a bid for the support of both parties. The California cross-filing system helped him in this, and in 1946 he was renominated by both Republicans and Democrats, an unprecedented political achievement.

The war and postwar booms gave Warren only problems of prosperity to solve. He paid off the state debt, but did not hesitate to increase the budget tremendously, with full confidence that California could pay its way at a new and unprecedented level of economic operation. He actively supported educational expansion and improvement of school facilities, road building, prison and institutional betterment, hospital construction, and old-age and unemployment insurance. His advocacy of health insurance aroused accusations that he favored "socialized medicine," and he supported revision of the Taft-Hartley Act, a federal fair-employment-practices act, and vigorous defense of civil liberties. Despite the fact that postwar California had a preponderance of registered Democrats, Warren's liberal policies attracted support from both parties to the extent that in 1950 he became the state's first third-term governor. He was not destined to complete this term, however, for on the death of Chief Justice Frederick M. Vinson of the United States Supreme Court, Warren was elevated to that exalted post, and in 1953 the governorship of California was turned over to Lieutenant-Governor Goodwin Knight, who was re-elected in his own name the following year. Knight proved to be less palatable to the liberals than his predecessor, though he made an active bid for the support of organized labor.

Another Californian who rose to national prominence during postwar years was Richard Milhous Nixon. A resident of Whittier in the southern part of the state, he began a legal practice there after service in the Navy, and was soon elected to Congress. His battle for a senate seat attracted much attention, largely because his opponent was Congresswoman (and former actress) Helen Gahagan Douglas, a pronounced liberal in politics. The campaign was conducted with no holds barred, and in 1950 Nixon was elected. He rapidly became an outspoken leader of the conservative wing of the Republican Party in Congress and gained new fame with his conduct of the Alger Hiss investigation, involving the notorious "pumpkin papers" and resulting in Hiss's imprisonment for perjury. In 1952 Nixon was Dwight D. Eisenhower's choice for running-mate, and with the latter's election, he became Vice-President of the United States. In this post Nixon rapidly won the reputation of being the most active Vice-President the nation had ever possessed, and served both as the President's political trouble-shooter and public-relations front man. At the same time his loyalty to Eisenhower's policies aroused doubts among his former conservative colleagues, and by the time he had followed Eisenhower to victory again, he was no longer the darling of the right wing. Yet his political position seemed fairly strong, and he apparently had the full confidence of the President.

The third national figure from the Golden State was William Fife Knowland. Son of Joseph Knowland, publisher of the *Oakland Tribune*, one of the state's powerful newspapers, Knowland became a member of the state legislature and a staunch supporter of Earl Warren. When Senator Hiram Johnson died in 1945, Knowland was Warren's nominee for the empty seat, and he was re-elected in 1946 and 1952. Despite his support of Warren and Eisenhower, Knowland had a political faith which was far more conservative than his patrons', and although he was majority leader of the senate during Eisenhower's honeymoon years and minority leader thereafter, he did not hesitate to differ with the President whenever he thought it necessary. Knowland early interested himself in the Far Eastern policy of the nation, was an outspoken critic of Truman's program in that area, and, to a certain extent, of Eisenhower's. He exhibited strongly nationalistic tendencies, discounted the virtues of the United Nations, and came out strongly for economy in government, an uncompromising attitude toward Communism both abroad and at home, and a generally vigorous foreign policy. As time passed, it became evident that he had a powerful constituency which supported his presidential aspirations and deeply respected his forthrightness, his vigor, his industry, and his air of unshakable integrity. In 1957 he announced that he would not again be a candidate for the senate, and declared his intention of running for the governorship, a development which forced Knight out of the race and led him to declare himself a candidate for Knowland's senate seat.

The election of 1958 was a Democratic landslide in California as well as in the rest of the nation. Knowland, tying his campaign to an anti-closed-shop initiative measure (Proposition 18, the "right-to-work" amendment) went down to defeat before Attorney-General Pat Brown, while Knight lost the Republican Senate seat to Democratic legislator Clair Engle. The legislature also became sweepingly Democratic in political hue.

Another political factor, harder to define and confront than that of candidates and issues, was that of the "pressure group." Lobbyists had been prominent in California politics for many years, but "influence peddlers" became so powerful during World War II that one of them, Arthur Samish, became a public scandal, and so much attention was attracted to the lobbying activities of industries and professional organizations that the lobbyists were sometimes referred to as the "Third House."

Following this brief analysis of the political leadership of the state, it remains to outline a few postwar political problems. One of these, unquestionably, was water. Always an issue in California, especially in the thirsty south, the water problem had two facets which periodically made the front pages: the struggle between California and Arizona over the flow of the Colorado River, and the Central Valley Project.

The Colorado River problem was basically simple. When the Colorado River flow had been originally divided by means of the Colorado Compact, California laid claim to a larger share than Arizona because of the population disparity. Arizona resented this and began a campaign based on the reasonable argument that although it was quite true that she had fewer people than California, it was equally true that she would never be able to increase her population unless she acquired more water. Arizona citizens made the additional point that while California had other sources to which she could turn (the Feather River, processing of sea water, etc.) Arizona had but one—the Colorado. California's arguments were equally clear-cut. Her major case was that while Arizona anticipated a future population, a surplus of people were already living in California, and they were currently thirsty. Nor did the alternative sources of water appear to be capable of easy development or possible of quick attainment.

While these arguments flowed on as monotonously as the Colorado River itself, California confronted another of her water problems with better prospects of early solution. The Central Valley Project, already described, served, through Friant and Shasta dams and miles of canals, to equalize the water distribution of California, so that the wet Sacramento Valley now shared some of its liquid wealth with the arid San Joaquin. The problems were not all solved, it was true. Devastating floods struck Yuba City and Marysville in 1956, showing that control was not complete and emphasizing the need for the Feather River Project and other planned solutions. Furthermore, the argument still raged over whether farms of more than 160 acres could utilize water from federally controlled sources, and the debate on this became so bitter that a movement to have the state buy the Central Valley Project from the federal government was seriously discussed. Finally, private power companies fought hard against any intrusion of the Central Valley Project into the power business, and this struggle promised to continue for some time. But, with all the controversy, construction on various water-control units, both public and private, went on, and benefits became evident.

Another major issue which involved the state during postwar years was the question of control over tidelands oil deposits. Legally this involved the perennial question of federal versus states' rights, the complexities of which extend far beyond the scope of this discussion. Briefly, however, the story ran as follows: when California was acquired by the United States, the federal government clearly acquired mineral rights in the new territory. Later, when California became a state, she obtained title to the beds of all navigable waters down to a minimum low-water mark under the so-called "equal footing" doctrine, by which, when a state entered the union, it did so on an equal footing with the original thirteen states. As early as 1897 undersea oil exploitation began at Summerland, and geological investigation showed that there were about one hundred square miles of possible subsurface development within the three-mile limit. California assumed that she owned these subsurface deposits and proceeded to lease them for production, so that by 1950 there were 483 producing wells in this "tideland" zone. Average royalties paid to the state in the late 1940's totaled about $7,000,000 per year.[7]

Numerous problems were faced by both state and federal governments and oil operators. There were attempts to control "whipstocking" or slantwise drilling from the shore which drained undersea oil pools. But by far the most serious complication arose from the fact that the federal government began to take an interest in these subsurface deposits. Eventually three Supreme Court cases declared the paramount authority of the federal government in tidelands oil: *United States v. California* (1947), *United States v. Texas,* and *United States v. Louisiana.* The California case was generally agreed to be the most important of the three, because of the legal precedents it set. In 1945 the federal government tried to obtain an injunction to prevent the Pacific Western Oil Company from continuing its operations in the submerged Elwood field near Santa Barbara. After some legal backing and filling, the federal authorities dropped the suit, but immediately followed it with an action filed in the Supreme Court against the state of California. Attorney-General Tom Clark stated that he hoped the California suit would constitute a test case whereby the authority of the federal government over state control of waters within the three-mile limit would be clearly determined.

The state of California responded with a three-volume, 800-page, three-and-a-half-pound document which defended state ownership and control of tidelands from every possible angle. Shortly thereafter the Supreme Court requested California to file a briefer statement, which was done. The Supreme Court decided in favor of the federal government, with Mr. Justice Black writing the majority opinion, while Justices Frankfurter and Reed dissented. Black's argument was based mainly on the paramount right of the federal government to control coastal areas in the interest of the safety and welfare of the nation as a whole, and he

---

[7] Ernest R. Bartley: *The Tidelands Oil Controversy* (Austin: University of Texas; 1953), pp. 62 f.

ignored some of the fundamental legal reasoning in both the filed action and the state's defense.

Although the state immediately filed petitions for a rehearing of the case, oil stock in California dropped sharply on announcement of the decision. So distraught were investors and operators that the state and federal governments hastily completed some interim arrangements, declaring, in an attempt to calm the panic, that certain areas were outside the scope of the court's decision. But in October 1947, the Supreme Court denied the California request for a rehearing. Political pressure, however, caused the federal government to reconsider the consequences of its victory, and in May 1953, Congress passed the Holland Bill, abandoning the rights of the federal government over the "tidelands" historically claimed by the states, but reserving all other rights on the continental shelf to the federal government.

Passage of the Holland Bill evoked a heavy forensic barrage between the proponents of states' rights (conservative Republicans and southern Democrats) and those who claimed the federal government was trading away its birthright. Maneuvering went on in Congress for long weeks, and was climaxed by one of the lengthiest filibusters ever attempted, a twenty-two-hour effort by Wayne Morse, senator from Oregon, who opposed the bill. But it passed eventually, and was followed by numerous test cases before the courts. However, at this writing the principle that the states retain their historic tidelands and undersea rights, together with the privilege of releasing impounded royalties, remains undamaged —a victory for the Jeffersonian tradition.

The state-versus-federal argument was carried on in other ways. Between Los Angeles and San Diego lay Camp Pendleton, 135,-000 acres on the old Santa Margarita Ranch currently devoted to training activities of the United States Marines. The Santa Margarita River, which supplied the camp with water, first flowed by the town of Fallbrook, a pleasant little inland agricultural community. In 1949 camp authorities and town fathers came to an amicable agreement to construct a dam to impound the waters of the river and to allocate 12,500 acre-feet of water to the camp, 7,500 to the community. The federal government was unwilling to accept this arrangement, and in 1951 demanded that the 14,-000 citizens of Fallbrook and its environs "cease and desist" from using waters of the Santa Margarita, which, it claimed, rightfully belonged to the Marines.

The consequences of this policy were explosive. Fallbrook citizens girded for battle, enlisted the aid of their Congressmen, and —more important—the sympathy of public opinion throughout the state and nation. National periodicals devoted attention to the matter,[8] and mass meetings and political pressure of all kinds finally brought about a ruling from the Comptroller-General's office that federal funds could not be used to prosecute stubborn water users on the Santa Margarita. Again the principle of states' rights triumphed, and California was in the thick of the melee.

A corollary to the conservation aspects of the tidelands controversy occurred in the election of 1956 when major oil producers of the state placed "Proposition 4" on the ballot as an initiative measure. This proposal, if passed, would have established a state-appointed board to regulate production, it would have given the largest landholders in an oil district the right to determine the rate of extraction, and it was presented to the voters as a "conservation" measure. Smaller producers and independents looked upon the bill as a means whereby large producers with foreign sources of supply could cut down on California output and increase the market for their foreign operations. Modern advertising media were used to the utmost, and emotional appeals were flashed on television and brought constantly before the voters through billboards, cartoons, and other means. Unfortunately, neither side made any attempt to explain logically what either passage or defeat of the proposition entailed, and the voters, irri-

---

[8] See Ed Ainsworth and Cameron Shipp: "Government's Big Grab," *Saturday Evening Post*, Vol. CCXXIV (Jan. 5, 1952), pp. 26 ff. "Fallbrook Case Explodes in the Bureaucrats' Faces," loc. cit. Vol. CCXXV (Oct. 11, 1952), pp. 10 f.

tated and confused, defeated the bill and retained the status quo.

An earlier chapter defined the 1930's as the "confused decade" because of the epidemic of aberrant and farfetched social panaceas that sprang up like weeds among California's discontented multitudes. True, no period since has seen a proper parallel to that wild era, but one aftermath must be reported. It concerned the aged, that group which made the Townsend Plan and Ham and Eggs significant factors in California politics.

One of the supporters of the Thirty Dollars Every Thursday scheme was a man named George McLain, natty, intelligent and persuasive. When Ham and Eggs failed to sweep the electorate, McLain shifted his sights to a more conservative venture, the Citizens Committee for Old Age Pensions, and through a skillful publicity campaign, appealing publications, persistent radio broadcasts, and efficient organization won the support of the California aged to the extent that he reportedly received contributions sometimes at the rate of $4,000 per day. By 1948 he had groomed his organization to a powerful enough position to place an initiative measure on the state ballot. The proposal involved shifting control of old-age pensions from county to state; decreasing the eligibility age from sixty-five to sixty-three; making it possible for persons owning $3,500 in real estate, a car and personal possessions, and $1,500 in cash to receive pensions; and declaring that relatives no longer had legal responsibility for providing for aged members of their immediate family. Another startling innovation was establishment of the principle that pension payments constituted a lien on state funds, and had priority over all other state obligations.

Much to everyone's surprise, the measure passed, and became Article 25 of the California constitution. Results were immediate and frightening to the California taxpayer. Within six months pensioners increased from 200,000 to 250,000, and at the end of six months the pension bill to the state had grown to $30,000,000, representing more than one third of the total case-load increase in the entire nation. Throughout the state, new and modishly furnished offices declared the entry of the state into the pension picture, and the new state director of the operation, a woman, was closely associated with George McLain.

Panicky voters repealed the measure at the end of 1949, returned pension control to the counties, and restored the sixty-five-year age limit. They retained only the new level of pension payments—seventy-five dollars per month—but limited the eligibility provisions. Again California had successfully turned away from a socialistic measure which threatened to bankrupt it—but this time its buckler had been down, and the state constitution had been altered, if only briefly. Californians were learning that eternal vigilance was the price of solvency and stability.

While California staunchly defended her rights against federal encroachment and tried to solve her internal social problems, she was never allowed to forget that she was a border state, close to Mexico. During World War II the excited Mexican youth of Los Angeles (which contained the second largest Mexican population of any city in the world) organized gangs dressed in picturesque garments—high-waisted, baggy trousers tight at the ankle, sport coats with padded shoulders and lengthy skirts, flat-crowned, broad-brimmed hats, and over-long watch chains. These were the insignia of the "zoot-suiters" or *pachucos* who fought and raided and made life difficult for the Los Angeles police force. The war seemed to create a hysteria which fostered delinquency, and these youth of a nationality occupying lower economic strata in the city's social pattern reacted to the crisis in an unfortunate manner. Lives and property were lost, and although Mexicans were clearly not the only offenders, public opinion in California assumed that they were the chief culprits.

Later, the nearness of the border was brought home to all the state's citizens in telling manner. California had long utilized Mexican agricultural labor on a seasonal basis, and to regulate this there was a 1951 agreement between the two governments permitting *braceros* or contract agricultural laborers to be recruited by Mexico and sent to the United States for service in the farm-labor market. This agreement ended in February of 1952, and although a three-month extension was agreed upon by the two governments, Mexican authorities refused to renew the agreement unless the United States tightened its restrictions and penalties against farmers who hired "wetbacks" or Mexicans who had smuggled themselves across the border. In 1951 there were 144,-000 Mexicans legally in the United States under the farm-labor agreement; but overbalancing this figure by far were 518,000 wetbacks who had entered illegally, and who were hired by American farmers at starvation wages in consequence of their uncertain status. Even so, the differential between American and Mexican farm wages was great enough to encourage many to risk illegal entry.

The refusal of the Mexican government to renew the arrangements caused the congregation of thousands of would-be *braceros* at the border, riots, additional illegal entries, and other problems. The Mexican government's viewpoint was clear and defensible; Mexico felt that the unconscionable treatment afforded wetbacks should be controlled and regulated by the United States government; the United States, on the other hand, hesitated to penalize farm-labor employers who were taking advantage of a labor supply which, though illegal, was purely voluntary. Meantime, the problem of arresting wetbacks and shipping them home reached wholesale proportions. "Coyotes," or middlemen, throve in the border towns, demanding high fees from Mexican laborers for arranging to get them across the border, legally or illegally. United States border patrolmen were increased from 130 to 730 to stem the pushing tide.

Finally, exchanges of notes between the Mexican and American government established a new basis of understanding, and the troubles calmed. The new agreement, in effect in 1955, included the principles that wages for Mexican agricultural labor in the United States would be the same as for American workers, employers were declared "ineligible" only through bilateral action of the two governments, there would be no further quarantining of whole districts or counties by the Mexican government, and a Joint Migrant Labor Commission was established. Mexico, meanwhile, expanded its recruiting set-up to six stations, in Durango, Irapuato, Guadalajara, Monterrey, Chihuahua, and Mexicali, to encourage Mexican farm workers to become *braceros* instead of wetbacks.

California's labor history had been skewed by the fact that San Francisco had surrendered first to the "closed shop" principle. Los Angeles, under the militant leadership of the *Times*, Harrison Gray Otis, the Merchants and Manufacturers' Association, and other forces, held out valiantly against the walking delegate and his colleagues. The combination of depression and war, however, coupled with vigorous competition between the two major national unions, the C.I.O. and the A.F. of L., served to spread unionism in California very rapidly during the decades of the 1930's and 1940's. By the 1950's California was a heavily industrialized state and a heavily unionized one. San Francisco and the Bay region still had more powerful and dominant union organizations, but Los Angeles was rapidly coming into the fold.

No one aware of California's twentieth-century trends expected anything but a continuation of union expansion and gradual strengthening of the entire labor front. But suddenly, in 1957, Senator William Knowland announced his candidacy for the governorship in 1958 and based his campaign on the "Right to Work" principle—the theory that although unionism should be permitted, the closed shop should not. This decision required clear courage on Knowland's part, considering the trend toward unionism in the state and the preponderantly Democratic registration. However, he seemed willing to stake his political future on the issue, and once again labor organization rose to prominence as an issue in California politics, leading, as has been stated, to Knowland's defeat.

One further problem, which had overtones in politics, society, and public attitudes, should be briefly mentioned. This was California's response to the postwar "red scare," which resulted in investigating committees of state and federal legislatures, blacklists, and loyalty oaths. In 1941 the state legislature organized an investigating committee headed by State Senator Jack B. Tenney. This body worked until 1949, industriously defining subversion and identifying organizations and individuals within the state which it considered were overly sympathetic or co-operative with the "Stalinist" viewpoint. It operated on a wholesale and inclusive, rather than a selective, basis, and consequently aroused much opposition. On Tenney's retirement from the committee chairmanship, the project was continued by another, more moderate, group. Meanwhile, loyalty oaths were demanded from Los Angeles city and county employees, persons connected with the University of California, and finally from all state employees.

The university loyalty oath, initiated in 1949, aroused protest from a sizable group of professors and others who considered their academic freedom endangered, and who based their claim on the simple, positive loyalty oath required by the state constitution and that document's guarantee that no further oaths would be required. Twenty-six professors were dismissed because of refusal to sign—a tiny minority in the huge university faculty. In 1952 the state supreme court declared the university's loyalty oath invalid, but upheld the oath required of all state employees, and the latter was inserted in the constitution by an amendment of 1952.

Most persons who were asked to sign these additional oaths did so without protest and considered that they might be an additional, worth-while safeguard against subversion. Others, however, felt that they constituted an infringement of civil and professional rights. It seemed clear, when emotions had cooled, that oaths were not a particularly effective bulwark against disloyalty to American ideals. Genuine Communists, trained in Machiavellian tactics, signed without question; idealistic liberals were often the ones most troubled by the test statements. The chief benefit was the possibility of prosecuting an oath-signer for perjury if he later proved to have Communist connections.

Other things have happened in California since the war. The old custom of cross-filing was abandoned, and party affiliations of all candidates for state office had to be designated. According to one observer,[9] this shift was not expected to have far-reaching results, but it did serve to strengthen party positions and responsibilities and changed somewhat the composition of the state legislature. Although there was no major postwar change in the state's tax structure, the ample funds available caused the state to assume financial burdens which were traditionally those of local government. Examples of this were the Collier-Burns Highway Act of 1947, apportioning highway users' revenues to cities and counties; the use of the state's bonding power for loans and grants for school construction; increased equalization aid for school support; and the Bradley-Burns Act, which provided for state administration of sales taxes for county governments as well as cities. Because of malpractice on the part of certain members, the State Board of Equalization, responsible for licensing and regulating sales of alcoholic beverages, was changed from an elected agency to a department responsible to the governor.

But these events, good and bad, failed to alter the opinion of the average California citizen that he lived in a great state with a great history, one which was worth celebrating. And as the centennial years of the gold rush and statehood approached, everyone made ready for a characteristic western pageant. In 1947, Senate Bill No. 610 provided for the creation of a Centennials Commission of five members appointed by the governor, who were to be assisted by one aide from the Senate and another from the Assembly. A Centennials Advisory Committee of twenty-five members was also formed, and these groups were instructed to

provide for, assist in, sponsor, and promote public celebrations and exhibits which may be of patriotic, educational, or economic benefit to the people of this State in order to commemorate and publicize the centennial and other anniversaries of significant events in the history of the State of California during the years 1948 to 1950, inclusive.[1]

After certain preliminaries, the main party began at Coloma on January 24, 1948, exactly a century after James Marshall had dis-

[9] Gilbert G. Lentz to Glenn S. Dumke, Jan. 21, 1957.
[1] California Centennials Commission: *California Centennials* (Sacramento: California State Printing Office; 1948).

covered "color" in Sutter's mill race. Hundreds of people gathered to watch a colorful pageant, graced by motion-picture and television celebrities, and an entire week end was occupied by western songs, dances, costumes, and horseplay reminiscent of days of the Argonauts. Town after town, county after county followed with local celebrations, some professionally polished and beautifully done, others amateurish and crude, but all with enthusiasm unbounded. Angels Camp had a "Jumping Frog Jubilee," Calaveras had a Centennial Fair, southern California sponsored a Portolá Trek, with a party of horsemen in morions and leather jackets following the trail of 1769 from San Diego northward. A "historical caravan" consisting of two large museum-buses toured the state bringing Drake's Plate of Brass, the golden spike of Promontory Point, and a portion of Portolá's actual diary, plus many other artifacts, to the school children and citizens of all California. Admission Day of 1950 was celebrated throughout the state with special verve and energy.

For although Californians have had their problems in the past and face ever more complex ones in the present, they are aware, most of them, of a memorable heritage. California has seen the flags of Spain, Britain, Russia, Mexico, and the United States fly over various portions of its lands, besides having its own bear-emblazoned banner. Early motion-picture tycoons were not the only ones who appreciated the contrasting terrain, ranging from the lava beds of Lassen and Shasta through the majestic redwood forests of the north to the warm, rich Central Valley lined by granite peaks backed by deserts, and descending to the semi-arid pleasant southlands. The state's economic potential has been valued by a variety of pioneers looking for cattle, gold, farms, oil, and factory sites. The region has been subject to a population migration of a persistency and duration that is hard to parallel anywhere in the world. It lives richly from its natural bounty and its popularity, yet precariously because of its dearth of water. Its culture has been adolescent and unpolished, offbeat, erratic—yet with overtones of high and rich sophistication. It has had big growth, big catastrophes, spectacular business developments, colorful leaders, and much violence. Yet the main story is not one of excesses, but rather of a rich region coming to fruition with the arrival of millions of industrious, constructive people.

At this mid-point of the twentieth century it can truthfully be said that California has matured, that its economy, industry, and attitudes are no longer those of the frontier. Yet to one who has lived in California, it is equally clear that there are new and challenging frontiers, and that the ultimate destiny of Borica's "most peaceful and quiet country" has not yet been written.

The Literature of California History

Because California history is so colorful and dramatic, collectors in this field have multiplied. In consequence, some of the more popular items have become almost unavailable in their original or early editions, but this trend has been neutralized by some excellent reprints of these and other items, and by the stimulus to publication afforded by the subject's popularity. The literature is vast and ranges from significant nuclear volumes to the marginal products of enthusiastic amateurs. The following list is by no means complete or even exhaustive, but it does contain some of the best references and sources of information. For the student who is assigned some reading it will serve as a guide; for the more fortunate individual who develops a genuine interest in California, it is no more than a serviceable springboard.

General Works

Basic to any library of Californiana is the seven-volume history of the state "by" Hubert Howe Bancroft (*History of California,* San Francisco: The History Company; 1884–90). Bancroft was an indefatigable collector and bibliographer, but he did not write all of the works published under his name. He and his staff, however, produced an essential reference work which, with its comprehensive notes and bibliography, nearly enables it to parallel, for a limited area, Justin Winsor's great *Narrative and Critical History of America.* Next to Bancroft, Theodore H. Hittell, a San Francisco attorney, wrote the best comprehensive history of the state. His *History of California* (4 vols., San Francisco: N. J. Stone & Company; 1885–97) is well done and especially valuable in connection with those episodes, such as vigilanteism and growth of democracy in mining communities, where a legal interpretation is enlightening. Somewhat lighter in vein is Zoeth S. Eldredge: *History of California* (5 vols., New York: Century History Company; 1915).

Shorter works on the history of the state are more numerous. Charles E. Chapman: *A History of California: The Spanish Period* (New York: The Macmillan Company; 1921) and Robert G. Cleland: *A History of California: The American Period* (New York: The Macmillan Company; 1922) are still valuable. Cleland's later volumes, *From Wilderness to Empire* (New York: Alfred A. Knopf; 1944) and *California in Our Time* (New York: Alfred A. Knopf; 1947), on which the present volume is based, provides a more up-to-date, though less detailed, survey, with emphasis on the twentieth century. John W. Caughey: *California* (2nd ed., New York: Prentice-Hall; 1953) is an excellent, well-balanced, one-volume treatment, and there are older single-volume histories by Arthur A. Gray, *The History of California from 1542* (Boston: D. C. Heath & Company; 1934), Rockwell D. Hunt and Nellie Van de Grift Sanchez: *A Short History of California* (New York: T. Y. Crowell Company; 1929), and Henry K. Norton: *The Story of California* (Chicago: McClurg; 1913). A series worth noting is *California,* edited by John Russell McCarthy (9 vols., Los Angeles: Powell Publishing Company; 1929–30), including Nellie Van de Grift Sanchez: *Spanish Arcadia;* Robert G. Cleland: *Pathfinders;* Rockwell D. Hunt and William S. Ament: *Oxcart to Airplane;* Owen C. Coy: *The Great Trek* and *Gold Days;* Robert G. Cleland and Osgood Hardy: *March of Industry;* Frank J. Taylor: *Land of Homes;* Harold C. Bryant: *Outdoor Heritage;* and Edwin Markham: *Songs and Stories.* Most of the titles are self-explanatory, and together the volumes constitute a well-written, somewhat popularized history and description of the state. The University of California Press started a series called *Chronicles of California,* listed as individual volumes and referred to hereafter as *C. C.*

Bibliographies of California history must be headed by Robert E. Cowan: *A Bibliography of the History of California and the Pacific West 1510–1906* (San Francisco: Book Club of California; 1914). Cowan's own collection was acquired by the University of California at Los Angeles Library. A second edition of the bibliography greatly lengthened the list of books; it was published in three volumes in 1933. One of the best essays on California bibliography appears in John W. Caughey: *California,* noted above. Other checklists include Phil Townsend Hanna: *Libros Californianos* (Los Angeles: J. Zeitlin, Primavera Press; 1931), Owen C. Coy: *A Guide to California History* (Dubuque: William C. Brown Company; 1951), and *The Zamorano Eighty: A Selection of Distinguished California Books Made by Members of the Zamorano Club* (Los Angeles: Zamorano Club; 1945). A list of important books relating to California prior to 1900 may be found in Cleland: *From Wilderness to Empire.*

Two picture-books of California history are of genuine significance: Jeanne (Skinner) Van Nostrand and Edith M. Coulter: *California Pictorial: A History in Contemporary Pictures, 1786 to 1859, with Descriptive Notes on Pictures and Articles* (Berkeley: University of California Press; 1948) and W. W. Robinson: *Panorama: A Picture History of Southern California* (Los Angeles: Title Insurance and Trust Company; 1953). A generally useful handbook is Federal Writers' Project of W.P.A.: *California: A Guide to the Golden State* (New York: Hastings House; 1939). See also Division of Mines, Bulletin 141, *Geologic Guidebook Along Highway 49—Sierran Gold Belt, The Mother Lode Country* (September 1948).

Spanish and Mexican California

This whole period was treated competently by Irving Berdine Richman: *California under Spain and Mexico, 1535–1847* (Boston: Houghton Mifflin Company; 1911). For the Indians whom the Spaniards encountered on their explorations the classical reference is Alfred L. Kroeber: *Handbook of the Indians of California* (Washington: Government Printing Office; 1925). Other useful sources on native peoples include Frederick W. Hodge's scholarly *Handbook of the American Indians North of Mexico* (2 vols., Washington: Government Printing Office; 1907–10) and Hubert H. Bancroft's outdated *The Native Races* (5 vols., San Francisco: A. L. Bancroft and Company; 1882). Occasional papers in the publications of the Bureau of Ethnology shed further light on California tribes. Two shorter items on Indians worth mentioning are Gerónimo Boscana: "Chinigchinich," reprinted in Alfred Robinson: *Life in California* (New York: Wiley and Putnam; 1846), and Hugo Reid: *The Indians of Los Angeles County* (Los Angeles: privately printed; 1926).

For the Spanish approaches to California, see Irving Berdine Richman: *The Spanish Conquerors* (New Haven: Yale University Press; 1919) and Edward G. Bourne: *Spain in America, 1450–1580* (New York: Harper & Brothers; 1904), surveys of the entire period of exploration and discovery; and one of the great historical classics of all time, William Hickling Prescott: *History of the Conquest of Mexico* (3 vols., New York: Harper & Brothers; 1843). Francis A. MacNutt: *Fernando Cortés and the Conquest of Mexico, 1485–1547* (New York: G. P. Putnam's Sons; 1909) and *Letters of Cortés* (2 vols., New York: 1908), together with Salvador de Madariaga: *Hernán Cortés,*

Conqueror of Mexico (2nd ed., Chicago: Henry Regnery Co.; 1956) constitute a trilogy of the best sources on this subject, while for a more personal view of the conquest, nothing can surpass Bernal Díaz del Castillo: *Historia Verdadera de la Conquista de Nueva España*, published in several editions and translations. For Mexican history following the conquest, see Arthur S. Aiton: *Antonio de Mendoza, First Viceroy of New Spain* (Durham: Duke University Press; 1927), J. Lloyd Mecham: *Francisco de Ibarra and Nueva Vizcaya* (Durham: Duke University Press; 1927), and Philip W. Powell: *Soldiers, Indians and Silver: The Northward Advance of New Spain, 1550–1600* (Berkeley: University of California Press; 1952).

Exploration and discovery have produced a vast literature. Henry Raup Wagner: *Spanish Voyages to the Northwest Coast of America in the Sixteenth Century* (San Francisco: California Historical Society; 1929) and his *Cartography of the Northwest Coast of America to the Year 1800* (2 vols., Berkeley: University of California Press; 1937) are definitive works by a capable investigator. Other good references include Herbert E. Bolton, ed.: *Spanish Exploration in the Southwest, 1542–1706* (New York: Charles Scribner's Sons, 1916; Barnes & Noble, 1952), and his *The Spanish Borderlands* (New Haven: Yale University Press; 1921). Individual explorers are treated in Fanny R. Bandelier: *The Journey of Alvar Núñez Cabeza de Vaca and His Companions from Florida to the Pacific* (New York; 1905), George P. Winship: *The Journey of Coronado* (New York: A. S. Barnes & Company; 1904), and Henry Raup Wagner: *Sir Francis Drake's Voyage Around the World: Its Aims and Achievements* (San Francisco: J. Howell; 1926).

For the Jesuits, Herbert E. Bolton: *Kino's Historical Memoir of Pimería Alta* (2 vols., Cleveland; 1919), *The Padre on Horseback* (San Francisco: Sonora Press; 1932), and *Rim of Christendom* (New York: The Macmillan Company; 1936), together with Rufus Kay Wyllys: *Pioneer Padre* (Dallas: Southwest Press; 1935), form an excellent foundation. For Lower California, see Miguel Venegas: *Noticia de la California* (3 vols., Madrid; 1757), and *Juan María de Salvatierra* (Margaret Eyer Wilbur, tr., Cleveland: Arthur H. Clark Company; 1929). More popular works include Arthur W. North: *The Mother of California* (San Francisco: Paul Elder; 1908), and a historically accurate novel, Antonio de Fierro Blanco: *Journey of the Flame* (Boston: Riverside Press for Houghton Mifflin Company; 1933). Fierro Blanco was in actuality Walter Nordhoff, of the famous family of writers who spread their talents from California to Pitcairn Island. Don Meadows: *Baja California, 1533–1950* (Los Angeles: Dawson's Book Shop; 1951) is an excellent short bibliography.

The expeditions of 1769 and their background can be traced in Charles E. Chapman: *The Founding of Spanish California* (New York: The Macmillan Company; 1916), while more specific approaches appear in Herbert I. Priestley: *José de Gálvez, Visitor-General of New Spain (1765–1771)* (Berkeley: University of California Press; 1916), and in *Publications* of the Academy of Pacific Coast History, I and II (Berkeley: University of California Press; 1910–11), the journals of Portolá, Costansó, Vilá, and others are printed. See also Douglas S. Watson: *The Spanish Occupation of California* (San Francisco: Grabhorn Press; 1934).

Men and institutions of Spanish California are described expertly by Serra's Boswell, Francisco Palou, who wrote *Noticias de la Nueva California,* translated by Herbert E. Bolton as *Historical Memoirs of New California* (4 vols., Berkeley: University of California Press; 1926). Palou's favorite subject, however, was *Junípero Serra* (C. Scott Williams, tr., Pasadena: G. W. James; 1913). Other biographies of Serra have been done by Abigail Fitch, Agnes Repplier, and MacKinley Helm. The church's version, encyclopedic and full of information, of the history of the missions is told by Fr. Zephyrin Engelhardt: *The Missions and Missionaries of California* (4 vols., San Francisco: James H. Barry Company; 1908–15). Anza is best presented by Herbert E. Bolton: *Anza's California Expeditions* (5 vols., Berkeley: University of California Press: 1930) and *Outpost of Empire* (New York: Alfred A. Knopf; 1931). Visitors to California often left good descriptions behind them, notably Jean François Galaup de la Pérouse: *Voyage de la Pérouse autour du Monde* (4 vols., Paris; 1797); Edith C. Galbraith: "Malaspina's Voyage Around the World," *California Historical Society Quarterly,* III (1924), 215–37; Lesley B. Simpson: *California in 1792: The Expedition of José Longinos Martínez* (San Marino: 1938); and George Vancouver: *A Voyage of Discovery to the North Pacific Ocean* (3 vols., London: printed for G. G. and J. Robinson; 1798). See also George Simpson: *Narrative of a Journey Round the World* (2 vols., London: H. Colburn; 1847); Charles Wilkes: *Narrative of the United States Exploring Expedition* (5 vols., Philadelphia: C. Sherman; 1844); and Eugène Duflot de Mofras: *Duflot de Mofras' Travels on the*

Pacific Coast (Marguerite Eyer Wilbur, tr., Santa Ana: Fine Arts Press; 1937). The Rezanov visit is described by Thomas C. Russell: *The Rezanov Voyage to Nueva California in 1806* (San Francisco: T. C. Russell; 1926) and *Langsdorff's Narrative of the Rezanov Voyage to Nueva California in 1806* (San Francisco: T. C. Russell; 1927). More popular treatments have been written by Hector Chevigny and Gertrude Atherton. A Californian who wrote about his own province is presented by Herbert I. Priestley: *A Historical, Political, and Natural Description of California by Pedro Fages* (Berkeley: University of California Press; 1937). Sanchez: *California Pastoral,* already noted, is a good source.

Yankees who came early to California also left interesting records. Richard Henry Dana: *Two Years Before the Mast* (New York: Harper & Brothers; 1840) is a classic account of the hide and tallow trade, and Richard J. Cleveland: *Narrative of Voyages and Commercial Enterprises* (2 vols., Cambridge: J. Owen; 1842), is a well-written account of the fur trade by sea. For the mountain men, see Hiram M. Chittenden: *The American Fur Trade of the Far West* (2 vols., New York: Press of the Pioneers; 1935); Stanley Vestal: *Mountain Men* (Boston: Houghton Mifflin Company; 1937); Robert G. Cleland: *This Reckless Breed of Men* (New York: Alfred A. Knopf; 1950) and *Pathfinders.* Individuals have been thoroughly studied: Maurice S. Sullivan: *Jedediah Smith, Trader and Trail Breaker* (New York: Press of the Pioneers; 1936) and Harrison C. Dale: *The Ashley-Smith Explorations and the Discovery of a Central Route to the Pacific, 1822–1829* (Cleveland: Arthur H. Clark Company; 1918) deal with perhaps the greatest of the mountain men; see also *The Personal Narrative of James O. Pattie* (Cincinnati: E. H. Flint; 1833 and several later editions). Stories of early migrants are told in numerous volumes, among them John Bidwell: *John Bidwell's Trip to California, 1841* (St. Louis; 1842); Susanna Bryant Dakin: *A Scotch Paisano:* Hugo Reid's *Life in California, 1832–1852* (Berkeley: University of California Press; 1939); Charles L. Camp: *James Clyman, American Frontiersman, 1792–1881* (San Francisco: California Historical Society; 1928); and Charles F. McGlashan: *History of the Donner Party* (Truckee: Crowley and McGlashan; 1879 and later editions). See also Alfred Robinson: *Life in California* (New York: Wylie & Putnam; 1846), reprinted as *Life in California Before the Conquest* (San Francisco: Private Press of T. C. Russell; 1925), William Heath Davis: *Sixty*

Years in California (San Francisco: A. J. *Leary;* 1889), and *Seventy-Five Years in California* (San Francisco: J. Howell; 1929), together with Andrew F. Rolle: *An American in California: The Biography of William Heath Davis, 1822–1909* (San Marino: Huntington Library; 1956). George P. Hammond, ed.: *The Larkin Papers* (5 vols., Berkeley: University of California Press; 1951–55), and Reuben L. Underhill: *From Cowhides to Golden Fleece: A Narrative of California, 1832–1858* (Stanford: Stanford University Press; 1939) give a portrait of one of the most important American pioneers.

Institutions are competently described by Herbert E. Bolton: "The Mission as a Frontier Institution in the Spanish-American Colonies," *American Historical Review*, XXIII (1917), 42–61, and Robert G. Cleland: *The Cattle on a Thousand Hills* (San Marino: Huntington Library; 1951). Cleland describes a typical large landholding in *The Irvine Ranch of Orange County, 1810–1950* (San Marino: Huntington Library; 1952).

The American Period

Up to quite recently this era of California history took second place to the earlier decades in popularity with writers. The last quarter century, however, has produced an increasing literature on the American period, and each year sees good items added to the list.

The acquisition of California by the United States is told by Cleland: "The Early Sentiment for the Annexation of California," *Southwestern Historical Quarterly*, XVIII (1914–15), 1–40, 121–61, 231–60; Allan Nevins: *Frémont, the West's Greatest Adventurer* (2 vols., New York: Harper & Brothers; 1928) and *Frémont, Pathmarker of the West* (New York: D. Appleton-Century Company; 1939); Justin H. Smith: *The War with Mexico* (2 vols., New York: The Macmillan Company; 1919); Philip St. George Cooke: *The Conquest of New Mexico and California* (New York: G. P. Putnam's Sons; 1878) by the commander of the Mormon Battalion; and William S. Emory: *Notes of a Military Reconnaissance in Missouri and California* (New York: George Long and Brother; 1848) by an officer under Kearny. There are numerous treatments of specific episodes and individuals, a good example being Arthur Woodward: *Lances at San Pascual* (San Francisco: California Historical Society; 1948).

The Gold Rush, an exception to the comparative lack of popularity of the American period, probably has been more written about than any other single episode in California history. Owen C. Coy's *Great Trek* and *Gold Days* are interesting treatments of the migration and the realization; a more up-to-date treatment, using results of recent scholarship, is John W. Caughey: *Gold Is the Cornerstone* (Berkeley: University of California Press; 1946, *C.C.*). Valeska Bari: *The Course of Empire* (New York: Coward-McCann; 1931) gathers selections from participants in interesting format, and Hubert Howe Bancroft: *California Inter Pocula* (San Francisco: The History Company; 1888) treats the rush as a social phenomenon and does some philosophizing. Journals of those who crossed the plains are legion; see Alonzo Delano: *Life on the Plains and Among the Diggings* (Auburn: Milner, Orton and Mulligan; 1854) for a real diary, and Archer B. Hulbert: *Forty-Niners* (Boston: Little, Brown & Company, 1931) for a synthetic one. William L. Manly: *Death Valley in '49* (San Jose: Pacific Tree and Vine Company; 1894), Ralph P. Bieber: *Southern Trails to California in 1849* (Glendale: Arthur H. Clark Company; 1937), and George W. B. Evans: *Mexican Gold Trail* (San Marino: Huntington Library; 1945) describe variants of the trail. An excellent account of the Isthmus route is given by Bayard Taylor: *Eldorado* (New York: Alfred A. Knopf; 1949), and the Cape Horn journey is described in Oscar Lewis: *Sea Routes to the Gold Fields* (New York: Alfred A. Knopf; 1949).

Problems of early statehood are narrated in Joseph Ellison: *California and the Nation, 1850–1869* (Berkeley: University of California Press; 1927) and Cardinal Goodwin: *The Establishment of State Government in California, 1846–1850* (New York: The Macmillan Company; 1914). See also William H. Ellison: *A Self-Governing Dominion: California, 1849–1860* (Berkeley: University of California Press; 1950, *C.C.*). The Broderick-Gwin feud is handled in James O'Meara: *Broderick and Gwin* (San Francisco: Bacon and Company; 1881) and in Albert Russell Buchanan: *David S. Terry of California, Dueling Judge* (San Marino: Huntington Library; 1956, *C.C.*). Vigilanteism is well described in Hubert H. Bancroft: *Popular Tribunals* (2 vols., San Francisco: The History Company; 1887); Mary Floyd Williams, ed.: *History of the San Francisco Committee of Vigilance of 1851* (Berkeley: University of California Press; 1921) and her *Papers of the San Francisco Committee of Vigilance of 1851* (Berkeley: University of California Press; 1919); Stanton A. Coblentz: *Villains and Vigilantes* (New York: Wilson-Erickson; 1936); and William Tecumseh Sherman:

Memoirs of General William T. Sherman (2 vols., New York: D. Appleton & Co.; 1875).

Filibustering is well treated by Rufus Kay Wyllys: *The French in Sonora* (*1850–1854*) (Berkeley: University of California Press; 1932); William O. Scroggs: *Filibusters and Financiers* (New York: The Macmillan Company; 1916); and Laurence Greene: *The Filibuster* (New York: The Bobbs-Merrill Company; 1937), an account of William Walker.

Transportation is another subject which has often appealed to the pen; various periods in its development are described in Ernest A. Wiltsee: *The Pioneer Miner and Pack Mule Express* (San Francisco: California Historical Society; 1931); William Banning and George Hugh Banning: *Six Horses* (New York: Century Company; 1930); Oscar O. Winther: *Express and Stagecoach Days in California* (Stanford: Stanford University Press; 1936); Leroy R. Hafen: *The Overland Mail, 1849–1869* (Cleveland: A. H. Clark Company; 1926); Arthur Chapman: *The Pony Express* (New York: G. P. Putnam's Sons; 1932); Roscoe P. Conkling: *The Butterfield Overland Mail, 1857–1869* (Glendale: Arthur H. Clark Company; 1947); and many others. Railroad history may be traced in U.S. Engineer Department: *Pacific Railroad Reports* (13 vols., Washington: Government Printing Office; 1855); Edwin L. Sabin, *Building the Pacific Railway* (Philadelphia: J. B. Lippincott Company; 1919); Glenn Chesney Quiett: *They Built the West* (New York: D. Appleton-Century Company; 1934); and Oscar Lewis: *The Big Four* (New York: Alfred A. Knopf; 1938). Travel accounts are interesting and of historical value; they include Horace Greeley: *An Overland Journey* (New York: C. M. Saxton, Barker and Company; 1860); Demas Barnes: *From the Atlantic to the Pacific, Overland* (New York: Van Nostrand; 1866); Mark Twain: *Roughing It* (Hartford: American Publishing Company; 1872); and Samuel Bowles: *Our New West* (Hartford: Hartford Publishing Company; 1869). The Southern Pacific's unique position in California is described in Stuart Daggett: *Chapters on the History of the Southern Pacific* (New York: The Ronald Press Company; 1922) and Frank Norris: *The Octopus* (New York: Doubleday, Page and Company; 1901).

Migration to California is dealt with in much promotional literature of the 1860's and 1870's, including such items as California Immigrant Union: *All About California and the Inducements to Settle There* (San Francisco: California Immigrant Union; 1870); Charles Nordhoff:

California for Health, Pleasure and Residence (New York: Harper & Brothers; 1872); and Benjamin C. Truman: *Homes and Happiness in the Golden State of California* (San Francisco: Central Pacific Railroad Company; 1883). The period of the 1880's is described in Glenn S. Dumke: *The Boom of the Eighties in Southern California* (San Marino: Huntington Library; 1944) and more humorously in Theodore S. Van Dyke: *Millionaires of a Day* (New York: Howard and Hulbert; 1890).

The water problem has many facets; some of the best sources include J. A. Alexander: *The Life of George Chaffey* (Melbourne: The Macmillan Company; 1928); William H. Hall: *Irrigation in California* (Sacramento: State Printing Office; 1888); *Complete Report on Construction of the Los Angeles Aqueduct* (Los Angeles: Department of Public Service; 1916); Willie A. Chalfant: *The Story of Inyo* (Chicago: the author; 1922); Remi Nadeau: *The Water Seekers* (New York: Doubleday & Co.; 1950); Robert W. de Roos: *The Thirsty Land: The Story of the Central Valley Project* (Stanford: Stanford University Press; 1948), and many others, some of which include journalistic criticism of certain episodes, such as Morrow Mayo: *Los Angeles* (New York: Alfred A. Knopf; 1933).

Other phases of California's political development are treated in George Mowry: *The California Progressives* (Berkeley: University of California Press; 1951); Walton Bean: *Boss Ruef's San Francisco* (Berkeley: University of California Press; 1952); Robert A. Walker and Floyd A. Cave: *How California is Governed* (New York: The Dryden Press; 1953), and Franklin Hichborn: *Story of the Session of the California Legislature of 1909, 1911 and 1913* (3 vols., San Francisco: James H. Barry Company; 1909–13). A special topic is dealt with in Charles Dwight Willard: *The Free Harbor Contest at Los Angeles* (Los Angeles: Kingsley-Barnes and Neuner Company; 1899), while comparable problems in the northern part of the state are described in Franklin Hichborn: *"The System"* . . . (San Francisco: James H. Barry Company; 1915); Fremont Older: *My Own Story* (San Francisco: Call Publishing Company; 1919); and J. Lincoln Steffens: *The Autobiography of Lincoln Steffens* (2 vols., New York: Harcourt, Brace & Company; 1931). Racial overtones are narrated in California State Board of Control: *California and the Oriental* (Sacramento: California State Printing Office; 1920); Thomas A. Bailey: *Theodore Roosevelt and the Japanese-American Crisis* (Stanford: Stanford University Press; 1934); and California, Mexican Fact-Finding Committee: *Mexicans in California* (Sacramento: California State Printing Office; 1930). For Japanese evacuation, see United States War Department: *Japanese Evacuation from the West Coast, 1942* (Washington: Government Printing Office; 1943); Dorothy S. Thomas and Richard Nishimoto: *The Spoilage* (Berkeley: University of California Press; 1946); Leonard Bloom and Ruth Riemer: *Removal and Return* (Berkeley: University of California Press; 1949); and Dorothy S. Thomas and others: *The Salvage* (Berkeley: University of California Press; 1952). Labor problems are treated by Ira Cross: *History of the Labor Movement in California* (Berkeley: University of California Press; 1935); Louis Adamic: *Dynamite* (New York: The Viking Press; 1931); Ernest J. Hopkins: *What Happened in the Mooney Case* (New York: Brewer, Warren and Putnam; 1932); Clarence S. Darrow: *The Story of My Life* (New York: Charles Scribner's Sons; 1932); and William M. Camp: *San Francisco: Port of Gold* (New York: Doubleday & Co.; 1947).

Recent economic growth is the subject of a vast and perhaps ephemeral literature. Periodicals and newspapers are valuable, and the following books treat of important themes: Cleland and Hardy: *March of Industry*; Ira B. Cross: *Financing an Empire* (4 vols., Chicago; 1927); Carey McWilliams: *Southern California Country* (New York: Duell, Sloan & Pearce; 1946), and, by the same author, *California, the Great Exception* (New York: Current Books; 1949), and *Factories in the Field* (Boston: Little, Brown & Company; 1939). McWilliams has a consistent pro-labor, anti-management bias. Also see Frank L. Kidner: *California Business Cycles* (Berkeley: University of California Press; 1946) and the *Los Angeles Times* "Midwinter Numbers" for a promotional view. For motion pictures, see Lewis Jacobs: *The Rise of the American Film: A Critical History* (New York: Harcourt, Brace & Company; 1939), and Maurice Bardeche and Robert Brasillach: *The History of Motion Pictures* (Iris Barry, tr., W. W. Norton & Company; 1932).

The Union Oil Company is described in Frank J. Taylor and Earl Welty: *Black Bonanza* (New York: Whittlesey House; 1950) and the automobile in Phil T. Hanna: "The Wheel and the Bell," *Westways*, Vol. XLII, No. 12 (December 1950), pp. 41–56.

INDEX

A NOTE ABOUT THE AUTHOR

A Kentuckian by birth (Shelbyville, 1885) and a descendant of two pioneer families, the Logans and the Clelands, Robert Glass Cleland at the age of four migrated to Duarte, California, where much of his childhood was passed in an adobe ranch house built in 1842. A later period found the Cleland family in the small boom town of Azusa. During those years spent roaming about California, young Cleland developed his avid interest in the history of his adopted state. At eighteen, he was graduated from Occidental Academy in Los Angeles and entered the college of the same name. After his graduation in 1907, he took two degrees at Princeton University—a second A.B. and a Ph.D. For nearly sixty years Dr. Cleland was an interested observer of California's development. Long a member of the History Department at Occidental College, and then vice-president and dean, he later became a member of the permanent research staff of the Huntington Library, San Marino. His published books included *From Wilderness to Empire: A History of California, 1542–1900* (1944); *California in Our Time, 1900–1940* (1947); *This Reckless Breed of Men: The Trappers and Fur Traders of the Southwest* (1950); and *A History of Phelps Dodge, 1834–1950* (1952), as well as a book for older children, *California Pageant: The Story of Four Centuries* (1946). Dr. Cleland died on September 3, 1957.

A NOTE ABOUT THE EDITOR

Glenn S. Dumke was born in Green Bay, Wisconsin, on May 5, 1917. He attended Occidental College (A.B., 1938; A.M., 1939) and the University of California at Los Angeles (Ph.D., 1942), and later taught at both, being a professor of history and dean of faculty at Occidental from 1950 on. He was President of San Francisco State College and is now Chancellor of California State College. His published books include *The Boom of the Eighties in Southern California, Mexican Gold Trail*, and *A History of the Pacific Area in Modern Times*. He has contributed widely to learned and popular periodicals.

A NOTE ON THE TYPE

The text of this book is set in Caledonia, a Linotype face designed by W. A. Dwiggins (1880–1956), who was responsible for so much that is good in contemporary book design. Though much of his early work was in advertising and he was the author of the standard volume Layout in Advertising. *Mr. Dwiggins later devoted his prolific talents to book typography and type design, and worked with great distinction in both fields. In addition to his designs for Caledonia, he created the Metro, Electra, and Eldorado series of type faces, as well as a number of experimental cuttings that have never been issued commercially.*

Caledonia belongs to the family of printing types called "modern face" by printers—a term used to mark the change in style of type-letters that occurred at the end of the eighteenth century. It is best evidenced in the letter shapes designed by Baskerville, Martin, Bodoni, and the Didots.

This book was composed, printed, and bound by Kingsport Press, Inc., Kingsport, Tennessee. Typography and binding designs based on originals by W. A. Dwiggins.

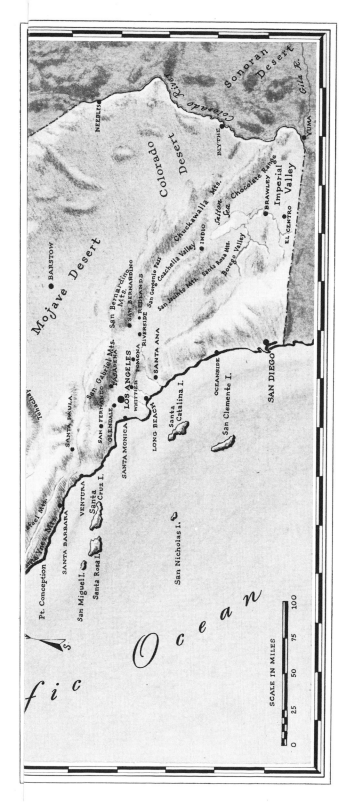

CALIFORNIA,

a map showing the principal topographic features, cities, and place names of the state.